An American Procession

ALFRED KAZIN

An American
Procession

Vintage Books
A Division of Random House
New York

First Vintage Books Edition, February 1985
Copyright © 1984 by Alfred Kazin
All rights reserved under International and
Pan-American Copyright Conventions.
Published in the United States by Random House,
Inc., New York, and simultaneously
in Canada by Random House of Canada Limited,
Toronto. Originally published by
Alfred A. Knopf, Inc., in 1984.

Acknowledgment for permission to reprint
previously published material appears on page 411.

Library of Congress Cataloging in Publication Data
Kazin, Alfred, 1915-
An American procession.
Includes index.
1. American literature—History and criticism.
I. Title.
[PS88, K3 1985]   810'.9   84-40517
ISBN 0-394-72923-4 (pbk.)

Manufactured in the United States of America

I dwell in Possibility—
A fairer House than Prose—
More numerous of Windows—
Superior—for Doors—
          EMILY DICKINSON
        #657, c. 1862

We grant no dukedoms to the few,
　　We hold like rights, and shall;—
Equal on Sunday in the pew,
　　On Monday in the mall.
For what avail the plough or sail,
　　Or land or life, if Freedom fail.
EMERSON, "Boston"

Contents

Part Three

Ruling by Style: History and the Moderns, 1900–1929

Acknowledgments

An American Procession was first worked out, in part, as the Christian Gauss lectures at Princeton, 1961, and in the lectures I gave as Beckman professor in 1963 at the University of California, Berkeley. Since that time I have been able to develop this book by drawing on my seminars at universities here and abroad, and on reviews, essays, and introductions I have written. In the course of more than twenty years I have been constantly stimulated by rethinking and recasting my early efforts.

The book has been aided considerably by the support of Dr. Gordon Ray and the John Simon Guggenheim Memorial Foundation, and by fellowships, 1977–78, from the National Endowment for the Humanities and the Center for Advanced Study in the Behavioral Sciences, Stanford University.

My students at Hunter College and the Graduate Center of the City University of New York have helped more than they know by fiercely arguing back.

I owe a special debt to my editor, Robert Gottlieb. He cares about these books as much as I do and, without regard for my feelings, has insistently demonstrated literary acumen beyond the call of duty.

Without my wife Judith, nothing would have happened.

Preface

One's-Self I sing, a simple separate person,
Yet utter the word Democratic, the word En-Masse.

WHITMAN, "One's-Self I Sing"

This book offers an interpretation of some major figures in American writing during the crucial century that began in the 1830s when Ralph Waldo Emerson left the church and founded a national literature on the basis of a religious revolution. I end my book on the eve of the 1930s with the triumph of modernism—Eliot, Pound, Hemingway, Fitzgerald—and with the revelation after the First World War of the "postponed power" among those who had been "modern" before their time—Adams, Melville, Whitman, Dickinson.

The literary century that began with Emerson's *Nature* (1836) closed (but not entirely) when the free spirit of the moderns was dissipated by war, depression, political ideology, academicism, "post-modernism." My book encompasses the two greatest periods in our literature. The first was before the Civil War; the second, just after what John Dos Passos unrelentingly called "Mr. Wilson's War." The earlier period includes the transcendental idealists (Emerson, Thoreau, Whitman) and the great romancers (Hawthorne, Poe, Melville). The later period includes the modernist poets, novelists, and critics—Eliot, Pound, Hemingway, Dos Passos, Fitzgerald, Edmund Wilson, Kenneth Burke—too many for me to do justice to in a book that ends with the 1920s. This literary century also encompasses our great realistic novelists of the period between the Civil War and the "Great" War—Mark Twain, James, Crane, Dreiser. And Emily Dickinson, the greatest realist in our literature of the "internal difference, / Where the Meanings, are."

This period of literary creation, unprecedented expansion, and national promise was to Henry Adams, who lived it all from 1838 to 1918, to be the most eventful and decisive period in the recorded history of the West.

America from Lincoln to Woodrow Wilson seemed unparalleled in its concentration of material power and the challenge this represented to the intellect. The rise of the United States was a planetary event and one by no means
to be welcomed blithely even by those fascinated by the "challenge." This
concern with power on a scale previously unknown to men is one reason
why Adams the great observer plays a large role in my narrative; he was
always near the seats of power. Another reason is that Adams, the most
original, imaginative, and provoking of American historians, was a bolder
and more accomplished literary artist than William Dean Howells and other
tame excellences of the period.

Emerson, in leaving the church and other mere "institutions," gained an
individual sense of power that now seems primordial. He found the universe
an "open secret." I begin with Emerson because Whitman (thereby giving
me my title) predicted correctly that "America in the future, in her long train
of poets and writers, while knowing more vehement and luxuriant ones, will,
I think, acknowledge nothing nearer [than] this man, the actual beginner of
the whole procession. . . ."

We have certainly known more vehement and luxuriant characters in the
procession of American writers since Emerson's day. Emerson is still
"nearer" because the astonishing sense of self that he incarnated in his early
writings created many a writer's confidence that the individual in America
is by himself equal to anything. And this at a time when the most penetrating
observer of America from a European, aristocratic, Catholic point of view,
Alexis de Tocqueville, recognized that democracy was the revolutionary
proposition of the time and that democracy in America was founded on a
faith in the individual that was unprecedented, wonderful, and dangerous.

> Americans acquire the habit of always considering themselves as standing
> alone, and they are apt to imagine that their whole destiny is in their hands.
> Thus not only does democracy make every man forget his ancestors, but it
> hides his descendants, and separates his contemporaries from him; it throws
> him back upon himself alone, and threatens in the end to confine him entirely
> within the solitude of his own heart.

This now-legendary sense of self in America is a principal character in
my narrative, along with the hopes of a "free man's worship" that came with
it, before the aggressive and ever more concentrated forces assimilated this
sense of self into capitalism as a theology. (As the end of "Self-Reliance"
shows, Emerson did not always know the difference.) But what Emerson
called his "one" doctrine—"the infinitude of the private mind"—nevertheless gave a special radiance to *Nature, Walden,* "Song of Myself," and even

Moby-Dick, a radiance that has allowed millions to remember "morning in America" and that sustains some sense of self in our very different world. The world is always new to those who can see themselves in a new light.

Emerson was a central source of that light. As Wright Morris has noted, "the simple separate person . . . is still our one inexhaustible source of energy." Emerson was Romanticism with a difference. Blake and Wordsworth remained outside English life and development. Karl Marx in his youth had the same revelation that "God" would at last "actualize" himself in man, but for some reason this has had no echo in the Soviet Union. Emerson, the radical romantic of *Nature, The American Scholar*, the Divinity School Address, "Self-Reliance," "The Poet," was a fomenter of social hope before the Civil War and the founder of a national idea. He was an intellectual father to men of genius from Thoreau and Whitman to William James; an extraordinary proof of mental solidarity to Nietzsche; a lasting figure in the minds of those who opposed him—Melville, Poe, Hawthorne. Emerson's faith in the self was inseparable from his hope that America would have an original destiny. In this "revolutionary age," as Emerson always called it, *Emerson* became another name for this expectation.

Near the end of the twentieth century it is necessary to remind literary critics that Emerson was not first and foremost a literary critic but a "God-intoxicated" man possessed by the spirit of innovation. His admirer Nietzsche summed up the paramount anxiety of their century as "the death of God." Nietzsche promptly offered up the thinker-as-hero as one who could allay that anxiety, filling up the vacancy with the figure of Zarathustra, the "overman"-who-must-now-be-more-than-man. Emerson and Whitman had created that Promethean figure for themselves. It was above all Melville who, writing to Hawthorne in the exultancy of finishing *Moby-Dick*, described them both as titanic figures, God's sentinels around the world.

Hawthorne never thought of himself as a demi-god. Quite the contrary; he was convinced that the literary career in America was a futile battle with greedy publishers and an unheeding public, and his career ended in a "crack-up" infinitely more sorrowful and paralyzing than the one Scott Fitzgerald recounted in the 1930s. Emerson was to have trouble reconciling the unfettered self with his later discovery of "Experience." He was to have greater trouble presenting his early "dream" with the national experience. Whitman, the omnipresent "I" in "Song of Myself," and especially Melville, playing the despot Ahab off against the dreamily passive Ishmael in *Moby-Dick*, showed that the emancipated American self was not above the pressures of society and the contradictions in human nature. Thoreau never worked out the consequences of the unlimited self. One reason for his early death, during

the Civil War that despite his enthusiasm for John Brown he was too peaceful to support, may well have been his inability to reconcile his romantic
genius with American power.

Melville, the greatest working mind in the literature of the period, was
not afraid to seek truth in the confrontation of man with the elemental and
in the terrors of his own heart. He thought this ruined him as a popular
author, and he was right. But Melville had that peculiar awareness of whatever is everlastingly "crossed" and "subterranean," as he liked to say. Whitman, for all his boundless ego, had that awareness on the plane of "solidarity." He owed this to his eroticism; as Auden was to say, Eros is the father
of cities. Whitman the New Yorker knew everything that goes on in a great
city. A dramatic sense of relationship haunted Whitman all his life as "the
fusing explanation and tie—what the relation between the (radical, democratic) Me . . . and the (conservative) Not Me . . . ?"

Just to pose that "relation" shows political imagination. It brought Whitman through the Civil War despite his public "failure" as a poet. The
"shut-in" Dickinson, with her wonderful contrast of "boundary" and "circumference," of the "body" and the "immortality" that is "the mind alone
without corporeal friend," had a more concentrated, more sibylline awareness of woman's relation to the nineteenth century than many a more active
and worldly woman. Mark Twain's greatest achievement in his best book
may very well be the contrast between Huck on the raft and Huck on shore
peering around the edges of a society at once genteel and murderous. What
must always fascinate us in Henry James is his sense of the *entanglement* of
New World types with the enduring character of the Old World.

Imagination on this level is so unlike ideology that it cannot tolerate
ideology. This is no doubt what Eliot meant when he said that James had
a mind so fine that no idea could violate it. And ideology is so much the rival
and destroyer of literature that, beginning my studies in the 1930s, I came to
know all too well why even an artist like Dos Passos could not function with
two contradictory ideas in his mind at the same time, so turned sharp right
after his disillusionment with the left. Scott Fitzgerald said that *he* could live
with the contradiction. He proved this not only in the mingled romanticism
and satire of *The Great Gatsby* and in the self-exposure and remorselessness
of *Tender Is the Night* but in the unequalled subtlety about Hollywood and
its "dreams" that he brought to the unfinished *The Last Tycoon*.

Those who have such imagination find others who have it. Whitman said
of Emerson that "his quality, his meaning has the quality of the light of day,
which startles nobody. You cannot put your finger upon it yet there is
nothing more palpable, nothing more wonderful, nothing more vital and

refreshing." Henry James sought the most ideal, the most receptive side of his talent in Balzac as well as in George Eliot, in Turgenev as well as in Hawthorne. Hemingway knew that he owed everything to Cézanne, Gertrude Stein—and *Huckleberry Finn*. T. S. Eliot as a youngster in St. Louis found the future ground of his poetry in foreign poets he could barely understand.

"For genius, all over the world, stands hand in hand, and one shock of recognition runs the whole circle round." Melville's great tribute to Hawthorne no longer gets much "recognition." A debased Freudianism is used to exaggerate the natural rivalry of writers. But writing *Moby-Dick*, which he would dedicate to Hawthorne, Melville in a letter to him spoke "now of my profoundest sense of being, not of an incidental feeling." In another, "Whence come you, Hawthorne? By what right do you drink from my flagon of life? . . . I feel that the Godhead is broken up like the bread at the Supper and that we are the pieces. Hence this infinite fraternity of feeling."

Emily Dickinson summed up her era and much of my argument when she wrote in a letter: "We thank thee, Father, for these strange minds that enamor us against thee." The death of "the old God" and the rise of "a new man" put the writer in America on his mettle. Thoreau, who was certainly jealous of Emerson and had reason to resent his Olympian serenity and detachment, perfectly described his bond to Emerson. He told a friend that in Emerson he had found "a world where truths existed with the same perfection as the objects he studied in external nature, his ideals real and exact."

Alfred Kazin
August 1983

An American Procession

Prologue, 1918:
Old Man in a Dry Month

I will show you fear in a handful of dust.

ELIOT, *The Waste Land*

It was 1918 and America was at war again. In his great house on Lafayette Square just across from the White House—for forty years the Square had been his favorite lookout on the presidents he joyfully despised—Henry Adams felt that as a survivor of the nineteenth century's "drama of human improvement," as a student of what he called History's mad acceleration into "chaos," he had come to the most dramatic moment of all. History in his century had replaced religion as the first drama of human existence. History had long been the greatest possible subject to his madly speculative mind. "That wonderful century," as the codiscoverer of natural selection Alfred Russel Wallace had called it, "the century of progress" hailed by Leopold of Belgium when he took over the Congo, had ended at last. As usual, Henry Adams was there to pick up the pieces.

He was eighty years old in February 1918, and he would be dead in March. Since his stroke six years before, he could write hardly anything but his wickedly brilliant letters relating Washington political gossip and the tendency of History to fulfill the sourest prophecies of Henry Adams. But surrounded by his Japanese vases, a great Turner, his color print of Blake's *Nebuchadnezzar Eating Grass,* his choice French impressionist works resting on chairs built to accommodate his tiny figure (he was just a little over five feet tall), his great library, and the Adams family portraits in one of the twin houses built for him and his friend John Hay by his Harvard classmate H. H. Richardson, Adams spent voluptuous hours listening to the beautiful young Aileen Tone singing the medieval French chansons to which he was still determined to find the original words. She was the last of those honorary nieces whom he hired for their excellent French, their pleasing voices, and a disposition (marked among bright young women in Washington) to admire without limit the flashing mind and prodigious interests of this fierce little old man who was venomous to everyone but a few friends yet was strangely fascinating to many. Elizabeth Cameron, the young wife of the Pennsylvania senator and political boss Don Cameron, had become his favorite woman in the world. But even she confessed, "It is a curious faculty you Adamses have of inspiring terror; it must be because you are frightened yourself and communicate it."

After his wife's tragic death in 1885 her real nieces had attended him. As they had grown away, his determination to discover words for the medieval chansons led him to France for seven months every year. How pleasant it was to bring together his passion for the medieval and his delight in handsome, witty, elegantly well bred young women competent to assist his researches and to enjoy his wittily abrasive views of his degenerate country. He was a great appreciator of Woman—never more so than after Marian's death, when he needled his friends at dinner by announcing the superiority of every woman present to her husband. For all his contemptuous ways and doomsday notions, Adams had a gift for friendship that singled out the wives of his friends the secretary of state, the British ambassador, the chairman of the Senate Foreign Relations Committee. No one in the rough-mannered new century would ever approach Adams's ingratiating way of sharing with intimates a mind alarmingly superior. "There is something voluptuous in meaning well." He had no friends who were not leaders of American society and enterprise, drivers of the "powerhouse." He liked to tell them to their faces that they lacked passion. But he was too special a case—privately wealthy, obsessively exclusive, the wholly intellectual spectator of a power in which he did not share—not to know that he was an oddity in America's governing class. A senator from Wisconsin—on the floor of the Senate!—had called him a begonia.

How much did he mean his public idolatry of women? How much did he mean anything he said after Marian—"Clover"—took her life thirty-three years before? For a scholar who had virtually founded the modern historical seminar at Harvard in the 1870s, a superb critical intelligence with a particular instinct for smelling out established untruths in American history, Henry Adams had certainly become a genius, or devil, at mystifying his friends. When his *Education* was finally released to the public after his death, he continued to mystify those he most fascinated.

This unbearably proud descendant of two of the most famous public men in American history now made a point of putting his best self into letters.

He had burned his diaries and his letters to Marian after her death. *The Education of Henry Adams,* begun in 1903, completed in 1907, privately printed in just one hundred copies, and sent out, as he put it with his usual mock deference, "to the persons interested, for their assent, correction, or suggestion," would make him famous, ultimately an American classic. Mark Twain said of his *Autobiography* (unlike the *Education* it was not a work of art but a tormented man's garrulity) that "only dead men tell the truth." Dead men do not tell the truth in the *Education.* Adams was not interested in telling the "truth" about himself—whatever that was. His aim was to present himself as History.

Like the economic swashbucklers of his generation—Rockefeller, Morgan, Whitney, Carnegie—Adams said "The public be damned." He said it often. His contempt for what his brother Brooks called "the degradation of the democratic dogma" was absolute. He was snobbishly pleased because he had had to pay Scribner's to publish his nine-volume *History of the United States of America During the Administrations of Thomas Jefferson and James Madison.* Such was the fate of the exceptional historian with a private income in a literary market dominated by mere novelists of the new American middle class.

How provocative and contemptuous Adams was in publishing his own pseudonovels. *Democracy* (1880), a satire on Washington society, was issued anonymously. *Esther* (1884), a story of New York society and his particular friends the artist John La Farge and the geologist Clarence King, was published under a feminine pseudonym. Adams encouraged rumors that his friend John Hay, and possibly others, had written each of the romans à clef. His favorite pose was to stay behind the scenes. Even when elected president of the American Historical Association in 1894, he managed to avoid delivering his presidential address, "The Tendency of History," by addressing it from Mexico. President Charles William Eliot of Harvard was exasperated by Adams's refusal to appear in person for an honorary degree. He thought Adams an overrated man and was the only one among Adams's hundred "friends" to return his copy of the privately printed *Education.*

Yet this immensely private, proud, unfathomably touchy person—"angelic porcupine" his friends called him—was the most public recluse in Washington. Living in his famous house opposite the president's, he knew everybody who in his considered opinion was worth knowing. He had been the closest friend of Secretary of State Hay during the McKinley and Roosevelt administrations and was supposed to have been Hay's secret advisor. Compared with grandfather John Quincy Adams and great-grandfather John Adams, Henry was just a rich eccentric scholar with mystifying interests in everything from Paleolithic art to the craze for a "science" of history. But this most superior and forbidding person so easy to dislike was Washington's most informed political gossip. Through the friends he had made in England during the Civil War as private secretary to his father the American minister, through his family connections and his all-important friends in politics, science, and literature, he was an informed and informing intelligence office. He had learned very early that Washington "usually had more to do with compromise than anything else." This made society interesting. No other American intellectual of the time was so much at the center of things while pretending to despise it. And he was at the heart of Washington power without any official position whatever.

Even as he approached eighty, Adams had a special grasp of the old century's struggles among the European powers, a grasp that after he took us into the war those struggles led to, Adams's fellow historian Woodrow Wilson was the last to admit. As usual, with his sharp intuitions of historical "acceleration" (his favorite theme), Adams expressed approval of nothing but the working out of a blind process. The nineteenth century was the "century of hope," Alfred North Whitehead was to say, because it invented invention. The release of new productive forces was almost beyond calculation. Adams was spellbound by inventions like the famous dynamo he virtually "prayed" to at the Paris Exposition of 1900. But he was less interested in their social use than he was in the emergence of new forces. At eighty he had lived long enough to see "a new universe of winged bipeds . . . British airplanes sailing up and down under my windows at all hours." That was not progress, just a new item to weigh in the scale of history.

In his "scientific" theory of history Adams emphasized the "law" of acceleration and the tendency of modern societies to go mad under the pressure of multiplicity. He grandly took the second law of thermodynamics to mean that in industrialized society, entropy signified a hemorrhaging of vital energy. The centralization vital to modern technology and politics would crack. He had long prophesied an uncontrollable explosion of energy expanding to reach the whole planet and likely to tamper with it. He was a better guesser than most Victorian prophets because he suspected that the system's call for ever more power was uncontainable, but it hid a death wish. America of the nineteenth century, the America that had made nonsense of the "eighteenth-century" Adams tradition of political reason in control of a wholly new society, now stood in Adams's mind for mechanical energy alone. It was *the* powerhouse. In 1917, with the once-provincial colonies about to rescue the British Empire—but not for long and certainly not for Britain's sake—Adams saw what he had guessed in England during the Civil War:

"Our good country the United States is left to a career that is positively unlimited except by the powers of the imagination." That "Maryland schoolmaster type" Woodrow Wilson, whom Adams hardly bothered to despise (Adams's own circle hated Wilson to the point of frenzy), was morally overwhelmed by this power. Wilson talked nonsense about saving for democracy a world that for the most part had never known democracy.

> We shall fight for the things which we have always carried nearest to our hearts,—for democracy, for the right of those who submit to authority to have a voice in their own Governments, for the rights and liberties of small nations, for a universal dominion or right by such a concert of free peoples as shall bring peace and safety to all nations and make the world itself at last free.

Wilson wept over the young men he sent out to die and trusted that the worst war in history would end war forever. Bad as William II sputtering *Gott mit uns,* Wilson was overheard at Paris saying, "If I didn't think God was behind me, I couldn't go on. . . ." For his own reasons Adams had gloated over Wilson's call to war. He had long sought a great Atlantic alliance. "It is really a joy," he wrote to an English friend, "to feel that we have established one great idea even though we have pulled the stars out of their courses to do it."

The war itself did not move him one way or another. All his life this perfect spectator had studied war and narrated war; he had supposed himself, from his family intimacy with power, capable of calculating the direction of war and the future of national power. The habit of "exclusion," which he said he had learned as a literary style at Harvard (it was in fact a family trait), had become his only style for life and thought. If Henry Adams felt anything in particular about the 116,708 Americans who were to die in the war, he left no word. The greatest American historian of his crucial century, the most versatile imagination among American scholar-historians, would have agreed with Randolph Bourne (had he bothered to hear of Randolph Bourne) that "War is the health of the state." He would not even have noticed Bourne's lonely protest against America-in-the-war; it was not in Adams's character or in his philosophy to worry over the two thousand prosecutions under Section 3 of the Espionage Act.*

---

*"And whosoever, when the United States is at war, shall willfully cause or attempt to cause insubordination, disloyalty, mutiny or refusal of duty in the military or naval forces of the U.S., or shall willfully obstruct the recruiting or enlistment services of the U.S., to the injury of the service of the U.S., shall be punished with a fine of not more than $10,000 or imprisonment for not more than twenty years, or both."

On the other hand, Henry James's hysterical espousal of England must have seemed to Adams uninformed. James, since 1876 settled in England, had in gratitude for "Europe" as the best vantage point for fiction taken England as the dream country of his eloquent heart and mind. In 1914 James almost died of shock, but before he did die in 1916 he became a British subject in order to show that *he* was in the war. On the outbreak of war he wrote to Howard Sturgis:

> The plunge of civilization into this abyss of blood and darkness by the wanton feat of those two infamous autocrats is a thing that so gives away the whole long age during which we have supposed the world to have been, with whatever abatement, gradually bettering, that to have to take it all now for what the treacherous years were all the while really making for and *meaning* is too tragic for any words.

He was to wish he had not lived on "into this unspeakable give-away of the whole fool's paradise of our past." This idealization of England, this total surprise that great-power rivalry could lead to war, would have made Adams laugh his death's-head cackle. Henry James may have had the "imagination of disaster," as he claimed of himself; the lasting disaster of the war was beyond his comprehension. Thomas Hardy, in his notes to *The Dynasts* on August 1914, wrote, "The human race is to be shown as one great network or tissue which quivers in every part when one point is shaken, like a spider's web if touched." That was more to the point of 1914, that onset of all our woe, when crowds in London and Berlin shouted "We want war! We want war!" D. H. Lawrence described the enthusiasm for war as "sensational delight posing as pious idealism."

Had Adams lived into the 1920s, he might have been able to read "Gerontion," the imaginary monologue of "an old man" composed by a thirty-year-old poet from St. Louis, now living in England, who had scornfully reviewed *The Education of Henry Adams* and then borrowed images from it for his poem. Unlikely as it is to imagine Adams recognizing his connection with the poem, he was certainly—like Eliot—another figure wasted by history in which he had played no part.

> Here I am, an old man in a dry month,
> Being read to by a boy, waiting for rain.
> I was neither at the hot gates
> Nor fought in the warm rain
> Nor knee deep in the salt marsh, heaving a cutlass,

Bitten by flies, fought.
My house is a decayed house,
And the jew squats on the window sill, the owner,
Spawned in some estaminet of Antwerp,
Blistered in Brussels, patched and peeled in London.

With his deadly gleefulness Adams once noted that he and his even more catastrophe-minded younger brother Brooks had discussed "the total failure of the universe, as usual, and especially of our own country, which seems to afford even more satisfaction." If there was no war, he wrote just before the war, the Middle West, all "stomach, but no nervous center,—no brains— would overwhelm America like an enormous polyp." War, he had argued, was necessary in order to institute "an Atlantic system," including Germany, from the Rocky Mountains to the Elbe, since this was "the energy center of the world." And the war, or at least a future war, might well be against a still-disorganized Russia before it was able to industrialize Siberia. When Adams reached England from France safely in August 1914, Bernard Berenson congratulated him: "I trust that you are satisfied at last that all your pessimistic hopes have been fulfilled."

Adams was not disheartened by the outbreak of hostilities. Henry James in Rye, on the Channel coast, constantly looked toward France as though he could share the war. Edmund Gosse:

The anguish of his execration became almost the howl of some animal, of a lion of the forest with the arrow in his flank, when the Germans wrecked Rheims Cathedral. He gazed and gazed over the sea southeast and fancied that he saw the flicker of the flames. He ate and drank, he talked and walked and thought, he slept and waked and lived and breathed only the War.

Yet no less than James, and no less than the thirty-year-old expatriate from St. Louis who had been prevented by the war, by his marriage to a distraught Englishwoman, and by his own growing "aboulie" from sailing home to defend at Harvard his dissertation on the philosophy of F. H. Bradley, Adams plainly projected his solitariness, his sexual sorrow, and his special dryness of heart and mockery onto a world at war. It had fulfilled all his anticipations of what nineteenth-century power struggles could lead to. He was a man so totally acid, embittered, enraged, that his dislike of the contemporary world had become a kind of ecstasy. In the 1890s he had thundered to his adored Elizabeth Cameron:

I expect troubled times for many years to come. On all sides, especially in Europe and Asia, the world is getting awful rickety. In our country we shall follow more or less the path of the world outside. For my own part, hating vindictively, as I do, our whole fabric and conception of society, against which my little life has squeaked protest from its birth, and will yell protest till its death, I shall be glad to see the whole thing utterly destroyed and wiped away.

Adams once confessed that his "instinct was blighted from babyhood." Yet as much as the expatriate Eliot, fifty years his junior, this gifted, equally antidemocratic American was to make his grateful audience in the twenties (when at last it heard of Henry Adams) think of the current world as a wasteland.

Adams the great historical dramatist was the widowed husband of a highly charged, acidly witty Boston patrician, Marian Hooper Adams, a gifted pioneer photographer. At the age of forty-two, on December 6, 1885, a Sunday morning "when all believers were safe in church," she drank the cyanide she kept for developing her pictures.

There is no reason to believe that Marian Hooper Adams, like Vivien Haigh-Wood Eliot, was in any way marred by a husband's sexual difficulties. We do not know as much about Henry Adams as we have learned about the gifted, troubled poet who wrote "The Love Song of J. Alfred Prufrock" before his marriage, "Gerontion" and *The Waste Land* after it. Adams, who felt that he had "finished my dinner" at forty-seven, when Marian died, had objective reasons, a great historian's expert reasons, for distrusting the modern age. He was another modernist who found a public only after the First World War confirmed his long-seated belief that the modern world was meaningless, insane, out of control. But unlike Yeats, Lawrence, Eliot, and Pound, Adams's ostensible subject *is* the historical process. His particular hope—dismissing every other—was to make a "science" of history. This was conjectured by a remarkable literary imagination that, he admitted, relied on images, not facts. Adams's real theme, like that of Eliot and all the great modernists, was the agony of change, the fear of the masses, the longing for an absolute. Long before he wrote the last sentence of the *Education*, Adams knew that if he and his like returned to the twentieth century, they would not "find a world that sensitive and timid natures could regard without a shudder." More and more indeed, the best were to lack all conviction, the worst to be full of a passionate intensity.

Adams omitted his wife from the book of his life. He concentrated on history as the mere acceleration of mechanical forces, ending in their uncontrollable dispersion. He was obsessed by the accumulation and centralization of power as the underlying theme of American history. But as though he had anticipated the nuclear age, he was also spellbound by the possibility of total destruction. His personal bitterness fed his malicious reading of History. The nineteenth century had given Western man—democratic, capitalist, "scientific" man—an unparalleled sense of power. In midcentury America, Whitman asserted in *Democratic Vistas* (1871), "It seems as if the Almighty had spread before this nation charts of imperial destinies, dazzling as the sun . . . making old history a dwarf." Adams's unhappy prophecy was that power stayed in the "powerhouse." So much centralization could not last. What Adams was saying below his breath, of course, was that power might prove suicidal because man could not be trusted. If History was always on his mind, suicide was never far away. A less cosmic version of so much disappearance, randomness, and destruction was Adams's writing near the end of his life, "All one has cared about has been a few women, and they have worried one more than falling empires."

Adams was fascinated by force, that prime image of nineteenth-century physics. In his own life, horribly as mechanical progress excited him, he knew no force more powerful than what he called Woman. Woman was outside and superior to the money-making routine of men. Woman was the virgin figure, the "goddess" in Adams's mythology, who in the Middle Ages was what the dynamo was now. (The American had incorporated the dynamo into himself.) Woman was the great exception to the materialist society, and Marian was the magnetic pull on Adams's "posthumous" existence from her death in 1885 to his in 1918. The image and terror of her death were to last long after the fact. Marian Adams's death by her own hand was to become the supreme instance in Adams's life of the "force" that can be exerted by a personal compulsion. All we know is that her love for her long-widowed father was more pressing than her love for her husband. When Dr. Hooper, to whom she wrote a full account of her doings every Sunday morning, died, she died with him. She bowed under this yoke and Adams bowed to the force of her necessity. Necessity, in good positivist style, was to become the theme of the last sections of his *History of the United States.* For Adams, sex was indeed to become "the sacred fount," the mysterious source of energy. Just as "Clover" became the all-disposing but especially all-forgiving Virgin in *Mont-Saint-Michel and Chartres,* so the *Education* projected her as Woman, a main force in history. The mysterious hooded figure he had Saint-Gaudens design over her (and later his) famous tomb in Rock Creek Cemetery is more a female figure than a male one.

In chapter 21 of the *Education,* "Twenty Years After (1892)," Adams pointedly takes up his life after Marian's death without saying a word about her. In "The Dynamo and the Virgin (1900)" he introduces the succession of force figures that dominated his historical imagination.

> . . . he turned from the Virgin to the Dynamo as though he were a Branly coherer. On one side, at the Louvre and at Chartres, . . . was the highest energy ever known to man . . . yet this energy was unknown to the American mind. An American Virgin would never dare command; an American Venus would never dare exist.
>   . . . The idea survived only as art. . . . Adams began to ponder, asking himself whether he knew of any American artist who had ever insisted on the power of sex, as every classic had always done; but he could think only of Walt Whitman. . . . All the rest had used sex for sentiment, never for force. . . . Society regarded this victory over sex as its greatest triumph. . . .

This victory symbolized to Adams the repressive spirit of modern capitalism. What he did not say (current religion bored him) was that so much propriety, so much conscious virtue on the part of America's upper classes, had replaced every possible tinge of supernatural religion. "God" was really "dead." What replaced Him was the immortality of Art. The nineteenth-century antagonists of progress who came to be considered modernists by the twentieth century can be identified by their belief, as Henry James put it to H. G. Wells, that "art *makes* life, makes interest, makes importance." Literature is the only life that has pattern, shape, meaning, the only life that may last; literature and art—this was Adams's reason for writing *Mont-Saint-Michel and Chartres*—are what religion leaves behind it. Only through literature is History embodied and the divine law recalled. To Henry Adams, as to all the House of Adams, History was still the first art.

Henry Adams had no respect for the new realistic fiction produced by his generation. To John Hay he was to write with easy superiority that "James knows almost nothing of women but the mere outside; he never had a wife. . . . Howells . . . cannot deal with gentlemen and ladies; he always slips up." In his manifesto "The Art of Fiction" (1884) James had hailed the novelist as succeeding to the "sacred office" of the historian. Although Adams never spoke of himself as an "artist," the Adamses, writers all (none of them was such a writer as Henry), accepted the ability to write as if it went with the offices they held and their command of intellectual and political history. Henry Adams never had to say that he was in command of his art, which in the United States was still called History.

Intellectual authority had belonged to historians because the writing of history was associated with the keeping of political tradition. Historians in

America were part of the history they lived to write, they were men of the world, the political world. It would not have occurred to Parkman, Prescott, Bancroft, or Adams that the work of such wild men as Poe and Melville, beggarly romancers, might be more lasting than that of historians. Marian Adams said of Henry James that it is "not that he bites off more than he chaws but that he chaws more than he bites off." James seemed to Adams to be setting the scene and arranging his effects with studied effort, to have *trained* himself to look at society through the eyes of the great European novelists of manners.

By the end of the First World War, when Henry Adams died and his *Education* came alive, History had ceased to be the narrative art that it had been to the nineteenth century. History as some Great Tradition, History as Intellectual Authority had become as much a Great Ruin as religion. This was certainly the idea of William Butler Yeats, T. S. Eliot, Ezra Pound, D. H. Lawrence, the Ernest Hemingway whose first important work was called simply *In Our Time.* Modernist literature would picture history exclusively as a Great Fall.

The young Henry James, afraid that a new country could not give a novelist the rich settings that old Europe did, had said apropos of Nathaniel Hawthorne that it takes a good deal of history to produce a little literature. Forty years later Eliot was writing in "Gerontion" that "History has many cunning passages." History Eliot would soon discount in the name of tradition. History was an immense panorama of futility and anarchy. Tradition was religion. The self would not suffice.

> I have seen the moment of my greatness flicker,
> And I have seen the eternal Footman hold my coat, and snicker,
> And in short, I was afraid.

In 1919 the thirty-one-year-old Eliot, caught by the war in England and happy to stay there, reviewed *The Education of Henry Adams* under the head, "A Sceptical Patrician." Eliot was unimpressed by the book, scornful of the man. He already had the sharp, impressively cutting air of critical authority that would please conservatives like Paul Elmer More. More could not understand why Eliot's poetry was so newfangled, so different from his prose. Eliot's reply: poetry deals with the world as it is. Eliot's severity as a critic was already a bit of an act, necessary to the postwar scepticism that would welcome as the very voice of itself Eliot's dislike of nineteenth-century sentiment.

The authoritative manner was also necessary to his secret despair as he wrote in a mosaic style and with gallows humor the poetry of a world more absurd than himself. Like Henry Adams, Eliot liked to deceive and mock the public. Nothing would have seemed more ridiculous to Eliot than Whitman's romantic democracy: "The soul of the largest and wealthiest and proudest nation may well go half-way to meet that of its poets." The poet in the modern world was damned. Damnation showed in the manic kaleidoscope of moods in "Prufrock," the desperate playfulness which is itself mimicked in stray couplets that tease the ear with their mock chords, as if forced from a hurdy-gurdy. The "indecisions" and "revisions" end on a helpless blank.

> And when I am formulated, sprawling on a pin,
> When I am pinned and wriggling on the wall,
> Then how should I begin
> To spit out all the butt-ends of my days and ways?
> And how should I presume?

When one considers Eliot's real emotions, and forgets the stern lawgiver who was soon to hypnotize English studies, it is touching to read Eliot's confession in *On Poetry and Poets* (1957) that he could not bear to reread his critical prose. To More's complaint that his poetry and criticism were disturbingly different, he replied that criticism describes the world as it should be.

The 1919 review of *The Education of Henry Adams* is insolent, clever, destructive. Eliot in America could never have written with such lordliness. No wonder the extraordinary lament of the "old man" of "Gerontion" reads like a cry from the soul of Henry Adams as much as it does one from the young Eliot, so quick to cry in "Prufrock" (1917), "I grow old . . . I grow old. . . ."

Why, unless he recognized himself in Adams and in Adams's own painful sense of tradition, did Eliot find him so unimpressive? But of course Adams *was* American history, and Eliot was trying to discharge himself of America.

He was much more refined than the equivalent Englishman, and had less vitality, though a remarkably restless curiosity, eager but unsensuous. . . . And his very American curiosity was directed and misdirected by two New England characteristics: conscientiousness and scepticism.

Here is precisely what makes the book, as an "autobiography," wholly different from any European autobiography worth reading. Adams is perpetually busy with himself. . . . But Adams is superlatively modest, diffident. . . . Conscience told him that one must be a learner all one's life, and as he had the financial means to gratify his conscience, he did so. This is conspicuously a Puritan inheritance. . . . Still, there are always others whose conscience lays upon them the heavy burden of self-improvement. They are usually sensitive people, and they want to do something great; dogged by the shadow of self-conscious incompetence, they are predestined failures. . . .

Wherever this man stepped, the ground did not simply give way, it flew into *particles*. . . . He was seeking for education, with the wings of a beautiful but ineffectual conscience beating vainly in a vacuum jar. He found, at best, two or three friends, notably the great John Hay, who had been engaged in settling the problems of China and Cuba and Manchuria. Adams yearned for unity, and found it, after a fashion, by writing a book on the thirteenth century.

The Erinyes which drove him madly through seventy years of search for education—the search for what, upon a lower plane, is called culture—left him much as he was born: well-bred, intelligent, and uneducated.

Eliot grasped, and was appalled by, Adams's preoccupation with self. This preoccupation haunted Eliot emotionally: the prisoner in his cell was to declare the highest aim of literature an escape from emotions and personality; escape from the self became the great theme of a religious striving that was more striving and cultural piety than it was belief.

> Because I do not hope to turn again
> Because I do not hope
> Because I do not hope to turn
> . . .
> (Why should the agèd eagle stretch its wings?)
> . . .
> And I pray that I may forget
> These matters that with myself I too much discuss
> Too much explain
> Because I do not hope to turn again

The prisoner in his self was even the subject of Eliot's doctoral thesis on F. H. Bradley's *Appearance and Reality,* and Bradley would be quoted in the notes to *The Waste Land* as a gloss on lines 411–17:

> . . . I have heard the key
> Turn in the door once and turn once only
> We think of the key, each in his prison
> Thinking of the key, each confirms a prison
> Only at nightfall, aethereal rumours
> Revive for a moment a broken Coriolanus

What provoked Eliot most in his review of the *Education* was his recognition that Adams's "scepticism" was his own. It was a despair of the modern world mounting to the "horror" of Mr. Kurtz as he finds himself in the heart of darkness. The children of the founding fathers are deracinated, besieged.

> Signs are taken for wonders. "We would see a sign!"
> The word within a word, unable to speak a word,
> Swaddled with darkness. In the juvescence of the year
> Came Christ the tiger
>
> In depraved May, dogwood and chestnut, flowering judas,
> To be eaten, to be divided, to be drunk
> Among whispers . . .

Does the prisoner in his self know how alone he is? Henry Adams would certainly have recognized himself as "a broken Coriolanus." The descendants of Puritans now adored the Middle Ages. The leadership of their country had long since passed the Adamses by. Eliot in England, who on the appropriate date wore a white rose in memory of Richard III, also bewailed John Quincy Adams's having had to yield the White House to Andrew Jackson. Adams the self-dramatizing "failure" became a terrible and terrifying old man who liked, as he said, to discuss the total failure of the universe. Eliot would have found superfluous Adams's "dynamic theory of history." But since Eliot was interested in history only as tradition, he would have agreed that the supposed dynamics of history lead to chaos, the dispersion of energy trailing out between the stars.

The center will not hold. "Hail nothing full of nothing, nothing is with thee," is Hemingway's lampoon at the end of "A Clean, Well-Lighted Place." A real or rhetorical bitterness would soon be the norm. But where was the primal fault—in the supposed absence of deity, in the revolt of the masses, in the eclipse of authority, in democracy itself? Or was it, horror of horrors, in the primal scene? As Adams said (and it was one of the more sincere sentences he ever wrote), "All one has cared about has been a few women, and they have worried one more than falling empires." Sex after the war would become a divine energy that would not suffer connection with other divinities. The Puritans had once insisted on a connection. The young Eliot lampooned Boston gentility, but "Prufrock" demonstrated the brilliant effect of repression. Adams and Eliot had excellent reasons not to free themselves of the New England virtue that was their pride, their minutest discrimination, their ability to pass judgment on the millions they despised.

The prisoner in his self, the self-exiled Coriolanus, is there because he chooses to be there. He is different from his pitiful age. The price he pays is sexual martyrdom, a familiar Christian forfeit, a distrust of woman that trembles through every reference by Eliot to a woman's hair.

> A woman drew her long black hair out tight
> And fiddled whisper music on those strings
> And bats with baby faces in the violet light
> Whistled, and beat their wings
> And crawled head downward down a blackened wall

It was a distrust that Adams also felt in his grief, in his guilt as a husband, and it resonated in his dinner-party glorification of Woman.

Sexual desolation is not hostile to wit and eloquence. Henry James was amazed by the power of self-revelation Adams displayed in old age. The young Eliot never wrote better than in "Prufrock," "Gerontion," *The Waste Land, The Hollow Men.* He was to show himself sublimely eloquent in the poem leading to his conversion, *Ash Wednesday,* and in the *Four Quartets* that closed his career with so many golden assurances.

> And all shall be well and
> All manner of thing shall be well
> When the tongues of flame are in-folded
> Into the crowned knot of fire
> And the fire and the rose are one.

One sometimes regrets the elder statesman who replaced mad but enduring Prufrock.

Eliot's famous assumption of "impersonality" was necessary to his early provocations in the absurdist style of Laforgue and Corbière, the harsh tensions of the Jacobean dramatists and the metaphysical poets. Baudelaire called drugs artificial paradises. (Eliot's favorite writers rather specialized in artificial hells.) In view of the sexual tragedy hidden within *The Waste Land* and its emphasis on dryness, it was certainly a great act that Eliot put up in the unrelieved gravity of his critical pronouncements. Finally, however, he admitted of the poem, misread by a generation with his encouragement, "To me it was only the relief of a personal and highly insignificant grouse against life; it is just a piece of rhythmical grumbling." The grouse was not insignificant, and Eliot's magnificent rhythmical sense, essential to his emotional power over the reader, expresses more than "grumbling." But equally resonant of Eliot's distrustful political soul was his famous early saying, "Poetry is not a turning loose of emotion, but an escape from emotion; it is not the expression of personality, but an escape from personality." It is only too clear why Eliot added, ". . . of course, only those who have personality and emotions know what it means to want to escape from these things." Other people do not suffer as we do.

Eliot sought at first to "escape" by turning many tortured fragments into scenes that positively drugged us as they flashed across an interior memory we discovered to be our own. The heap of broken images, the "little voices," as he brilliantly called them, showed us the refrain of buried words beating against the public world. The musicality was insidious but totally captivating as the phrases echoed and varied themselves. Here was a tour de force that depended on the shock effect of discontinuity without letup. "The thousand sordid images / Of which your soul was constituted," his great lines in "Preludes," came through in a haunting aura of music. Like Stravinsky, Eliot knew how to jar the reader with a force that made connection with the reader's own life.* When Eliot said in disparagement of Henry Adams that "it is the sensuous contributor to the intelligence that makes the difference," he was referring to his own poetic strategy. He knew how to borrow for sensuous contribution even when he reversed what he borrowed.

In chapter 18 of the *Education*, "Free Fight (1869–1870)," Adams begins:

The old New Englander was apt to be a solitary animal, but the young New Englander was sometimes human. Judge Hoar brought his son Sam to Washington, and Sam Hoar loved largely and well. He taught Adams the charm of Washington spring. Education for education, none ever compared with the delight of this. The Potomac and its tributaries squandered beauty. Rock Creek was as wild as the Rocky Mountains. Here and there a negro log cabin alone disturbed the dogwood and the judas-tree, the azalea and the laurel. The tulip and the chestnut gave no sense of struggle against a stingy nature. The soft, full outlines of the landscape carried no hidden horror of glaciers in its bosom. The brooding heat of the profligate vegetation; the cool charm of the running water; the terrific splendor of the June thunder-gust in the deep and solitary woods, were all sensual, animal, elemental. No European spring had shown him the same intermixture of delicate grace and passionate depravity that marked the Maryland May. He loved it too much, as though it were Greek and half human.

In "Gerontion," published in *Poems* (1920), Adams's excited roaming became

> In depraved May, dogwood and chestnut, flowering judas,
> To be eaten, to be divided, to be drunk
> Among whispers; by Mr. Silvero

---

*Eliot would say that he heard in *Le Sacre du printemps* "that vanished mind of which our mind is a continuation—the primitive mind still survives in the absurdities of the soul."

> With caressing hands, at Limoges
> Who walked all night in the next room . . .

Later the speaker complains, in some of Eliot's most wonderfully shaped and affecting lines,

> I have lost my passion: why should I need to keep it
> Since what is kept must be adulterated?
> I have lost my sight, smell, hearing, taste and touch:
> How should I use them for your closer contact?

The judas-tree became a favorite symbol of betrayal, and "Gerontion" himself an image not only of aged impotence and despair but of the difficulty, perhaps the impossibility, of reaching Christ the Saviour rather than Christ the tiger, whose terrible force leaped out at us "in the juvescence of the year," in "depraved May." "Gerontion" is a wonderfully effective and penetrating poem in Eliot's most clamorous, stricken early style. It does not matter that he made ominous those images in Adams that were joyful with "passionate depravity." It is funny to read Eliot's final dig at Adams in his review of the *Education:* "There is nothing to indicate that Adams's senses either flowered or fruited; he remains a little Paul Dombey asking questions." Adams, remembering "the dogwood and the judas-tree, the azalea and the laurel," showed that his senses had indeed flowered and fruited in the primitive nature that once surrounded Washington.

Eliot was thirty-one when he wrote his poem, as was Adams when he exulted in the Washington spring of 1869. The Adams whom Eliot reviewed with so much distaste could only have been the speaker in "Gerontion." What a transference that would have been between these Puritans born half a century apart who yet were artistically two ends of the same thought. Both suffered the inaccessibility of God. That is the deepest strain in "Gerontion": it is easier for God to devour us than for us to partake of Him in a seemly spirit. Nowhere in Eliot is the God for whose eclipse he blames the modern world real and apparent to Eliot himself; it is religion, not faith, that will give him assurance, and religion will be valued for the "culture" it leaves. Eliot admitted that he was as ready to become a Buddhist as a Christian after the turmoil leading to *The Waste Land,* a poem that ends in Buddhist imperatives and the Upanishad cry for peace. Adams in *Mont-Saint-Michel and Chartres,* as in his poem "Buddha and Brahma," shows the same pluralism—religion is culture rather than belief, religion is literature that attests the unbelief Adams never denied and was even sardonically proud of. History is the only master! Eliot, even as a Harvard undergraduate studying Oriental religion, always sought something "higher."

Adams, citing Whitman as the only American artist "who had ever insisted on the power of sex," omitted to say that Whitman found democratic America the correlative of his sensuous energy. Whitman the old believer, the "sweet democratic despot," thought of democracy itself as a form of sex. It went without saying that sex was a form of democracy. Adams and Eliot emphasized the defeat of both. But what makes "Gerontion" so impressive is that in the speaker's privation one does hear worlds revolving, one does see the stars. The *Education* astonished postwar readers by revealing a sense of the "failure" of America, bitterly insisted on by Adams, that the best-placed Americans were feeling. This would soon be interpreted as the *modern* failure. Eliot in "Gerontion" made his war-besotted generation see history as nothing but human depravity.

> After such knowledge, what forgiveness? Think now
> History has many cunning passages, contrived corridors
> And issues, deceives with whispering ambitions,
> Guides us by vanities.

The disconnection between the self and the modern world was not as general as Adams and Eliot said it was. It was in themselves as men and artists, refined to the point of pain by their need to embrace an absolute. An unmoved mover—Dynamo or Virgin!—was just a literary idea to their indifferent contemporaries. They saw themselves as the embodiment of history in a world rushing to the death of the past.

What made Adams and Eliot great—and kept them solitary—was their ability to hear in their minds those "little voices" that they made others hear in a work of art. One hears these voices in the *Education*, in *Mont-Saint-Michel and Chartres*, and in Adams's extraordinary letters from Boston to Tokyo, Washington to Palermo, London and Paris to Samoa. Although Adams had once presumed to make a science of history, it was the art of history he was best at—history as the actual appearance and complication of mankind; history as manner, pretense, personal ambition, and undying hatred. These voices made a revolution in poetry when they were heard in "The Love Song of J. Alfred Prufrock." They were to dominate the generation that recognized itself in *The Waste Land*.

Our buried feelings, even in their humiliated state, can make the triumph of literature. Poetry, Rilke said, is the past that breaks out in our hearts. "Poetry" in the largest sense—the personal voice that Emerson inaugurated as a national tradition—became in Adams and Eliot a form of submission rather than the revolution in human affairs that Emerson identified with America. We must decipher what history has made of us. This can become a way of despair, as it was in Adams, who reversed the belief in progress that had established the House of Adams, and in Eliot, who in England mourned the last of the Plantagenets as though America had killed off the Middle Ages —which indeed it had. Too respectful and submissive a sense of tradition brought Henry Adams to lament the "unity" of the Middle Ages falling into the "multiplicity" of the terrible nineteenth and twentieth centuries, and it brought Eliot to the beautiful articulation that was his genius:

> . . . De Bailhache, Fresca, Mrs. Cammel, whirled
> Beyond the circuit of the shuddering Bear
> In fractured atoms. Gull against the wind, in the windy straits
> Of Belle Isle, or running on the Horn,
> White feathers in the snow, the Gulf claims,
> And an old man driven by the Trades
> To a sleepy corner.
> Tenants of the house,
> Thoughts of a dry brain in a dry season.

Yet mere suspension in the universe, these wonderful images of a power greater than ourselves that makes for anonymity, owed something to the reversal of the "century of hope" with which American literature had begun in an age of faith, at the hands of Ralph Waldo Emerson.

PART ONE

The Self as Power:

America When Young

1830–1865

The self: "Miracle of miracles, beyond statement, most spiritual and vaguest of earth's dreams, yet hardest basic fact, and only entrance to all facts."

WHITMAN, *Democratic Vistas*

1

The Priest Departs, the Divine Literatus Comes: Emerson

Prometheus's confession—"in a word, I detest all gods"
—is its own confession, its own slogan against all Gods
in heaven and earth who do not recognize man's consciousness of himself as the highest divinity.

KARL MARX, *On the Difference Between
Democritus' and Epicurus' Philosophy of Nature*
(Doctoral Dissertation, 1841)

I

When Ralph Waldo Emerson lay dying in 1882, a friend who watched by his bedside on one of the last nights was astonished to hear him "repeating in his sonorous voice, not yet weakened, fragments of sentences, almost as if reciting. It seemed strange and solemn in the night, alone with him, to hear these efforts to deliver something evidently with a thread of fine recollection in it, his voice as deep and musical as ever."

The old enchanter was dying, as he had lived, by words. Emerson the writer had lived from day to day by talking to himself in his journal. What was instinctive to him, elemental, was the fragment, the stray observation, the aphorism or epigram that came from an absolute confidence that his perfect freedom made him a vessel of truth and a link to the divine mind. No wonder Emerson found any right sentence sufficient to itself. Though his memory began to fail long before his death, the lack of continuity in his thought was not a hindrance. He was Orpheus, playing what music he liked. Even in his best days as one of the most active lecturers in America, he did not always think it necessary to read a manuscript consecutively. In full sight of an audience he would shuffle pages as if he were looking for some favorite passage superior to argument. When he was unable to write anything new, his daughter Ellen and James Elliot Cabot strung together passages from his old lectures. Emerson had been doing the same thing for years. Ellen was so embarrassed by his reluctance to follow a manuscript that she once sewed his pages together to keep him to the original text.

Strict organization had never been Emerson's strong point, and in fact it had little to do with his genius for dreaming his way into a subject, for finding himself in his own depths. "A man finds out," he wrote in his journal for 1859, "that there is somewhat in him that knows more than he does. Then he comes presently to the curious question, Who's Who? which of these two is really me? the one that knows more, or the one that knows less? the little fellow or the big fellow?" In his "savings bank," the journal from which he winnowed his best sentences (this was more than Yankee thrift), he formed public utterance from single sentences and passages that were sudden stabs "at the very axis of reality." Emerson was an organic writer and instinctive stylist who even on the platform seemed to be waiting for his own voice to astonish him. Reading him in an age that finds exotic his insistence that the independent "soul" is all man's freedom, intelligence, and power, we can still hear the man who dazzled so many brave minds in the nineteenth century. Emerson was the contemporary who discovered them to themselves.

> A man is a god in ruins. When men are innocent, life shall be longer, and shall pass into the immortal as gently as we awake from dreams. Now, the world would be insane and rabid, if these disorganizations should last for hundreds of years. It is kept in check by death and infancy. Infancy is the perpetual Messiah, which comes into the arms of fallen men, and pleads with them to return to paradise.

> There are innocent men who worship God after the tradition of their fathers, but their sense of duty has not yet extended to the use of all their faculties.

> Every spirit builds itself a house, and beyond its house a world, and beyond its world, a heaven. Know then the world exists for you. For you is the phenomenon perfect. What we are, that only can we see. All that Adam had, all that Caesar could, you have and can do. . . . Build therefore your own world. As fast as you conform your life to the pure idea in your mind, that will unfold its great proportions.

The years after the Civil War were to be one long anticlimax to rhapsodies from Emerson's genius for personal faith. Then Emerson himself became "a god in ruins," reduced to the elegance of style that never failed him.

The apostle of perfect personal power—to be gained from the energy and imagination no longer sacrificed to formal religion—was to be misunderstood as a preacher of rugged individualism. Emerson's unchurched, free, visionary, and ideal "man thinking" would not be the lodestar for twenty million driven Americans. "Things are in the saddle," he noted as early as the Mexican War (1846), "and ride mankind." Emerson would eventually be understood as a moralist only. Even before the Civil War there was a subtle shift in his own thinking from the individual as supreme power to power's proving the worth of the successful individual. Yet in the great early days of *Nature, The American Scholar,* the Divinity School Address, and "Self-Reliance," when he was the rising American oracle and a threat to the orthodox, he was all too aware that he wrote by "inspiration," in short flights that excited him but left him wittily resigned to the accidents of composition. After all, it was at his desk that he discovered what a miracle life can be. To his friend Carlyle, whose furious talk-style he admired:

> Here I sit and read and write, with very little system, and as far as regards composition, with the most fragmentary result: paragraphs incompressible, each sentence an infinitely repellent particle.

> For my journals, which I dot here at home day by day, are full of disjointed dreams, audacities, unsystematic irresponsible lampoons of systems, and all manner of rambling reveries, the poor drupes and berries I find in my basket after endless and aimless rambles in woods and pastures. I ask constantly of all men whether life may not be poetic as well as stupid?

In 1851 he noted to himself that "I found when I had finished my new lecture that it was a very good house, only the architect had unfortunately omitted the stairs." Emerson had the highest confidence in the perceptive powers of his "soul"—in his intellectual gift as a seer. It was the "self-trust" that the founders of a new religion expect of their followers—and that the followers adapt to their own temperament and interest. Once he had found himself in his isolation, a young widower who had the courage to leave the ministry and the church, he became anything but modest or a respecter of modesty. "Take egotism out and you would castrate the benefactors." To write so much by fits and starts, to make the orphic his method, made him believe in the virtues of passivity. "I am a natural reader, and only a writer in the absence of natural writers. In a true time, I should never have written."

Whenever that true time may have been, the times now needed an Emerson. New England, the home of our first American saints, did not suit Emerson's perfectionism. Its intellectual class—the first thing he looked for in any examination of society—was confined to ministers and pedants. Emerson, whom the old Whitman in Camden summed up shrewdly, "He is best as critic, or diagnoser," did not think of himself as a "prophet" even when he wrote like one in *The American Scholar* and the Divinity School Address. He was a clairvoyant, a throwback to the great ages of faith who, by identifying faith with the individual soul's gift for faith, addressed himself to a future of miraculous "self-actualization," as the young Karl Marx called it. Emerson thus left everything open to the self that Whitman in the first raptures of *Leaves of Grass* called "miracle of miracles, beyond statement, most spiritual and vaguest of earth's dreams, yet hardest basic fact, and only entrance to all facts." Nothing was to prove more various than this self, nothing more indeterminate than self-actualization. No American writer ever played more roles than Emerson the inspirer, the "mystic," the poet, and the inhuman perfectionist. On the lecture platform he was blandness itself, the sage on all subjects. Reporting his mind in his journal, he astonished and disconcerted himself. His mind was porous, plastic, shrewd; his situation in rough, indifferent, hard-drinking Concord was one of isolation.*

Emerson's disposition was to sit back, to let the world come to him. "Society" was a problem.

> I, cold because I am hot—cold at the surface only as a sort of guard and compensation for the fluid tenderness of the core—have much more experience than I have written there, more than I will, more than I can write. In silence we must wrap much of our life, because it is too fine for speech, because also we cannot explain it to others, and because somewhat we cannot yet understand.

His real life was "poetic," ceaseless thought. "Life consists in what a man is thinking of all day." He would have to be the eternal spectator, making judgments on people from his private mountaintop. Carrying this disposition into society, he knew how it affected others. It mattered less to him than the

---

*One of literary America's best-kept secrets. "Always remember that the literary men of Concord have never been popular there during their lives. The Concord people were ignorant, low lived, unambitious save in the money making line, and many large estates were squandered by farmers who neglected their farms, and lounged in the Tavern bar rooms week in and week out.... Do not forget that Emerson began this work, that his first work was to educate his townsmen, to uplift them, that the literary history of Concord has grown up entirely since 1829, or the birth of the lyceum." (*Remembrances of Concord and the Thoreaus: Letters of Horace Hosmer to Dr. S. A. Jones*, edited by George Hendrick, 1977)

Hosmer noted acidly that taverns in Concord were scarcely a mile apart, that there were three large taverns in the center of town, and that all stores sold liquor by the gallon or quart. The manufacture of rum barrels was the chief industry; "ministers drink and *got drunk*, helplessly so."

objectionableness of society. "We descend to meet." A priggish saying. The great man never quite left off being the great man. But he was far from considering himself the best kind of writer—he was just one peculiarly necessary to "This Age, This Country, Oneself." "Natural writers" were perhaps those, like Isaiah and Jesus, who did not have to write to be understood. Only such represented a "true time."

Emerson respected prophets too much to regard himself as one. He did identify all good writing, his own not least, with some fundamental charge of spirit that gave new life to the reader. He "greeted" his contemporaries as an age of hope. Democracy in America was only one revolutionary challenge of the time. If limitless faith in the individual seemed natural to the century's progress, the individual would transcend the slavish societies of the past by finding divinity within himself. Marx and Engels in *The Communist Manifesto* (1848) hailed the century as mankind's greatest material triumph, made possible by the triumph of middle-class individualists over feudalism and its handmaiden, religion. Freed from religion, opium of the people, mankind would rise to unparalleled heights of creativity and subject nature completely to its material needs. The elder Henry James (a utopian socialist) noticed that "the kingdom of man is at hand." The great gospel of the nineteenth century was *inevitable* progress, confirmed by evolution and promising, with the release of man from physical drudgery and superstition, his moral improvement. Marx was to suggest that man would be free to confront his religious yearnings only when relieved of the struggle for existence. The ascent of man was not to be doubted. The "religion of humanity," as George Eliot called it, would be the free man's worship.

Emerson, with his invincible belief that the universe is on man's side and that there is "compensation" for our losses, remained loftily spiritual in his tastes. He despised fiction because it was mundane; in every "romantic" novelist of his time he saw mere contrivance. Though himself an occasional poet and even one for public occasions, his own taste in contemporary poetry was indifferently conventional. The famous exception remains *Leaves of Grass*, which Emerson found

the most extraordinary piece of wit & wisdom that America has yet contributed. I am very happy in reading it, as great power makes us happy. It meets the demand I am always making of what seemed the sterile & stingy nature, as if too much handiwork or too much lymph in the temperament were making our western wits fat & mean. I give you joy of your free & brave thought. I have great joy in it. I find incomparable things said incomparably

well, as they must be. I find the courage of treatment, which so delights us,
& which large perception only can inspire.

Nothing here suggests how much Emerson valued Whitman as a poet.
Whitman's "message" must have been glimpsed by Emerson as the farthest
extension of his own, Whitman's ecstatic lines a startling complement to
rhapsodic paragraphs of *Nature*. Emerson the anthologist never thought to
include "the most extraordinary piece of wit & wisdom that America has yet
contributed." (It would have blown up a tedious schoolbook like *Parnassus*.)
When Whitman was preparing a third edition in 1860, Emerson went to see
him in Boston and attempted to dissuade him from including *Children of
Adam*. Emerson had responded fervently to Whitman's first edition because
of its "great power," which made him throw off all his usual boredom with
polite letters in New England. "I find the courage of treatment, which so
delights us, & which large perception only can inspire." Thoreau called
Whitman's second edition "a great primitive poem—an alarum or trumpet-
note ringing through the American camp." Emerson would have liked this
said about himself. He felt his own literary power to be "aboriginal." In his
great essay "The Poet" (1844) he wrote out what he thought *he* was—a poet
of the type before literary specialization, a poet in the "original" sense of the
word, a poet who spoke directly to other men out of his representative
nature. All true writers were types of "*the* poet," not subdivided and clas-
sified but integral of mind and spirit, able to see life whole and to express
the "All."

Walt Whitman in 1871 was still trying to explain himself to an unheeding
country. He insisted in *Democratic Vistas*, though his voice was diminished
in hope from 1855, that "the problem of humanity all over the world is social
and religious, and is to be finally met and treated by literature. The priest
departs, the divine literatus comes." This is just what Emerson thought.
Divine or not, the literatus (only Whitman could have given such elevation
to the word) had a literary mission to his raw new country. It was to be
founded on the comprehensive power released to the individual by his emancipation from institutions. Justification by faith, crucial to Protestantism, was
to leave self and soul, every person and every mind, free. After all, Emerson
had made himself free, had addressed himself to every opportunity. "Ours
is the revolutionary age," he wrote in 1839, "bringing man back to consciousness." Emerson in his great early period was exalted, perfectly confident, as
he confronted every difficulty under the American sun. To this day his

readers cannot find the right name for his composite role. He was indifferent to labels and in 1850 shrugged them off—"Call yourself preacher, pedlar, lecturer, tinman, grocer, scrivener, jobber, or whatever lowest name your business admits, and leave your lovers to find the fine name."

Emerson was not just an "essayist," and his ideas were not original enough to make him a "philosopher." The literary categories that Emerson derided are now so fixed that Emerson's role as a thinker-at-large (who became a presiding influence) seems more complex than in fact it was. America does not have names for literary men like Diderot who are foment-ers of a new consciousness; Victorian "prophets" like Arnold, Ruskin, Mill, Carlyle; rebels of thought like Nietzsche, William James, Shaw, Sartre.

Emerson as much as anyone in his time—and perhaps a little more—remains one of them. His whole effort as writer and speaker was to persuade "the American this new man" to *be* a new man. He could not imagine literature's *not* seeking to uproot society by changing the individual. He could not imagine a new world of thought without literature as its medium. Literature was central, and literature was transformation. The writer was a sacred figure through whom new life passed to the people. Without Carlyle's storminess at the degradation of modern man, but with just as much author-ity, Emerson tacitly considered himself as much of a hero as his country needed. The nineteenth-century cult of genius touched everyone of the "more prophetic" sort. Even Melville ("Nay, I do not oscillate in Emerson's rainbow") had to admit that

> Emerson is more than a brilliant fellow. Be his stuff begged, borrowed, or stolen, or of his own domestic manufacture, he is an uncommon man. Swear he is a humbug—then is he no common humbug. . . . There is a something about every man elevated above mediocrity, which is, for the most part, instinctively perceptible. This I see in Mr. Emerson. And, frankly, for the sake of the argument, let us call him a fool;—Then had I rather be a fool than a wise man.—I love all men who *dive*.

Emerson sometimes called himself a "speaker." As in any age of a new Gospel, his effective voice was valued before it was read, was "published before it was printed." Emerson said that the age was revolutionary because it was "bringing man back to consciousness." But as his surly friend Carlyle told him, he was "a new man in a new country," and he regarded himself, as many an American then did, as a novelty—the Robinson Crusoe of this island, its first settler and prime discoverer. And it was a country of the spirit as well as a new world. The ex-minister preaching "self-reliance" in all things, starting with organized religion, was God-intoxicated. What went out of him in letters of fire became far more material in the eyes and ears of the American congregation. To himself and for himself, Emerson was many things. His habitual benevolence and insistent optimism made him suspect, even in his own time, as a type of confidence man. But in his great beginning, when the minister of Second Church in Boston unfrocked himself and then offered himself as "man thinking" to any lecture audience that would have him, he was that rarest of all modern intellectuals—an ecstatic, a primitive Christian: "For this was I born & came into the world to deliver the self of myself to the Universe from the Universe: to do a certain benefit which Nature would not forego, nor I be discharged from rendering, & then immerge again into the holy silence & eternity, out of which as a man I arose."

If in his authority he remained a clergyman and something too self-righteous for a man of genius (the "proof" of his private and pure religion was the "moral sentiment," which he thought universal and permanent, a "law" of nature confirmed by science), his own faith was deep and wild, sometimes beyond his own reach.

II

On September 9, 1832, the twenty-nine-year-old minister of Second Church in Boston preached to his regretful congregation a farewell sermon in which he explained why he could not regard the communion service as ordained by scripture. The Lord's Supper was nothing more than the Jewish Passover feast. Emerson then resigned his pastorate. By the end of the year he was off to Europe; like Melville's Ahab, he sailed on a Christmas day. When he returned almost a year later, he was ready to publish his first book, *Nature*. Emerson's real ministry had just begun.

The formal grounds on which Emerson resigned his pastorate were hardly enough to explain his leaving the church *and* the ministry. He had really left all formal religion behind him. Emerson was beginning to understand that total "self-reliance"—from his innermost spiritual promptings—would be his career and his fate. The death from tuberculosis of his wife, Ellen, at nineteen, after less than two years of marriage, had increased his intellectual isolation and downright boredom as he went his clerical rounds. He, too, had been in danger from tuberculosis, the New England calamity of the time that was to kill two of his brothers. He and Ellen had loved each other wildly amidst her many frightening "scaldings" of blood. He never got over Ellen. Losing her made him even more impatient with his old way of life, destroyed many clerical cautions.

Emerson always maintained a preacher's professional unction, but any established creed he found intolerable. Remote and a shade too literary as he often seemed, he awed a majority of his congregation. They pressed him to stay, kept putting off acceptance of his resignation; for a year after he left he continued to receive his salary. Emerson was always to have a positive effect on people who did not know what he was talking about.

If it was hard for Second Church to let its minister go, he also recognized his going as strange. The rumor in Boston was that he had gone mad. The former president John Quincy Adams was to charge that

> a young man named Ralph Waldo Emerson . . . after failing in the every-day vocations of a Unitarian preacher and schoolmaster, starts a new doctrine of transcendentalism, declares all the old revelations superannuated and worn out, and announces the approach of new revelations and prophecies. Garrison and the non-resistant abolitionists, Brownson and the Marat democrats, phrenology and animal magnetism, all come in, furnishing each some plausible rascality as an ingredient for the bubbling cauldron of religion and politics.

No one had ever been more truly born to the ministry than Emerson, and when had an Emerson not been in the ministry? For nine successive generations in New England, Emersons had been ministers. To go over the formal record of Emerson's leaving—his farewell sermon on the Lord's Supper, the affectionate letter of resignation, the reluctant vote to accept the resignation —is to summon up the departure scene on an old Greek frieze. A young man is leaving his family; they hold out their hands to him; though already on his way, he looks back to them. Even after Emerson's resignation had been accepted he was occasionally to appear in his old pulpit and many another. "I like a church; I like a cowl," he was to begin a famous poem in 1839. "Yet not for all his faith can see / Would I that cowlèd churchman be."

"In Massachusetts," Emerson wrote in 1839, "a number of young and adult persons are at this moment the subject of a revolution.

> Not in churches, or in courts, or in large assemblies; not in solemn holidays, where men were met in festal dress, have these pledged themselves to new life, but in lonely and obscure places, in servitude, in solitude, in solitary compunctions and shames and fears, in disappointments, in diseases, trudging beside the team in the dusty road, or drudging, a hireling in other men's cornfields, schoolmasters who teach a few children rudiments for a pittance,

ministers of small parishes of the obscurer sects, lone women in dependent condition, matrons and young maidens, rich and poor, beautiful and hard-favored, without conceit or proclamation of any kind, have silently given in their several adherence to a new hope.

These people were Christians who no longer needed a church—moralists and pietists, earnestly independent souls in the oldest Protestant tradition of the "priesthood of all believers." They were not wholly emancipated, like the George Sand of whom Emerson noted enviously that she "owes to her birth in France her entire freedom from the cant and snuffle of our dead Christianity." Emerson was not the first and certainly not the last minister to make conscience and imagination his church. He was simply more gifted, startlingly the literatus—unlike George Ripley, who was to establish Brook Farm and later become the *New York Tribune*'s literary critic under Horace Greeley, or the passionate reformer Theodore Parker, who was for the most part excluded from the churches. Emerson's marked literary grace in the pulpit had created a bond between him and the congregation. This accord was based more on the man's extraordinary presence than on an understanding of his mind; it foretells the respect his lecture audiences were to feel for the "mystic" who impressed them by talking over their heads. After he had spoken for the first time on the West Coast in a San Francisco church, a paper reported, "All left the church feeling that an elegant tribute had been paid to the creative genius of the Great First Cause, and that a masterly use of the English language had contributed to that end."

Emerson's estrangement from doctrinal Christianity was absolute. All his teaching as a sage-at-large and the exaltation that can still be felt behind the style of *Nature, The American Scholar,* the Divinity School Address, "Self-Reliance," "The Poet," reflect the "dignity" that impressed even a hostile T. S. Eliot and that rests on the minister's revelation that he did not need a church. Not "God" was dead but the church! And since the church was the Past, it was really only the Past that was "dead." Freed from obedience to superstition, dogma, hierarchy, and Sunday routine, man on the crest of his inborn faith would find in himself all that men had ever meant by God and thereby become more-than-man-had-ever-been: types of Prometheus and Zarathustra and, from the mountaintop of the Superman or Hero, deliverers of mankind.

New England as a society had been founded on the church. Pilgrims and Puritans had arrived as bodies of organized belief. Amidst the solitude and fright of the wild Western shore, it was always to the church, the essential "body" of believers, the church as emblem, justification, release, that Emerson's ancestors had clung. The minister was their visible connection to the faith. Wherever radical Protestantism returned to the austerity and directness of the Gospels, it identified the whole people as the "Lord's People." The preacher reinforced this identity. By giving out the Word to his people, he assured continuity to their spiritual life, became the teacher of his tribe, a "vessel" to all those dependent on his soul-restoring eloquence.

Emerson looked as if he had been born to this role. His remoteness assured him of success even on the lecture platform. The classic New England minister was not a sweaty actor like Henry Ward Beecher but, like Hawthorne's Dimmesdale, an oracle suitably distant from the souls he never ceased to instruct. Emerson lamented his inability to reach people easily but was not downcast by this traditional failing. He looked the Puritan minister in his "lofty" bearing, his very leanness—the Yankee leanness which someone said made him look like a scruple. The photographs of him in his prime show a face so assured that it now looks archaic. William James eventually came to adore and even to "represent" Emerson in the succession of American thinkers. But in 1874 he wrote that Emerson's "refined idiocy seems as if it must be affectation." The contribution of spirituality to so much self-respect was widely noted. Condescension toward those lacking in grace was also marked. The serenity famous in every decade seemed impermeable to admirers and suspicious critics. "O you man without a handle!" the elder Henry James burst out. "Shall one never be able to help himself out of you, according to his needs, and be dependent only upon your fitful tippings-up?" An inhuman equanimity continued into his letters, which always tried to correct the general impression of his remoteness. Every report of his conversation is surprising—he is cagey, clever, unweariedly performing.

Emerson was to have the greatest possible influence on his contemporaries, on other writers, on the myth of the American as being uniquely free. Whitman was eventually let down by Emerson's prudish objections to *Leaves of Grass,* but he would have been nothing without Emerson's presence in the American picture. He sized up Emerson's temperament as "almost ideal." Talking to Horace Traubel in Camden, the old man appreciated in Emerson a "transparency" properly mysterious.

His quality, his meaning has the quality of the light of day, which startles nobody. You cannot put your finger upon it yet there is nothing more palpable, nothing more wonderful, nothing more vital and refreshing. There are some things in the expression of this philosoph, this poet, that are full mates of the best, the perennial masters, and will so stand in fame and the centuries. America in the future, in her long train of poets and writers, while knowing more vehement and luxuriant ones, will, I think, acknowledge nothing nearer [than] this man, the actual beginner of the whole procession —and certainly nothing purer, cleaner, sweeter, more canny, none, after all, more thoroughly her own and native. The most exquisite taste and caution are in him, always saving his feet from passing beyond the limits, for he is transcendental of limits, and you see underneath the rest a secret proclivity, American maybe, to dare and violate and make escapades.

Emerson left the church because he was happy with his mind as it was. He could subsist outside the church because, living on his mind and being responsive to its every prompting, he was satisfied that the "active soul" was an actual mirror of the world. The Greeks may have discovered that the "world" replicates the human mind; Emerson lived this fact without philosophy's sense that perception can be duplicitous. The "soul" or "mind" had for him such total access to reality that it virtually replaced it. Nature is there to serve man. Mind is everywhere the master. The soul as pure perception, pathway into All Things, became for Emerson the *universe* as an "open secret." Once he discovered this secret, he saw that there was no secret. The soul was not just the perfect knower but the real medium of existence. We live in disembodied consciousness as God does. No wonder that John Jay Chapman, who thought Emerson the last barrier to the mob spirit, admitted that

> if an inhabitant of another planet should visit the earth, he would receive, on the whole, a truer notion of human life by attending an Italian opera than he would by reading Emerson's volumes. He would learn from the Italian opera that there were two sexes; and this, after all, is probably the fact with which the education of such a stranger ought to begin.

The French biologist Jacques Monod attributed the success of religion to the fact that it makes it possible for us to love the world. Emerson, by placing the world at the disposal of our "ripe perceptive powers," certainly made it lovable.

This was a creative mind's sweet illusion—the world is forever moving in the direction of our thought. For Emerson everything came back to the personal sense of power that seized the universe at large as its corollary and friend. "Nature," everything outside of us, waiting on us alone, perceived and possessed by us alone, easily makes itself known. God speaks through us alone, so He must be in us. We share His power. Even to radical Protestantism, whose hope for emancipation from worldly institutions like the church was finally achieved (and perhaps terminated) in Emerson, his insistence on "the infinitude of the private mind" ("the only doctrine I have ever taught") was understandably shocking. In his intoxication with the religious sufficiency of his creative powers Emerson paraded before all men a doctrine sufficient only to great creative talent. The farmers and shopkeepers at his lectures were no doubt glad to hear that the individual in America had no limit but the sky.

Emerson aroused something more specific in creative minds from Matthew Arnold to Nietzsche. In America, Thoreau and Whitman, reverberating to Emerson's revelation, were the nearest to him, the most gifted and lasting in the American line that took the unlimited self as its greatest resource. Thoreau told Moncure Conway that he found in Emerson "the same perfection as the objects he studied in external nature, his ideals real and exact." Matthew Arnold was moved to write on the flyleaf of Emerson's *Essays:*

> Strong is Soul, and wise, and beautiful:
> The seeds of godlike power are in us still:
> Gods are we, Bards, Saints, Heroes, if we will—

(Only Melville among American writers would have thought of Arnold's next line: "Dumb judges, answer, truth or mockery?")

Emerson naturally associated his gospel with a great Protestant tradition of independence. He would have associated himself gladly with Keats's letter of May 3, 1818, on the peculiarly Protestant virtues of Milton and Wordsworth:

> In [Milton's] time Englishmen were just emancipated from a great superstition and Men had got hold of certain points and resting places in reasoning which were too newly born to be doubted, and too much opposed by the Mass of Europe not to be thought etherial and authentically divine. . . . The Reformation produced such immediate and great benefits, that Protestantism was considered under the immediate eye of heaven. . . .

And Emerson would have sniffed at T. S. Eliot's condemnation of D. H. Lawrence (a rebel against the Congregationalist Church, like so many New Englanders):

> We are not concerned with the author's beliefs, but with the orthodoxy of sensibility and with the vast sense of tradition. . . . And Lawrence is, for my purposes, an almost perfect example of the heretic.
> . . . The point is that Lawrence started life wholly free from any restriction of tradition or institution, that he had no guidance except the Inner Light, the most untrustworthy and deceitful guide that ever offered itself to wandering humanity.

Emerson, relying on a broad tradition of religious independence, may have carried it so far as to end its connection with religion. His revelation —which became his esthetic as well as his religion—was that the important things come easily to the man who just waits for them. God is easy to achieve —"It," the "Over-Soul," the "First Cause." Lawrence, though he recognized the "inrushes" Emerson got from his God, laughed that Emerson was connected only on "the Ideal phone." This may explain Emerson's hold on sceptics.

Emerson provided relief from the commercial round and from the most politicized society of the nineteenth century. His appeal, like that of so many rare spirits in the history of religion, was that he was altogether exceptional. Neither Thoreau nor Whitman, nor any one of his many acolytes and admirers, resembles Emerson in his gift of total conviction. William James in a positivist climate had great trouble finding objective reasons for his religious promptings. He was to conclude in *The Varieties of Religious Experience* (1902) that such promptings must not be denied as evidence of God's existence. From despising Emerson's attitude of fixed benevolence, James came to admire him, even to envy him. Religiously, Dr. William James the professional scientist could never go the whole way. Emerson began with such an absolute of personal conviction that he left himself no room in which to develop.

Emerson's God-intoxication was communicated to most people without his performing miracles. Emerson never admitted—he never understood— that so much belief in the soul is a gift. He never doubted that his conviction must pass into his audience and become the gospel of a New World. But was it "religion" or the "word" that he imparted? Was he more the evangel or the always immaculate stylist? Near the end of the twentieth century the rebellious Catholic theologian Hans Küng was to concede that if his was the church of the sacraments, Protestantism was "the church of the word." Emerson would have liked that. "Golden sentences" came out of his mouth even when he was dying. He had been trained in pulpit eloquence, of course, but his innate artist's sense of elegance and discrimination, rhetorical strategy and effect, gave him a particular taste for prophetic upwelling and scriptural cut and thrust. He confidently assumed that "soul" is the same as style, for he was so natural a stylist that conventional writers could be put down as conventional souls. No one can miss in the "saintly" Emerson the immodesty of a superb artist on familiar terms with inspiration and thus with "God": "The maker of a sentence, like the other artist, launches out into the infinite and builds a road into Chaos and Old Night, and is followed by those who hear him with something of a wild, creative delight."

How spontaneously Emerson reported the explosion of spirit behind his appearance of restraint. The connection between faith and creativity is now so dim that we jealously wonder what Yeats meant when he said that "belief makes the mind abundant." Emerson himself no longer fortifies a free personal religion. God is dead even for Allen Ginsberg. Emerson may have helped to kill "self-reliance" in religion by dispensing it too confidently from his own subjectivity. But he did recognize himself as a revenant from early ages of faith—a primordial, "aboriginal" kind of early Christian, thoroughly tuned into his unconscious, who knew how to awaken dead souls, to *strike*, as only the God-intoxicated can.

"I like," he wrote in his journal, "dry light, and hard clouds, hard expressions, and hard manners." If Emerson looked and sounded the sage (the wise man of the American tribe who showed his ever more secular countrymen where to look for faith), it was because of his genius for compression. He reduced his style, like his life, to fundamentals. Unlike his literary son Thoreau, he did not train himself to live the absolute. Emerson lived in his study and in mild walks around Concord farms. Thoreau constantly dared himself to invade and master inhospitable country. Thoreau showed a lifelong need to *live* nature, to roll himself up in it, to enjoy "to the full" woods and fields as his erotic complement. He carried everywhere—even in Concord village, where he despised his neighbors for not being spiritual enough—the myth so dear to the American heart. The solitary man is the virtuous man as well as the more curious explorer of existence. A key sentence in Thoreau's lifelong journal: "The world appears to me uninhabited." Another: "It was not always dry land where we dwell." Emerson gave Thoreau and Whitman the satisfaction—so strange to the European mind—of being not merely an original but the incarnation of originality.

Even Whitman, so amazed by his gifts that he pretended he had invented them—even Whitman, with his posturing and his need to sell himself—made use of the American penchant for turning oneself into Adam. In America, Adam was not just the first man but sometimes the only man, the true God-man, Osiris and Christ and other masquerades for Whitman in his gallery. We know that Whitman was original, for his own literary culture resembles a musty secondhand bookstore. (Whatever is not firsthand in Whitman is fake.) His greatest lines are truly "a song of myself."

Emerson's compound of ideas—taken from Plato and neo-Platonists, Kant, Coleridge, Wordsworth, Carlyle—could have made him just another New England minister in the "ice house of Unitarianism" trying to keep up an intellectual front in the face of religious doubt. In fact Emerson impressed even the most hostile critics by his lonely certitude. Originality of thought

Emerson did not claim or even want. Nor was it authority of style, which he took for granted, that made Emerson the teacher of the tribe and "the actual beginner of the whole procession." It was his paramount discovery that in an increasingly faithless world he possessed the gift of faith. Belief was something else, formal, a creed; belief usually owed everything to someone else. It was secondary to the heart's natural loyalties. Though Emerson's fame and influence came from the joyous ease with which he imparted the "open secret of the universe," the nature of his appeal, attested even by people who did not claim to understand him, was that it was himself he was imparting. He was the enraptured realization that no one *now* was in this original relation to nature and a new country.

Emerson as an eponym for freshness, discovery, openness, for all that was hopeful in his country and his century, has survived his actual message because people can still take from him the cardinal theme: a brave beginning. And no one can read *Nature* or his early essays and journals without sharing his thrill that in this great, intelligent, sensual, and avaricious America, "glad to the brink of fear," he recognized in himself a vessel of the Holy Spirit. The thrill, the positive exultation in all the early writings, lies not in any delusion of intellectual originality but in the primacy that he shared with Nature and America itself.

America itself was the original. The confrontation with it by even the most seasoned men—explorers, missionaries, worldly philosophers and cynics—made things new. When John Locke said, "In the beginning all things were America," that was a figure of speech. But the constant raid on the vast emptiness made a person of Nature for even the practical and superstitious. Nature was wild but waiting to be exploited; as Emerson noted contentedly, it exists to serve. Many men were to make practical use of the unique opportunity; many more, expecting bonanza, fell by the wayside. (It was also typical of the Yankee Emerson to note that the actual founders of small towns in the West invariably failed.) But the first men of literary genius—Emerson, Thoreau, Whitman, and Melville—characteristically turned *their* raid on Nature into a book, the world at large into a fable. In their own mythology they acted out the role of primal man. Emerson in his journal, 1840: "I dreamed that I floated at will in the great Ether, and I saw this world floating also not far off, but diminished to the size of an apple. Then an angel took it in his hand and brought it to me and said, 'This must thou eat.' And I ate the world."

The genius of primitive Christianity lent itself to Emerson's belief that his soul was the center of a cosmic drama. John Milton seems to have infused his spacious mind into American Puritans whose influence over their new country he could not have predicted. Emerson certainly felt himself to be of the greatest possible importance to the cosmos. Which may be why he conceived of empty nature surrounding him as the unutterable stretches of space through which Satan fell. The American as "first man" was a hero of this drama because of all that he could lay his hand to. The gift of conviction that made a new age possible occurred for Emerson in the instant connection between faith and the word. The word alighting in his mind was more than a signal and symbol of faith; it was evidence that his faith was real, that it lived in the word as well as by the word. By the word he passed out faith. And in this century of the word, when literature was still central to thinking men, the word was open to all.

Emerson's sense of his own authority—so strong that one can hardly miss the exultation behind it—has been dismissed by conservative critics who charge that transcendentalists in the age of Jackson felt themselves to be superfluous. In fact they were simply out of touch with the hard new boisterous times of democratic emergence. Emerson's contempt for the organized church still gives offense; one churchly literary critic was capable of saying in the 1950s that Emerson was responsible for Hitler. Not to see that Emerson's life work began in a religious crisis that he shared with the age, that the stream of his writings began because by leaving the church he felt that he also had a solution for others, is to miss Emerson's central need to overcome *all* scepticism.

As there was God before the church existed, so God might be rediscovered by striking out on one's own. The Kingdom of God is within you or it is nowhere. Tolstoy as a young officer during the Crimean War wrote:

> A conversation about Divinity and Faith has suggested to me a great, stupendous idea, to the realization of which I feel capable of devoting my life. That idea is the founding of a new religion corresponding to the present stage of mankind: the religion of Christ but purged of dogmas and absolutism—a practical religion, not promising future bliss but giving bliss on earth.

2

Things Are in the Saddle and Ride Mankind: Emerson

Every one for himself, driven to find all his resources,
hopes, rewards, society and divinity within himself.

EMERSON, "Historic Notes of Life
and Letters in New England"

I

Since he was in the habit of giving sermons, in 1832 the ex-minister became a lecturer. For the better part of the next fifty years, Emerson was to earn much of his living by lecturing and to prepare first in the form of lectures most of his essays and books. As everyone knows, he lectured on *The American Scholar* before Harvard's Phi Beta Kappa chapter in 1837, and before the Harvard Divinity School's senior class in 1838. He lectured to the literary societies of Dartmouth the same year, and to the Society of the Adelphi in Waterville College, Maine, in 1841. In Boston, on January 25, 1841, his topic before the Mechanics Apprentices' Literary Association was "Man the Reformer," and on December 2 he read a lecture "On the Times" at the Masonic Temple, only to return a week later with a lecture on "The Conservative."

He did not always depend on the Lyceum circuit or on invitations from colleges and associations. Soon he was giving his own lecture series in Boston and elsewhere, became his own lecture bureau. He placed notices in the papers, hired the hall, wrote out the tickets of admission. In two weeks during the winter of 1855, he appeared in twelve towns. In the course of one season alone, 1865–66, he lectured in Massachusetts, New York, Pennsylvania, Michigan, Indiana, Illinois, Wisconsin, and Iowa. The next season found him in Minnesota and Kansas. He lectured in Canada, in cities as far west as St. Louis—where he met the grandfather-to-be of T. S. Eliot, William Greenleaf Eliot, the Unitarian minister and founder of Washington University, who had left New England to tend to the cultural-religious needs of the hinterland and was known as "the Saint of the West." Emerson valued Eliot but believed "no thinking or even reading man" was to be found "in the 95000 souls" of St. Louis.

The railroads were coming in after 1840; there were more and more people to hear the great word from the celebrated Mr. Emerson. He lectured at cattle shows; in churches, barns, lyceums; at Ripley Female College in Wisconsin. When, after the Civil War, Harvard at last forgave him for the Divinity School Address, the least systematic of writers even gave lectures in "philosophy" at his old college. It was with the expected, the inevitable address by Ralph Waldo Emerson, that Concord celebrated the centenary of the shot heard round the world—and the opening of its free library. Emerson could be called upon to commemorate with a ringing address the emancipation of the slaves in the British West Indies, New England's firm opposition to the Fugitive Slave Act, the assault on Senator Charles Sumner, the martyrdom of John Brown, the arrival in this country of the Hungarian liberator Kossuth, the consecration of Sleepy Hollow Cemetery, the arrival of the first Chinese ambassador. He lectured in Concord more often than anywhere else, but he was always ready to address farmers in the Midwest, clerks in New York, and the American people at large on Eloquence, Manners, Immortality, Woman, Shakespeare, the Over-Soul, and other topics at once so large and yet so close to the interests of both lecturer and audience.

Hawthorne, who hated to open his mouth and was no admirer of Emerson, satirized the lecture vogue in "The Celestial Rail-road." Of the "new divines," the last and greatest is Dr. Wind-of-doctrine.

> The labors of these eminent divines are aided by those of innumerable lecturers, who diffuse such a various profundity, in all subjects of human or celestial science, that any man may acquire an omnigenous erudition, without the trouble of even learning to read. Thus literature is etherealized by assuming for its medium the human voice; and knowledge . . . becomes exhaled into a sound, which forthwith steals into the ever-open ear of the community. These ingenious methods constitute a sort of machinery, by which thought and study are done to every person's hand, without his putting himself to the slightest inconvenience in the matter.

In *The Blithedale Romance* Hawthorne pictured "one of those lyceum-halls, of which almost every village has now its own, dedicated to that sober

and pallid, or rather drab-colored, mode of winter-evening entertainment."
Provincial gratitude for lectures and "other exhibitions" ("Here comes the
ventriloquist, with all his mysterious tongues . . .") obviously depressed his
spirits. But after all these years, there is something about this familiarly
innocent chapter in American life that suddenly takes one back to the classic,
the prophetic beginning of nations. Emerson was on a mission to his own
people; he was preaching now to the whole American congregation. To
recall these village lyceums, these rude country halls, evening meetings in
odd churches, barns, schools, and banquet rooms, tents spread in preparation
for the idyllic summer's opening of the college year, the advertisements
Emerson wrote and placed himself, the garbled and breathless summary in
a Cincinnati paper ("His lecture is not to be reported—without his own
language, his manner, his delivery, it would be little—to essay to reproduce
it would be like carrying soda water to a friend the morning after it was
drawn, and asking him how he relished it . . . "), is to imagine a time when
people still looked to literary men for guidance. The lecture committee
waited grimly on the speaker to pronounce that he had given satisfaction,
then presented him with a basket of apples. Emerson made a thousand
appearances, crossed the Mississippi on ice in dead winter to deliver a lecture
in Iowa, was bumped, jostled, frozen in wagons, carriages, flatboats, steam-
boats, trains (where he felt so solitary that he vowed he would go over to
any man reading a book and hug him).

The country was still so new to itself that it seemed "fabulous"; ministers,
scholars, poets were expected to remind Americans of their high historic
mission. America was still so empty that prophecy was needed to encourage
it. Emerson certainly acted as if he was needed. He was exceptional, he felt
blessed. To see everything from a private revelation was to see that America,
this new situation, was waiting for men of genius, "heroes," to complete it.

Herman Melville in the excitement of writing *Moby-Dick* informed Nathaniel Hawthorne that they were both demi-gods, outposts on the farthest
boundary of consciousness, "God's spies." Melville did not see himself as
ministering to a still-uncreated country. Emerson did. Before the Civil War,
when he and America seemed to be starting out together, he thought that
the country had to satisfy his loftiest ideals or be declared a failure. As early
as 1838, he could sum up (without reference to actual leaders and issues)
Jacksonian democracy:

This country has not fulfilled what seemed the reasonable expectation of
mankind. Men looked, when all feudal straps and bandages snapped asunder,
that nature, too long the mother of dwarfs, should reimburse itself by a brood

of Titans, who should laugh and leap in the continent, and run up the mountains of the West with the errand of genius and of love. But the mark of American merit in painting, in sculpture, in poetry, in fiction, in eloquence, seems to be a certain grace without grandeur, and itself not new but derivative, a vase of fair outline, but empty—which whoso sees may fill with what wit and character is in him. . . .

"Great country, diminutive minds," he complained to himself in 1847. "America is formless, has no terrible and no beautiful condensation." Emerson wrote a public letter to President Martin Van Buren protesting the expulsion of Cherokee Indians from their ancestral lands in Georgia. He was to be inflamed by the Fugitive Slave Act; he turned fiery patriot ("sometimes gunpowder smells good") during the Civil War. It took him a long time to feel that "politics" in the usual American sense was his business. The ordinariness of Americans troubled him more than slavery. Tocqueville concluded his observations of democracy in America—that great new fact in an old world—by admitting that "Men in general are neither very good nor very bad, but mediocre." That was Emerson's complaint; the actual state of society did not fit his excited discovery that the private mind had infinite possibilities. Emerson's central belief in compensation, or the eternal fitness of things, was easier for the individual than for society to measure itself by. His apocalyptic thinking about politics is shown in his angry identification with Jesus. "If Jesus came now into the world, he would say, You, YOU! He said to his age, I." About manners in a still deeply class-conscious society, he could be equally lofty. Democracy in America, as Tocqueville demonstrated, found in a European, Catholic, aristocratic temper its most acute analysis. Emerson took his audience for granted. He wanted them to "rise" to his level, but he did not particularly love them. To his friend Carlyle (who after Joseph De Maistre was probably the most reactionary man of the nineteenth century) Emerson was to write with the ease of one genius to another:

> I fancy my readers to be a very quiet, plain, even obscure class,—men and women of some religious culture and aspirations, young, or else mystical, and by no means including the great literary and fashionable army, which no man can now count, who now read your books. . . . I had rather have fewer readers and only such as belong to me.

He virtually began his important lecture on "Fate" (1846), a significant revision of his first enthusiasm, with "Let us honestly state the facts. Our America has a bad name for superficialness."

As it would turn out, America was not an idea in Emerson's mind. His difficulty was with the application of his favorite ideal. The "active soul" was not easy to fit in with so much aggressive self-interest. Tocqueville, who was in America when Emerson left the church, saw in the populace what Emerson asked of intellectuals in *The American Scholar:* "The Americans now accept tradition only as a means of information." Tocqueville from his aristocratic perspective saw that America was more revolutionary than Americans knew. The religion of equality was fundamental, for it asserted as "rights" the most primitive self-importance. Unfettered democracy was a danger exactly to the lofty perceptions that Emerson expected of the individual. After Emerson's early rhapsodies over self-reliance, Tocqueville reads like a warning against mass society.

> Everyone shuts himself up tightly within himself and insists upon judging the world from there.

> Every revolution has more or less the effect of releasing men to their own conduct and of opening before the mind of each one of them an almost limitless perspective. . . . Everyone then attempts to be his own sufficient guide and makes it his boast to form his own opinions on all subjects. Men are no longer bound together by ideas, but by interests; and it would seem as if human opinions were reduced to a sort of intellectual dust, scattered on every side, unable to collect, unable to cohere.

> Far from thinking that [intellectual authority] will disappear, I augur that it may readily acquire too much preponderance and confine the action of private judgment within narrower limits than are suited to either the greatness or happiness of the human race. In the principle of equality I very clearly discern two tendencies: one leading the mind of every man to untried thoughts, the other prohibiting him from thinking at all. And I perceive how, under the dominion of certain laws, democracy would extinguish that liberty of the mind to which a democratic social action is favorable; so that, having broken all the bondage once imposed on it by ranks or by men, the human mind would be closely fettered to the general will of the greatest number.

Emerson was never to face directly the consequences in society of the "self-trust" that was all-important to his own gifts. It was easier to complain (how Melville enjoyed this!) that "the calamity is the masses."

> When I spoke or speak of the democratic element, I do not mean that ill thing, vain and loud, which writes lying newspapers, spouts at caucuses, and sells its lies for gold. . . . There is nothing of the true democratic element in what is called Democracy; it must fall, being wholly commercial. I beg I may not be understood to praise anything which the soul in you does not honor, however grateful may be names to your ear and your pocket.

Why are the masses, from the dawn of history down, food for knives and powder? The idea dignifies a few leaders, who have sentiment, opinion, love, self-devotion; and they make war and death sacred—but what for the wretches whom they hire and kill? The cheapness of man is every day's tragedy.

. . . the key to all ages is—Imbecility; imbecility in the vast majority of men at all times, and even in heroes in all but certain eminent moments; victims of gravity, custom and fear. This gives force to the strong—that the multitude have no habit of self-reliance or original action.

Emerson liked to say that "Life consists in what a man is thinking of all day." Melville's Ishmael, who did a lot of thinking at sea, snapped back in the opening of *Moby-Dick:* "Who ain't a slave? Tell me that." "Life" for Emerson was indeed nothing but what the "great man" is thinking of. The great man, he told Bronson Alcott, fills up "the whole space between God and the mob." What he did not have to tell the all-too-spiritual Alcott is that this whole space is the domain of spirit. Spirit for transcendentalists was the dream of a world entirely responsive to oneself. "Immortality," though improbable, is real, because what is constant in life is consciousness, from which we cannot separate ourselves. But our difficult relation to things is the philosophical problem that the Romantic philosopher waved aside in favor of a rapturous self-affirmation. "Power"—the crucial aspiration in Emerson —meant the individual's own profound sense of himself, the highest, freest, most abounding consciousness.

"Soul" power, Emerson assumed with the confidence of all religious founders, must pass into those who hear us. Soul was leadership, appointed to give out fresh life to the people. Emerson owed much of his influence to his private aura; he impressed by seeming inaccessible. William Dean Howells in *Literary Friends and Acquaintances* (1902) remembered that "It would be hard to persuade people now that Emerson once represented to the popular mind all that was most hopelessly impossible, and that in a certain sense he was a national joke, the type of the incomprehensible, the byword of the poor paragrapher." By remaining "impossible" he gave the "wholly commercial element in what is called Democracy" its favorite image of the literary man as someone removed from "real" life while remaining an embodiment of the idealism professed as the essence of America. Emerson's "golden sentences" were to be quoted on the schoolroom wall and in the treasurer's report; he became, as is the fate of religious founders, a sanction for the double life.

The "scribbling class," as Whitman liked to call it, recognized Emerson as one of its own. The once-dangerous oracle was to become of the greatest personal importance to a host of superbly creative people. Emerson's appeal was felt in Europe as late as the existentialist demand for greater personal liberty in all moral decisions. Albert Camus told an American friend in the 1940s how astonished he had been to discover the effect on him of Emerson's "tonic" power. In his own century, which for many admirers he personified as the peak of true individualism, he was the shaman and diviner of the many who were struggling with religious doubts. James Russell Lowell, who was no Emersonian and indeed became a very worldly fellow, nevertheless remembered that in his youth

> we used to walk in from the country to the Masonic Temple . . . through the crisp winter night, and listened to that thrilling voice of his, so charged with subtle meaning and subtle music, as shipwrecked men on a raft to the hail of a ship that came with unhoped-for food and rescue. . . . The delight and benefit were that he . . . made us conscious of the supreme and everlasting originality of whatever bit of soul might be in any of us. . . .

The emphasis on originality was to become a fixture of American expression; in conservative Europe, Emerson became a byword for whatever real newness might be streaming in from America's barbaric shore. Britons and Europeans contemptuous of American timidity (or brashness) in the arts made Emerson their personal discovery. Emerson alone stood out for them as something free and wild, stunningly appropriate to the New World. Carlyle gleefully told Emerson that a Swiss lady, kinswoman to Madame de Staël, had come to regard Emerson "with a certain love, yet a *shuddering* love." "He is the kind of American," the lady breathed, "who after having beaten down the forest with the blows of his axe thinks that the same will conquer the intellectual world!"

It was an age when genius was "representative," as Emerson liked to say. Goethe was Germany (Germany would soon be Wagner); France, having been Napoleon, was to become Victor Hugo. Mark Twain and Henry James, meeting Turgenev in France, easily concluded that the sweet sad giant was Russia. Emerson represented *the* "newness" to those who not only were confident of their originality but suffered it and suffered for it. Nietzsche, the most isolated of German literary thinkers, who wrote only for the prescient few, typically "discovered" Emerson as if no one else had had the wit to do so. But hating all established truths, especially those reverenced in Christianity (he, too, was a minister's son), Nietzsche became addicted to Emerson. He carried Emerson's works on his endless nervous travels in search of health; the American was the unseen friend who personified radiant intellectual liberty. And incidentally, for Nietzsche Emerson was one of just four writers—with Leopardi, Landor, Mérimée—"worthy to be considered a master of prose."

Carlyle despised America and Americans, supported slavery, and thought all moral order came to an end because Parliament in 1867 enfranchised the working class in the towns. He would sneer that Whitman thought he was a big poet because he came from a big country. Emerson as early as 1833, on his first trip abroad, had made his way to solitary Craigenputtock to see a writer whom he had come to admire long before the literary public did. Carlyle recognized Emerson as another "sky-messenger" and was to write to Concord:

> My friend! you know not what you have done for me there. It was long decades of years that I had heard nothing but the infinite jangling and jabbering and inarticulate twittering and screeching, and my soul had sunk down sorrowful, and said there is no articulate speaking then any more, and thou art solitary among stranger-creatures?—and lo, out of the West, comes a clear utterance, clearly recognisable as a *man's* voice, and I *have* a kinsman and brother: God be thanked for it! I could have *wept* to hear that speech [*The American Scholar*]; the clear high melody of it went tingling thro' my heart. . . .

Carlyle recognized in Emerson at thirty a strange, solitary, and enigmatic force long before Emerson in his and America's middle age became the altogether too acceptable American sage. It is significant that Carlyle should have seen in himself so many parallels with Emerson the spiritual loner, another believer in heroes and hero-worship, when Carlyle despised Emerson's country as a mobocracy and could not have liked Emerson's faith in "the party of hope." Carlyle in opposition to the "slavish" popular currents of his time, Carlyle howling in cascades of magnificent rhetoric against democracy (in which he saw the extinction of faith, mind, the great tradition), nevertheless recognized Emerson, in regard to the "people," to be as supercilious as himself. And Carlyle's hot speech-prose, erupting in folk rhythms, mimicry, joking exaggerations, was in fact so much more "democratic" than Emerson's was—more aware of the readers with whom he was plainly uniting himself and to whom he was making furious appeal—that his significant criticism of Emerson was Emerson's way of removing himself. In 1841 he complained:

> You seem to me in danger of dividing yourself from the Fact of this present Universe, in which alone, ugly as it is, can I find any anchorage, and soaring away after Ideas, Beliefs, Revelations, and such like. . . . Surely I could wish

you returned into your poor nineteenth century, its follies and maladies, its blind or half-blind, but gigantic toilings . . . and trying to evolve in some measure the hidden Godlike that lies in it. . . . Alas, it is so easy to screw one's self up into high and ever higher altitudes of Transcendentalism, and see nothing under one but the everlasting snows of Himmalayeh. . . .

Well, I do believe, for one thing, a man has no right to say to his own generation, turning quite away from it, "Be damned!" It is the whole Past and the whole Future, this same cotton-spinning, dollar-hunting, canting and shrieking, very wretched generation of ours. Come back into it, I tell you! . . .

No truly great man, from Jesus Christ downwards, as I often say, ever founded a Sect—I mean wilfully intended founding one. What a view must a man have of this Universe, who thinks "he can swallow it all," who is not doubly and trebly happy that he can keep it from swallowing him!

Emerson did indeed think he could swallow it all. Could Carlyle have guessed that Emerson once dreamed that an angel commanded him to eat the world?

Emerson the "spiritual libertine," as church conservatives derogated him, Emerson the all-out personification of a religion founded on nothing but the promptings of the individual soul, was only indirectly a democrat and reformer. Carlyle, as one self-assertive genius to another, recognized Emerson's underlying contempt for those who could not live up to his revelation for them. Emerson shared with Carlyle a belief in the writer as master teacher to the age, the reinforcer of the spirit in an age when faith was too weak to be left to the churches. Carlyle the radical absolutist sought to fortify Emerson against opposition from "all the Popularities." He understood Emerson's problem; Emerson's insurrection in American life was easily underrated. He knew that in the beginning Emerson had had an audacious mission—by words alone, to inspire belief in a God Who Had No Name and could easily be confused with the findings of Science as the "First Cause" or the "Supreme Cause." What Carlyle did not know or even want to know was America and what made America thrilling to its own people, which was the strange new egalitarian faith of "democracy."

Emerson's distracted relation to society he defined perfectly in an early journal entry. "The problem which life has to solve is, how to exist in harmonious relation to a certain number of perceptions, such as hunger, thirst, cold, society, self, God:—it is the problem of three bodies."

He did not yet understand that most people—certainly all societies—did not think of *life* as a "problem" to be solved. Life demanded a "solution" only to the religious mind. Emerson not only saw a problem; he thought he had solved it, once and for all, by a faith that came to absolute self-trust. Why then, when everything about some twenty million rugged individualists and land-starved immigrants proclaimed the release of some overpowering new energy, did the soul and society remain so tantalizingly parallel and apart? Why—Emerson brooded over this question without asking it—was it possible for so many to absorb his message without practicing it? Why was it so difficult to exist in harmonious relation to so many different perceptions? Why, alas, were there so many *bodies* to take care of?

The contradiction between the soul and society, which helped to kill Thoreau during the Civil War, did not kill Emerson. It did not even change him significantly. It muted his enthusiasm and darkened his vocabulary, intensified his belief in history as biography, so that he could produce his wonderful hymns to genius in *Representative Men* (1850). He turned his gift as a social analyst and wit into his ironic but essentially admiring portrait of England at the apex of Victorian self-satisfaction. During the Civil War he condescended to be a patriot in the company of conventional New England divines whom he had once fled. Emerson thoroughly enjoyed the Civil War, and from time to time, as benefitted a Brahmin too idealistic for ordinary politics, derogated Lincoln as snobbishly as did the London *Times*.

Nevertheless, the orphic Emerson knew, in the long anticlimax to his early rhapsodies, that life was no longer a problem *he* knew how to solve. The advancing country had got beyond its oracle. The most eventful century in history (everyone agreed on this), the most hopeful (especially in America), certainly the most productive, revealed one aim of the times to be the tireless exploitation of nature—and not nature as the language of God.

Did the lofty believer shift his ground like many another under the pounding of a raw new country's furious rush to dominate a continent, to push out the Indian, to defend and expand slavery as it welcomed unlimited immigration? The "newness" with which Emerson has identified himself made him deliverer to an uncreated culture. The expectant masses that had given him an audience were now ready to obliterate anything outside their "manifest" need to make up for the privations of past history and the Old World. But in making rawness a model for the future, America needed institutions; nowhere would the "church," sometimes any church, be so necessary as on the frontier. Emerson's scorn for institutions and the state was not even a prophecy. More significantly (like so many other nineteenth-century antagonists of formal religion who thought that the energy once given to ritual and obedience would now be released in "Promethean" thunder for the *spiritual* emancipation of mankind) he overlooked the century's grasp of technology for its material salvation. The individual's life became more real than God's life. All sense of time was infected by anxious mortality.

In the face of overwhelming secularism, Emerson's trust in the spiritual life somehow came down to the absolute necessity of his own freedom. The "word," once given out, never lost its sanctity for Ralph Waldo Emerson. But not always received in the spirit that sent it forth, it made him seem even loftier—a special case among Americans. Emerson in his later phase was taken for a mahatma, a great soul, rather than the instigator of a revolutionary consciousness. The only limit he would admit to his horizon was "Fate." We do not enjoy *perfect* freedom.

Thoreau in his strenuously self-centered way was to realize that it is not always right to "slander the outward." Emerson never condescended to the external world, which like everything else was subject to the "ripe perceptive powers." But as early as 1844 he began an extraordinary admission in an essay on "Experience":

> Where do we find ourselves? In a series of which we do not know the extremes, and believe that it has none. We wake and find ourselves on a stair; there are stairs below us, which we seem to have ascended; there are stairs above us, many a one, which go upward and out of sight. But the Genius which according to the old belief stands at the door by which we enter, and gives us the lethe to drink, that we may tell no tales, mixed the cup too strongly, and we cannot shake off the lethargy now at noonday. Sleep lingers all our lifetime about our eyes. . . . All things swim and glitter. Our life is not so much threatened as our perception. Ghostlike we glide through nature, and should not know our place again.

With the clerical unction that never left him, Emerson consoled his audience. It was already too late in the American day—though the Fugitive Slave Act of 1850 (the only political outrage that ever disturbed his saintly composure) was yet unthinkable—to fool himself. In "Montaigne; or, The Skeptic" he had confessed:

> The astonishment of life is the absence of any appearance or reconciliation between the theory and practice of life. Reason, the prized reality, the Law, is apprehended, now and then, for a serene and profound moment amidst the hubbub of cares and works which have no direct bearing upon it—is then lost for months or years, and again found for an interval, to be lost again. . . .

The "prized reality" was "the Law," man's ideals in unison with the universe. The moral law proved the existence of Emerson's God—it showed the divine truth that had the human soul for its messenger. But to our "flickering" perception it did not last. The problem was as old as the inconstancy with which their prophets belabored the Jews. In his most exultant period, Emerson had told the Divinity School (in the peremptory terms Coleridge had taken from German idealists): "There is no doctrine of the Reason which will bear to be taught by the Understanding." Jesus alone in all history estimated the greatness of man, Jesus alone was true to what is in you and in me. Jesus was *the* Poet, Prophet, Hero-Genius. But "the understanding caught this high chant from the poet's lips, and said, in the next age, 'This was Jehovah come down out of heaven. I will kill you, if you say he was a man.' "

There was really no defense when sublime reason (the unity of creation incarnated in exceptional persons) was brought down, *materialized*, by the mere understanding. As Captain Ahab was impatiently to say to his "doltish" crew, "Hark ye, yet again,—the little lower layer." Society was the little lower layer. Emerson's great gift—accepting everything his mind "received" —stood him well when he retreated from the sublime to the America that would not survive half slave and half free. Of course he sounded condescending about it; how *could* people be so obtuse to the moral law as not to understand that it should dissolve all political conflict? But seeing defective humanity as the rule, he could be witty, elastic, ironic about the selfishness and turbulence of professed Christians. He spoke in New York against the Fugitive Slave Act:

> I fear there is no reliance to be put on any kind or form of covenant, no, not on sacred forms, none on churches, none on bibles. For one would have said that a Christian would not keep slaves;—but the Christians keep slaves. . . . They quote the Bible, quote Paul, quote Christ, to justify slavery. If slavery is good, then is lying, theft, arson, homicide, each and all good, and to be maintained by the Union societies. . . .
> . . . Whenever a man has come to this mind, there is no Church for him but his believing prayer; no Constitution but his dealing well and justly with his neighbor. . . .

Emerson turned out to be a more minute observer of society than of literature, where he was brilliant, even orphic, only on forms resembling his own. He was a far shrewder and of course a more interested student of politics than Thoreau. In the years of the Mexican War he was still lordly about the state's necessary inferiority to the soul of Ralph Waldo Emerson.

> The State is a poor, good beast who means the best; it means friendly. A poor cow who does well by you—do not grudge it its hay. It cannot eat bread,

as you can; let it have without grudge a little grass for its four stomachs.
. . . You, who are a man walking cleanly on two feet, will not pick a quarrel
with a poor cow. Take this handful of clover and welcome. But if you hook
me when I walk in the fields, then, poor cow, I will cut your throat.

If the Fugitive Slave Act shocked him, Daniel Webster's support of it particularly irritated him. He had always esteemed Webster, as was common
practice in New England, because of Webster's immense force. Webster
was the great Yankee. But Webster the Unionist at any price, whose support was vital to the Compromise of 1850 (and the Fugitive Slave Act), had
blended into the state and was now as mechanical a patriot as he was an
orator.

Emerson was soon resigned to the lack of perfectionism in this ever more
driven society. The "double consciousness" that he kept during his still-
exalted flights was to keep him always curious about a world that every day
contradicted his inner world. But why did he never write a book about
American life and manners as sustained as *English Traits* (1856)? *English
Traits* is remarkable among Emerson's works for being a *book;* it is worldlier,
shrewder, wittier than anything else by this God-intoxicated man. The
subject, for once, was all outside him. Obviously it was good for Emerson
to get away from woodsy Concord and fellow minds that did not have *his*
mind. Emerson turned out to be a brilliant tourist, and one with a vengeance
against England's superior wealth and superior ways. The vengeance subsides into sheer wonder at the strangeness to American eyes of so much
power in conservation.

England was the bank and workshop of the world, the first and still the
prize example of the industrial revolution and mass labor. America was not
just provincial but empty.

On the way to Winchester, whither our host accompanied us in the afternoon, my friends asked many questions respecting American landscapes,
forests, houses—my house, for example, . . . There, I thought, in America,
lies nature sleeping, over-growing, almost conscious, too much by half for
man in the picture, and so giving a certain *tristesse,* like the rank vegetation
of swamps and forests seen at night, steeped in dews and rains, which it loves;
and on it man seems not able to make much impression. There, in that great
sloven continent, in high Allegheny pastures, in the sea-wide sky-skirted
prairie, still sleeps and murmurs and hides the great mother, long since driven
away from the trim hedge-rows and over-cultivated garden of England. And,
in England, I am quite too sensible of this. Everyone is on his good behavior
and must be dressed for dinner at six.

Nothing Emerson wrote about America betrays what he missed in it so much as does his tribute to English robustness, traditionalism, self-confidence, independence of thought. Like the "international" novels of Henry James, *English Traits* works as a continuing contrast of civilizations. The book is personal testimony to far more than Henry James saw missing to the American storyteller—"No sovereign, no court, no personal loyalty, no aristocracy, no church, no clergy, no palaces, no castles, nor manners, nor old country houses. . . ."

Emerson not only found tradition in England; he played up each item of it into an English character. His book shows what he could do on a purely social canvas with his usual suavity of impression. Obedient to his aphoristic style, he tosses off ridiculously smooth pronouncements. Praising the English newspapers' power to expose, he concludes that "there is no corner and no night. A relentless inquisition drags every secret to the day . . . the whole people are already forewarned. Thus England rids herself of those incrustations which have been the ruin of old states. . . . No antique privilege, no comfortable monopoly, but sees surely that its days are counted. . . ."

One would like to have seen Dickens reading this. Of course Emerson never minded contradicting himself; he was making the picture of a nation out of the different images England presented to his mind. His starting point is England as John Bull. This, when we consider how much England under its aristocratic leadership had turned into the dominating bourgeois of the century, was not *simpliste*. As Emerson keeps touching up the too solid flesh that stands for England, he is saying that America does not have enough "character." Even if Emerson had been able to read fiction (to say nothing of his being able to write it), he would have been right to think that America was not yet ripe for the inclusive character he gave England. Far from anticipating America's industrial eclipse of England by the end of the century (the first figures on this made Henry Adams reel), Emerson would have agreed with Sydney Smith in the *Edinburgh Review*—"In the four quarters of the globe, who reads an American book?"

With his essential concern for power, Emerson in his literary way did approach the fundamental question that foreigners in England (like Karl Marx) were always asking. What makes this people, in material terms, "great"? Not being Karl Marx, Emerson thought that India fell to English "character."

The problem of the traveller landing at Liverpool is, Why England is England? What are the elements of that power which the English hold over other nations? If there be one test of national genius universally accepted, it is success; and if there be one successful country in the universe for the last millennium, that country is England.

Emerson's answer to his question—for all his concern with individual freedom, he did not understand laissez-faire—was the materialism of the English, which he associated with physical strength like an athlete's. This was their essence and their idiosyncrasy. Was emphasis on the physical an attempt to correct in Emerson what Carlyle had mocked as "sky-blue idealism"? Was it an inability to measure in America the social use of "self-reliance"?

In any event, Emerson turned witty and sportive on his favorite theme: John Bull's heartiness, implacability, brazenness. At times he actually diverged into the kind of brightness that Henry James was to display in every impression of English formality. "In short, every one of these islanders is an island himself, safe, tranquil, incommunicable. In a company of strangers you would think him deaf. . . . He does not give his hand. He does not let you meet his eye. It is almost an affront to look a man in the face without being introduced."

Emerson's concern with power did not extend to the process by which it was gained. When Emerson is not awed by England, he is sly. "Twenty thousand thieves landed at Hastings. These founders of the House of Lords were greedy and ferocious dragons, sons of greedy and ferocious pirates." He is irreverent about England's national saint, George, who in Asia Minor began his career "as a low parasite who got a lucrative contract to supply the army with bacon." The heartiness, the "healthiness," the supposedly pervasive roast beef and ale are his theme. He did not miss the brutality that shrieked out of England's indifference to its many casualties. He was just not one to identify himself, as the young Melville did in *Redburn*, with the outcasts, the near-dead, of Liverpool. Emerson's eye is mainly on English energy as thriving, pushing, prospering, aggressive. English character is synonymous with realism. "How realistic or materialistic in treatment of his subject is Swift. He describes his fictitious persons as for the police." Though Emerson often favors his elegant style over the facts, the too-comfortable scholar guesses, in the wake of the Chartist riots and the first mobilization of the working class, the underlying social struggle.

They have no revolutions; no horse-guards, dictating to the crown; no Parisian *poissardes* and barricades, no mob; but drowsy habitude, daily dress-dinners, wine and ale and beer and gin and sleep.

With this power of creation and this passion for independence, property has reached an ideal perfection. It is felt and treated as the national life-blood. . . . Whatever surly sweetness possession can give, is tasted in England to the dregs.

He fastened with pleasure on every display of English self-importance.

When you see on the continent the well-dressed Englishman come into his ambassador's chapel and put his face for silent prayer into his smooth-brushed hat, you cannot help feeling that he believes himself to have done almost the generous thing, and that it is very condescending in him to pray to God.
. . . Their religion is a quotation; their church is a doll. . . . In good company, you expect them to laugh at the fanaticism of the vulgar; but they do not, they are the vulgar.

11

Representative Men is Emerson's self-portrait within a group portrait of genius. He plainly recognizes his own egotism in Napoleon the hero of the ascendant middle class, in Goethe the intellectual Zeus of a Weimar small and prim enough to be confused with Concord, in Swedenborg the mad magus whose passion for classifying spiritual phenomena in the style he learned as a scientist presented an immodest analogy with Emerson's habit of adducing the moral sentiment from natural history. In Europe great men seemed to produce each other; America had to summon up men who believed in the possibility of being great. Measuring himself against America, Emerson realized he was a great man. He is the only American in his gallery of great men.

In the age-old way of Puritan America, Emerson regarded himself as one of the Elect because a divine message had come through him. It was not just as the founder of a new spiritual consciousness that Emerson recognized himself; it was as a link between man and God. The poet-prophet-clairvoyant-hero was more than a spokesman for the divine; he was the living proof that God could be realized in every man. Although he professed himself bored by Hegel, Emerson was in the stream of German Romantic philosophizing that led Hegel to affirm that God is not God until He comes to consciousness of Himself. Where but in man? While *Representative Men* and *English Traits* show Emerson's appreciation of great men as historical actors, he saw nothing in Hegel's insistence that men acting on history, bringing it out, are working out God's own passage to self-knowledge. History is only biography, Emerson thought. He did not show how men create history.

The only doctrine he ever taught, said Emerson, was "the infinitude of the private mind." Would the private mind be alone with its infinitude so long as it remained "private"? Emerson gave his whole heart to this dream of possessing infinity. History was the public drama, and all things public were in conflict and demanded compromise. As the slavery question heated up, Emerson finally recognized in the Fugitive Slave Act attached to the Compromise of 1850 that the ideal freedom he had always taken for granted, had almost worshipped, was in fact not ideal. It was not his to keep. The release of men from their age-old obedience to the church would be not the free man's worship but the "private" man's superiority.

As a leader of democracy Emerson came to seem as providential as Lincoln. He defended what was sacred in individual liberty—its relation to the infinite—long after it had been confused with self-assertion. But the more he joined himself to New England's agitation over slavery, the more he despised the halting and awkward democratic process. Like future radical idealists and conscientious objectors to American wars and mass hysteria, he was sickened by the easy drift of popular opinion. Once the Civil War was on, he became more warlike than the soldiers. Despite all his "preaching" to the American public, he turned out to have little faith in democratic persuasion. "Leave this hypocritical prating about the masses," he had written in 1841.

> Masses are rude, lame, unmade, pernicious in their demands and influence, and need not to be flattered but to be schooled. I wish not to concede anything to them, but to tame, drill, divide and break them up, and draw individuals out of them. The worst of charity is that the lives you are asked to preserve are not worth preserving. Masses! the calamity is the masses!

Twenty years later he could not decide just how capable Lincoln was. He disapproved of the president's conviviality, but when the Emancipation Proclamation met with his approval, he confessed in the *Atlantic* (November 1862) that "we have underestimated the capacity and virtue which the Divine Providence has made an instrument of benefit so vast. . . . Forget all that we thought shortcomings, every mistake, every delay. In the extreme embarrassments of his part, call these endurance, wisdom, magnanimity; illuminated, as they are, by this dazzling success." Yet a month later he could write to Carlyle—that most ferocious supporter of slavery!—that "all our bright young men go into [the war], to be misused and sacrificed hitherto by incapable leaders." By autumn 1863 he was again impatient with Lincoln as well as condescending.

We must accept the results of universal suffrage, and not try to make it appear that we can elect fine gentlemen. . . .

You cannot refine Mr. Lincoln's taste, or extend his horizon; he will not walk dignifiedly through the traditional part of the President of America, but will pop out his head at each railroad station and make a little speech, and get into an argument with Squire A., and Judge B. He will write letters to Horace Greeley, and any editor or reporter or saucy party committee that writes to him, and cheapen himself.

But this we must be ready for, and let the clown appear, and hug ourselves that we are well off, if we have got good nature, honest meaning, and fidelity to public interest, with bad manners,—instead of an elegant *roué* and malignant self-seeker.

III

Emerson's "Illusions" (1860) is a poem in which he just barely manages to console himself for the indifferent drift that he now sees as the first law of life.

> Know the stars yonder,
> The stars everlasting,
> Are fugitive also. . . .

William Butler Yeats thought these the most beautiful lines he had ever read. Yeats improved them by recalling them as "the stars, the stars everlasting / are fugitive also." (He does not seem to have commented on the rest.) Typical of an Emerson poem, this one flashes, then subsides. It pictures the world as impervious change:

> Old man and young maid,
> Day's toil and its guerdon,
> They are all vanishing,
> Fleeing to fables,
> Cannot be moored.

Nothing stays. Yet

> When thou dost return
> On the wave's circulation,
> Beholding the shimmer,
> The wild dissipation,
> And, out of endeavor

> To change and to flow,
> The gas become solid,
> And phantoms and nothings
> Return to be things,
> And endless imbroglio
> Is law and the world,—
> Then first shalt thou know,
> That in the wild turmoil,
> Horsed on the Proteus,
> Thou ridest to power,
> And to endurance.

Yeats would never have opened a poem with

> Flow, flow the waves hated,
> Accursed, adored,
> The waves of mutation;
> No anchorage is.

The heavy adjective *hated* on which the first line ends actually sinks it; *mutation* is an even heavier word, and too abstract, to end a line on. But Yeats did not write poems to "dramatize" ideas and to exhort the reader: "Then first shalt thou know." Emerson said a "metre-making argument" makes the poem; his argument was sometimes stuffed *into* metres. And transformation as the first law of life was easier on Yeats's theosophy than on Emerson's demand of the universe. Like so much that Emerson wrote in his growing scepticism, "Illusions" is about the drifting off of his illusions. The poet-prophet, the all-seeing Me, now finds himself *in* the wild turmoil. Far from being a medium of God, a passive receptable for the "divine rays," he is horsed on plunging Proteus and in the wild turmoil rides to *power*. And to *endurance*.

The "open secret" of the universe had become the open universe itself. It was not just the newly discovered self as the harbinger of cultural revolution that made Emerson the sign and herald of an American future; it was the Emerson who had betrayed his own wildness in his salute to *Leaves of Grass*. "I am very happy in reading it, as great power makes us happy. It meets the demand I am always making of what seemed the sterile and stingy nature, as if too much handiwork, or too much lymph in temperament, were making our western wits fat and mean."

Here he was divested of his usual unction, of his terrible benevolence. So in the struggle against slavery and the Civil War he was to be excited that things had come to a verge. As there subtly faded his great revelation that the liberated self, directly in touch with God, will change the world, Emerson enjoyed the ultimate clash of ideas in the war. Holy War was as delicious to the old Puritan as Christian "love." It claimed the whole universe for its ideals.

Proteus would not be still, though Emerson remained himself. A year after the war, he was admitting in his journal, "for every seeing soul there are absorbing facts,—*I* and *The Abyss*." Was this what Whitman's "Me and the Not Me" would come to?

Without quite registering the fact, the later Emerson was thinking like any other space-mad American. The open road, so easy for an American to call his own, was more akin to his sympathies than the historical world of sin and error. This was Emerson's real gift to the untamed American visionaries who came after him. But the enterprising self glorified by American business and its many yes-men was hardly his end point. Emerson really concluded with an admission that man was an "isolato" (Melville's word) in an endless sea of determined voyaging and heroic failure. Nature is not limited to serving man. Of course he had begun by wanting it so. But long before he died, as he had lived, to the purr of his honeyed sentences, Emerson admitted that the infinite universe cannot be domesticated to man's religious needs. This became the lonely stoic note of America's problem writing in Melville, Dickinson, Mark Twain, Stephen Crane, Wallace Stevens.

Nature was truly "masterless." Still, man's claim on it remained obstinate. In the nineteenth century the classically American moment occurs in the "First Lowering" chapter of *Moby-Dick*.

So, cutting the lashing of the waterproof match keg, after many failures Starbuck contrived to ignite the lamp in the lantern; then stretching it on a waif pole, handed it to Queequeg as the standard-bearer of this forlorn hope. There, then, he sat, holding up that imbecile candle in the heart of that almighty forlornness. There, then, he sat, the sign and symbol of a man without faith, hopelessly holding up hope in the midst of despair.

In the twentieth century it would be the conclusion of Wallace Stevens's "Sunday Morning":

> We live in an old chaos of the sun,
> Or old dependency of day and night,
> Or island solitude, unsponsored, free,
> Of that wide water, inescapable.

The American, D. H. Lawrence was to write in *Studies in Classic American Literature*, "is hard, stoic, isolate, a killer." Melville in his fierce struggle

against his "island solitude" certainly entertained thoughts of killing. Killing
is one of the great themes in Melville—and in many another American
thinker who was to prove untamable. Emerson's sense of his "power" never
descended to anything so rough. His Puritan lordliness could not admit that
even though God was always in him, this was a happy accident. D. H.
Lawrence mocked Emerson for writing (obviously in his younger days), "I
am surrounded by messengers of God who send me credentials day by day."
Lawrence snorted: "The fact of the matter is, all those gorgeous inrushes of
exaltation and spiritual energy which made Emerson a great man, now make
us sick."

It is not hard to understand why Emerson, old before his time, broke up
mentally like his own vision of the Godhead. God had become a matter of
pieces, fragments, glowing moments. Emerson was a spiritual and literary
genius who worked by dreams and audacities. These moments became his
God. These moments, he must have realized, sealed off *his* island solitude.
On the other hand, he could not have known how much, in serving his own
God-seeking, he had been translated into other men. His message would be
received by his countrymen and his age with a relish that worshipped not
the "First Cause" but a nation. In that sense it was true, as Emerson said in
ending "The Over-Soul," that he carried the whole future in the bottom of
his heart.

3

A Lover and His Guilty Land: Thoreau

All that a man has to say or do that can possibly concern
mankind, is in some shape or other to tell the story of his
love,—to sing; and, if he is fortunate and keeps alive, he
will be forever in love. This alone is to be alive to the
extremities.

THOREAU, *Journal*, May 6, 1854

This world is more wonderful than convenient.
THOREAU, Commencement Oration,
Harvard, 1837

When he thought he was dying, the savage Queequeg in *Moby-Dick* had the ship's carpenter make him a coffin.

He then called for his harpoon, had the wooden stock drawn from it, and then had the iron part placed in the coffin along with one of the paddles of his boat. All by his own request, also, biscuits were then ranged round the sides within; a flask of fresh water was placed at the head, and a small bag of woody earth scraped up in the hold at the foot; and a piece of sail-cloth being rolled up for a pillow, Queequeg now entreated to be lifted into his final bed, that he might make trial of its comforts, if any it had. He lay without moving a few minutes, then told one to go to his bag and bring out his little god, Yojo. Then crossing his arms on his breast with Yojo between, he called for the coffin lid (hatch he called it) to be placed over him. The head part turned over with a leather hinge, and there lay Queequeg in his coffin with little but his composed countenance in view.

In the Morgan Library in New York you can see the box that Thoreau (always his own handyman) built to hold his journals. This work runs to thirty-nine manuscript volumes, was printed in fourteen volumes, and contains nearly two million words in more than seven thousand printed pages.

It is not the longest writer's journal only because Thoreau, who kept it fiercely from the time he was twenty, died before he was forty-five—not altogether of the lung disease made worse by his tramping about in the worst weather and the graphite he inhaled when making pencils. Thoreau helped to kill himself by what Emerson deplored as his fanaticism—his daily struggle to find a beloved object equal to his insatiable demands.

For most of his life Thoreau was to make nature his beloved, the perfect Other. Like the moral perfection he took for granted as a characteristic of himself, a necessity he demanded of man in society, even "Great Nature" turned out to be a denial of his demands. He always ended up with himself alone. His journal became the most unflagging example—even among American writers—of a man's having to write his life in order to convince himself that he had lived it. Thoreau came to shape his life by the fiercest control words could exert. He hoped these words would be taken for his life. He was the first reader he had to convince.

The greatest part of Thoreau's life was writing and preparing himself to write. The modern need to make a career out of literature was not his ideal. Thoreau was looking not for prominence, money, access to the "good life," but the absolute—the marrying of the self to its object. If a man will "follow his own dreams," Thoreau liked to say, he will finally lead the life he imagines. What gives such severity to Thoreau's life is that the one book he was writing became a search for something great and dependable to love. The work of art he was seeking to create was himself. The most resonant version he achieved—*Walden*—proclaimed that he had "found it," that he had closed every gap, that he was perfectly at home with himself and a world that conveniently consisted of himself and nature.

Thoreau's basic experience was of an object directly before him. "Sometimes it is some particular half-dozen rods which I wish to find myself pacing over, as where certain airs blow; then my life will come to me, methinks; like a hunter I walk in wait for it." "My life will wait for nobody," he noted in his 1841 journal, "but is being matured still irresistibly while I go about the streets."

This hardly describes the incessant effort of will, day after day, with which Thoreau pursued his life.

> I long ago lost a hound, a bay horse, and a turtle-dove, and am still on their trail. Many are the travellers I have spoken concerning them, describing their tracks and what calls they answered to. I have met one or two who had heard the hound, and the tramp of the horse, and even seen the dove disap-

pear behind a cloud, and they seemed as anxious to recover them as if they had lost them themselves.

He mischievously threw this passage into "Economy," the decisive first chapter of *Walden,* with his usual condescension toward beings less private than himself. He had a secret and defied them to guess it. His real emphasis, though he tried to pretty it up, was not on private symbols. "I am still on their trail." He would call himself an "inspector of snow-storms and rain-storms," chuckle like a professional Yankee over his hardihood and the shrewdness he displayed in keeping himself aloof. This was Thoreau in his favorite literary guise—that of the man who had solved the problem of life by living in a hut at Walden Pond and telling everyone how to conduct his life. It was not the most certain gospel for those with a strong interest in the other sex.* But it was literature, delightful, mounting to such absorption in the landscape that the felt hallucination was more telling than Thoreau's saying it was.

Writing and the constant preparation for writing became for Thoreau access to some "higher," divinelike energy. Writing was parallel to living; unlike living, it was a promise that became greater and even sublime. Thoreau's existence had a theme; it was the search. He transcribed it day after day, seeking to capture experience in just one form: the sensations of a man walking about all day long. To this daily round he was restricted by his own experience; he magnified what happened but did not wish to invent anything and in fact was incapable of doing so. (Of course he scorned novels—transcendentalists always did.)

"I should not talk so much about myself," he crowed at the beginning of *Walden,* "if there were anybody else whom I knew as well. Unfortunately, I am confined to this theme by the narrowness of my experience." He was even more confined: he had no experiences to report except those of being a writer and looking for topics in nature. Thoreau never married. (And neither did his brother, his sisters, his cousins, or his aunts.) Wherever possible, as he told the world in his most famous book, he lived alone. This was in fact rarely possible, for since other members of the Thoreau family preferred to cling together, they imposed themselves on him through the

---

*A Concord neighbor, Horace Hosmer, noted with Victorian delicacy that Thoreau "did not have the 'love-idea' in him: he did not appear to feel the sex-attraction." Hosmer also noted that the passion for nature ran so strong in the Thoreau family that the parents were off in the woods or fields together whenever they had a moment to spare. They spent so much time botanizing that Thoreau was almost born in the open.

family's pencil business—and his mother's cooking. The family kept a kind of boardinghouse.

Escaping the family when he could, Thoreau at least went about alone; he became a naturalist in his own independent style, an observer who could find his material on every solitary walk. Emerson laughed that Thoreau "lived extempore, the only man of leisure in the town." At twenty-three he boasted in his journal:

> I am freer than any planet; no complaint reaches round the world. I can move away from public opinion, from government, from religion, from education, from society. . . . Shall I raise corn and potatoes in Massachusetts, or figs and olives in Asia Minor? sit out the day in my office in State Street, or ride it out on the steppes of Tartary? . . .
>
> These are but few of my chances, and how many more things may I do with which there are none to be compared!

The airiness was juvenile—and lucky. His turning every "saunter" into a fable, even a search for some holy land (à la sainte-terre, he playfully derived the word), says as much about the village's lack of pressure as it does about Thoreau's freedom from wage-slavery. But Thoreau's perfect independence was assured by Concord's indifference to him. Horace Hosmer wrote that "the Concord people did not understand Emerson, or Thoreau, or wish to, even. . . . The people did not know whether Emerson and Thoreau were fluid or solid, neither did they care." When Thoreau, in one of the more mysterious episodes of his life, managed to set fire to Concord woods while cooking a catch of fish on the shore of Fair Haven Bay, he attained greater independence by being scorned as the town nut.

"I think I could write a poem to be called 'Concord,' " Thoreau wrote in his journal for 1841. "For argument I should have the River, the Woods, the Ponds, the Hills, the Fields, the Swamps and Meadows, the Streets and Buildings, and the Villagers."

The Villagers, of course, came last. Thoreau not only lived with quotations to support his moral vision of nature, he depended on wise sayings as if they were his own. He copied out close to a million words in his commonplace books. He was also very much a literary naturalist, constantly seeing purpose in the smallest phenomena. He anxiously read up on things before he "discovered" them; he was no Robinson Crusoe having to make everything for himself. He had that large family he never wrote about, full of eccentrics like himself, who nevertheless provided the home base he went back to night after night, even when he was living at Walden, apart from "civilized life." There were all those secondhand transcendentalists like Ellery Channing, his pilgrims rather than his friends. Emerson was his some-time employer and patron, hardly a friend. Both men recorded the constant friction so necessary to Thoreau's relationship with the great man who was his model in everything except temperament. Otherwise Thoreau might have felt that he was betraying his ideal life, the life that he lived in the epiphanies of his journal. It was a life that nobody could live except with himself alone.

Since books were personal tools and friends were invariably to betray his design for life, there remained for subject matter, in a book of two million words, Nature the American God, the only god left to these self-communing transcendentalists in the New England of the 1840s. For spiritual life Thoreau depended so much on his daily and hourly search of fields and streams that he sometimes felt he was wearing nature out even as it was wearing him out. By 1854 he could admit: "We soon get through with Nature. She excites an expectation which she cannot satisfy. The merest child which has rambled into a copsewood dreams of a wilderness so wild and strange and inexhaustible as Nature can never show him." Nature would not live up to Thoreau's visionary demands.

> This earth which is spread out like a map around me is but the lining of my inmost soul exposed. In me is the sucker that I see.... There was a time when the beauty and the music were all within, and I sat and listened to my thoughts, and there was a song in them. I sat for hours on rocks and wrestled with the melody which possessed me. I sat and listened by the hour to a positive though faint and distant music, not sung by any bird, nor vibrating any earthly harp. When you walked with a joy that knew not its own origin.

Thoreau told Moncure Conway that he found in Emerson "a world where truths existed with the same perfection as the objects he studied in external nature, his ideals real and exact as antennae and staminae"; he did not separate "truths" from "ideals." Nature for Emerson meant everything not himself; for Thoreau it became the other self he walked into. When he and a companion accidentally set Concord woods afire, burning over a hundred acres and destroying much young wood, he laughed off the anger: ". . . I felt that I had a deeper interest in the woods, knew them better and should feel the loss more, than any or all of them." He gloated that "the rest of the town have had their spirits raised." Nature was *his*. Nature afforded him the public jobs he took as a surveyor from time to time to keep him in some practical relation to the neighbors he scorned. Nature made him call himself a scientist, though he was just more dogged than other New Englanders passionate for natural history. He did note every minute change in the hillsides. He came to know them with the familiarity that another man had about the body of his wife.

Above all, Nature revealed his immortal destination—his transcendence of what he studied every day. Nature was the great permissive space around Concord, in those still-early days of American settlement when villages were "a single long street lined with trees, so straight and wide that you can see a chicken run across it half a mile off." Nature was perfect *rest* as well as freedom; it was constant health and interest; it was the perfection of visible existence and the only link left (how lucky for God's own country) to an invisible one. Nature was the ideal friend, the perfect because always predictable experience. It was ease and hope and thought such as no family, certainly no woman, not even another writer, would ever provide. Why all this? Because Nature seemed consistency, order, system. It answered to man's fondest wish, that the human mind and the "Not Me" outside it reflected each other in perfect harmony. Ethan Allen, the old revolutionary fighter and homespun deist, put it in a line much quoted in Concord—"there is an eternal fitness of things." Nature in America justified the ways of God to man even when God had become a figure of speech. It was the divine principle still disclosing itself. God to Thoreau meant not the perfect Other, what is most unlike us, but perfect satisfaction.

This is what God had begun to mean to Emerson's "children"—who were assured (for a season) that God lives in us and as us. God is manifested by our power and trust alone. Emerson, who really had access to Otherness, became the oracle of a faith that depended on him alone. Emerson's faith was pure inspiration. Without His presence to give testimony, God had to be approximated by disciples who, as Mark Twain was to say of his wife's efforts at swearing, had the words but not the spirit. Without his incomparable serenity, his living voice, Emerson was never to inspire in later generations what the magnetism of his presence had created in his own day—the sense that here was the founder of American originality.

Except for anxiety about the growing intervention of the slave interest, which he recognized as a threat to his own absolute freedom as well as an affront to his private Christianity, Thoreau was so contemptuous of society that he was interested in his village only as an observer of a different species. He noted not people but striking personalities. The condescension to the ne'er-do-well Irish settler who sold him the remains of his own dwelling for Thoreau's Walden cabin typifies Thoreau's zeal to notice people for their peculiarity. In *Cape Cod* he emphasized farmers who regularly spat into the fireplace; in *The Maine Woods* Indian guides who are not noble savages forget the point of the story they are telling and are shockingly fond of money.

Society was ludicrous. But God was private to Thoreau, not to be taught or shared with anyone else. *It* was imaginative pure power, Thoreau's one real acquisition in a life narrowed to the hardness of saintship by a temperament flogging itself to find pure morality, pure love, pure creation.

God to Henry David Thoreau was the fulfillment you sensed in the woods as you passed. He was synonymous with a certain feeling. Of course other poets were saying this in the first half of the nineteenth century in England, Germany, and the United States. What Thoreau said, in prose of exceptional vibration, was that *he* had this fulfillment, this immanence in the woods, for and to himself whenever he wanted it. He had only to walk in the woods, to sit on the cliffs and look out over the Concord River and the Conantum hills, for perfect satisfaction to return. As late as 1857, he could note:

> Cold and solitude are friends of mine. . . . I come to my solitary woodland walk as the homesick go home. This stillness, solitude, wildness of nature is a kind of thoroughwort or boneset, to my intellect. This is what I go out to seek. It is as if I always met in those places some grand, serene, immortal, infinitely encouraging, though invisible companion, and walked with him.

The satisfaction lay in ready access to revelation. None of Emerson's moony followers equalled Thoreau in the ease with which he found "correspondences" in nature to every wish. It is this testament to perfect happiness that gives *Walden* its glowing surface. Nothing untoward, nothing really "personal" was allowed to break through. Style accomplished the perfect pastoral of the century. Walden Pond was a perfect mate. The contemplativeness at the center of the book dreamily fills up everything Thoreau sees, makes nature incandescent. "Life in the woods" shows man perfectly at home.

> In such a day, in September or October, Walden is a perfect forest river, set round with stones as precious to my eye as if fewer or rarer. Nothing so fair, so pure, and at the same time so large, as a lake, perchance, lies on the surface of the earth. Sky water. It needs no fence.
> . . . Paddling gently to one of these places, I was surprised to find myself surrounded by myriads of small perch, about five inches long, of a rich bronze color in the green water, sporting there, and constantly rising to the surface and dimpling it, sometimes leaving bubbles on it. In such transparent and seemingly bottomless water, reflecting the clouds, I seemed to be floating through the air as in a balloon. . . .

Walden is a meticulously manufactured altarpiece. A sense of deliverance is its subject matter, and the grateful reader acquires this as a spiritual gift from Henry David Thoreau. Reverie is its real persona. Dreamy as the book is (it seems to have had some effect on the "ouverture" to *A la recherche du temps perdu*), Thoreau fills up every space he sees with evidence of design, growth, meaning. The beautiful fiction of *Walden*, its "plot," is that Thoreau did nothing but live with perfect attachment to the pond and woods. He created the figure of Nature as a single organism with the irresistible tendency to explain itself to him. This sweet American myth, man and Nature in perfect congress, was Thoreau's fulfillment. No one else at the time—"morning in America"—not the explorers, the settlers, the professional naturalists and nature-painters, ever fashioned so smooth and unrufflable an icon.

Thoreau even managed to make living in a cabin and writing a book a contribution to "political economy." The most significant sentence in *Walden* touches not on man gazing at Nature but on man being consumed by time. "The cost of a thing is the amount of what I will call life which is required to be exchanged for it, immediately or in the long run." Thoreau's success in *Walden* is not as philosopher but as illusionist; he can persuade us that we can "spend" our lives just as we like. Romanticism remains a vital expression of the modern mind because it prolongs into the world of actual necessity every criticism made by our dreams.

The visible surface in *Walden* glows with magical transformation. All things become related to Thoreau. His alignment with nonhuman forms is so intense that they seem to be arranging themselves to please an eye that could not have been more purely loving even as it searches details to exhaustion. Emerson, whose ministerial habit of finding sermons in stones never left him, sometimes shows more curiosity for its own sake than the Thoreau who disparaged the methodicalness of Humboldt and Darwin. But Thoreau created the perfect romance between man and Nature—what he sought from Nature was not knowledge but the possibility of loving.

The perfect satisfaction in *Walden* could not continue away from life; faintly reported in the journal are the inevitable days of bleakness, bafflement, weakness. Thoreau really believed he could make his life by writing it. Although his writing took the form of remembrance transfigured, his idyll in *Walden* was complete because he sought to commemorate experience by replacing it. Thoreau always believed that a word can entirely equal an experience. That is perhaps all he meant when he wrote, "I long ago lost a hound, a bay horse, and a turtle-dove, and am still on their trail." The writer was in pursuit of the man. The ecstatic flash, the real thing in life, was always getting dim. But what was lost could always be fashioned on the page as though it had been experienced with the same intensity. This, even more than his tight control, explains the charm of *Walden*. Loving at last becomes as real as the dream of loving. A memory that transcended the merely personal was Thoreau's power of imagination. The dreaming mind of this writer, imagining his life as if there were nothing else in the world to imagine, at last created a life.

This effort called for the most relentless ordering of every experience, by constant fireworks of epigram, pun, paradox, ingenious derivation, which he recognized as his characteristic fault of style. It quite wore him out. Even the most devoted reader of Thoreau is likely to weary of his stylistic repertoire. Yet the felt need to produce "life" becomes overwhelming and feeds his enduring appeal. *Walden* yokes together many passages written separately. Some of them are positively hallucinating in their ability to evoke a moment. And Thoreau can hold us to the glory of a moment.

Thoreau was always a young man until he deteriorated suddenly in his late thirties. He was certainly oriented, as Thornton Wilder put it, to childhood. All transcendentalists had a way of peaking and then fading. Perhaps Thoreau anticipated this when he addressed his most famous book to "poor students." *Walden* is read mostly in schools, and Thoreau's most admiring readers, young or missing their youth, respond to the inner feeling of youth in its pages—the restlessness, the peremptory impatience with authority, the expectation of some different world just over the horizon. Students recognize in Thoreau a classic who is near their own age and condition. All his feelings are absolutes, as his political ideas will be. There is none of that mocking subtlety, that winning ability to live with contradiction, that one finds in Emerson. Thoreau in 1851 admitted that

> no experience which I have today comes up to, or is comparable with, the experiences of my boyhood. . . . As far back as I can remember I have unconsciously referred to the experiences of a previous state of existence. . . . Formerly, methought, nature developed as I developed, and grew up with me. My life was ecstasy. In youth, before I lost any of my senses, I can remember that I was all alive, and inhabited my body with inexpressible satisfaction.

This glow is what Thoreau's readers will always turn to him for—it is that special consonance of feeling that exists between the pilgrim and his landscape. Ecstasy was not so much achieved as rewritten; whatever the moment was, his expression of it was forged, fabricated, worked over, soldered from fragmentary responses, to make those single sentences that created Thoreau's reputation as aphorist and fostered the myth that in such cleverness a man could live.

> I should not talk so much about myself if there were anybody else whom I knew as well. . . . I have travelled a good deal in Concord; and everywhere, in shops, and offices, and fields, the inhabitants have appeared to me to be doing penance in a thousand remarkable ways. . . . I see young men, my townsmen, whose misfortune it is to have inherited farms, houses, barns, cattle, and farming tools; for these are more easily acquired than got rid of. . . . Who made them serfs of the soil? Why should they eat their sixty acres, when man is condemned to eat only his peck of dirt? Why should they begin digging their graves as soon as they are born?

Each of Thoreau's famous sentences in *Walden* is a culmination of his life, the fruit of his all-too-perfect attachment to his local world. Each was a precious particle of existence, existence pure, the life of Thoreau at the very heart. Each was victory over the long unconscious loneliness—and how many people, with far more happiness in others than Thoreau ever expected or wanted, can say that their life is all victory? In the end was the word, only the word:

> When I was four years old, as I well remember, I was brought from Boston to this my native town, through these very woods and this field, to the pond. It is one of the oldest scenes stamped on my memory. And now tonight my flute has waked the echoes over that very water. The pines still stand here older than I; or, if some have fallen, I have cooked my supper with their stumps, and a new growth is rising all around, preparing another aspect for new infant eyes. Almost the same johnswort springs from the same perennial root in this pasture, and even I have at length helped to clothe that fabulous landscape of my infant dreams, and one of the results of my presence and influence is seen in these bean leaves, corn blades, and potato vines.

The details in this key passage are so intimate, woven out of Thoreau's ardor, that the rhythms—"and even I have at length helped to clothe that fabulous landscape of my infant dreams"—seem as inevitable as a man talking in his sleep. A student once wrote about Thoreau: "This man searched to exhaustion a scene that sometimes appeared empty." Years later another student, as if to answer the first, noted that after writing *Walden*, Thoreau could look about him (as we do today when we visit Walden Pond amidst a litter of beer cans) with the feeling that he had produced the place. Thoreau did create Walden Pond; the hut along its shores became, as Ellery Channing said, the wooden inkstand in which he lived. The attachment to Walden became as total and single in its all-absorbing attentiveness as that of a baby to its mother, a prisoner to his cell. *Walden* records a love blind to everything but the force of its own will. That is why we recognize in *Walden* the beauty of youthful feeling that is haunted by doom but not by tragedy—the feeling that death seems easier than any defeat from the social compact.

For youth the center of the world is always itself, and the center is bright with the excitement of the will. There is no drama like that of being young, for then each experience can be overwhelming. Thoreau knew how to be young. He knew how to live deep and how to suck all the marrow out of life. "I went to the woods because I wished to live deliberately, to front only the essential facts of life, and see if I could not learn what it had to teach, and not, when I came to die, discover that I had not lived. I did not wish to live what was not life, living is so dear; nor did I wish to practice resignation, unless it was quite necessary."

That is youth speaking; only youth thinks that it can "live deliberately," that a man's whole life can be planned like a day off, that perfect satisfaction can be maintained without friction, without friends, without sexual love, with a God who is only and always the perfect friend—and all this in relation to a piece of land and a body of water on whose shores one practices the gospel of perfection. Only the individual in the most private accesses of his experience knows what a "perfect" moment is—a unit too small for history, too precious for society. It belongs to the private consciousness. And Thoreau's predominating aim was to save his life, not to spend it; he wanted to be as economical about his life as his maiden aunts were about the sugar in the boardinghouse they ran (they kept the sugar spoon damp so that sugar would cling to it). He wanted to live, to live supremely, and always on his own terms, saving his life for still higher things.

Enter the State and the coming of modern times. Nature Thoreau could always transcendentalize. No storm or loneliness or discomfort could turn him out of his fanatical control there. He felt at home in the primitive: he could project any fancy onto it. If he was in any sense the scientist he wanted but dreaded to be, it was when he felt superior to and untouched by dumb things in nature. The only physical apparition that seems genuinely to have frightened him was Mount Katahdin in Maine. Describing the night he spent on the summit, he significantly confessed:

I stand in awe of my body, this matter to which I am bound has become so strange to me. I fear not spirits, ghosts, of which I am one . . . but I fear bodies, I tremble to meet them. What is this Titan that has possession of me? Talk of our life in Nature—daily to be shown matter, to come in contact with it —rocks, trees, wind on our cheeks! the *solid* earth, the *actual* world! the *common sense!* Contact! *Contact! Who* are we? *where* are we?

Still, he could always get off that mountain and return to the village of which he said, "I think I could write a poem to be called 'Concord.'" Searching himself "to exhaustion," he tried to convince himself that "Concord" was the book he was writing in his journal. But the State, represented by men whose overreaching frightened him, was to become the Other that he could not domesticate as he did nature. In the eighth chapter of *Walden*, "The Village," he describes his arrest in July 1846, as he was on his way to the cobbler's. He was arrested for not paying the poll tax that was still exacted by the State in behalf of the church. Thoreau's father had been enrolled in the church; Henry's name should not have been on the roll. He spent one peaceful, dreamy night in jail. In "Civil Disobedience" he reports that "the night in prison was novel and interesting enough. . . . It was like travelling into a far country, such as I had never expected to behold, to lie there for one night. . . . It was to see my native village in the light of the Middle Ages, and our Concord was turned into a Rhine stream, and visions of knights and castles passed before me."

"At the request of the Concord selectmen" he filed a statement after he had demanded that his name be dropped from the church rolls: "Know All Men By These Presents, That I, Henry Thoreau, Do Not Wish To Be Regarded As A Member Of Any Incorporated Society Which I Have Not Joined." The experience was not a traumatic one; on being released, he "returned to the woods in season to get my dinner of huckleberries on Fair Haven Hill." But he says truly, "I was never molested by any person but those who represented the state."

In *Walden* Thoreau was to say of his prison experience that it showed the inability of society to stand "odd fellows" like himself. In "Civil Disobedience" he said in a most superior way that the State supposed "I was mere flesh and blood and bones, to be locked up," and since it could not recognize that his immortal spirit was free, "I saw that the State was half-witted, that it was timid as a lone woman with her silver spoons . . . and I lost all my remaining respect for it, and pitied it."

What gives "Civil Disobedience" its urgency is that between 1845, when Thoreau was arrested for a tax he should have paid in 1840, and 1848, when he wrote the essay, the State had ceased to be his friend the Concord sheriff, Sam Staples, who had so pleasantly taken him off to the local hoosegow, and had become the United States government. Under the leadership of the imperialist president James Polk and Southern planters determined to add new land for their cotton culture, it was making war on Mexico and would take away half its territory in the form of California, Texas, Arizona, New Mexico, and parts of Colorado and Wyoming. The Mexican War was notoriously one for plunder, as Congressman Abraham Lincoln and many other Americans charged. But the war was the first significant shock to Thoreau's complacent position that the individual can be as free as he likes, in and for himself—especially when he has persuaded his neighbors to think him odd.

Oddity was no longer enough to sustain total independence from society. Despite Thoreau's opposition to slavery in principle, he knew no Negroes and had never experienced the slightest oppression.* As a radical individualist he was very well able to support this privilege in Concord; he was not confined by his share in the family's pencil and graphite business, and he was indeed free as air—free to walk about all day long as he pleased, free to build himself a shack on Walden Pond and there to prepare to write a book, free to walk home any night for supper at the family boardinghouse. Up to the Mexican War—and more urgently, the Fugitive Slave Act of 1850, the act of 1854 permitting "squatter sovereignty" in Kansas and Nebraska, and John Brown's raid on Harper's Ferry in 1859—Thoreau's only social antagonist was the disapproval, mockery, or indifference of his Concord neighbors. He never knew what the struggle of modern politics can mean for people who identify and associate with each other. Thoreau was a pure idealist, living on principle: typical of New England in his scorn for Irish immigrants, properly indignant about slavery in far-off Mississippi, but otherwise, as he wrote *Walden* to prove, a man who proposed to teach others to be as free of society as himself.

"Civil Disobedience" stirs us by the urgency of its personal morality. As is usual with Thoreau, he seems to be putting his whole soul into the protest against the injustice committed by the State. He affirms the absolute right of the individual to obey his own conscience in defiance of an unknown law. But despite his compelling personal heat, he tends to moralize all political relationships and to make them not really serious. He turns the State into a wholly ridiculous object, its demands on him into a pure affront, and then archly tells it to stop being so overbearing and please to disappear.

---

*The English biographer and critic of Thoreau Dr. Alexander H. Japp started the fiction that Walden was a "secret station for the underground railroad." Horace Hosmer pointed out that "the Pond was the worst place for a station in the town. Thoreau had no privacy. His house was never locked. . . . How could a man who was roaming the woods and fields of Maine, Canada attend to this business. I never heard or saw a 'fugitive' till after the passage of the Fugitive Slave Law and the publication of Webster's speech on it."

Thoreau's creed is refreshing. But anyone who thinks it a guide to political action at the end of the twentieth century will have to defend the total literary anarchism that lies behind it. Gandhi used "Civil Disobedience" a century ago because, as a young leader of the oppressed Indians in South Africa, he was looking for immediate tactics with which to sidestep a totally repressive regime. There were no laws to protect the Indians. Thoreau's essay is a noble, ringing reiteration of the highest religious individualism as a self-evident social principle. The absolute freedom of the individual is his highest good, and the State is not so much the oppressor of this individual as his rival. How Dare This Power Get In My Way? For Thoreau the problem is simply one of putting the highest possible value on himself rather than on the State. This is essential: we are all individuals first, and at many junctures it may be necessary to obey oneself rather than the State. Thoreau never shows he is aware that the individual's problem may be how to resist the State when he is already so much bound up with it (he can hardly just turn his back on what he involuntarily depends on). Thoreau denied that he owed *anything* to community, state, country.

The significantly political passages in the essay have to do with what Thoreau calls "slavery in Massachusetts." He of all people could not grant that property is the greatest passion and the root of most social conflicts and wars. Yet he insisted "that if one thousand, if one hundred, if ten men whom I could name—if ten *honest* men only—ay, if *one* Honest man, in this State of Massachusetts, *ceasing to hold slaves,* were actually to withdraw from this co-partnership, and be locked up in the county jail therefor, it would be the abolition of slavery in America." With his marvellous instinct for justice, for pure Christianity, for the deep-rooted rights of the individual soul, he said: "Under a government which imprisons any unjustly, the true place for a just man is also a prison." Morally invigorating as this is, it would perhaps not have helped the fugitive slave, or the Mexican prisoner on parole, or the Indian come to plead the wrongs of his race when, as Thoreau said, they came to the prison and found the best spirits of Massachusetts there. Thoreau estimated the power of individual example to be beyond any other device in politics, but he did not explain how the usefulness of example could communicate itself to people who were in fact slaves and were not free.

The fury of the coming war could already be felt in Massachusetts. The Kansas-Nebraska Act made Thoreau explode. "There is not one slave in Nebraska; there are perhaps a million slaves in Massachusetts." But he still attacked every possible expediency connected with politics. "They who have been bred in the school of politics fail now and always to face the facts. They put off the day of settlement indefinitely, and meanwhile, the debt accumulates." The "idea of turning a man into a sausage"—the purpose of slavery—is not worse than to obey the Fugitive Slave Act.* In the pulsations of a prose no longer idyllic or smugly ironic, he pounded away at the State, the Press, the Church—institutions all leagued, he felt, by the infamous conspiracy to send runaway slaves back to their masters. He mimicked the timorous, law-obeying Massachusetts citizen:

> Do what you will, O Government! with my wife and children, my mother and brother, my father and sister, I will obey your commands to the letter. It will indeed grieve me if you hurt them, if you deliver them to overseers to be hunted by hounds or to be whipped to death; but nevertheless, I will peaceably pursue my chosen calling on this fair earth, until perchance, one day, when I have put on mourning for them dead, I shall have persuaded you to relent.

Each sentence is, as usual with Thoreau, an absolute in itself; each is a distillation of the most powerful feelings. The violence inextricable from the slavery issue—even in Concord—was taking over the quietist who in Maine was shocked by his cousin George Thatcher's killing a cow moose. "The afternoon's tragedy, and my share in it, as it affected the innocence, destroyed the pleasure of my adventure." The killing suggested "how base or coarse are the motives which commonly carry men into the wilderness. . . . Our life should be lived as tenderly and daintily as one would pluck a flower."

Now John Brown brought to the surface what had long been buried in the soul of Henry David Thoreau. The most passionate single utterance of his life was "A Plea for Captain John Brown," delivered in the Concord Town Hall on the evening of October 30, 1859. (Brown had attacked Harper's Ferry on October 16; he would be hanged on December 2.) Emerson's son Edward heard Thoreau read the speech as if it "burned" him. There is nothing so inflamed elsewhere in Thoreau's work. All the dammed-up violence of the man's life came out in sympathy with Brown's violence. Brown's attack on Harper's Ferry clearly roused in Thoreau a powerful sense of identification. Apocalypse had come. John Brown's favorite maxim was, Without the shedding of blood there is no remission of

*Emerson said the purpose of slavery was to turn a man into a monkey.

sins. Brown's raid was exactly the kind of mad, wild, desperate, and head-long attack on the authority of the United States, on the support it gave to the slave system, that Thoreau's ecstatic individualism sympathized with. It was too violent an act for Thoreau himself to have committed; he had long since given up the use of firearms and was more or less a vegetarian. But Brown represented in the most convulsively personal way the hatred of injustice that was Thoreau's most significant political passion—and this was literally a *hatred*, more so than he could acknowledge to himself, a hatred of anyone as well as anything that marred the perfect design of his moral principles.

All his life Thoreau had been saying that there are only two realms. One is the realm of grace, which is a gift and so belongs only to the gifted; the other is the realm of mediocrity. One is of freedom, which is the absolute value because only the gifted can follow it into the infinite, where its beauty is made fully manifest; the other is of acquiescence and conformism, another word for which is stupidity. One is of God, whom His elect, the most gifted, know as no one else can ever know Him; the other is of the tyranny exacted by the mediocre in society. John Brown, whom all leading historians, judges, lawyers, and respectable people have always solidly denounced as mad, John Brown, who indeed had so much madness in his background, nevertheless represented to Thoreau the gifted man's, the ideal Puritan's, outraged inability to compromise between these two realms. Even worse than evil is the toleration of it, thought John Brown, so he tried to strike at evil itself. To Thoreau, this directness proved Brown's moral genius. Then, as the state of Virginia and the government of the United States rallied all their forces to crush this man and to hang him, it turned out, to Thoreau's horror, that another exceptional man was not understood. The State, which would do nothing to respect the slave's human rights, and had in deference to Southern opinion acknowledged its duty to send back every runaway slave, would indeed obliterate John Brown with an energy that it had never shown in the defense of helpless blacks.

It was this that roused Thoreau to the burning exaltation that fills "A Plea for Captain John Brown." He had found his hero in the man of action who proclaimed that action was only the force of the highest principles. Thoreau's "plea" indeed pleads principle as the irresistible force. The pure, vehement personalism that had been Thoreau's life, in words, now sees itself turning into deeds. The pure love of Christ, striking against obstinately uncom-prehending, resisting human heads, turns into pure wrath. God has certain appointed souls to speak and fight for Him, and that is the secret of New England.

We aspire to be something more than stupid and timid chattels, pretending to read history and our Bibles, but desecrating every house and every day we breathe in. . . . At least a million of the free inhabitants of the United States would have rejoiced if [his last act] had succeeded. . . . Though we wear no crape, the thought of that man's position and probable fate is spoiling many a man's day here at the North for other thinking. If any one who has seen him here can pursue successfully any other train of thought, I do not know what he is made of. If there is any such who gets his usual allowance of sleep, I will warrant him to fatten easily under any circumstances which do not touch his body or purse.

For himself, Thoreau added, "I put a piece of paper and a pencil under my pillow, and when I could not sleep I wrote in the dark."

He wrote in the dark. Writing was what he had lived for, lived by, lived in. And now, when his unseen friend was being hanged in Charlestown prison, he could only speak for him. The word was the light, the word was the church, and now the word was the deed. This was Thoreau's only contribution to the struggle that was not for John Brown's body but for righteousness. He called the compromisers "mere figureheads upon a hulk, with livers in the place of hearts." He said of the organized church that it always "excommunicates Christ while it exists." He called the government this most *hypocritical* and *diabolical* government, and he mimicked it, saying to protesters like himself, "What do you assault me for? Am I not an honest man? Cease agitation on this subject, or I will make a slave of you, too, or else hang you." He said, "I am here to plead his cause with you. I plead not for his life, but for his character—his immortal life; and so it becomes your cause wholly, and is not his in the least. Some eighteen hundred years ago Christ was crucified; this morning, perchance, Captain Brown was hung. These are the two ends of a chain which is not without its links."

There was nothing Thoreau could do except to *say* these things. Brown, who was quite a sayer himself, had said to the court:

Had I so interfered in behalf of the rich, the powerful, the intelligent, the so-called great . . . it would have been all right. . . . I am yet too young to understand that God is any respecter of persons. I believe that to have interfered as I have done—as I have always freely admitted I have done— in defense of His despised poor, was not wrong but right.

Yet we in our day cannot forget that Brown was punished for a direct assault on the government, for attempting insurrection. Melville, putting his dispassionate elegy on John Brown at the head of his poems of the Civil War, *Battle-Pieces*, called Brown "The Portent."

Hidden in the cap
  Is the anguish none can draw;
So your future veils its face,
  Shenandoah!
But the streaming beard is shown
  (Weird John Brown),
The meteor of the war.

Brown did as much as any one man did to bring about the Civil War—
which Thoreau rejected as immoral. Concord snickered at his inconsistency.
Of course he was already ill when the war broke out (he was to be dead in
a year). If Thoreau died of the war as well as of the terrible struggles with
himself that hastened his disease, he did not die a martyr. "The cost of a thing
is the amount of what I will call life which is required to be exchanged for
it, immediately or in the long run." By that test Thoreau paid much to
become the writer he was. But the cost of nonviolence—which Thoreau
returned to as his gospel—is so great in the face of the all-powerful twentieth-
century state that Thoreau, who once in his life was astonished by power
that was not his individual spiritual power, does not help us in the face of
the state power which we supplicate for the general "welfare" and dread for
snooping into our lives.

Thoreau did not anticipate the modern state. He distrusted all government and understood it far less than did Jesus when He counseled the Jews
under the Roman heel, Render unto Caesar the things that are Caesar's.
When the Civil War broke out, Thoreau advised an abolitionist friend to
ignore Fort Sumter. "Be ye perfect, even as your Father in Heaven is
perfect." That was the only power Thoreau knew and believed in—outside
the writer's power that made him a life. He would not have believed it
possible that the United States could become a superpower, a superstate, and
that young people in this state would be reading and "imitating" Thoreau
in order *not* to do anything about the government.

4

The Ghost Sense: Hawthorne and Poe

Why does Hawthorne give us the afternoon hour later
than anyone else?—oh late, late, quite uncannily late, as
if it were always winter outside?

HENRY JAMES, "The Lesson of Balzac"

I

Nathaniel Hawthorne was not quite sixty when in 1864 he died suddenly
during the Civil War—a war in which he felt no zeal for either side. For at
least four years before his death, Hawthorne was tormented by his inability
to finish any of his last projected novels and by the oncoming dissolution of
the Union. To both of these he reacted with a feeling of personal dread and
political helplessness.

The past, usually nearer to Hawthorne than "the Present, the Immediate,
the Actual," was coming apart in his mind even before the guns made it
unreal. Hawthorne's obsessive symbols now seemed to him disconnected,
artificial, outworn machinery that he had never before exploited for melodramatic effect (as had Poe). The aborted "romances"—*Dr. Grimshawe's
Secret; Septimius Felton, or The Elixir of Life; The Ancestral Footstep*—all
projected fantastic themes that Hawthorne could never work out to his
satisfaction. They became personal obsessions, failed attempts to put the past
into order. Hawthorne dimly recognized that his themes were the turbid past
baffling the present. Unable to separate himself from his own symbols, he felt
haunted as a man and humiliated as an artist.

One story presented an elixir that would keep a man alive forever. Another featured the print of a bloody footstep left on a house step by a
Protestant martyr persecuted by Bloody Mary. Another represented an

American in England, there to claim an ancient inheritance. Still another told of a woman's corpse that in the coffin turned into masses of golden hair. These romances had many interchangeable features—always a sign that an author is pursuing some separable idea from book to book rather than working out a situation in its own terms. Characters were discarded only to pop up again under new names. The cast included spiders, buried treasure, indecipherable markings on tombstones, and gave the impression that Hawthorne had long carried in his mind certain atmospheric "effects" as deadweight. It was not clear from Hawthorne's indecisiveness, his many desperate attempts to secure a story by making repeated outlines and frantic notes to himself in the margins of his manuscripts, whether he had ever taken his last plots seriously. He may have just felt himself closeted with his own contrivances. But once it had become complicated, plot offered him the chance to work out his rich excursions into existence as a moral mystery.

Even in 1850–51, the time of *The Scarlet Letter* and *The House of the Seven Gables,* of his sudden success as an author, Hawthorne had never been confident that success would continue. He was distrustful of the literary career in America, sardonic about his own efforts as a "mere storyteller" in preachy New England and among his transcendentalist neighbors in Concord—who could not read him. His sometime neighbor Herman Melville came to identify himself with a tragic young French author's bitterness: "The literary career seems to me unreal, both in its essence and in the rewards which one seeks from it, and therefore fatally marred by a secret absurdity." Hawthorne would have agreed with every word. Nothing was more uncertain and "absurd" than to attempt to support a family by the pen. In the preface to *The Scarlet Letter*—Hawthorne was always writing bluff, blunt, "sensible" prefaces to his novels, as if to assure his countrymen that the real New Englander should not be confused with the "fanciful" and "visionary" author—he admitted that even though his Puritan ancestors would have scorned such an "idler" and "writer of story-books," "yet, let them scorn me as they will, strong traits of their nature have intertwined themselves with mine."

But he was never to be sure that this was entirely so. Had he been accepted and even "forgiven" for telling stories in so many subtle and enigmatic ways that they could have been taken as mischievous, even dangerous to the moral tradition which New England thought special to itself? Of all the many forms and realities of guilt that Hawthorne had taken as his subject matter, none was perhaps so unexpected as that of being a "mere" storyteller in the new Israel whose most famous and self-liberated man of letters, Ralph

Waldo Emerson, could not read fiction. Emerson thought that Hawthorne's reputation was really a tribute to the man, for his romances were "good for nothing."

Hawthorne continued to live in the country of his imagination long after he had written himself out. From his first stories to the last novel he published, *The Marble Faun* (1860), his work had been "haunted" by the themes of sin, crime, guilt, murder. There was always some dread secret, some real or projected violation of the human order, some unimaginable solitude in society. What Melville in the 1850s saluted at the center of Hawthorne's work as "the power of blackness" deteriorated even before the Civil War into some mysterious personal blankness. His isolation expressed itself in a total exasperation with the American political process and the abolitionist sympathies in Concord. He was a pragmatic party Democrat easily made cynical by the jockeying for power. We do not know how much he approved of President Franklin Pierce's pro-Southern administration, but he owed his consulship in Liverpool to Pierce, his college classmate and lifelong friend. During the Civil War, when Pierce was generally discredited in his native New England, Hawthorne made a point of dedicating to Pierce his English reminiscences, *Our Old Home*, and summoned up his last strength to defy the outraged protests of Emerson and others.

Hawthorne was living out his last years as a Hawthorne character. He had been an extraordinarily attractive man and was an adored husband; but solitude was always more natural to Hawthorne than "society" of any kind beyond his wife and children—even the amiable superficial society of other authors in Concord and the Berkshires. He was the surliest and most fractious of Yankees, a hermit crab with a Timon-like contempt for his idealistic contemporaries (he excepted Thoreau, as a boating companion) and a gift for tripping up others with his grim silences that disconcerted professionally genial people like Dr. Oliver Wendell Holmes. This trait amused Emerson, who in Concord was a sacred object. He enjoyed walking with the silent, bilious Hawthorne. "In his conversation, as in his books, you feel there is some bitter fairy, which is biting him all the time, and which he is unable to conceal."

The mysterious breakdown of Hawthorne's imaginative capacity suggests the ominousness of a Hawthorne story: everything is suspended until the catastrophe. The catastrophe is usually the one violence in the story, something that human nature has willed after keeping it long withheld, and the disclosure is of some secret long buried within the soul.

Hawthorne wrote of one of his last projects, *The Dolliver Romance*, "I cannot finish it unless a great change comes over me; and if I make too great an effort to do so, it will be my death, not that I should care much for that, if I could fight the battle through and win it, thus ending a life of much smoulder and scanty fire in a blaze of glory." Now his own "catastrophe" was on him: extreme uncertainty, mental dislocation, great difficulty in his physical movements, a marked abdication of his vital resources. The war was his despair, chewing everything up for a national ideal Hawthorne did not believe in. He would have let the South go if it had left peacefully. "New England is as large a lump of earth as my heart can hold." "I must say that I rejoice that the old Union is smashed. We never were one people and never really had a country since the Constitution was formed." Only Hawthorne, indifferent to all agitation over slavery, would have been equally contemptuous of the constitutional compromise under which the South counted a slave as three-fifths of a person in determining a state's representation in Congress.

Nevertheless, a terrible Civil War was raging. No other writer in New England sounded so cold to the national cause. And the war was helping to kill him. The war was a violation and destruction of what little order there was around him. With his usual melancholy dependence on time past as more real than the present, he felt himself sinking into some general confusion. In a disdainfully independent essay for the *Atlantic Monthly*, "Chiefly About War Matters—by a Peaceable Man," Hawthorne described a visit to the Southern theater of war without any of the usual patriotic trumpetings. "This dismal time, when our country might seem to have arrived at such a dead standstill."

In his campaign biography of Pierce (1852), Hawthorne described slavery as "one of those evils which divine Providence does not leave to be remedied by human contrivances, but which, in its own good time, by some means impossible to be anticipated, but of the simplest and easiest operation, when all its uses have been fulfilled, it causes to vanish like a dream." It would soon vanish, though not like a dream, and Hawthorne might easily have anticipated this as one result of the war. But with his grave faith in doing nothing, Hawthorne found everything about the war painful to his conservative mind. His relief was to find military pomp ludicrous.

Only Hawthorne would have written that the country in general "was more quiet than in ordinary times, because so large a proportion of its restless element had been drawn toward the seat of the conflict." "The air was full of a vague disturbance." He sorrowed over the "lines of soldiers, with shouldered muskets, putting us in mind of similar spectacles at the gates of European cities. . . . Will the time ever come again, in America, when we may live half a score of years without once seeing the likeness of a soldier, except it be in the festal march of a company on its summer tour?" He bitterly anticipated the "preponderance of military titles and pretensions. . . . It behooves civilians to consider their wretched prospects in the future, and assume the military button before it is too late." Deriding the mighty preparations for battles which Northern generals were usually too cautious to win, Hawthorne said that

> the whole business, though connected with the destinies of a nation, takes inevitably a tinge of the ludicrous. The vast preparation of men and warlike material,—the majestic patience and docility with which the people waited through those weary and dreary months,—the martial skill, courage and caution with which our movement was ultimately made,—and, at last, the tremendous shock with which we were brought suddenly up against nothing at all.

Hawthorne was equally unimpressed by Lincoln. He derided the unpredictable electoral process which permitted the voters to choose a candidate they knew nothing about.

> It is the strangest and yet the fittest thing in the jumble of human vicissitudes, that he, out of so many millions, unlooked for, unselected by any intelligible process that could be based upon his genuine qualities, unknown to those who chose him, and unsuspected of what endowments may adapt him for his tremendous responsibility, should have found the way open for him to fling his lank personality into the chair of state,—where, I presume, it was his first impulse to throw his legs on the council-table and to tell the Cabinet ministers a story.

Hawthorne's equally unflattering remarks about Lincoln's appearance were suppressed by the *Atlantic Monthly* when it reluctantly published "Chiefly About War Matters" in July 1862. Since Hawthorne's lack of patriotic fire made the magazine uneasy, he cheerfully added unsigned footnotes, purporting to come from the editors, that protested passages in his own text. But he denounced John Brown as a "blood-stained fanatic" and roundly declared that "Nobody was ever more justly hanged. He won his martyrdom fairly, and took it firmly." Then he ridiculed the wartime exaltation of Brown by saying that "any common-sensible man, looking at the matter unsentimentally, must have felt a certain intellectual satisfaction in seeing him hanged, if it were only in requital of his preposterous miscalculation of possibilities."

.   .   .

Hawthorne saw the war as a totally tragic event and, in failing health and spirits, identified his crisis with the national crisis.

> The Present, the Immediate, the Actual, has proved too potent for me. It takes away not only my scanty faculty, but even my desire for imaginative composition, and leaves me sadly content to scatter a thousand peaceful fantasies upon the hurricane that is sweeping us all along with it, possibly, into a Limbo where our action and its polity may be as literally the fragments of a shattered dream as my unwritten Romance.

Yet had there ever been a time in his life when the social world was less than a grim duty, the political world not repulsive? Hawthorne's enduring solitude after leaving college in the "dismal chamber" of the Salem home where he had practiced his art, was more than a personal habit; it was a commitment to the wholly mental life of his own characters. What he most despised in John Brown—the "preposterous miscalculation of possibilities" —paralleled what had gone wrong with his own last projects. In each unfinishable novel he was working less with an inherent dramatic situation than with a controlling idea that the characters were to represent and the final catastrophe to make clear. The characters, having this awful symbolic weight to bear, kept turning into each other and getting lost. With so much hanging on the too-abstract "meaning" behind each story, Hawthorne tried for shock effects—a bloody footstep visible after centuries in a stone step, a corpse dissolving into golden ringlets of hair, a villain falling dead after swallowing the elixir he thinks will make him young again.

Allegory, some "higher" meaningfulness and moral purpose, had been central to Hawthorne's work from the beginning. He was the one great artist of New England's religion—of people who walked a world where every gesture as well as every action came under the eye of a totally sovereign Deity. The solitude of Hawthorne's characters was more than physical in the bare, still uncharted world of Boston in *The Scarlet Letter*, caught between the sea and the wilderness. There everyone felt himself endlessly accountable; the individual knew that his aloneness was of supreme interest to God. Solitude was not exclusion from society but the condition of a life incessantly moralized. The individual was always deliberating, inspecting, and challenging to make sure that a highly suspicious divinity would in fact not exclude him.

So much solitude lived in anxious self-confrontation and self-study meant a totally interior life. Consciousness could become an infliction. It finally did to Hawthorne, an artist who had to balance his characters' incessant mental striving against their high sense of purpose. He was entirely matter-of-fact about a world that was legendary. The crux of the matter was that his people were always so alone; they felt damned. And so did he. Emerson, despite his dismissal of Hawthorne's fiction, may have guessed the agony of Hawthorne's last years when he wrote on hearing of his death, "I thought there was a tragic element in the event, that might be more truly rendered—in the painful solitude of the man, which, I suppose, could no longer be endured, and he died of it." To be that much alone was to be in contradiction. The subject Hawthorne inherited was the purposefulness (once one came under the sovereign eye of God) that actual life and human passion could no longer demonstrate. Allegory was inherent to his characters. They practiced it every day, for the human world was to find its justification only in the moral order.

But what if that moral order did not really exist? had come to seem a human construction like any other? The memory of so much "order" and purpose, once set by the supreme mind that created the universe, remained with people long after the sacred connection had vanished. The life once *lived* as allegory could disappear into history, becoming fragments to be put together only in a story. The ancestral religion had in fact turned its ancient duties and inflictions into legend, the matter of New England, a remote regional culture like that of the Basques or the Celts.

What Hawthorne seized as his natural subject was New England's historic remoteness, New England as a legend to itself after the ancient fires of belief had burned out in the nineteenth century. Utterly opposed to Emerson, Hawthorne did not believe that in the absence of the church, man's natural faith asserts itself. Personally indifferent to religion, Hawthorne kept the old Puritan distrust of society and Nature. Nature in the human heart, not in Concord woods, was really quite terrible. Moreover, New England Democrats were never aroused by democracy as the promise of equality. Few things were less to Hawthorne's taste than Emerson's blithe assurance to his listeners that any farmer or small trader was potentially a genius like himself. Hawthorne distrusted the American people politically and excluded most American types from his fiction. He did not think that literature consisted of personal ideals. His lifelong insecurity as a professional author reflected his suspicion of the public as well as of publishers. He was more isolated even than Poe, who *had* to work the public through magazines. To write dramatic fiction in a New England that had remained self-righteous while doubting religion—that was simply not natural. Only in New England could so pure a work of art as *The Scarlet Letter* have aroused a busybody minister to cry

out, "There is an unsound state of public morals when the novelist is permitted, without a scorching rebuke, to select such crimes and to invest them
with all the fascination of genius and all the charms of a highly polished
style."

But only in New England could *The Scarlet Letter* have been written.
From the beginning, when he spent ten—or was it twelve?—years in his
Salem room learning to write "tales," Hawthorne instinctively fixed on New
England as his tradition, his subject, his fate. He tried for many years to
interest publishers in collections of interrelated tales variously called *Seven
Tales of My Native Land, Provincial Tales, The Storyteller*. The publishers, as
it usually happened, wanted only Hawthorne's best stories. The rascally
book merchant Samuel C. Goodrich took for his gift annual *The Token* in
1832 "The Gentle Boy," "The Wives of the Dead," "Roger Malvin's Burial,"
and "My Kinsman, Major Molineux" without Hawthorne's name so as to
deceive readers into the belief that they were getting several authors instead
of just one. It was not until *Twice-Told Tales* (1837) that Hawthorne's name
appeared over his works.

Hawthorne's fixation on New England, his sense of solitude as a fatality
—not least in his own life—and above all his sense that we are determined,
located in ourselves forever, by the past as human sinfulness, acting on us
as second nature, was to make him a puzzle to the realists who came after
the Civil War. What is special in Hawthorne is the belief that even though
no moral order may exist, the responsibility for it has fallen on the sinner
himself. So his relation to it in faithless times is problematical, endlessly
difficult. It is some strange preoccupation that we must live with. There is
nothing to guide us in this "forest" (a refrain in Hawthorne) but the heart.
"Heart" is as central in Hawthorne as "soul" is to the transcendentalists. It
stands for the loneliness of sexual love and its attendant affections, con-
strained by the spell of the past that still makes many of the living unable
to love. The struggle to *love* makes Hester and Dimmesdale in *The Scarlet
Letter* more dramatic than any newly "liberated" self rebelling against nineteenth-century convention.

Hawthorne would have agreed with Marx: the dead generations weigh
on the living like an incubus. Unlike Marx, Hawthorne felt that the past, not
the future, was his opening to the imagination. He did not trust the future
in America; the buoyancy and thrust of nineteenth-century ambition never
interfered with his creative bent. Hawthorne is not modern: the drama in his
works is located in the past or is wholly determined by it. In his last desperate
period the historical pitch of his mind became his curse. Almost everything
in Hawthorne turns on old legends, myths, chronicles, "twice-told tales,"

"mosses from an old manse," England as "our old home." *The Blithedale Romance* (1852) is the only one of his four major novels that is concerned wholly with issues and personalities of Hawthorne's own nineteenth-century America, still struggling with pastoral images of itself that were soon to be destroyed in the fires of the Civil War. *The Scarlet Letter* is of course a story of seventeenth-century Boston. *The House of the Seven Gables*, though set in nineteenth-century Salem, is about the hold of the past on some elderly characters and the struggle of the young to free them from the "grip" (a favorite word in Hawthorne) of the past. The last novel Hawthorne published in his lifetime, *The Marble Faun*, laid in contemporary Italy, is really about the unlosable past, the baleful and ominous past that stands in the way of two pairs of ill-matched and unbelievable lovers. The past represents guilt —guilt for the past. The way out is dark, uncertain, a labyrinth like the narrow passages, dreamlike monuments, and tombs of historic Rome.

Even after his marriage, Hawthorne felt himself a prisoner of his native Salem. Sophia Hawthorne said it was "dragging at his ankles." But as imaginative dream and subject material, he could not leave it alone. In "The Custom House," preface to *The Scarlet Letter*, he wrote that the village lingered in his mind with "only imaginary inhabitants to people its wooden houses, and walk its homely lanes." He was no sooner back for a visit to the "dismal chamber" in Herbert Street than he took out his quire of paper and prepared "to cover it with the accustomed nonsense." The imaginative connection with the past was instantaneous, a kind of fatality. Hawthorne was not a "historical" novelist. (As Faulkner said, the past is not even past.) But the fascination in Hawthorne is that the past is all determination and all picture. One can never forget, from *The House of the Seven Gables*, the innocent Matthew Maule on the scaffold, the halter around his neck, crying out to horrible Governor Pyncheon on horseback, grimly watching him, "God will give you blood to drink!" It is the enduring leitmotif of the novel.

In an early sketch for a story that never really came off, "Alice Doane's Appeal," Hawthorne harks back, as he often did, to the hanging of "witches" on Gallows Hill.

> In the rear of the procession rode a figure on horseback, so darkly conspicuous, so sternly triumphant, that my hearers mistook him for the visible presence of the fiend himself; but it was only his good friend, Cotton Mather, proud of his well won dignity, as the representative of all the hateful features of his time; the one blood-thirsty man, in whom were concentrated those vices of spirit and errors of opinion, that sufficed to madden the whole surrounding multitude. And thus I marshalled them onward, the innocent who were to die, and the guilty who were to grow old in long remorse—

tracing their every step, by rock, and shrub, and broken track, till their
shadowy visages had circled round the hill-top, where we stood. I plunged
into my imagination for a blacker horror, and a deeper woe, and pictured the
scaffold—

Hawthorne called himself not novelist but "storyteller" and described
what he wrote as "romances" in those prefaces to his books that were
apologies for his strange calling and his attempts to bridge the gap between
himself and his audience. As a storyteller, choosing to represent psychic
situations rather than to explain them, Hawthorne suggested uncertainties
where there had always been God's truth; he drew shadows and hinted at
abysses where there had always been clarity; he strained to find images
of the imponderable, the blackness, and the vagueness, even the terror that
waits in what he called "the dim region beyond the daylight of our perfect
consciousness."

In Hawthorne's best work—his short stories and his first two novels,
The Scarlet Letter and *The House of the Seven Gables*—the past still possessed
the unity, dominion, force formed by Puritanism. Hawthorne told his publisher James Fields that, *The Scarlet Letter* "being all in one tone, I had only
to get my pitch and could then go on interminably." It was so much of one
piece, he said, that by keeping so close to its point, it was "diversified no
otherwise than by turning different sides of the same dark idea to the
reader's eye."

Edgar Allan Poe insisted that "unity of effect" was the highest aim of
literature and was possible only in short forms like the tale and the lyric
poem. This was the public version of Poe's obsessive belief that the artist
must manipulate his audience. "Unity of effect" was a hypothetical idea,
subjective rather than esthetic; Poe was always too conscious of his audience
and of his need to absorb it into his will.

Hawthorne, by contrast, wrote *The Scarlet Letter* as if hypnotized by it.
With his usual need to protect his feelings, he pretended to scoff at his own
efforts. Seventeenth-century Boston produced in him a concentrated force
of impression—the scaffold on which the book opens and concludes, the
town imprisoned between the ocean and the forest, the scarlet letter itself,
the mirror, the pillory, the jail, the "sad-colored garments, and gray, steeple-
crowned hats, . . . assembled in front of a wooden edifice, the door of which
was heavily timbered with oak, and studded with iron spikes." The past fell
into shape—a marshalling of images that developed into a single figure,
putting the past into relief. The reader can look at it from every side, as if

it were a piece of sculpture. This is a freedom that Poe never willingly gave his reader.

The dramatic logic and progression of *The Scarlet Letter,* the overwhelming sense it exerts on the reader of the harsh Puritan past as the "dark necessity" that works on everyone's life, the particular way in which images of the past are felt by us as present psychological and human inflictions—this effect is so keen and inexorable that Hawthorne's "ghost sense," as Eliot called it, becomes the psychic stream in which we live. But Hawthorne has not, like Eliot, been torn from the past; he is clearly afraid of it. It is more of a "ghost" than Eliot knew. There is in Hawthorne's best stories a subtle removal from the past he has called up. He just cannot sever himself from it. Puritanism is America's Middle Ages, and in Hawthorne its details are finally as ungraspable as those gargoyles on Gothic cathedrals, those knotted images in Dante, that are so much the mind of another period that we never fully see them, however cleverly we explain them.

There are many writers, far more removed from us in time, who reach us more directly than Hawthorne does. If the historical sense, as Eliot put it in a famous essay, consists in bringing certain past works into the daylight of present consciousness, then Hawthorne is not easily assimilable by us. That is why there are so many theological and psychoanalytical interpretations of Hawthorne—they fill the vacuum created by our modern uncertainty about the use and relevance of Hawthorne's art.

What this means, in terms of that art, is that Hawthorne's images of the past are autonomous yet cling to their original texture. Something irrecoverable of the past clings to them, as in "My Kinsman, Major Molineux" and "Young Goodman Brown." There is indeed a "dim region beyond the daylight of our perfect consciousness." Hawthorne's "ghost sense" can be a turning of the present into the past—for the delight of the dream itself, for the sense of severity, the "brass studded spikes on the door of the prison house." Far from turning the past into still another symbol of ourselves, Hawthorne's art relies on his extraordinary pictorial sense. The rose bush set against the dismal prison door at the opening of *The Scarlet Letter* and the intimidating gleam of the swords and armor in "The Governor's Hall" chapter are as startling as the scarlet of the letter, Pearl's "crimson velvet tunic, of a peculiar cut, abundantly embroidered with fantasies and flourishes of gold-thread." In the hall "there was a steel headpiece, a cuirass, a gorget, and greaves, with a pair of gauntlets and a sword hanging beneath; all, and especially the helmet and breastplate, so highly burnished as to glow with white radiance, and scatter an illumination everywhere about upon the floor." In "Young Goodman Brown" flame is at the heart of the forest; in "My Kinsman, Major Molineux," even before we come to the brilliant scene, lit up by torches and the prostitutes' red petticoats, of the major's public undoing,

> a redder light disturbed the moonbeams, and a dense multitude of torches shone along the street, concealing by their glare whatever object they illuminated. The single horseman, clad in a military dress, and bearing a drawn sword, rode onward as the leader, and, by his fierce and variegated countenance, appeared like war personified; the red of one cheek was an emblem of fire and sword; the blackness of the other betokened the mourning which attends them.

Hawthorne's attention to allegory is incessant; as James said in his biography, it amounted to "importunity." With so much symbolizing and symbolism at our disposal, contemporary critics have had no trouble showing what Hawthorne should have known about his symbols. But for all Hawthorne's symbolizing (and even his anxious moralizing), such extraordinary scenic effects as the grappling for Zenobia's body at the end of *The Blithedale Romance,* the aged, pathetic, shrivelled brother and sister in *The House of the Seven Gables* fleeing their house, and the night scenes of Rome in *The Marble Faun* become the imaginative space in Hawthorne's work, a perfect historical dreamwork, which is his real achievement.

Everyone recognizes that whatever is most profound in New England is somehow bound up with Puritanism. In Hawthorne we see an artist's natural emancipation from it and also a Victorian's turning back to it as the material of legend, an allegory of the human heart. The automatic moralizing of the New England mind, the sententiousness of its intellectual manner in its nineteenth-century descendants, the consciousness of being God's elect that is evident in Emerson's belief that his orphic manner could instruct a "plain" people—these realities were turned by Hawthorne into fanciful, elusive, symbolic elements of human nature. But surrounded by so many moralists and religionists who thought they commanded the reality principle, Hawthorne created more memorably than he did anything else a sense of the *unreality* of existence—its doubleness, its dreaminess, its unrealizability except through the symbol-haunted tale. In Hawthorne, Puritanism returned to its secret core: the hidden God, not just the all-sovereign one; the ungraspable God, not just the lawgiver and taskmaster whom the anxious Puritan, not altogether sure of his salvation, had constantly to satisfy. Reality for the storyteller was like the forever unknown God who lies beyond our ken and may be "hidden" because He *is* beyond our ken.

It was this sense of the elusive, of the mystery right before our eyes, that made the remarkable writer who thought himself archaic haunting to the late James. James had begun by agreeing that Hawthorne was archaic, and as he confessed in his autobiography, he wanted him out of the picture. There is an obvious parallelism to Hawthorne in the heavy symbolism of late novels like *The Wings of the Dove* and *The Golden Bowl* and in the intense self-scrutiny of characters who in the international leisure class have as much time as the Puritans did for perpetually examining their conscience. But when Eliot on James's death defined as the "Hawthorne aspect" their feeling for the "deeper psychology" (apparently every nineteenth-century novelist lacked this except two Americans), he was really upholding the peculiar isolation on which so much American literature rests.

Eliot thought that Hawthorne's distinction was his ability "to grasp character through the relation of two or more persons to each other; and this is what no one else, except James, has done." Obviously Eliot was still defining himself as an American poet when he wrote this; his enthusiasm for James's *The Sense of the Past* was peculiar but strangely apt in the context of the "Hawthorne aspect." Just as Hawthorne could not finish his last works, so James left unfinished a wholly mental romance like *The Sense of the Past*. The theme of a young man's exchanging places with the subject of an ancestral portrait and stepping into the world of a hundred years before leads to so many unreal gyrations of plot that it is easy to see why James left it unfinished: he had nowhere to go. What is most chilling about this wholly mental construction is that James was contriving his "sense of the past." He had nothing like Hawthorne's saturation in a definite time and place.

Hawthorne's tales affect us as primitive memory. Certain episodes we seem to have dreamed in common. Of all the American classics, Hawthorne is still the standard for those readers who think that a piece of writing should have the mysterious authenticity and the self-sufficient form of a dream.

I I

It is an odd fact—to those who do not know America from within—that this wholly modern society should have produced as its rarest, profoundest artists writers who were most concerned with the inner life, with the many strange theaters for mental consciousness alone. Although our writers have naturally found their abundant subject matter in unprecedented transformations, one operating force had to be the struggle with ancestral symbols. Many ghosts haunted the American mind in the nineteenth century. Whatever transcendentalists might say of their kinship with divine Nature, Hawthorne was to portray the half-remembered forest as the repository of what is forever unknown, inhuman, unrecognizable.

Hawthorne—like Poe—became a kind of virtuoso in the fiction of the inner life: the only novelist from New England as subtle as Emerson and Dickinson. He was able to present in the current style the extraordinary burden on the New England mind of the past, its moral introspection, its unending self-confrontation. Poe, his only equal in the "tale," was really a convert to esthetic medievalism, an apologist for slavery, order, and hierarchy, a writer of "grotesques and arabesques" who saw the power of blackness as personal damnation and a way of practicing literary terror. It is the force of the repressed that Poe made his drawing card, the power not of the past but of the dead, as phantoms preying on unsleeping guilt.

Hawthorne remained a child of Puritanism, rooted in the village, the theocracy, the rule of law, the numbing force of convention. Poe, by contrast, is forever homeless, landless, seeking a visionary home in some Platonic heaven of eternal Beauty, writing his most poignant poems out of a profound homesickness that operated as a curse.

Damnation was a great stimulator of literary effect. No one would ever match Poe's ability to share his terror with the reader. In a sense Poe never felt that he lived here; his contempt was absolute. As a lordly instructor of the susceptible American people (who made their education out of magazines, as Poe found in them his livelihood and his one chance to enthrall and bamboozle), Poe was still caught up in his favorite pose of being someone Other—a great public personage trailing his mysterious origins, like Alexander Hamilton from the West Indies or Count Rumford (Benjamin Thompson) from Massachusetts. Poe's haunted castles are all European, like his alter ego, Dupin, the private genius of detection who inaugurated a genre by telling the dumb police where to look.

But if the stage trappings are European, the sense of personal isolation is all too familiar—and even magnified by the abstractness of his ambition and his grandiloquence. Baudelaire, who thought he was Poe's double, nevertheless understood that

> dazzling a young and unformed country by his mind, shocking men who considered themselves his equals by manners, Poe was fated to become a most unhappy writer. Rancors were aroused, solitude settled around him. In Paris, in Germany, he would have found friends; in America, he had to fight for his bread. Thus his drunkenness and nomadic habits are easily explained. He

went through life as if through a Sahara desert, and changed his residence like an Arab.

"The terror of which I write," Poe needlessly admonished his contemporaries, "is not of Germany, but of the soul." The most expert American critic of his time, a poet so routinely professional that his famous effects are more those of a virtuoso musician indifferently tootling away than those of a thinker *in* poetry, a mesmerist in his ability to spellbind and intimidate the reader, Poe was of course right to believe in the Romantic cult of genius. To demonstrate his originality in all genres *and* the sciences, however, Poe had to erect his literally fantastic abilities on his own wretchedness. *Eureka*, his one-man theory of the universe, his supreme effort to put existence and cosmology together as Melville would do in *Moby-Dick* and Whitman in *Leaves of Grass*, is a dazzling catastrophe. Which, as we know from his longest, most sustainedly brutal, least "supernatural" fiction, *The Narrative of Arthur Gordon Pym*, he thought the universe to be.

Pym is anything but the "pure" fiction Poe said he delighted to write and of which he thought himself the master. It is artificially prolonged, mechanical to a degree, and it suspends the reader on such a chain of crises (several of them borrowed from sailors' narratives) that despite violent excitements, it remains the strangest possible chronicle. Pym (the monosyllable rings in our mind like "Poe") is a dummy without individual mind or emotion. Any craft he gets into suddenly ensnares him, and everyone else on board, in dangers more extreme and complex than could have been fabricated by anyone but Edgar Allan Poe.

Nevertheless, *Pym*—like so much in Poe—is "remarkable" and startling. Because it is not "supernatural" until the very end, when in the Antarctic it stops short on "a shrouded human figure, very far larger in its proportions than any dweller among men," it is repeatedly and satisfyingly frightening. As always with Poe at his most fervid, we are held down (quite literally in one stowaway scene), narrowed to the confrontation that is Poe's necessary image of life. We are brought to see life as nothing but anxiety; for the story consists of one near-fatal disaster after another, from which not only Arthur Gordon Pym but *we* are saved at the last possible moment.

Pym is a young man of whom we get to know nothing. In himself (and, so far as Poe cared to go into the matter, *to* himself) Pym is less a person than the occasion of the most desperate encounters. He no sooner goes to bed after a drinking party with his friend Augustus Bernard than this friend (so drunk that he is walking in his sleep) routs him out of bed to go sailing in the middle of the night.

> It was blowing almost a gale, and the weather was very cold—it being late in October. I sprang out of bed, nevertheless, in a kind of ecstasy. . . .
>
> . . . I perceived at once that, in spite of his assumed *nonchalance*, he was greatly agitated. I could see him distinctly by the light of the moon—his face was paler than any marble, and his hand shook so excessively that he could scarcely retain hold of the tiller. I found that something had gone wrong, and became seriously alarmed.

That something had gone wrong is definitely an understatement. As the gale dismasts and splinters their boat, Augustus is "insensible" and Pym ties him—and himself—up to keep them from drowning. Whereupon a whaler rides over them, and though they are picked up almost dead, they recover quickly enough to appear at Augustus's home for breakfast without having to say a word about their escapade.

These rapid shifts, climactic and anticlimactic to the point of farce, are characteristic of Poe's excited quickness of mind. They intimidate and even awe us through Poe's self-hypnotizing genius for the unexpected detail. It was the most natural thing in the world for his characters to be in extremis. A sentence like "It is hardly possible to conceive the extremity of my terror" ran off his pen as a matter of course. "Never while I live shall I forget the intense agony of terror I experienced at that moment. My hair stood erect on my head—I felt the blood congealing in my veins—my heart ceased utterly to beat. . . ."

What will never seem a matter of course is Poe's ability to imagine what Pym looked like after the whaler had obliterated the skiff to which he had tied himself before passing out:

> It appeared that one of the timberbolts having started and broken a passage through the copper, it had arrested my progress as I passed under the ship, and fastened me in so extraordinary a manner to her bottom. The head of the bolt had made its way through the collar of the green baize jacket I had on, and through the back part of my neck, forcing itself out between two sinews and just below the right ear.

That on returning to shore Pym is able to trot off cheerfully to breakfast, without a sign of injury, is as improbable as what happened to his neck. But we accept the first because we understand early in the story that Pym's eating breakfast is not of the slightest significance. Only the far-out, the totally bizarre and unexpected, counts for Poe. When, as with "the head of the bolt" making its way through Pym's neck, something so violent occurs *on* the human body, Poe's fascination with infliction does not so much suspend our disbelief as it arrests us—and then just as quickly lets us go. Poe's ability to imagine not only extremes but a *succession* of them was his genius. As a critic he insisted that a plot should be constructed as perfectly as God made the universe: "we should aim at so arranging the incidents that we shall not be able to determine, of any one of them, whether it depends from any one other or upholds it." This hardly pertains to *Pym*, which has no plot and is a chain of episodes.

But what episodes! Violent storms, shrieking drunkenness, murder with axes, murder by drowning, death from heat prostration, hunger and thirst ending in cannibalism. Yet none of these butcherings, stabbings, battles, and man-made earthquakes is so devastating as the account, soon after Pym is safely restored to shore, of how Augustus Bernard hides Pym aboard his father's ship, the *Grampus*. It never occurs to Poe to give us any very convincing explanation of why Captain Bernard will not tolerate another young man on board; what interests Poe is not motive but sensation. Augustus stows Pym into the tiniest possible space, thus inviting the reader into a box that is not just Pym's hiding place but represents Poe's favorite horror —burial alive. To be trapped in a world altogether foreign to it was to Poe the condition of genius. The superior intellect tests itself by enduring the tomb, proves itself by describing every facet as such horror has never been described before, and raises itself through the power of mind alone.

Poe's obsession with "premature burial" can easily be traced to every form of confinement, early and late, that a character so frightened and proud had to endure. But its central meaning is made clear in the cherished details and didactic tone that Poe brings to the contemplation of such horror. This was a man for whom every particle of his consciousness was infinitely precious, much as he felt *buried* in it. Poe so urgently surrendered his "human" and emotional immaturity to the act of thinking that he called his season in hell the "thinking age" and wondered if men before him had ever thought at all. "Thinking" to Poe was more a test than a result. It was a form of showmanship, but even more it was ultimate proof of identity. Thinking alone enabled him to escape from some persisting sense of isolation, of exile, of having been put away. It was a retrieval from death to a life that raised one's self-esteem to the highest power. It thrived on agony.

Every occasion for thinking became a test—testing is repeated in *Pym* to the point of hysteria. Freud said that the emotional life is characterized by repetition. Pym has no emotional life, just visceral reactions to butchery and the like. What dominates the story is Poe's own insatiability: his need to set a problem for his character, to prolong it to the last endurable moment—and to dash quickly on to another.

The main ordeal in *Pym* begins with Augustus Bernard's leading his friend down through increasingly narrow spaces to the hold and the box that will be his hiding place. First Augustus shows Pym a cabin

> fitted up in the most comfortable style—a thing somewhat unusual in a whaling-vessel. . . . The ceiling was full seven feet high, and, in short, everything appeared of a more roomy and agreeable nature than I had anticipated. Augustus, however, would allow me but little time for observation, insisting upon the necessity of my concealing myself as soon as possible.

They descend into the hold down a trap concealed by a carpet, make their way through the darkness with a small taper, and at last, "after creeping and winding through innumerable narrow passages," reach an ironbound box, "such as is used sometimes for packing fine earthenware."

> It was nearly four feet high, and full six long, but very narrow. Two large empty oil casks lay on the top of it, and above these, again, a vast quantity of straw matting, piled up as high as the floor of the cabin. In every other direction around was wedged as closely as possible, even up to the ceiling, a complete chaos of almost every species of ship-furniture, together with a heterogeneous medley of crates, hampers, barrels, and bales, so that it seemed a matter no less than miraculous that we had discovered any passage at all to the box.

Pym has reached his true home. "My companion now showed me that one of the ends of the box could be removed at pleasure. He slipped it aside and displayed the interior, at which I was excessively amused." This coffin contains a mattress, books, blankets, a large jug full of water, three or four immense bologna sausages, cordials and liquors. It reminds the reader of the Egyptian tomb stored with everything the dead would need in the next world. Since the story line consists of the most contrary sensations in tandem, Pym proceeds "immediately to take possession of my little apartment, and this with feelings of higher satisfaction, I am sure, than any monarch ever experienced upon entering a new palace."

The watch Augustus thoughtfully left him quickly runs down. Soon Pym will not know whether it is day or night or how many days and nights he has spent in his box. As is natural to a Poe character, Pym at first finds half-suffocation interesting. It is susceptible to subtle differentiations, it stimulates the reasoning power, it is not only Poe's highest proof of power but just now Pym's one power. Pym's patience seems unnatural only if one forgets how many thoughts can occur to a man buried alive.

> Pondering in this manner upon the difficulties of my solitary and cheerless condition, I resolved to wait yet another twenty-four hours, when, if no relief were obtained, I would make my way to the trap, and endeavour either to hold a parley with my friend, or get at least a little fresh air through the opening, and a further supply of water from his stateroom.

Sick with thirst, he falls into a stupor and has dreams "of the most terrific description." These dreams are rather too terrific, overcolored nightmares that fail to impress us. What does work is the unbearable sharpness of Pym's "thinking faculties" as he tries to discover what has happened to Augustus. (He does not know that a mutiny has broken out above.) He feels increasingly blocked by the stowage on every side. In the most excruciatingly drawn out suspense, he has to find and then decipher in darkness a message that Augustus has thoughtfully sent down with Pym's dog Tiger.

The cipher is another of Poe's favorite obsessions; like entombment, it requires for a solution to the problem some special display of reasoning power. Poe certainly piles it on. Pym in the darkness has to read a message not very conveniently threaded on the dog's back. First Tiger tries to tell Pym that he bears a message by lying on his back with his paws uplifted. Thinking that the dog may be signalling an injury, Pym examines his paws. Thinking him hungry, he feeds him a large piece of ham—which the dog devours, then promptly returns to his "extraordinary manoeuvres." Thinking him thirsty, and "about adopting this conclusion as the true one," Pym finally, not neglecting to give us every step in his reasoning, gets to the paper fastened beneath the left shoulder of the animal. Which he has now to read in darkness.

> What to do next I could not tell. The hold was so intensely dark that I could not see my hand, however close I would hold it to my face. The white slip of paper could hardly be discerned, and not even that when I looked at it directly; by turning the exterior portions of the retina towards it, that is to say, by surveying it slightly askance, I found that it became in some measure perceptible.

In vain his brain revolves

> a multitude of absurd expedients for procuring light—such expedients precisely as a man in the perturbed sleep occasioned by opium would be apt to fall upon for a similar purpose—each and all of which appear by turns to the

dreamer the most reasonable and the most preposterous of conceptions, just as the reasoning or imaginative faculties flicker, alternately, one above the other.

He places the slip of paper on the back of a book, collects the fragments of phosphorus matches together upon the paper, and with his palm rubs the whole over quickly yet steadily. Nothing. In rage he tears the paper and throws it away. Then he comes to his senses, finds a small piece of the note, holds it to Tiger's nose so that the dog will bring him another piece, figures out that the other side of the paper must contain writing, and eventually, after a more extensive investigation of the *thickness* of the paper than would occur to anyone except a prisoner studying every crevice of the window through which he plans to make his escape, recovers a fragment of the warning Augustus had sent down. There has been a mutiny above. Pym must "lie close."

Dostoevsky, though admiring of Poe, complained that his "fantastical-ness" was merely external. "Not fantastic should he be called but *capricious*. . . . He chooses as a rule the most extravagant reality, places his hero in a most extraordinary or psychological situation, and, then, describes the inner state of that person with marvellous acumen and amazing realism." Dosto-evsky concluded that Poe's imagination was too material. "Even his un-bounded imagination betrays the American."

Baudelaire, to the contrary, thought Poe a victim of America. Poe was too concerned with the ideal not to suffer from his native land. His vision was of "paradise—a unique land, superior to all others, as Art is to Nature, where Nature is reformed by the dream, where it is corrected, embellished, remodelled."

Dostoevsky and Baudelaire were both right. Poe spent so many of his days in a private hell that his most touching poems and some of his most visionary stories look directly at "paradise." In *Pym* his bitter longing for another world shows itself, all too brutally, in the shock after shock of violence that men and the sea administer to the survivors on the *Grampus*. That voyage ends in cannibalism. Pym, as always, is rescued just in time for him to be flung into more adventures. He never initiates any of them but is moved about so as to show Poe's longing for what the Romantics called the "untrodden." Poe the self-declared "scientist," the insatiable analyst, the inventor of the detective story, the spellbound captive of his own imagina-tion, finally carries Pym to the bottom of the world, the Antarctic. Nothing is left to discover. This is the famous and enduringly mysterious conclusion: "And now we rushed into the embraces of the cataract, where a chasm threw itself open to receive us. But there arose in our pathway a shrouded human figure, very far larger in its proportions than any dweller among men. And the hue of the skin of the figure was of the perfect whiteness of the snow."

Why *that* figure at the end? Poe did not extend or explain; the shock at which he always aimed had turned up as an effect on himself, leaving him nothing more to say. The passage begins as a threat of extinction and nothingness, then veers to a vision that leaves us gasping. Poe has his triumph. As he solemnly affirmed in the equally extraordinary conclusion to his theory of the universe, *Eureka*, the universe was all in God's mind, and man in "this thinking age" had become God. There was no universe except as the mind created one.

III

Unlike Poe, Hawthorne did not believe that hell was a state of mind; one of his most impressive characters is the Devil in us, the Devil as the other side of a small-town existence. Poe's characters seek order desperately; Hawthorne's are weary of it. It is this small-town, "provincial-land" background of Hawthorne's fiction, the dominating image of the Salem that was hateful to him but unlosable in every crooked corner, that makes the same impression on us as Joyce's dark old Dublin and Kafka's cabalistic Prague. Only Joyce and Kafka have duplicated Hawthorne's power to invest one's rigid, creepy, boringly stultified home town with the force of a religion that has lost every attraction to a writer except its ancestral markings. The restrictiveness of the setting has pushed the characters into a wholly mental existence. Poe's characters make speeches at each other; each supreme egotist does not quite believe he faces another. In Hawthorne people just talk to themselves more than they do to other people, talking to others only to report what they have already told themselves. And they talk to others as though they were talking to themselves.

This is Puritanism, where the space around each individual existence reaches up to the Great Ruler and Taskmaster. But it is dense with the probings and preoccupations that led so many Puritans to count up their failings at the end of the year as if reporting to an invisible court. This is literally a communing of the self with the self in a world where the individual in his solitude is more real to himself than anything else is.

The "public" speech of Hawthorne's characters is intensely formal, as indeed everything pertaining to style is in Hawthorne. There is so little *public* world—so few institutions, especially of the English kind that young Henry James lamented the absence of in Hawthorne and thought essential to the modern social novel. Puritanism put the greatest possible strain on the individual, for by its scheme of things he was convinced of the total depravity of mankind yet had to find a chink in this darkness, some outlet to salvation, in the report of worthiness that his incessant effort at probity was meant to impress God with. James did all he could with the realistic novel, and then he found himself in old age back in a world like Hawthorne's where the human mind must pursue itself as the external world comes more and more unstuck.

This is the situation portrayed over and again in Hawthorne—as it is in many stories out of Catholic Ireland and in many European Jewish writers brought up to find their material in orthodoxy. All perceptions become troubling to the sinner convinced of his sinfulness, even when he disbelieves in the moral order that once supported the idea of sin. Where everything was once an image of God's omnipresence, commonplace things show the rule of strangeness. Hawthorne's addiction to masks and veils—emblems, shadows, ruins, blackness—his need of fiction machinery involving the American claimant to an English estate, the missing will, the bloody footprint left on the threshold of the noble mansion, the scaffold, the pillory, and the forest, show how instinctively he thought of obstructions to be cleared as claims upon the past that could never be satisfied. Hawthorne, a strikingly uncooperative imagination in a "new" country, recognized that men could never discharge ancestors from their minds. The past contained the one secret they were always looking for.

5

A More Perfect Union:
Whitman to Lincoln

> There are two classes of men whose names are more
> enduring than any monument—the great writers; and the
> men of great achievement, the founders of states, the
> conquerors.
>
> NICOLAY AND HAY, *The Life of Abraham Lincoln*

I

On the eve of the Civil War, Thoreau advised the abolitionist Parker Pillsbury to have nothing to do with it. He hoped that "a prospective reader" "ignores Fort Sumter, and 'Old Abe,' and all that; for that is just the most fatal, and indeed the only fatal weapon you can direct against evil, ever; for, as long as you *know* of it, you are *participes criminis.* What business have you, if you are an angel of light, to be pondering over the deeds of darkness, reading the New York Herald, and the like?"

Walt Whitman, no angel of light, heard on Broadway the news of the attack on Fort Sumter as he was on his way back to Brooklyn, having been to the opera on Fourteenth Street. Describing the first news of war in his "memoranda book," *Specimen Days* (1882), he typically surrounds himself with the New York crowd that was to play chorus to all his solitary declamations in *Leaves of Grass.*

> I heard in the distance the loud cries of the newsboys, who came presently tearing and yelling up the street, rushing from side to side even more furiously than usual. I bought an extra and cross'd to the Metropolitan hotel (Niblo's) where the great lamps were still brightly blazing, and, with a crowd of others, who gather'd impromptu, read the news, which was evidently authentic. For the benefit of some who had no papers, one of us read the

telegram aloud, while all listen'd silently and attentively. No remark was
made by any of the crowd, which had increas'd to thirty or forty, but all stood
a minute or two, I remember, before they dispers'd. I can almost see them
there now, under the lamps at midnight again.

In the shock of Bull Run and the North's unrelieved series of defeats, the
prospects of his country were of the greatest anxiety to Whitman. But they
were still so much brighter than his own that it was urgent as well as natural
(he had always been a great patriot) for him to identify his career with the
survival of the Union. To see himself politically, to be the poet of the people
and to act the poet in public, had been his instinct and strategy from the time
he excitedly moved into the writing of *Leaves of Grass*, as if under the force
of revelation, from his unstable life in the midst of the New York crowd as
printer, speculative house builder, journalist, editor, hack novelist, stump
speaker for the radical wing of New York's Democratic stalwarts.

His failure to reach the public and his fellow writers was of burning
concern to Whitman at forty-two. In 1861, despite three successive editions
(1855, 1856, 1860) of *Leaves of Grass* that contained virtually all his best poetry
before his elegy on Lincoln, Whitman was only notorious for having written
an eccentric and "dirty" book. He was known on Newspaper Row for being
undependable, for displays of temperament that did not consort with his
being "lazy as a mosquito," for taking marked pleasure in his physical person,
and for posing himself next to the drivers as the omnibuses sped up and down
Broadway.

This busybody from the political clubs, a vehement, almost professional
nationalist, an always flighty editor and newspaperman, had actually
launched himself (in the loudest possible voice) as a poet. He had printed his
book himself, and in "Song of Myself" (though he did not yet call it that)
he trumpeted the most amazing insinuations.

> Stop this day and night with me and you shall possess the origin of all
>   poems,
> You shall possess the good of the earth and sun. . . . there are millions of
>   suns left,
> You shall no longer take things at second or third hand. . . . nor look
>   through the eyes of the dead. . . . nor feed on the spectres in books,
> You shall not look through my eyes either, nor take things from me,
> You shall listen to all sides and filter them from yourself.

He had had his book "distributed" (there was not much distribution) by
Fowler and Wells, the phrenologists of lower Broadway, on July 4, 1855. This

"disgraceful" book, as Emily Dickinson in far-off Amherst was told to consider it, was certainly launched as an oddity. The names of author and publisher (the same person) were omitted from the title page, which read LEAVES OF GRASS: BROOKLYN NEW YORK. 1855. Opposite it was the engraved daguerreotype of a bearded man who was thirty-six years old in 1855, had one hand on his hip, posed as a workman who needed no coat or waistcoat, and had his shirt thrown open at the collar. As the engraver said, the man wore his hat with "a rakish kind of slant like the mast of a schooner."

It was typical of Whitman's pleasure and pride in his physical appearance to present himself as a *portrait*. Only on page 29 of the first edition, in the middle of his rhapsody over his existence and its sacred tie to everything surrounding him, did the author identify himself as "Walt Whitman, an American, one of the roughs, a kosmos."

Whitman never claimed anything more significant about himself than when he began his opening poem, "Song of Myself."

> I celebrate myself,
> And what I assume you shall assume,
> For every atom belonging to me as good belongs to you.

His street pals in Brooklyn must have spoiled him, then become his type of sexual complement; many a Victorian eminence (Tennyson, Swinburne, Hopkins, George Eliot) was moved by Whitman's erotic lines but was abashed by his direct appeal to the reader. Whitman made his mark by addressing and including another in the bountifulness of his love-talk and appeal for love.

> Who need be afraid of the merge?
> Undrape. . . . you are not guilty to me, nor stale nor discarded,
> I see through the broadcloth and gingham whether or no,
> And am around, tenacious, acquisitive, tireless. . . . and can never be
>   shaken away.

The connections Whitman made to every surrounding—the countryside and his unnamed companion ("God comes a loving bedfellow"), every listable occupation, opponents and sceptics no longer to be feared, the American scene at large—these were such friendly items in Whitman's mind that they had sexual warmth. The reader might be baffled by the constant shift of Whitman's subject, but the steady "hum" on the page was unmistakable. The reader was not addressed, he was being seduced. There were certainly a lot of hints in what Whitman genially called "the atmosphere."

The atmosphere is not a perfume. . . . it has no taste of the distillation.
     . . . it is odorless,
It is for my mouth forever. . . . I am in love with it,
I will go to the bank by the wood and become undisguised and naked,
I am mad for it to be in contact with me.

No wonder Emerson was "very happy" in reading *Leaves of Grass*, "as great power makes us happy. It meets the demand I am always making of what seemed the sterile and stingy Nature, as if too much handiwork, or too much lymph in the temperament, were making our Western wits fat and mean." Emerson for the moment overlooked the sexual flamboyance. In acclaiming the great power that "makes us happy," he also overlooked Whitman's genius for relating himself to "ordinary" people and the most commonplace things in life. But because he was a wonderfully intuitive critic, Emerson drew the right conclusions from the poem's effect on himself—he recognized the "power" of the primitive that Whitman was to inspire in readers, generation after generation. No other American writer was to have quite this particular sense of the reader as "friend and comrade," or to make such an appeal within poem after poem without mawkishness.

This was the triumph of a "role"—that of the "rough," the barbarian who broke through the proprieties to boast that he was clean inside and out and to "lean and loafe at my ease. . . . observing a spear of summer grass." Whitman was never a "rough," but in opposition to what he called the "scribbling class," he was proud to announce himself one of New York's million plebs. While he identified himself with the crowd, as he did with his own family of mental defectives, bruisers, alcoholics, he was an exception to everyone. He was incomprehensible to his "normal" brother George. The questioning and beseeching of identity in Whitman's poetry shows that he was a mystery to himself. This was turned to creative advantage. The journey motif in his work is a quest in a world he must dominate in order to find himself. The pleasure in his uniqueness surely began in his lording it over young men. One feature of his style in "Song of Myself" is just declamatory. Another is the putting of "big" questions to the unseen "you" who is always in his mind. He sets riddles, is genially enigmatic to those he would call his "eleves."

Apart from the pulling and hauling stands what I am,
Stands amused, complacent, compassionating, idle, unitary,
Looks down, is erect, bends an arm on an impalpable certain rest,
Looks with its sidecurved head curious what will come next,
Both in and out of the game, and watching and wondering at it.

This haughtiness also takes care of the "linguists and contenders," the "trippers and askers" with whom, before he became the poet Walt Whitman, "I sweated through fog." The self-propelling line that gives Whitman's poetry its backbone is a form of assertion that he first practiced on street pals and waited a long time to practice on the world. His sense of physical preeminence—"I find no sweeter fat than sticks to my own bones"—is always in the picture, as is the boastful health that (up to his collapse after serving in the Civil War hospitals) leads him to refer to himself with open admiration. The general scorn for his poetry did not keep him from being one of the most photographed men of his time in America. There are so many photographs of Whitman in different poses that he was obviously a willing model. He had learned very early to regard himself as a physical wonder: "I dote on myself. . . . there is that lot of me, and all so luscious."

Yet for all this "celebration" of self and Whitman's constant addressing of himself to "you," "Song of Myself" makes its effect as a whole by its indirectness, its air of mystery. Even the listing of American types and occupations, mechanical in itself, contributes to the mysterious effect, since the lists have no clear relation to the greatest lines in the poem, like those in sections 5 and 6 of the final version of 1881, which reveal a genuine vision, sexual, natural, religious. Yet these lists support the panorama, the constant shift of scene that was his life-need and became his poetic strategy.

Whitman was to say of his Civil War poems, *Drum-Taps,* that they expressed "the pending action of *this Time & Land we swim in.*" "Pending action" is the clue to Whitman's effect. Despite the heavy sexual breathing throughout "Song of Myself," he is always more purely suggestive than erotic. He may coax the reader to join him, but what the reader is really expected to do is to finish Whitman's thought for him. The constant impression of latency produces Whitman's favorite image of boundlessness— one where all items (metaphysical and earthly) become equal to each other. Whitman in relation to the reader is a tease, but in relation to love itself he is a petitioner. Although his lines begin as declaration, their showy parallelism is deceiving. Individual lines often close in on themselves. What follows one line may so little continue a thought or mood that if we fall in with the rapid shift, we get a sense of life playing itself out before our eyes.

The "atmosphere" is certainly sexual, but desire is rarely fulfilled. The progression of effect depends on the "celebration" remaining elusive. We must believe him when he says, "Only the lull I like, the hum of your valved voice." He is "daring" to the uttermost.

I mind how we lay in June, such a transparent summer morning;
You settled your head athwart my hips and gently turned over upon me,
And parted the shirt from my bosom-bone, and plunged your tongue to
    my barestript heart,
And reached till you felt my beard, and reached till you held my feet.

Only to fly up into the great *agnus dei* passage: "Swiftly arose and spread around me the peace and joy and knowledge that pass all the art and argument of the earth." This depends on the pulsing repetition of "and" for the launching of his ecstasy. Whitman clinches the effect by the amazingly right lineup of details in the lines

And limitless are leaves stiff or drooping in the fields,
And brown ants in the little wells beneath them,
And mossy scabs of the wormfence, and heaped stones, and elder and
    mullen and pokeweed.

Whitman's time sense is one of suspension. There is a longing somehow not to be fulfilled. (The reader must help Whitman.) "The universe has only one complete lover," he boasted in the 1855 preface, "and that is the poet." But the poet remains uncompleted, always in search. The great journey can never end. Nothing so beautifully terminates a Whitman poem as the last lines of "Song of Myself" on skipping out just ahead of the reader:

I bequeath myself to the dirt to grow from the grass I love,
If you want me again look for me under your bootsoles.
    . . .
Failing to fetch me at first keep encouraged,
Missing me one place search another,
I stop some where waiting for you.

In Whitman's best-sustained "long" poem, "Crossing Brooklyn Ferry" (1856), suspension is what the poem is about. The ferryboat between Brooklyn and Manhattan hovers between the shores. The poet in the crowd invokes the crowd of the future. But the people of the future will be just as "questioning" of themselves as Walt Whitman:

I too felt the curious abrupt questionings stir within me,
In the day among crowds of people sometimes they came upon me,
In my walks home late at night or as I lay in my bed they came upon
    me,
I too had been struck from the float forever held in solution,
I too had receiv'd identity by my body . . .

And in the body,

> I am he who knew what it was to be evil,
> I too knotted the old knot of contrariety . . .

The current flowing with the flood tide, receding with the ebb tide, eventually reassures him more than the many who call to him with love. "What gods can exceed these that clasp me by the hand, and with voices I love call me promptly and loudly by my nighest name as I approach?" The flow is the medium of life: "Suspend here and everywhere, eternal float of solution!" And now the passage from shore to shore, from present to future, becomes the passage *through* appearances to the true reality. "You have waited, you always wait, you dumb, beautiful ministers." Which is what we crave most —not to complete the journey but to understand why we have undertaken it; not to make an end but in the perfect middle of our life to hover between two worlds, our present selves in time and immortality:

> We fathom you not—we love you—there is perfection in you also,
> You furnish your parts toward eternity,
> Great or small, you furnish your parts toward the soul.

Whitman's greatest longing was for "unity." Looking back on his work after the Civil War, he wrote William D. O'Connor: "I can hardly tell you why, but feel very positively that if anything can justify my revolutionary attempts & utterances, it is such *ensemble*—like a great city to modern civilization & a whole combined clustering paradoxical unity, a man, a woman."

Although Whitman was not in the abstract sense a *political* thinker, no other American writer in the "democratic century" made America so resonant a character and inspiration. Whitman made the nation truly part of Walt Whitman. If his favorite verbs are transitive and sexual, his ideas presuppose the sacredness of American union and the "comradeship" made possible to millions by their common situation as Americans.

The "ensemble" that was Whitman's deepest longing generally suffuses his work not as reality but as reverie. Occasionally, *very* occasionally, as in "Out of the Cradle Endlessly Rocking," poem matches form with content, rhythm with longing, memory, dream. "Out of the Cradle" is extraordinary but should be more unsettling than it is. The finale of Whitman's "aria and recitative," sweeping us into the arms of Mother Death as if such incest were our happiest finale, is altogether more believable than the bird-aria. Whitman's perfect opening

Out of the cradle endlessly rocking,
Out of the mocking-bird's throat, the musical shuttle,
Out of the Ninth-month midnight,
Over the sterile sands and the fields beyond, where the child leaving his
    bed wander'd alone, bareheaded, barefoot . . .

convinces us that he is speaking as "A man, yet by these tears a little boy again." The truly pregnant images of some maternal persona behind the poem, "From under that yellow half-moon late-risen and swollen as if with tears," move us far more than the rhythmic push of the opening lines, which is skillful but on the point of seeming mechanical. The images that make the connection to the almighty "mother" are effective because they are shadowy and reveal the struggle that forced them out of the most submerged memories of the child.

The aria sinking,
All else continuing, the stars shining,
The winds blowing, the notes of the bird continuous echoing,
With angry moans the fierce old mother incessantly moaning . . .

Whitman never wrote more rendingly of his "perturbations," his actually inchoate sexual feeling, than when he announced his birth as a poet in accepting the loss of the bird's mate that came home to him on the beach at night as *his* loss.

O you singer solitary, singing by yourself, projecting me,
O solitary me listening, never more shall I cease perpetuating you,
Never more shall I escape, never more the reverberations,
Never more the cries of unsatisfied love be absent from me,
Never again leave me to be the peaceful child I was before what there in
    the night,
By the sea under the yellow and sagging moon,
The messenger there arous'd, the fire, the sweet hell within . . .

What a revelation! And yet this recognition, "the destiny of me," is not enough. "O if I am to have so much, let me have more!" The mother sea, whispering it "all the time . . . from your liquid rims and wet sands . . . /Lisp'd to me the low and delicious word death."

The connection with death as *the* word, *the* key, supplies "the unknown want." Death is

Hissing melodious, neither like the bird nor like my arous'd child's heart,
But edging near as privately for me rustling at my feet,

> Creeping thence steadily up to my ears and laving me softly all over,
> Death, death, death, death, death . . .

the most private and solitary Eros. The singer is "solitary," as the boy on the sands at night knew he always would be.

The solitariness of the boy, the poet, the lover of death is another of Whitman's trinities. The grand summation and synthesis of "lilac and star and bird" in "When Lilacs Last in the Dooryard Bloom'd" is stagey, Whitman's attempt at a choral symphony. The poignancy of "Out of the Cradle" lies in the identification of love (for the mother) with death (the embrace of the mother sea). Death becomes the necessary connection into which erotic solitude must merge.

The constant affirmation of death in Whitman is not just erotic or psychological, as twentieth-century taste would have it. Death certainly appealed to Whitman because it was the greatest possible "idea" in his mental existence. Even more, death was still an open fact. Unlike Emily Dickinson, who made death the chief drama of a woman's domestic existence, Whitman saw it everywhere. It made connection within the heedless cycle of mass birth, mass production, mass extinction. In "Song of Myself" he erotically linked with hair—young men's hair—the grass springing up everywhere, covering the globe. And like every other poet of the century who sang the end of the Christian heaven, he could spiritualize death to his heart's content.

But Whitman's hymning death went beyond the personal and erotic; he understood its relation to mass life in the nineteenth century, the ferocity of the city, the indifference of the new and unstopping productive forces. As these forces turned the Civil War into mass fratricide on a scale never known before, his love of country became protective. He was aroused from the "failure" of *Leaves of Grass* and his waiting life in New York. When "fire eaters" in South Carolina could no longer contain themselves and precipitated the war by firing on Fort Sumter, Whitman at forty-two was already "old" Walt Whitman, on his way to becoming "the good gray poet." His countrymen ignored him; the "scribbling class" detested him.

Did Whitman really expect that the *Calamus* and *Children of Adam* poems in the 1860 edition would be accepted and praised? He had once excited Emerson, but that great man now kept urging him to censor himself. Thoreau even before the *Calamus* poems appeared had complained of Whitman's "sensuality"—"I do not so much wish that those parts were not written, as that men and women were so pure that they could read them without harm, that is, without understanding them." Whitman was out of step. Then the outbreak of war interrupted a communion with himself that was in danger of growing stale. He was living with his mother in Brooklyn, and his days were filled with the money squabbles and the emotional turbulence in his disturbed family. It had been a point of pride with him to remain relatively detached—to enjoy his superiority—while identifying with his mother and acting as her voice. The most pressing danger to Whitman in remaining with his family was that he so easily fell in with its sloth. But his brother George was missing after a battle, and this at last prodded Whitman to get out of Brooklyn.

11

John Hay, the president's private secretary, said of Washington during the Civil War that nothing so dramatic had been seen since Paris during the French Revolution. "There was never such a strange multitude, jumbled and incongruous . . . as that which swarmed in Washington from 1861 to 1865. . . . Through it all, the plot of the world-drama worked itself out." Washington in December 1862 was muddy and disorganized. Like the torn besieged Republic, the city was unfinished and threatened to be unfinishable. The Capitol dome, from which Thomas Crawford's bronze figure of Freedom was to surmount what poor Herman Melville, vainly looking for a job from Lincoln's new administration, had admired as "noble buildings, by far the richest in marble of any on the continent," would not be in place for another year. Washington was as distraught as the country it was trying to keep together. More than ever did it seem to justify Dickens's ridicule that the City of Magnificent Distances was the City of Magnificent Intentions.

The enemy was at the gates, and in addition to its regular cast of bitterly divisive politicians, the city was crammed with Confederate sympathizers, office seekers free to molest Lincoln in the White House, camp followers, relatives and friends of soldiers seeking passes through the enemy lines. A great many people, celebrated and not, seemed free to look in on the war. Emerson, Hawthorne, Melville, Henry Adams before he joined his father the American minister to England, Dr. Oliver Wendell Holmes searching for his wounded son the future justice, were just a few of the great army of civilians that came and went as casually as the newsboys who walked among the wounded after a battle, crying their papers. Matthew Brady the photogra-

pher parked his wagon in the midst of the troops as though it were an
ambulance. Winslow Homer flitted about, easily sketching for *Harper's
Weekly* even a sharpshooter hidden in a tree.

Washington at the end of 1862 was the place in which to make a deal, to
get a commission or a "preferment." Washington was a circle of hospitals,
many of them temporary shelters. The army was made up of volunteers and
would largely remain so even after the bitterly resented draft law was passed
the next year. (In New York it created the worst riot in American history;
troops had to be brought in to quell it.) The noncombatants were everywhere. They included all the major American writers old enough to fight
(except Mark Twain, who was briefly and jocosely a Confederate volunteer
in Missouri) and all the leading American capitalists of the postwar era.
Henry James in his autobiography lamented eloquently the "horrid even if
an obscure hurt" that had overtaken him "at the same dark hour" in which
Lincoln first called for seventy-five thousand volunteers. But none of the
following fought in the Civil War either: William Dean Howells (born 1838),
Henry Adams (1838), William James (1842), John D. Rockefeller (1839), J.
Pierpont Morgan (1837), Philip D. Armour (1832), John Wanamaker (1838),
Grover Cleveland (1837), James D. Blaine (1830), John Hay (1838), Alexander
Agassiz (1839), Roscoe Conkling (1829), Whitelaw Reid (1837), Clarence King
(1842), Jay Cooke (1821), Jay Gould (1836), Henry Hobson Richardson (1838),
John La Farge (1835), Jim Fisk (1835), Senator Don Cameron (1833), Gustavus
Swift (1839).*

Wartime Washington was a turbulence trying to hold on to the coattails
of the vast armies and wheeling movements it had set in motion. At the
center of the turbulence, always in the spotlight, nothing about him concealed from the great democracy that had made him its figurehead as well
as chief executive, was that assailable and by no means yet hallowed figure
known to the opposition papers as the Gorilla.

His vacillations, his lack of willpower and distinctive intelligence were
cited by well-placed observers as one more proof of the dangers in democracy. To the opinion-making class the most obvious thing about Abraham
Lincoln was that he was a mere politician with no settled convictions. He
swayed from moment to moment; he was weak; he had a deplorable tendency to wait on public opinion. Although he had always found slavery
repugnant, he would not alienate the vast pro-Union majority that was not
yet ready to approve emancipation. His concern for the Union dominated

---

*Hemingway in 1949: "Both my grandfathers fought all through the Civil War (no one who has
any money in America had a grandfather who fought)."

every moral and constitutional issue. He would not keep ahead of the masses whom he so much resembled.

What it came to in the eyes of his critics, foreign and domestic, was that he was ordinary. In England, where the governing class was impatient to recognize the Confederacy, the London *Herald* pointed out that Lincoln's predecessors had all been gentlemen. "Mr. Lincoln is a vulgar, brutal boor, wholly ignorant of political science, of military affairs, of everything else which a statesman should know." The London *Standard:* "Never were issues so momentous placed in so feeble a hand; never was so great a place in history filled by a figure so mean."

At home the contempt for Lincoln (he had been nominated as a compromise candidate and was elected only because he divided the vote with three opponents) was general among New England's intellectuals. The aristocratic abolitionist Wendell Phillips dismissed Lincoln as "the white trash of the South spawned on Illinois," "a first-rate second-rate man . . . waiting to be used." The Brahmin historian Francis Parkman complained in 1862 that Lincoln was the very type of character which democracy had given to the world, the "feeble and ungainly mouthpiece of the North." Thirty years later Parkman was deploring Lincoln's displacement of Washington as a hero to schoolboys.

Hawthorne, observing Lincoln in 1862 for the *Atlantic Monthly,* jocularly noted that

> there is no describing his lengthy awkwardness, nor the uncouthness of his movement; and yet it seemed as if I had been in the habit of seeing him daily, and had shaken hands with him a thousand times in some village street; so true was he to the aspect of the pattern American, though with a certain extravagance which, possibly, I exaggerated still further by the delighted eagerness with which I took it in.

The *Atlantic* did not choose to publish Hawthorne's condescension. Emerson, also observing Lincoln in 1862, allowed that the president was "correct enough, not vulgar, as described." Lincoln's delight in telling stories reminded Emerson of Harvard reunions.

In Lincoln's lifetime Whitman was the only major writer to describe him with love. Whitman identified Lincoln with himself in the worshipful fashion that became standard after Lincoln's death. That Lincoln was a class issue says a good deal about the prejudices of American society in the East. A leading New Yorker, George Templeton Strong, noted in his diary that while he never disavowed the "lank and hard featured man," Lincoln was "despised and rejected by a third of the community, and only tolerated by the other two-thirds." Whitman the professional man of the people had complicated reasons for loving Lincoln. The uneasiness about him among America's elite was based on the fear that this unknown, untried man, elected without administrative experience (and without a majority) might not be up to his "fearful task."

After his death, Lincoln's supreme competence and firmness became such an article of American faith that he was enshrined as the purest type of American. Henry James, recalling the war period in his autobiography, condemned Lincoln's unhappy successor, Andrew Johnson, because he was common and lackluster by contrast with the "mould-smashing mask" of Abraham Lincoln. It was the underlying political despair, the doubt that the federal government could maintain itself, that centered so much understandable anxiety on Lincoln. Slavery had for forty years divided the country: it was not until slavery died in the war, until the country under his leadership proved that "a new birth of freedom" was real, that Lincoln could be seen to be the very reverse of "vacillating."

Lincoln was not a revolutionary but a supreme nationalist. The Union had to be preserved at any cost. Since democracy in America was a revolutionary fact in the nineteenth-century world—Whitman always referred to Europe as "feudal"—there were too many powerful interests at home and abroad opposed to what Lincoln the campaigner joined as "free soil, free labor, free men," for Lincoln the war president not to recognize that he was upholding more than a national cause. "Thanks to all: for the great republic —for the principle it lives by and keeps alive—for man's vast future—thanks to all." If it was difficult in the century of American superpower for an Edmund Wilson to share Lincoln's fear for his threatened nation, it was still difficult to understand Lincoln's reluctance to press emancipation when he honestly believed in the promise of equality in the Declaration of Independence. And how to reconcile the "suffering" and "Christlike" Lincoln with the driving and even authoritarian president who suspended habeas corpus and violated individual rights granted by the Constitution? Although steel was not manufactured in great quantity until near the end of the war, Lincoln was capable of saying, "My mind is like a piece of steel—very hard to scratch anything on it, and almost impossible after you get it there to rub it out."

It was Lincoln's peculiar honesty—the total reliance on his innermost promptings that one associates with genius, least of all with politicians captive to public relations—that still makes him unfathomable and endlessly interesting. None of the contemporary literary folk who could have analyzed Lincoln's writings as a subject worthy of themselves ever did so. Henry

Adams's feisty elder brother, Charles Francis Adams, Jr., was the first to lead black troops through captured Richmond, and may have had enough experience of war to know what went into the Second Inaugural Address. From the field he wrote to his father, the American minister in London, who was not an admirer of the president.

> What do you think of the inaugural? That rail-splitting lawyer is one of the wonders of the day. Once at Gettysburg and now again on a greater occasion he has shown a capacity for rising to the demands of the hour which we should not expect from orators or men of the schools. This inaugural strikes me in its grand simplicity and directness as being for all time the historical keynote of the war; in it a people seemed to speak in the sublimely simple utterance of ruder times. What will Europe think of this utterance of the rude ruler, of whom they have nourished so lofty a contempt? Not a prince or a minister in all Europe could have risen to such an equality with the occasion.

It was Lincoln's poised, patient, and unswervable spirit of command, triumphing finally over the bloodiest American factionalism, that made him important to Whitman. Lincoln was the greatest possible example to the "failed" poet whose life was a perpetual crisis. Until the war released him from having to create his own legend, Whitman had proclaimed himself in transcendentalist fashion the author of his own fate. The expanding energies and manifest destiny of "these States" had been the counterpoint to his vaunted harmony and even supremacy within himself.

The war now moved him on, sweeping him into the anxiety and suffering of civil war. Before Whitman could locate his brother, says Whitman's biographer Gay Wilson Allen, "he had to pass a huge pile of amputated arms and legs lying under a tree in front of an army hospital. This would have been a shocking encounter at any time, but at the moment the thought that some of George's own limbs might be in that horrible heap almost overcame him."

Wounded, sick, dying soldiers were being overlooked; crippled and discharged soldiers seeking their back pay were uselessly trudging to the army paymaster's office. There Whitman took a job copying documents and soon settled on the hospital visits that became his wartime service. He was to call himself a "wound dresser," a title given by a disciple arranging Whitman's wartime letters to his mother. He was nothing of the sort. But although Whitman made a myth of "his" war, as he did of everything else, it is impossible to imagine Whitman without the war, his charged personal observations of soldiers in *Drum-Taps,* and his vivid prose record in *Specimen Days.* Everything Whitman wrote about the war shows what it did to age

him, ripen him, and perhaps finally kill him. To kill him not through the
paralysis the boastful man previously in "perfect health" felt he had incurred
in the hospitals, but through the mass suffering that was smashing its way
past all the pretenses of his lonely ego.

In Whitman's wartime letters to his mother and his old "gossips and
darlings" we see what Whitman was like with his family and familiars: "Lew
I wish you was here with me, and I wish my dear comrade Elijah Fox in ward
G was here with me—but perhaps he is on his way to Wisconsin—Lewy I
came through from Washington to New York by day train, 2nd Nov., had
a very pleasant trip, everything went lovely."

Whitman's "reports from the front," as he liked to call them, show a
strong sense of fact. Lincoln's prominent "ugliness" and sallow complexion
startled most observers. Whitman came up with "I think well of the President. He has a face like a Hoosier Michael Angelo, so awful ugly it becomes
beautiful, with its strange mouth, its deep cut, criss-cross lines, and its doughnut complexion." In his notebooks of the war period, *Specimen Days*, Whitman gives us an endearing glimpse of the president on horseback, returning
from the Soldiers Home where he slept on hot summer nights.

> Mr. Lincoln . . . is dressed in plain black, somewhat rusty and dusty, wears
> a black stiff hat, and looks about as ordinary in attire, etc. as the commonest
> man. A lieutenant, with yellow stripes, rides at his left, and following behind,
> two by two, come the cavalry men in their yellow-striped jackets. . . . The
> sabres and accoutrements clank, and the entirely unornamental *cortege* as it
> trots toward Lafayette Square arouses no sensation, only some curious stran-
> ger stops and gazes.

Whitman felt that *Drum-Taps* (1865), the cycle of war poems finished
before Appomattox, was a decided improvement on his earlier poems. He
had become self-conscious about the emotional abandon of the first three
editions of *Leaves of Grass*. Writing to his great friend and supporter in
Washington, William D. O'Connor, he explained *Drum-Taps* as

> more perfect as a work of art, being adjusted in all its proportions, & its
> passion having the indispensable merit that though to the ordinary reader let
> loose with wildest abandon, the true artist can see it is yet under control. But
> I am perhaps mainly satisfied with *Drum-Taps* because it delivers my ambi-
> tion of the task that has haunted me, namely, to express in a poem (& in a
> way I like, which is not at all by directly stating it) the pending action of this
> *Time & Land we swim in*, with all their large conflicting fluctuations of
> despair & hope, the shiftings, masses, & the whirl & deafening din, (yet over
> all, as by invisible hand, a definite purport & idea)—with the unprecedented

anguish of wounded & suffering, the beautiful young men, in wholesale death & agony, everything sometimes as if blood color, & dripping blood. . . . *Drum-Taps* has none of the perturbations of *Leaves of Grass*.

The war scene obviously gave Whitman confidence that he was moving into something more "objective"—and less scandalous—than his passionate early poetry. He was only forty-six in the year of the great summing up, 1865, but he was retreating so far from his former outcries of "wildest abandon" that he took premature aging as a sign of acceptability. He, too, wanted to be part of the American Union. Describing Lincoln on horseback returning to the White House, he imagined Lincoln returning his bow. In letters to his newfound friend Peter Doyle, a Washington streetcar driver, Whitman called him "dear son and loving comrade."

Whitman's sexual fires—the urgency behind his prewar poems and his seeking connection with everything that was "Not Me"—were being damped. In his profound solitude he had created the identity of his life with a book. He now saw the hammer blows of war on the soldiers around him, and they were hardly rousing little drum-taps. War was the concussion of young men on each other, a terrible parody of the dreamy love play Whitman had celebrated. War was cruel but exciting, full of what Whitman (and Melville in *Battle-Pieces*) called "portents." Whitman's most shattering recognition was that the life so precious to himself that it felt immortal could be thrown away by the thousand in a single hour. All this was humbling to the sacred ego founded on sexual showmanship, to the writer who had proclaimed himself the voice of so many young men.

Drum-Taps without "When Lilacs Last in the Dooryard Bloom'd" (the main feature of the "sequel" Whitman called *Memories of President Lincoln*) reflects the gift for on-the-spot reporting that he brought off fully in his "prose memoranda" of the war, *Specimen Days*. Like so many pieces in that rambling nineteenth-century construction called *Leaves of Grass*, *Drum-Taps* has to be read in terms of what Whitman called "ensemble." Perhaps he hoped that the ambition of the whole book would make the reader indulgent to every part. All poems were joined in the same "purport." In *Drum-Taps* "war glimpse" follows "war glimpse" in the casual tread of soldiers, in the ordinariness of war when not on parade: "Cavalry Crossing a Ford"; "Bivouac on a Mountain Side"; "A Sight in Camp in the Daybreak Gray and Dim." Of course Whitman had to round out these unpretentious pieces with his usual choral symphony of religious sacrifice. Whitman emerges from his tent "so early sleepless" to walk near a hospital tent, sees three forms wrapped in gray blankets, and lifting one blanket after another, sees an "elderly man so gaunt and grim, with well-gray'd hair, and flesh all sunken about the eyes"; a "sweet boy with cheeks yet blooming," and at last "a face nor child nor old, very calm, as of beautiful yellow-white ivory." "I think this face is the face of the Christ himself, / Dead and divine and brother of all, and here again he lies."

Whitman could not come near death without "ennobling" and eroticizing it. Lincoln's death assured the literary perfection of the Civil War as the American Iliad. Whitman could not absorb the shock without setting himself a love address to the dead, yet the elegy would have to remind his readers and *listeners* that they were joined in a communion of grief. Thanks to Abraham Lincoln, Whitman at last made perfect connection with his countrymen. "When Lilacs Last in the Dooryard Bloom'd" was composed to the reverberation of America's losing Abraham Lincoln. It is now so much a part of the Civil War that one cannot read it without reliving the delirium of April 1865. The triumph of "freedom's cause" and the murder of its leader follow each other in bursts. The melding of the man into his death, into the processional bearing Lincoln back to Springfield, becomes the millions attending the theophany of Lincoln the perfect chief and the sacred tie of the American people that he created by dying.

> Coffin that passes through lanes and streets,
> Through day and night with the great cloud darkening the land,
> With the pomp of the inloop'd flags with the cities draped in black,
> With the show of the States themselves as of crape-veil'd women
>   standing,
> With processions long and winding and the flambeaus of the night,
> With the countless torches lit, with the silent sea of faces and the
>   unbared heads . . .

The merging effect Whitman seeks is not altogether in the poem. It is in the reliving of history, of the war's emotion, of Whitman's grief. One of Whitman's many wonderful titles, "When Lilacs Last in the Dooryard Bloom'd," itself displays the poet positioning himself at home in order to begin his set piece, his ceremonial creation. Whitman is at his best not in the "trinity" of lilac, bird, and star, but in something directly observed. The lilacs of the title, blooming in the dooryard when Whitman heard that Lincoln was shot, take us to the pastoral ground whose images of spring convey, after Lincoln's death, the promise of renewal.

> In the dooryard fronting an old farm-house near the white-wash'd
>   palings,
> Stands the lilac-bush tall-growing with heart-shaped leaves of rich green,

With many a pointed blossom rising delicate, with the perfume strong I
   love,
With every leaf a miracle . . .

Although Lincoln is the "star" of Whitman's poem, he remains the
biggest symbol in symbol land. In death he perfects the role of the "Re-
deemer President" that Whitman had foretold in his 1856 blast against the
established order, "The Eighteenth Presidency." There is nothing complex
or even *gifted* about the only too human figure in Whitman's many cele-
brations of Lincoln. Whitman the writer never has anything to say about
Lincoln the writer. Lincoln, the most noble man, is now just nobly dead.

Whitman was always at his best when he could surprise the reader by
surprising himself. This usually occurred as an upwelling of primitive
sources in Whitman. The unity he strains for in the Lincoln elegy is formal,
hieratic; it starts by symbolizing Whitman's hero as well as Whitman's grief.
Yet Whitman binds himself to the complex network of his theme by tapping
our own associations with the dead man. An elegy is a public offering that
succeeds when the departed hero is already a public offering. "When Lilacs
Last in the Dooryard Bloom'd" is as much a monument as the Lincoln
Memorial.

On a lower level, *Specimen Days* shows Whitman always at the scene, in
the streets and hospitals of wartime Washington, so intimate and involved
an observer that thanks to his account, he becomes the important presence
that he wanted to be—in this war-torn, often "seditious" capital, at last a
participant. *Specimen Days,* the one record of the time by a first-rate writer,
reflects the national fervor. Whitman's curious, spasmodic book is a fascinating personal document. Distended, like all of Whitman's prose, it becomes
part of the passion of the Civil War and of the madness of war. By the 1880s,
when Whitman was at last able to put his "memoranda" of the war together
with saintly reminiscences of his youth that were meant to bind future
biographers to this self-portrait, the war had become a retrospective glow.
Specimen Days reflects the victorious spirit and the aggressive ego that were
shaping the North as defeat was shaping the South.

Whitman related himself to the popular passion released by war and gave
himself to this passion as a political cause. He understood popular opinion
in a way that Emerson, Thoreau, and Hawthorne did not attempt to understand it. Emerson said, like any conventional New England clergyman, that
the war was holy. He could not speak for the masses who bore the brunt of
the war. Whitman was able to get so much out of the war, to create a lasting
image of it, because he knew what people were feeling. He was not above

the battle like Thoreau and Hawthorne, not suspicious of the majority like his fellow New Yorker Herman Melville, who in "The House-top," the most personal poem in *Battle-Pieces,* denounced the "ship-rats" who had taken over the city in the anti-draft riots of 1863.

Despite Whitman's elusiveness—he made a career out of longings it would have ended that career to fulfill—he genuinely felt at home with soldiers and other "ordinary" people who were inarticulate by the standards of men "from the schools." He was always present, if far from available, presenting the picture of a nobly accessible and social creature. He certainly got on better with omnibus drivers, workingmen, and now "simple" soldiers (especially when they were wounded and open to his ministrations) than he did with "scribblers." By the time Whitman went down after Fredericksburg to look for brother George, the war was becoming a revolution of sorts and Whitman's old radical politics were becoming "the nation." This made him adore Lincoln as the symbol of the nation's unity. An essential quality of Whitman's Civil War "memoranda" is Whitman's libidinous urge to associate himself with the great, growing, ever more powerful federal cause. Whitman's characteristic lifelong urge to join, to combine, to see life as movement, unity, totality, became during the Civil War an actively loving association with the broad masses of the people and *their* war. In his cult of the Civil War, Whitman allies himself with a heroic and creative energy which sees itself spreading out from the people and their representative men, Lincoln and Whitman.

Hawthorne's and Thoreau's horror of America as the Big State did not reflect Whitman's image of the Union. His passion for the "cause" reflected his intense faith in democracy at a juncture when the United States at war represented the revolutionary principle to Marx, the young Ibsen, Mill, Browning, Tolstoy. Whitman's deepest feeling was that his own rise from the city streets, his future as a poet of democracy, was tied up with the Northern armies.

In *Specimen Days* he united himself to the war, he illuminated the war as a striving organism with which even nature was in sympathy. He made it a living cause through his capacity for turning the homeliest, commonest details of his daily life in the Washington hospitals into a vision of the unity of all things. One night he stood in the darkness and saw "shadowy columns moving through the night," through deep mud, laden with their packs and weapons. As they "fil'd by," Whitman felt that never before had he "realized the majesty and reality of the American people en masse." A hundred years later, no American writer would see in soldiers the majesty and reality of the American people en masse. But Whitman was writing from the battlefront in their own country. The survival of *his* country was at stake. Whitman felt that the Union soldiers, most of them volunteers, were by hardship and sacrifice helping to create an "American people."

Whitman's instinct for the "beauty of the natural," what Henry James admired in his wartime letters, is the key to *Specimen Days*. He had an amazing ability to suggest the "divinity" inherent in ordinary life lived in the midst of the great modern crowd that was now an American army. All things and persons as well as "days" are "specimens" to him—all instances are mysteriously expressive of more than themselves. So it is the rumor of battle, the march at night, a storm over the Capitol, frightened soldiers rushing away from Bull Run to drop in the Washington streets—detail upon detail that Whitman loves to get down, confident that everything in this national drama will prove the mysterious sympathy of all things in the order of nature.

In *Specimen Days* Whitman indulges in romantic speculation—so strange to our generation—that nature may join in the drama, express martial energies, and be sympathetic to man's "purposes." (In modern realistic writing about war, the more beautiful the weather, the more it symbolizes cosmic indifference.) Whitman's harping on the weather brings home the all-absorbing crisis that the war represents to him. He sees as many omens and portents as Caesar saw before his murder.

Other features of *Specimen Days* are far from being realistic. Whitman was a volunteer, bringing small gifts and occasionally writing letters, but he allowed the picture to stand of a "wound dresser" and a Christlike presence. The wounded soldiers with whom he made special friends, and on whom he freely bestowed kisses, do not talk *to* Whitman; they form the chorus to his patriotic arias. Whitman's receptive genius turned the sick lonely soldiers into stilted bedside scenes of brave dying soldiers watched over by a bearded saint. The wounded seem exactly alike; one can tell that Whitman formed no deep personal relationships in the hospitals. But what is "new" and a foretelling of modern descriptions of war is the emphasis on the "average." Though Whitman intended to show the soldiers as images of popular greatness, his rapid descriptions of so many faces in the crowded hospitals show his passion for documenting the masses—a modern taste.

Equally so is the utterly spontaneous reporting *sur le vif*, the prose rhythms with which Whitman captures the headlong dash of events. This is the war book not of "realism," as Stephen Crane was to practice it in *The Red Badge of Courage*, but of experience. It is intensely personal reporting. Calling up many action scenes in "Song of Myself," Whitman exulted: "I am the man, I suffer'd, I was there." This time Whitman *was* there. In

Winslow Homer's sketches from the field for *Harper's Weekly*, one is always charmed by the immediacy. All his life Whitman had been pretending: "I have been everywhere." Now he could glorify his having been in Washington when it counted. It is this warmth of the moment, his pleasure in being on the spot, that gives his war notes their old-fashioned humanity. One always seems to see Whitman living so many specimen days; the observer is always in sight, and you know all he is feeling.

Of course we suspect today that Whitman made too much of his hospital visits, that he was an intruder even by the lax hospital standards of the time. The Organized Sanitary Commission, which Whitman disdains as coldly impersonal and repellent to his favorites, did in fact finally establish some basic standards. We know now that the Sanitary Commission inaugurated bureaucratic controls that were copied by corporations after the war. But no professional aide of the Sanitary Commission would have lingered in the hospitals as Whitman did—or would have captured so strongly what Wilfred Owen called "the pity of war." Whitman was already an anachronism. He was able to describe in close detail scenes of individual suffering that would never again matter so much to the recorders of mass killing. When we compare the "old" Whitman in the Washington hospitals with the invented "Walt Whitman," the Godlike seer in the early editions, we see that *Specimen Days* moves us from the archaic America Whitman grew up in to modern times.

In Whitman's account of war, the sense of numbers is fundamental. The overcrowded hospital wards where so many boys are dying in agony, the crowds in the Washington streets, the Grand Army of the Republic in victory parading down Pennsylvania Avenue for two full days—all this has suddenly filled up the old, bare, provincial American scene. We are on the threshold of the modern mass world, where people have become as numerous as leaves of grass and are as easy to ignore. Whitman ignores nothing and nobody; he is no cold "realist." The Civil War was the first great modern war of mass armies and mass killing. For Whitman the common soldier—the patiently suffering American volunteer—is more a hero than Jeb Stuart was to the South. The wounded are faithfully itemized, with Whitman's strange loving passion for the soldier as archetype. Every death retains its supreme mystical significance to Whitman. He writes of "the million dead summ'd up," and his belief in sacrifice, death as fulfillment of nature, wins over his horror at so many corpses.

The dead in this war—there they lie, strewing the fields and woods and valleys and battle-fields of the South—Virginia, the Peninsula—Malvern Hill

and Fair Oaks—the banks of the Chickahominy—the terraces of Fredericks-
burgh—Antietam bridge—the grisly ravines of Manassas—the bloody prom-
enade of the Wilderness—the varieties of the *strayed* dead . . . the dead, the
dead, the dead—*our* dead—or South or North, ours all, (all, all, all, finally
dear to me)—or East or West—Atlantic coast or Mississippi Valley—somewhere they crawl'd to die, alone, in bushes, low gullies, or on the sides of
hills . . . the infinite dead—(the land entire saturated, perfumed with their
impalpable ashes' exhalation in Nature's chemistry distill'd, and shall be so
forever, in every future grain of wheat and ear of corn, and every flower that
grows, and every breath we draw).

So the million dead prepared the way, by their "sacrifice," for Lincoln
the fallen star whom Whitman celebrated in "When Lilacs Last in the
Dooryard Bloom'd." The connection of war with sacrifice is overwhelming
in *Specimen Days*. Whitman does intrude the sacrifice of his own health. (He
may have been too intimate with sources of infection!) But we cannot mind
this, for the theme of sacrifice is fundamental to Whitman's "national" idea
of a people's war. Whitman's honest sense of his own comparative insignificance, his attempt at the same time to express the willing sacrifice of so many
"unknown, forgotten" men, lifts his favorite theme, man's democratic destiny,

> One's-Self I sing, a simple separate person,
> Yet utter the word Democratic, the word En-Masse

to a new height of shared emotion.

III

Whitman's genius in "old age" was to describe a world in transition. It went
with his slowing up. In his now-archaic youth he had personified for the first
three editions of *Leaves of Grass* primeval energy. The corruption of democracy in the Gilded Age pushed him to the absolute affirmation of the poet
as the savior of his country. This was reminiscence. In 1871, a time when
nothing was more improbable in the age of Crédit Mobilier and Jay Gould,
Whitman was insisting in *Democratic Vistas* that "the problem of humanity
all over the civilized world is social and religious, and is to be finally met and
treated by literature." Was Whitman, who during the war had been discharged from a clerkship for writing an obscene book, and this by the
secretary of the interior himself, just being obstinate now, holding out to the
last? "Above all previous lands, a great original literature is surely to become

the justification and reliance, (in some respects the sole reliance,) of American democracy." In what can be taken as the low point of his career, Whitman insisted on identifying America with democracy and democracy's "lessons of variety and freedom," with poetry as their ideal expression. By the standards of modern realism and modern poetry's alienations, Whitman had created himself a "supreme fiction" and had replaced America with the most lovable fantasy. But Whitman's thinking, as always in his embattled career, identified the supreme fiction not with the imagination's desperately asserting itself over an unfriendly world but with ideal development. In the end, poetry for him was not subjective at all. It was Nature itself, operating within reality to bring it to an ideal conclusion.

Few writers in America have been so isolated as Whitman was within his own country; no writer was ever less "alienated." Although the prose of *Democratic Vistas,* his greatest political utterance, sometimes breaks under the strain of admonishing and affirming America in the same breath, this great pamphlet against the times is witty, highly charged, and bitterly to the point. Under Whitman's righteous indignation at "tepid amours" and the "infidelism" of current fashion, he enjoys putting himself in the wrong with the leaders of popular opinion. America is now a parvenu to Whitman's eyes. The country, unknowingly sitting for its portrait, emerges as a great flaccid body, ridiculously overdressed and flamboyant, looking like someone's vulgar mistress parading the United States Hotel or the Grand Union at Saratoga as Roscoe Conkling and Boss Tweed sit on the verandah smirking over their cigars.

> The depravity of the business classes of our country is not less than has been supposed, but infinitely greater. The official services of America, national, state, and municipal, in all their branches and departments, except the judiciary, are saturated in corruption, bribery, falsehood, mal-administration; and the judiciary is tainted. The great cities reek with respectable as much as non-respectable robbery and scoundrelism. In fashionable life, flippancy, tepid amours, weak infidelism, small aims, or no aims at all, only to kill time. In business, (this all-devouring modern word, business,) the one sole object is, by any means, pecuniary gain. . . . Money-making . . . [remains] to-day sole master of the field. The best class we show, is but a mob of fashionably dress'd speculators and vulgarians. . . . Behind this fantastic farce, enacted on the visible stage of society, solid things and stupendous labors are to be discover'd, . . . to advance and tell themselves in time. Yet the truths are none the less terrible. I say that our New World democracy, however great a

success in uplifting the masses out of their sloughs, . . . in a certain highly-deceptive superficial popular intellectuality, is, so far, an almost complete failure in its social aspects, and in really grand religious, moral, literary, and esthetic results. In vain do we march with unprecedented strides to empire so colossal, outvying the antique, beyond Alexander's, beyond the proudest sway of Rome. In vain have we annex'd Texas, California, Alaska, and reach north for Canada and south for Cuba. It is as if we were somehow being endow'd with a vast and more and more thoroughly-appointed body, and then left with little or no soul.

Whitman rises out of this complaint to proclaim the "divine literatus." Never before the administration of President Grant did he need so urgently to proclaim his living and soon dying faith. The poet, the most comprehensive mind, stands for democracy, the most comprehensive political faith. As there is always more to democracy than appears, so there is always more to the poet and his work. (It is notable that Whitman refers to "the poet" more confidently than he does to poetry.)

Whitman convinces the reader of *Democratic Vistas* that democracy in America made Whitman himself possible. Democracy in the most unlimited sense is what made Walt Whitman *necessary.* Democracy creates the new human dimension by which the reader understands him.

"Democracy *ma femme,*" democracy in the most unlimited sense, democracy as ideal equality through unexpected freedom, democracy as the purest aspiration for the "evolution" of the individual within the mass. Here comes everybody! At long last! This grave, great hope for a democracy that was just as despised in the classical republic as it was elsewhere—this was Whitman's way, a one-man "party of hope," of joining himself to his country. Democracy had made possible his self-discovery as a poet, democracy was a way of recognizing his subject matter in himself, democracy was the masses out of whom Walt Whitman came. Democracy was openness to oneself, to others, to the God within oneself whom he deciphered as past and present at once, the universal experience that as heirs of all time we carry in our hearts.

Democracy was above all the promise of the future for the human race so long restricted by what Whitman liked to call "feudalism"—medieval privilege and inequality that he came to identify with European class society and class thinking at all times. Europe was still the ancien régime that *Democratic Vistas* will help to supplant. Feudalism was the past, a deadly contempt for ordinary human beings. Even the poets of feudalism, in his easy roll call of the great poets of the past, Whitman honored as his ancestors: he put himself into the great line. As we do now. His ambition, never so clear as in his last trumpet-call, *Democratic Vistas,* was to write the epic of the new, the modern, America.

So it was democracy all over again, Whitman's favorite because all-inclusive theme, that became, at the end, Whitman's desperate human claim for himself. Sixteen years after he had first put *Leaves of Grass* to press, Whitman was still seeking to *create* his reputation as the first great *modern* poet. He was presenting *Leaves of Grass* as his "visiting card to the coming generations in the new world."

He had been more confident in 1855: "An individual is as superb as a nation when he has the qualities which make a superb nation. The soul of the largest and wealthiest and proudest nation may well go half-way to meet that of its poets."

PART TWO

Modern Times

1865–1900

It seems as if the Almighty had spread before this nation charts of imperial destinies, dazzling as the sun . . . making old history a dwarf.

WHITMAN, *Democratic Vistas*

Seeking to conquer a larger liberty, man but extends the empire of necessity.

MELVILLE, "The Bell-Tower"

6

"Melville Is Dwelling Somewhere in New York"

The drama's done. Why then here does any one step
forth?—Because one did survive the wreck.

MELVILLE, *Moby-Dick*, Epilogue

I

In the aftermath of the Civil War, when so many were seeking a fresh start,
Herman Melville was appointed a district inspector of customs in New York
Harbor. On December 5, 1866, he was assigned badge number 75 and began
his nineteen years' service at four dollars a day. (This was later reduced by
forty cents.) Working out of an office at 470 West Street, off Gansevoort
Street, now the wholesale meat district where nineteenth-century cobble-
stones can still be seen, Melville regularly inspected cargoes on ships tied up
at piers all the way to Harlem.

Gansevoort Street was named after Melville's grandfather, a hero of the
Revolutionary War. One day in 1870 Melville visited the Gansevoort Hotel,
corner of Little Twelfth Street and West Street, and asked the man at the
desk who sold him a paper of tobacco: "Can you tell me what this word
'Gansevoort' means?" He was informed that "this hotel and the street of the
same name are called after a very rich family who in old times owned a great
deal of property hereabouts." Reporting this to his proud embittered mother
with the leaden irony that now marked his personal communications, Melville added:

The dense ignorance of this solemn gentleman—his knowing nothing of the
hero of Fort Stanwix, aroused such an indignation in my breast, that disdain-
ing to enlighten his benighted soul, I left the place without further colloquy.

Repairing to the philosophic privacy of the District Office I then moralized
upon the instability of human glory and the evanescence of—many other
things.

He lived on East Twenty-sixth Street with his wife and four children.
In the front hall there was a colored engraving of the Bay of Naples, its still
blue dotted with tiny white sails. A large bust of Antinoüs, beloved to the
emperor Hadrian, stood on a pedestal. In the evenings, "nerve-shredded"
with fatigue, Melville worked at poetry that his relatives paid to publish. The
last novel he was to publish in his lifetime, *The Confidence Man* (1857), had
failed with critics and public even more disastrously than *Moby-Dick* (1851)
and *Pierre* (1852). A brother-in-law reported Melville's saying that "he is not
going to write any more at present & wishes to get a place in the N.Y.
Custom House." He had failed to get the consulship in Florence from the
Lincoln administration.

The district inspector of customs wrote in his bedroom. His granddaughter Eleanor Metcalf described "the great mahogany desk, heavily bearing up
four shelves of dull gilt and leather books; the high dim book-case . . . ; the
small black iron bed, covered with dark cretonne; the narrow iron gate."
There were prints, bronzes, a Claude Lorrain—a painter whose primary
subject was light drawing the eye into vast panoramas of land and sea. The
room seemed dark and forbidding to his granddaughter. Grandmother Liz-
zie's room was a very different place—"sunny, comfortable and familiar,
with a sewing-machine and a *white* bed like other people's."

Melville's eyes were weak: "like an owl I steal about by twilight, owing
to the twilight of my eyes." Even in his thirties he often wrote "keeping one
eye shut & wink at the paper with the other." His handwriting was regularly
misread by printers. In *Pierre* he described a young author overwhelmed by
all the errors in his proofs and finally "jeering" at them. The posthumously
published *Billy Budd* had to be deciphered again and again. Writing
"blindly," his eyes turned away from the paper, symbolized to wretched
Pierre Glendinning "the hostile necessity and distaste, the former whereof
made of him the most unwilling states-prisoner of letters."

Melville wore dark glasses in the street. In the evenings he walked up and
down the Battery to rest his eyes; he refused all social engagements. His
daughter Frances and later his granddaughter Eleanor were dutifully taken
on walks in the new Central Park and to the tip of Manhattan in what is now
Fort Tryon Park. Eleanor remembered her grandfather teasing her if she
slowed up—"the cop will get you!" Melville as a customs inspector, feeling
that he had somehow survived himself, was generally remembered as being

silently grim. As a "romancer" exploiting his adventures in the South Seas, he had been exuberant and racy. Then, marrying the daughter of the chief justice of Massachusetts and trying to keep his family afloat by knocking out book after book, sometimes two a year, he had become desperately humorous about himself. In 1850 he moved to Pittsfield in the Berkshires, where he wrote his greatest book and where, before he moved back to New York to make a living, his career somehow stopped. He was now known around his numerous clan—Melvilles, Gansevoorts, Shaws—for being "nervous" and for making his timidly loyal wife "nervous." It was a troubled family.

Melville in New York was an oppressive presence. One son was to shoot himself in what may have been an accident; another disappeared into the West. His oppressiveness passed into family history. His great-grandson Paul Metcalf, who never knew him, wrote that to the family Melville was "a poison, potent and to be feared . . . a sepsis. . . . Most personally, because of my relation to him, Melville was the monkey on my back. . . . I could never come to terms with myself until relieved of him."

In May 1867 Elizabeth Shaw Melville tried unsuccessfully to separate from Melville. Although she was often afraid of her husband, her half-brother Samuel Shaw recognized that she was even more afraid of how a separation would look "in the eyes of the world, of which she has a most exaggerated dread." Shaw wrote to the minister of the local Unitarian church to which both Melvilles belonged, asking that he assure Elizabeth of her good name. The minister had been so concerned for Elizabeth that he proposed a fake kidnapping to get her out of the house. Elizabeth never made the move.

While still in Pittsfield, Melville was already under such strain that Dr. Oliver Wendell Holmes, who had an early interest in psychiatry, had been called in to examine him—an episode that Melville satirized in the story "I and My Chimney." The Melvilles were always hard up, but money was found in the family circle—it usually was—to send him to Europe and the Holy Land. In one of the "gnostic" poems he was to write in New York after hours, Melville sufficiently noted:

> Found a family, build a state,
> The pledged event is still the same:
> Matter in end will never abate
> His ancient brutal claim.

The narrator of "I and My Chimney" is a contentedly slow and backward old man who says: "In a dream I go about my fields, a sort of lazy, happy-go-lucky, good-for-nothing, loafing, old Lear." He is beset by an enterprising wife who wants him to demolish the celebrated but useless oversized chim-

ney which dominates everything in the house: "From this habitual prece-
dence of my chimney over me, some even think that I have got into a sad
rearward way altogether; in short, from standing behind my old-fashioned
chimney so much, I have got to be quite behind the age, too, as well as
running behind-hand in everything else." When a Mr. Scribe is called in to
estimate the cost of removing the chimney, he discovers that there is a "secret
chamber, or closet" in it. The more the wife insists on having the chimney
"abolished," the more the old man is determined to keep his old chimney just
as it is:

> It is now some seven years since I have stirred from home. My city friends
> all wonder why I don't come to see them, as in former times. They think
> I am getting sour and unsocial. Some say that I have become a sort of mossy
> old misanthrope, while all the time the fact is, I am simply standing guard
> over my mossy old chimney; for it is resolved between me and my chimney,
> that I and my chimney will never surrender.

For all her fear of him, Elizabeth Melville was helplessly sensitive to her
husband. His "nervousness" was a constant subject of her family correspon-
dence. She may not have entered into all he wrote, but she felt the injustice
of his life. Like his favorite "villain," Ahab, he was "a valor-ruined man."
When Elizabeth reported his mental state around the family, it was clear that
they had all been afraid for his sanity: "poor fellow he has so much mental
suffering to undergo (and how *all* unnecessary). I am rejoiced when anything comes into his life to give a moment's relief."

"Herman has taken to writing poetry," she wrote in a letter of 1859. "You
need not tell any one, for you know how such things get around." But if she
had little clue to his "mental suffering," neither did he. Vehement in thought,
he had to go to the limit in book after book, pitting himself against "the
fates." His first and lasting image of the self was heroic, scornfully independent of the suffering that came with his sense of constant struggle. His life
was as tumultuously up-and-down as his work. After his first best-selling
adventure tales of the South Seas, *Typee* and *Omoo*, *Mardi* bewildered his
public. *Redburn* and *White-Jacket* tried to get it back. *Moby-Dick* alarmed
most who bothered to read it. *Pierre* disgusted the critics, *The Piazza Tales*
went unregarded, *The Confidence Man* merely baffled. Melville was perpetually adrift; even his effort to write a potboiler based on the adventures in
England of a Revolutionary War soldier captured by the British, *Israel Potter*,
betrayed a superior talent and his subversive ability to put even Benjamin
Franklin and John Paul Jones into comic relief.

Some uncanny drama seeped into his life, as if from his books. The drama was to mark his revival in the next century. All his terms became absolutes as he pushed some personal quest after an unnamable goal, pitted himself against this "wolfish world" with "my splintered heart and maddened hand." At the peak of his life, the end of 1851, when the writer he most admired, his Berkshire neighbor Nathaniel Hawthorne, praised *Moby-Dick* in a "joy-giving and exultation-breeding letter," Melville burst out to the elusive self-contained Hawthorne, the perfect Other he would never entirely reach, "Lord, when shall we be done growing? As long as we have anything more to do, we have done nothing. So, now, let us add Moby-Dick to our blessing, and stop from that. Leviathan is not the biggest fish;—I have heard of Krakens."

Five years later, stopping off in England on his way to Egypt and Palestine, he told Hawthorne on a walk along the Irish Sea (Hawthorne was then American consul in Liverpool) that he had "pretty much made up his mind to be annihilated." Hawthorne noted in his English notebooks:

> But still he does not seem to rest in that anticipation; and, I think, will never rest until he gets hold of a definite belief. It is strange how he persists—and has persisted ever since I knew him, and probably long before—in wandering to and fro over these deserts, as dismal and monotonous as the sand hills amid which we were sitting. He can neither believe, nor be comfortable in his unbelief; and he is too honest and courageous not to try to do one or the other. If he were a religious man, he would be one of the most truly religious and reverential; he has a very high and noble nature, and better worth immortality than most of us.

This is almost all we have from Hawthorne about Melville. Melville destroyed whatever Hawthorne may have replied to Melville's rapturous letters when writing *Moby-Dick*. But Hawthorne's quietly compassionate portrait sums up Melville's "problem" as no one near him ever grasped it. The proud discoverer of his own talent who wrote in *Moby-Dick*, "I try all things; I achieve what I can," was a wanderer who found himself adrift on all the oceans of thought. Life picked him up with one book and dropped him with another. He went where each new book took him but was always dogged by his early success, the best-selling *Typee*. "Let me be infamous; there is no patronage in that," he grumbled to Hawthorne. "What reputation H. M. has is horrible. Think of it! To go down to posterity is bad enough, anyway; but to go down as a 'man who lived among the cannibals!'"

He had become a troublesome quantity with his third book, *Mardi* (1849), a thin-spun fantasy and political allegory that few people could read. (This is still the case.) The book is a quest round and round a world—of symbols. This was Melville's tiresome intellectual habit in the few books he wrote (another is *The Confidence Man,* at the end of his public career as an author) without an external story to tell. His sense of being spiritually violated by a totally "white," empty world often left him to brood on symbols. He was not modest about this, just frantic on occasion. Though he tried another crowd-pleaser with *White-Jacket* (1850), he became a "failure" for the rest of his life with *Moby-Dick.* Still, it was more his need of money than of reputation that troubled Melville. Discovering the full range of his powers in *Moby-Dick,* he laughingly described himself to Hawthorne as an aristocrat of the brain unable to make a living.

> But Truth is the silliest thing under the sun. Try to get a living by the Truth —and go to the Soup Societies.

> **In a week or so, I go to New York, to bury myself in a third-story room, and work and slave on my "Whale" while it is driving through the press. *That* is the only way I can finish it now,—I am so pulled hither and thither by circumstances. The calm, the coolness, the silent grass-growing mood in which a man *ought* always to compose,—that, I fear, can seldom be mine. Dollars damn me; and the malicious Devil is forever grinning in on me,— I shall at last be worn out and perish, like an old nutmeg-grater, grated to pieces by the constant attrition of the wood, that is, the nutmeg. What I feel most moved to write, that is banned,—it will not pay. Yet, altogether, write the *other* way I cannot. So the product is a final hash, and all my books are botches.

> **What's the use of elaborating what, in its very essence, is so short-lived as a modern book? Though I wrote the Gospels in this century, I should die in the gutter.

In the long silent evening of his life (he was so completely forgotten that his death in 1891 went unnoticed by the leading literary journal of the day; the *New York Times* took some days to learn that "Henry" Melville had died) Melville managed to endure and ride out his "decline." The ill-fated Maurice de Guérin, who died at twenty-nine, had written that "There is more power and beauty in the well-kept secret of one's self and one's thoughts, than in the display of a whole heaven that one may have inside one. . . . The literary career seems to me unreal, both in its essence and in the rewards which one seeks from it, and therefore fatally marred by a secret absurdity." Melville's marginal comment: "This is the finest statement of a truth which everyone who thinks in these days must have felt." By 1885 he was writing to an

English admirer: "the further our civilization advances upon its present lines so much the cheaper sort of thing does 'fame' become, especially of the literary sort."

Unlike Walt Whitman, for whom New York would always be the great world, Melville returned to his native city as to a brutal necessity—the "Babylonish brick-kiln" in which he might find "regular employment." Back in New York, the end of all his outward voyaging, he was finished with it even as Grub Street. For him it was no longer the city of coldly predatory publishers he had lampooned in *Pierre*, but the wall blocking a writer's window. It was the screen behind which Bartleby the Scrivener had entombed himself in his employer's office. New York was immigrant "ship-rats," as he called them in his poem "The House-top," who in 1863 protested the Draft Act by lynching blacks all over the city and created the worst insurrection in American history.

Melville had made a nightmare of the scene in which Pierre Glendinning arrives in New York with the most ridiculous expectations in the world, only to achieve the destruction of himself and the two women clinging to him. Since New York was already the city most expert and ruthless in destroying its past, Melville satirically endured the eclipse of his ancestral class, the Gansevoorts and the Melvilles. A captive to the commercial capital, he identified New York at its lowest with the Tombs, where Bartleby the Scrivener starved himself to death in ultimate protest against the prevailing condition of life. New York at its "best" was Grace Church on lower Broadway, consecrated to the rich and well-born. In another bitter sketch, "The Two Temples," Melville was pursued by the beadle for daring to enter the church.

Melville's New York long ago vanished from New York. Even as Melville was forced back into the city, his own New York was eroded as a physical landscape and as a society. New York's aristocracy before the Gilded Age had consisted of solid old-fashioned merchants, preferably with some Dutch ancestry. It would soon be replaced by Society—the ostentatious new-rich of the Four Hundred. If Melville's father, in the business on lower Broadway of importing fine French dry goods, had not failed and then died of the shock (his son was fourteen), Melville would never have gone to sea. Like his well-placed relatives and in-laws, like George Templeton Strong and the father of Theodore Roosevelt, he might have become another of those weighty New Yorkers whom Edith Wharton would portray in all their external wealth and private melancholy. Melville looked on his literary career as an accident—which did not lighten his grim humor at becoming a slave to it. He saw himself more pursued by chance than Moby-Dick was by Captain Ahab—into a world without precedents and rules.

New York's top layer was disappearing, becoming what Melville's fellow New Yorker Henry James would in horror call the "swarm." This, along with the immigrant masses who found Tammany a benevolent despot, already meant the money-men. Wall Street came to represent New York just when Melville, by living in New York, vanished from sight. He ignored all external change in his native city. A minor sketch, "Jimmy Rose," describes a bon vivant turned bankrupt. Melville's own New York does not exist in his works. They are an allegory of his life in his most familiar roles: orphan, castaway, renegade from orthodox Christianity and the West, "isolato," the white savage driven out by his society and contemptuous of it. With his old-fashioned merchant's sense of honor, the bankrupt father had died of shame. The desperate son would find his positive ideal in men older and more harmonious than himself: the Englishman Jack Chase, captain of the maintop on the navy vessel that brought Melville home in 1844, and Nathaniel Hawthorne. But like the lonely killer Ahab, Melville could not believe that anyone had authority over this world—or within it. Heroes were such through strength of will. They had no objective ideal, only the magnetism of being superior persons. There was no father in heaven and only the resentful memory of one on earth.

The bereaved family broke up. Maria Gansevoort Melville wrote to the jurist Lemuel Shaw, one day to be Melville's father-in-law, that her husband's family had "deserted" her eight children. The loans advanced to Allan Melville during his lifetime were charged against the children.

At sixteen Herman was a clerk in Albany; at seventeen, a teacher in a country school; nearing twenty, he shipped as a cabin boy to Liverpool. In *Redburn* (1849), the record of this voyage, he described a customs officer in Liverpool. "A man of fine feelings, altogether above his situation; a most inglorious one, indeed; worse than driving geese to water." At twenty-one he shipped out in a New Bedford whaler, the *Acushnet*, for the South Seas. New Bedford whaling captains were the worst slave drivers on the seven seas.

II

Now began Melville's grand initiation: the three-and-a-half-year voyage that never left him and became his imaginative life. To read Melville is to go round and round the earth in magnified and mythified versions of that voyage. It took him from New England round Cape Horn to the lunar-looking but "enchanted" Galápagos six years after Darwin, exploring them, had been struck by the subtle variations that led certain birds and animals to thrive when others did not and to develop into new species. Melville already knew all he needed to know about the struggle for existence at sea and in the horrible fo'c'sle of an American ship—a byword for hardship, oppression, and desperate characters from all nations who would not have been employed elsewhere. American ships were known as floating jails.

In the Marquesas Melville deserted, became the "white man who lived among the cannibals" (for a month), was taken off by an Australian whaler, went to Tahiti, mutinied with other hardbitten types, was briefly and farcically jailed. After further escapades in the company of deserters, drifters, drunks, castaways, "mongrel renegades . . . and cannibals," he ended up in Honolulu as a clerk, as a pinboy in a bowling alley, before returning home on an American man-of-war, the *United States*. Melville's record of the return voyage is *White-Jacket*, half documentary and half lampoon. His biting description of flogging is supposed to have ended the practice in the American navy. The captain is incompetent and a martinet, the surgeon a sadist, the midshipmen "terrible little boys." The American navy provided "evils which, like the suppressed domestic drama of Horace Walpole, will neither bear representing, nor reading, and will hardly bear thinking of." But in the captain of the maintop he found his ideal man—bluff, hearty, poetry-spouting Jack Chase.

Melville's three-and-a-half-year voyage made him see Western man in confrontation (his favorite activity) with the primitive in society, the elemental in nature. His underlying antagonist was the conventional in white middle-class America and its Christianity. The great voyage furnished material for a lifetime. *Billy Budd*, Melville's last work, written in the last years of his life and not discovered until 1919, was "Dedicated to Jack Chase, Englishman, Wherever that great heart may now be, here on Earth or harbored in Paradise, Captain of the Maintop in the year 1843 in the U.S. Frigate *United States*."

So central and dominating for the rest of his life was Melville's great voyage that his prototype became a wanderer, an exile, a sailor, while his work takes us on an endless journey. It leads to South Sea islands and prisons; to the gigantic tortoises and reptiles of "The Encantadas"; to Liverpool in *Redburn*, where in the desolate cellars off the docks the poor die under the eyes of the indifferent police; to the slums of London, where Israel Potter spends most of his life trying vainly to get home; to the waters off the coast of Chile where Benito Cereno is held prisoner by rebellious slaves who dupe the kindly American Captain Delano into thinking that Cereno still has authority; to the seamy streets of old New York in *Pierre* and the desolation of Wall Street on Sunday in "Bartleby the Scrivener"; to the Mississippi in *The Confidence Man;* to Egypt and Palestine in Melville's extraordinary *Journal up the Straits* and his narrative poem *Clarel;* to ancient Italy in the virgin astronomer's passionate lament over wasted womanhood in the monologue "After the Pleasure Party."

This narrative journey, the most imaginative single span of the earth in American writing, ends in midocean with the sacramental crucifixion in *Billy Budd* of a son by his father.

"Heureux qui, comme Ulysse, a fait un beau voyage," wrote the Renaissance poet Joachim du Bellay. "Happy the man who, like Ulysses, made a good journey and then came home full of experience and wisdom to live out his life among his family!" No other significant writer of his time and place came anywhere near Melville's absorption of the imperial midcentury world in which New England whalers and cargo ships made portions of the Pacific an American preserve. New England devised the clipper ships that traded with China and newly opened Japan. New England whalers stripped Japan's seas of whales in the 1830s and 1840s. America first went to Japan in Commodore Matthew Perry's "black ships" in 1852–54, opening a reluctant, fearful country to the outside world after centuries of seclusion. (Perry's aim, Japanese scholars say, was to obtain water and coaling stations for American whalers.)

Melville had reason to become jeeringly sceptical of Western civilization and Protestant moralism; he had seen the missionaries at work.* Because young gentlemen sometimes developed trouble with their eyes and had to

---

Omoo, chapter 45: "In fact, there is, perhaps, no race upon earth, less disposed, by nature, to the monitions of Christianity, than the people of the South Seas. . . . 'The Great Revival At The Sandwich Islands,' about the year 1836 . . . [was] brought about by no sober moral convictions; as an almost instantaneous relapse into every kind of licentiousness soon afterward testified. It was the legitimate effect of a morbid feeling, engendered by the sense of severe physical wants, preying upon minds excessively prone to superstition; and, by fanatical preaching, inflamed into the belief, that the gods were taking vengeance upon the wickedness of the land. . . .

"Added to all this . . . [was] a quality inherent in Polynesians . . . more akin to hypocrisy than to anything else. It leads them to assume the most passionate interest in matters for which they really feel little or none whatever; but in which, those whose power they dread, or whose favor they court, they believe to be at all affected."

Protestant "triumphalism"—the belief that the entire world would be Christianized as it was getting Westernized—would delude a president of the United States as being representative of solid middle-class American values. President McKinley justified the Spanish-American War because it would "Christianize the Philippines." Fifty years earlier Melville saw that the missionaries themselves

leave Harvard for a spell, Richard Henry Dana had gone to sea and produced that superbly healthy and objective record of life at sea and in California before it was American, *Two Years Before the Mast*. But Melville cannot be relied on to give us straight facts. Conrad, asked in 1907 to write a preface to *Moby-Dick*, refused. "It struck me as a rather strained rhapsody with whaling for a subject and not a single sincere line in the 3 vols of it." Melville's significant imagination captured well the highs and lows of manifest destiny in its time: the exuberance of discovering the "world" and the disgust of sharing in the imperial grab that made Melville's great voyage possible. No other American writer served such an apprenticeship. Melville never forgot the human flotsam and jetsam around him. American literature was still captive to "high culture," was self-consciously genteel, and, in the fading of authentic belief, was replacing religion with moralism. The literary class was still homogeneous and unaware that it lacked muscle. Social power was in other hands. Melville on reading Emerson: "To one who has weathered Cape Horn as a common sailor what stuff all this is."

Melville's experience before he was twenty-five not only gave him material for a lifetime, it created his basic image: the inconclusive nature of reality, man forever driven back on himself as he seeks a fixed point. Melville's linked orphanage and "fall" from status, his sense of social injury and his maritime world of wonders, were urgent symbols to the ex-sailor who became a great reader only after discovering that he was a writer. He was never to write one of his semidocumentary novels without other men's voyages at his side.

Of all the many surprises in his life, probably none was so startling to Melville as his need of books and his passion for ideas. He proudly said that he "swam through whole libraries" to write *Moby-Dick*. He borrowed other men's narrative experiences in *Typee, Redburn, White-Jacket, Moby-Dick;* this was necessary not only to his extensive imagination but to his need to parody other writers' limitations. A corrosive humor became as important to his pride as his assertion of mental homelessness. And so did his sense of the ferocity of life at sea—"I have had to do with whales with these visible hands." He was a Darwinian by intuition. As he was to say, "Luther's day had expanded into Darwin's year." Original sin was behind natural selection. Predestination was in the genes as well as in the "soul."

---

had an excessive sense of sin and, believing in the total depravity of the natives, mercilessly tried to uproot their society.

It was in the South Seas, as Raymond Weaver first pointed out, that Melville learned that the white man had the dubious honor of being "the most ferocious animal on the face of the earth." In Tahiti he learned to despise the missionaries, who returned the compliment in the abusive reviews of *Moby-Dick* in the missionary papers.

Melville was unlike the gentle Darwin, who resisted his own awareness of the killer instinct in nature and was often made ill by the conclusive evidence he piled up. A year before the *Origin of Species* appeared, Darwin wrote: "It is difficult to believe in the dreadful but quiet war of organic beings going on in the peaceful woods and smiling fields." "It is like confessing a murder," Darwin wrote to the botanist Joseph Hooker, confiding his suspicion that species are not immutable. Ten miles outside Pittsfield, Melville was living in the Berkshires' peaceful woods and smiling fields when he produced Ahab's hymn to the killer instinct in nature. He was remembering his youth at sea. Killers cannot help themselves.

> By heaven, man, we are turned round and round in this world, like yonder windlass, and Fate is the handspike. And all the time, lo! that smiling sky, and this unsounded sea! Look! see yon Albicore! who put it into him to chase and fang that flying-fish? Where do murderers go, man! Who's to doom, when the judge himself is dragged to the bar?

Melville's "Darwinism" brought to his books a complex sense that human beings were futile yet heroic. His career was an example. The man who wrote in *Mardi*, "Oh, believe me, God's creatures fighting fin for fin a thousand miles from land, and with the round horizon for an arena, is no ignoble subject for a masterpiece," jauntily wrote to Hawthorne: "Genius is full of trash." A significant side of Melville is the scorn he developed for his early fame. Just before he landed in England in 1849, to sell *White-Jacket,* he derisively noted in his diary that ten years before he had sailed there as a common sailor; now he was "H. M., the author of Pee-Dee, Hullabaloo and Pog-Dog."

Melville was "posthumous" by the time he finished *Moby-Dick.* He was thirty-two. The problem was his incessant development after leaving the sea—a wholly personal matter not to be correlated with worldly success. He confessed his premonitions to Hawthorne as he was completing *Moby-Dick.*

> My development has been all within a few years past. I am like one of those seeds taken out of the Egyptian pyramids, which, after being three thousand years a seed and nothing but a seed, being planted in English soil, it developed itself, grew to greenness, and then fell to mould. So I. Until I was twenty-five, I had no development at all. From my twenty-fifth year I date my life. Three weeks have scarcely passed, at any time between then and now, that I have not unfolded within myself. But I feel that I am now come to the inmost leaf of the bulb, and that shortly the flower must fall to the mould.

The restlessness, the *interminability* of his personal quest, saw truth only in the sea's maddening beat. "Poor Rover!" cries Pip the cabin boy when he jumps out of the boat in fright and goes mad, "will ye never have done with all this weary roving? where go ye now?" "Annihilation" for Herman Melville meant never to be done voyaging, searching; never to lose the heart's dissatisfaction and the mind's inconclusiveness. We hear this in *Moby-Dick* from the frantic preparations for the voyage: "all betokening that new cruises were on the start; that one most perilous and long voyage ended, only begins a third, and so on, for ever and for aye. Such is the endlessness, yea, the intolerableness of all earthly effort."

"Annihilation" appears in book after book. The killer instinct that is so strong in *Moby-Dick* is first of all annihilation of the known limits, of the land, of the familiar self. Waiting for the *Pequod* to get off and meet its destiny, Ishmael senses the design to which, like another Ulysses forever roaming the world, he is caught.

> The port would fain give succor; the port is pitiful; in the port is safety, comfort, hearthstone, supper, warm blankets, friends, all that's kind to our mortalities. But in that gale, the port, the land, is that ship's direst jeopardy; she must fly all hospitality; one touch of land, though it but graze the keel, would make her shudder through and through. With all her might she crowds all sail off shore; in so doing, fights against the very winds that fain would blow her homeward; seeks all the lashed sea's landlessness again; for refuge's sake forlornly rushing into peril; her only friend her bitterest foe!

Moby-Dick is the product of a powerfully crossed mind—imitating the bursting century, expanding America, the manifest destiny out of which it came. It is an epic of mixed motives, of unyielding contradictions. And it is always histrionic. Ahab's dream of perfect freedom demands total mastership. Yet he admits himself subject to predestination in all things. It is "Nature's decree." Man and Nature must fight each other up and down the watery waste. Although Melville finds "linked analogies" in every observation—in this he is a good American of the transcendentalist church—Nature for Melville is not Emerson's word for man's *moral* nature. The great beasts of the sea—and the sea is the greatest beast—give the rule of things. They are the first and last of the earth. The antediluvian world is still with us, frightening, and in perpetual creation. The animal kingdom, the sea kingdom, is totally itself and aboriginal. It cares nothing for death. Nature was the killer from the beginning.

But now it is confronted by the ironic, weary, expectant mind of the nineteenth century. There are two principal voices in *Moby-Dick:* the excessively assertive Faust from Nantucket who pursues the sperm whale that bit his leg off and the passively contemplative, quietist, all-enduring survivor. He is the lost son and eternal wanderer Ishmael, whom his father Abraham ordered with his concubine mother Hagar into the wilderness—where, Genesis tells us, he became an archer.

Moby-Dick is the most memorable confrontation we have had in America between Nature—as it was in the beginning, without man, God's world alone—and man, forever and uselessly dashing himself against it. It is a confrontation peculiarly American and of the nineteenth century, for it connects the still-present "wilderness," the ferocity of brute creation, with the anxiously searching mind that has lost its father in heaven. *Moby-Dick* is full of symbols that unlike those of Emerson and Thoreau do not exhaust the natural facts from which they are extracted. The power of the book, the rolling, endlessly conjunctive style rushing to do justice to all this hunting, gashing, killing, devouring—and sexual cannibalism—gives us the full measure, brimming over in Melville's prose, of what the narrator's mind brings to the primordial scene.

The detachment essential to storytelling does not confine Melville's style. He certainly lacked Emerson's doubt of the final sufficiency of language. Melville luxuriates in language, looks to "Vesuvius for an inkwell," a "condor's wing" to write with. The extraordinary rhythm of the book is the wavelike pull, forward and back, between the expansive human will and the contraction of necessity. Freedom and necessity battle throughout the book. The mind naturally thinks itself free, but necessity is the deeper rhythm of things. Nature's "tiger heart" is just beneath the surface while, at his ease in the masthead, Ishmael "takes the mystic ocean at his feet for the visible image of that deep, blue, bottomless soul, pervading mankind and nature."

Like Carlyle, Melville shows sexual abandon in fitting his language to his subject matter. His shipmates address whales with a harpoon, Ishmael with a pen. The "fiery hunt" of the mightiest beast demands a style that from the opening of *Moby-Dick* conveys a sense of abundance that is easy, full, peculiarly rich in suggestion of the universal fable in the background and the epic stretching the narrative line. If ever there was a style that belonged to America's own age of discovery, a style innocently imperialist, romantic, visionary, drunk on symbols, full of the American brag, this is it. We come to feel that there is some shattering magnitude of theme before Melville as he writes. He has been called to a heroic destiny.

But it is a ponderous task; no ordinary letter-sorter in the Postoffice is equal to it. To grope down into the bottom of the sea after them; to have one's hands among the unspeakable foundations, ribs, and very pelvis of the world; this is a fearful thing. What am I that I should essay to hook the nose of this Leviathan! The awful tauntings in Job might well appal me. "Will he make a covenant with thee? Behold the hope of him is vain!" But I have swam through libraries and sailed through oceans; I have had to do with whales with these visible hands; I am in earnest; and I will try.

Moby-Dick is the greatest epic we have of the predatory thrill. Long before Americans completed their conquest of a continent and its aborigines, they had reached out to the Orient. But the savages the white man replaced entered into his soul—and they are all present on the *Pequod*. Power in every human guise is the norm in *Moby-Dick*. Ahab's dream of absolute power wrecks everything and almost everyone. The book overpowers by an uncontainable force, an appropriation that is instinctive and unashamed. It is a hymn to the unequalled thrust that lifted America to the first rank, and it is equally a hymn to the contemplativeness that was left to its literary men, its sensitive consciences, its lonely metaphysicals and seekers after God. It is at once Ahab's book, fiercely masculine, yet from the beginning rooted in Ishmael's passive, wonder-struck gaze. The reader is caught up by these different sides of Melville—the androgyny that American writing suffers in respect to American power. Ishmael constantly reports Ahab but never seems to meet him. There is no confrontation between the daemonic father and the lost son. There will be none between Captain Vere and Billy in *Billy Budd*, where Isaac *praises* his father Abraham for loving the law more than he loves his son. If there *is* a father, he is a disaster to Melville; yet Melville's despairing sense of "God" is that "God-like" minds are without a God. So his love and adoration for Hawthorne ended in the suspicion that he was writing to a father figure who was not really there.

Moby-Dick is *the* book of nineteenth-century American capitalism carried to the uttermost. Yet everything is encompassed by the dreaming mind of Ishmael, the last transcendentalist. Ishmael has no power whatever; but he thinks and thinks because he is residue of a Calvinism that has emptied itself out into as much dread as wonder. It is not God who is absolute sovereign but the whale. "Though in many of its aspects this visible world seems formed in love, the invisible spheres were formed in fright."

No wonder that the missionary papers disliked the book, or that Melville never quite recovered from the effort his "mighty" theme required. His struggle was not with the "daemonic" elements in the book, Ahab's "deliriously howling" as he baptized his harpoon *"in nomine diaboli."* The devil stuff in the book is imitation Gothic, boring and melodramatic; the only significance of Fedellah and the Parsee crew is the "exotic" tinge they give to Melville's determinism. The real struggle of the book was to create a great body of fact, learning, and humor around a theme ultimately nihilist. Melville admitted that his book "is not a piece of fine feminine Spitalfields silk—but it is of the horrible texture of a fabric that should be woven of ships' cables & hawsers. A Polar wind blows through it, & birds of prey hover over it." It is also a celebration of American enterprise and a grand joke on the ultimate futility of so much energy, will, and death-dealing bravado in the face of "eternal fates." Between Ahab as the maddened Faust seeking to exert his will and the indifferent beast-God he chases around the world only to sting him into contemptuous retribution, lies the sea, even more indifferently waiting to receive us all. But if there were no beast or God to pursue, there would be nothing. The sea in itself to human eyes is nothing. And nothingness is the "fright" behind the book.

III

Without Nathaniel Hawthorne, *Moby-Dick* might have remained the whaling yarn Melville started out to write. Hawthorne became the greatest, most direct inspiration in Melville's literary life; he was the only other man of genius in the neighborhood. Between the summer of 1850, when the Melvilles moved to Pittsfield, and November 1851, when the Hawthornes left Lenox, Melville rose to the height of his power as an artist, to all possible fervor as a man. But after the failure of the book coincided with the Hawthornes' leaving, Melville could never be sure that there had been a Hawthorne in his life.

It was not Hawthorne's fault that Melville came to think of him as being absent. Absence, vacancy, the "divine inert," the nothingness which a human being must constantly assail in "the now egotistical sky; in the now un-haunted hill," was forever in Melville's mind. Ahab *is* his greatest character, despite the bombast crowding this wholly literary, all-too-willed characterization, because Ahab is not so much a person as an idea—pursuing an idea. The "fiery hunt" carries no hope that there is anything out there; it is just the essential human effort. The great beast is from the beginning a metaphor by which we challenge ourselves. *Moby-Dick* (to the great delight of twentieth-century readers brought up on symbolism) is a pretext for Ahab's fanaticism. The "God-like" presence that finally emerges, in all his "Jove-like" beauty, is—like so many things in the book—unrelated to the abstraction Ahab first summons his crew to hunt: "Sometimes I think there's naught beyond. But 'tis enough. He tasks me; he heaps me; I see in him outrageous strength, with an inscrutable malice sinewing it. That inscrutable thing is chiefly what I hate."

The *Pequod* is condemned by Ahab to sail up and down the world in search of a symbol. And everyone but the necessary narrator will die in the attempt; such is the burden on the mind seeking an Other in our narcissistic existence. The "world" seems to be easy to grasp but never is. Man continually mounts the world in its appearance as Nature but never really joins it. The failure is what torments us. It kills the illusion that we are part of what we see.

Hawthorne, just by being there for Melville at the crux of his life, gave Melville the bliss of meeting a genius. Hawthorne filled the vacancy that had been Melville's residual image of the father, of the "divine inert"—and of the hopeless chase for fame and money that was the literary career in America. Melville could not believe his luck—his letters run over with jubilant surprise: "Whence come you, Hawthorne? By what right do you drink from my flagon of life? And when I put it to my lips—lo, they are yours and not mine. I feel that the Godhead is broken up like the bread at the Supper, and that we are the pieces. Hence this infinite fraternity of feeling."

Melville heartily joined himself to his century's easy belief in genius. Like Carlyle, he advanced a high and mighty idea of the writer as hero. But where the secret nihilist Carlyle shouted at a world it was too late to redeem, Melville was overcome by the discovery of his own gifts. In the tumbling, rhapsodic letters he wrote to Hawthorne during their brief acquaintance, he constantly projects his own literary temperament. Melville to the conservative, resigned, decidedly nonthundering Hawthorne:

There is the grand truth about Nathaniel Hawthorne. He says No! in thunder; but the Devil himself cannot make him say yes. For all men who say *yes,* lie; and all men who say *no,*—why, they are in the happy condition of judicious, unincumbered travellers in Europe; they cross the frontiers into Eternity with nothing but a carpet-bag,—that is to say, the Ego. Whereas those *yes*-gentry, they travel with heaps of baggage, and, damn them! they

will never get through the Custom House. What's the reason, Mr. Hawthorne, that in the last stages of metaphysics a fellow always falls to *swearing*
so? I could rip an hour.

Hawthorne was not Melville. Melville's response was to raise Hawthorne
to royalty, out of *everyone's* reach. Hawthorne's own image of himself was
that of a spy, a peeping Tom, lurking everywhere without being discovered.
"The most desirable mode of existence," he wrote in "Sights from a Steeple,"
"might be that of a spiritualized Paul Pry, hovering invisible round man and
woman, witnessing their deeds, searching into their hearts, borrowing
brightness from their felicity, and shade from their sorrow, and retaining no
emotion peculiar to himself."

Julian Hawthorne said his father always reflected the person he was with,
was a mixture of

> a subtle sympathy . . . and a cold intellectual insight . . . the real man stood
> aloof and observant. . . . Seeing his congenial aspect towards their little
> rounds of habits and belief [other people] would leap to the conclusion that
> he was no more and no less than one of themselves; whereas they formed but
> a tiny arc in the great circle of his comprehension.

Sophia Hawthorne, who idolized her husband, probably reflected something of Hawthorne's opinion of Melville as well as her own limitations
when she wrote to her sister Elizabeth Peabody that Melville's gushing
tributes to Hawthorne on *The House of the Seven Gables* showed Melville

> a boy in opinion—having settled nothing as yet—unformed—ingenue—& it
> would betray him to make public his confessions & efforts to grasp,—because
> they would be considered perhaps impious, if one did not take in the whole
> scope of the case. Nothing pleases me better than to sit & hear this growing
> man dash his tumultuous waves of thought up against Mr. Hawthorne's
> great, genial, comprehending silences. . . . Yet such a love & reverence &
> admiration for Mr. Hawthorne as is really beautiful to witness—& without
> doing any thing on his own part, except merely doing, it is astonishing how
> people make him their innermost Father Confessor.

IV

In 1883 Julian Hawthorne, in search of his father's letters for the biography
he was writing of his parents, called on Melville "in a quiet side street in New
York, where he was living almost alone." Melville said with a melancholy
gesture that Hawthorne's letters to him "had all been destroyed long since,

as if implying that the less said or preserved, the better! . . . He said, with agitation, that he had kept nothing; if any such letters had existed, he had scrupulously destroyed them. . . . When I tried to revive memories in him of the red-cottage days—red-letter days too for him—he merely shook his head."

Julian Hawthorne did not feel that he had learned much from the visit. He did give us a rare view of the "forgotten" Melville in New York:

> He seemed nervous, and every few minutes would rise to open and then to shut again the window opening on the court yard. . . . He was convinced Hawthorne had all his life concealed some great secret, which would, were it known, explain all the mysteries of his career . . . some secret in my father's life which had never been revealed, and which accounted for the gloomy passages in his books. It was characteristic in him to imagine so; there were many secrets untold in his own career.

Melville's bitterness was to come out in his poem "Monody."

> To have known him, to have loved him
>   After loneness long;
> And then to be estranged in life,
>   And neither in the wrong;
> And now for death to set his seal—
>   Ease me, a little ease, my song!

Melville probably considered this the final word—it was his only word —on his relation to Hawthorne. But the writer resurrected in the 1920s was in for a surprise. A great many people turned out to know so much about Melville's "secret" that it also became Hawthorne's "secret." In a poem celebrating Melville, W. H. Auden explained that "Nathaniel had been shy because his love was selfish."

v

In the late 1850s, as his wife revealed, Melville had "taken to writing poetry." If, as one reviewer complained about *Moby-Dick,* its expansive prose was "so much trash belonging to the worst school of Bedlam literature," poetry was certainly Melville's way of contracting his style by enclosing himself. But more than ever would he argue with himself. Even the prose fiction he wrote after *Moby-Dick*—the sometimes hysterical parody of the genteel style in *Pierre,* the stories and reveries he collected in *The Piazza Tales,* the shut-in terseness of *The Confidence Man*—show a restless waywardness of form, an exasperated need to try anything at hand, that finally came to rest in poetry privately published, poetry in which and for which he did not have to answer to anyone.

This was to be true of the posthumous *Billy Budd*, which Melville left unfinished, perhaps not wanting to see it finished and published. When it was discovered in 1919 by Raymond Weaver, who was tracking down Melville for the first biography, *Mariner and Mystic*, it was in a confusing state in Melville's most crabbed hand. Concealed in a tin breadbox, says Melville's great-grandson Paul Metcalf, it had to be "dug loose from the tight seaweed of Melville's heirs and descendants."

"Crabbed" is the word for Melville's poetry—and for the peculiar syntactical complexity of style in *Billy Budd*, which for all its drama betrays an instrument long unused as well as the grave slowness and quizzicality into which Melville's youthful force had subsided in "retirement."

The poetry is in every sense occasional. Even his most unforced, his easiest poem, "Billy in the Darbies," which concludes *Billy Budd* and in its humorous stoicism at the approach of death sums up Melville's work (and life) with all his old grace, answers to a kind of occasion: April 19, 1891, the date Melville added to "End of Book." "Billy in the Darbies" is a truly personal poem, "dramatic" in its monologue, since it is Billy speaking from his last night on earth. So many of Melville's poems—about history, vaguely historic personages, "fruits of travel long ago," Melville's burrowing in historical myths—proceed from some grave meditative center. By contrast with "Billy in the Darbies,"

> But me they'll lash in hammock, drop me deep.
> Fathoms down, fathoms down, how I'll dream fast asleep . . .

most of Melville's poems are altogether too "philosophic," too far above the battles that composed Melville's life and formed the strenuousness of his mind.

Reading Melville's verse, one cannot help picturing him, evening after evening, wreathed in cigar smoke as he measures his way from line to line, rhyme to rhyme. In one of his *Battle-Pieces*, "Commemorative of a Naval Victory," he was surely thinking of himself when he wrote:

> But seldom the laurel wreath is seen
> Unmixed with pensive pansies dark;
> There's a light and a shadow on every man
> Who at last attains his lifted mark—

Nursing through night the ethereal spark.
Elate he never can be;
He feels that spirit which glad had hailed his worth,
  Sleep in oblivion.—The shark
Glides white through the phosphorous sea.

"The shark / Glides white through the phosphorous sea" certainly breaks up the evening labor wreathed in cigar smoke; Melville is full of wonderful lines.

There are no outcries from this long-haunted man like the middle passages of baffled love in "After the Pleasure Party." "Amor threatening," he calls it in this remarkable piece about a woman astronomer in ancient Italy who suddenly awakens to the cost of her virginal existence. This is an unusually *felt* monologue. With the sudden brilliance that can flash across a Melville poem, his preoccupation with sexual ambiguity now asserts itself in urgent tones.

Could I remake me! or set free
This sexless bound in sex, then plunge
Deeper than Sappho, in a lunge
Piercing Pan's paramount mystery!
For, Nature, in no shallow surge
Against thee either sex may urge,
Why hast thou made us but in halves—
Co-relatives? This makes us slaves.
If these co-relatives never meet
Self-hood itself seems incomplete.
And such the dicing of blind fate
Few matching halves here meet and mate.
What Cosmic jest or Anarch blunder
The human integral clove asunder
And shied the fractions through life's gate?

The weary, inexperienced poet was his old self, if not his once-Promethean self: he still took on big "historical" themes. But they were now occasions for reflection, not scenes of action. The requisite subject after 1865 was the Civil War, which stirred Melville to write *Battle-Pieces* out of a sense of national tragedy rather than patriotism. In "America"

Valor with Valor strove, and died:
Fierce was Despair, and cruel was Pride;
And the lorn Mother speechless stood,
Pale at the fury of her brood.

The end of slavery stirred him less than the deaths of "young collegians." But even Melville's serial portraits of America's slaughtered youth, like many poems in *Battle-Pieces* commemorating battles and leaders of the Civil War, seem composed in a gray light. They lack the involvement (real or hoped) that Whitman brought to *Drum-Taps*. Melville's noble compassion for both sides shows no strong political resolve in response to America's finest hour and everlasting hurt.

The great exception is "The House-top," Melville's bitter response to the July 1863 anti-draft riots; it jolts the reader after so many shadowy genre paintings of war. Melville as Coriolanus, standing on the roof of his house in New York, describes with the most concentrated contempt for the mob its "Atheist roar of riot." The poem voices an embittered Toryism that is not altogether surprising. In his early works Melville's most obvious political reflex was a jeer at conventional Western values; missionary repressiveness and pettiness in the South Seas appalled him, as the natives certainly did not. He is disgusted by the city's "new democracy," its masses, and scornful of

> . . . the Republic's faith implied,
> Which holds that Man is naturally good,
> And—more—is Nature's Roman, never to be scourged.

He says with gritted teeth that

> The Town is taken by its rats—ship-rats
> And rats of the wharves. All civil charms
> And priestly spells which late held hearts in awe—
> Fear-bound, subjected to a better sway
> Than sway of self; these like a dream dissolve,
> And man rebounds whole aeons back in nature.

In "The Conflict of Convictions," a poem about the anxious "secession winter" of 1860–61, Melville obviously remembers his futile efforts, in sight of the unfinished Capitol dome, to obtain a consular appointment from the Lincoln administration. But the irrepressible conflict has turned his personal failure into political bleakness. His disenchantment, as in "The House-top," laments the vanished dream of the Founders:

> Power unanointed may come—
> Dominion (unsought by the free)
>   And the Iron Dome,
> Stronger for stress and strain,
> Fling her huge shadow athwart the main;

But the Founders' dream shall flee.
Age after age shall be
As age after age has been,
(From man's changeless heart their way they win);
And death be busy with all who strive—
Death, with silent negative.

VI

Why did Melville turn to poetry? It was not just because his novels had failed;
or, as soft-minded critics once thought, because Melville's "subjective" and
"intellectual" side had become "excessive." He had been willing to try any
form, sometimes within a single "novel," because his greatest literary need
was to express contraries. As Hawthorne noticed, Melville never tired of
"wandering to and fro" over "intellectual deserts." The condensation of
thought that poetry makes possible now appealed to a strenuous if no longer
frantic thinker. He was aging, he was "retired," in just that drop of American
idealism after the Civil War that saw—nowhere more sharply than in Herman Melville—a reversal of the Enlightenment. Verse offered the increasingly conservative ex-novelist the possibility that life could be contained as
epigram. He anticipated at the end of "The Conflict of Convictions" (and
in capital letters) the kind of jeering little "lines" that Stephen Crane called
poetry:

> YEA AND NAY—
> EACH HATH HIS SAY;
> BUT GOD HE KEEPS THE MIDDLE WAY.
> NONE WAS BY
> WHEN HE SPREAD THE SKY;
> WISDOM IS VAIN, AND PROPHESY.

Melville offered a riposte to Blake in a poem from *Timoleon*, "Fragments
of a Lost Gnostic Poem of the 12th Century."

> Indolence is heaven's ally here,
> And energy the child of hell:
> The Good Man pouring from his pitcher clear,
> But brims the poisoned well.

Melville in the long evening of his life needed such terseness as he came
to the end of his roaming. His long search within himself and his need to

elude the fate of Narcissus had ended in a reconciliation with certain fundamentals.*

What could not have changed was the need to storm "the axis of reality." As an exuberant young author just in from the Pacific, Melville had sought to transcend limits, to escape confines, to find in the heroic age of his young country the last undiscovered place. As a fugitive from the great American marketplace, Melville then "reduced" himself to stories for magazines, to soliloquies in his travel notes on Egypt and Palestine, to the contemptuous "masquerade" of *The Confidence Man,* to octosyllabics in his long narrative poem *Clarel.* In his last three years he was to reduce himself to the anonymity of *Billy Budd* and its theme, the father's compliance in the death of the son.

In the wild flight of writing *Moby-Dick,* Melville had praised himself (while praising Hawthorne) for embodying "a certain tragic phase of humanity. . . . We mean the tragedies of human thought in its own unbiassed, native, and profounder workings . . . the apprehension of the absolute condition of present things as they strike the eye of the man who fears them not, though they do their worst to him."

Melville the great American agonist, forever trying to recapture his belief in the God-given unity of all things, was a thinker unmistakably in search of the elemental. In his first, romantic books, this quest made him go to the ends of the earth. In the triumphant moment of his life, when he was finishing *Moby-Dick,* he avowed to Hawthorne that his own deepest concern was with the beginning and end of things. As a sailor he had had the merest glimpse of the Galápagos, but in the marvellous sketches and tales of "The Encantadas" Melville recreated a biblical scene—the first days of creation. In his journal of Egypt and Palestine, the intensity of his lifelong association with the Bible led him to put his impressions into the starkest personal shorthand.

Pyramids still loom before me—something vast, indefinite, incomprehensible, and awful. Line of desert & verdure, plain as line between good and evil. A long billow of desert forever hovers as in act of breaking, upon the verdure of Egypt. Grass near the pyramids, but will not touch them. Desert more fearful to look at than ocean. Theory of design of pyramids. Defense against desert. A line of them. Absurd. Might have been created with the creation.

Ride over mouldy plaine to Dead Sea—Mountains on both sides—Lake George—all but verdure——foam on beach & pebbles like slaver of mad dog —smarting bitter of the water,—carried the bitter in my mouth all day—

*"And still deeper the meaning of that story of Narcissus, who because he could not grasp the tormenting, mild image he saw in the fountain, plunged into it and was drowned. But that same image, we ourselves see in all rivers and oceans. It is the image of the ungraspable phantom of life; and this is the key to it all." (*Moby-Dick,* "Loomings")

bitterness of life—thought of all bitter things—Bitter is it to be poor & bitter, to be reviled, & Oh bitter are these waters of Death, thought I—Old boughs tossed up by water—relics of pick-nick—nought to eat but bitumen & Ashes with desert of Sodom apples washed down with water of Dead Sea.—Must bring your own provisions, as well, too, for mind as body—for all is barren.

Melville *had* to make his way to the Holy Land after his nervous crisis of the 1850s, just as when a young man, "having little or no money in my purse, and nothing particular to interest me on shore, I thought I would sail about a little and see the watery part of the world." Melville's instinct made him sink the *Pequod* in the deepest waters of the Pacific. With like instinct he sought nature in its most savage aloofness from man. Yet even in the Holy Land, "the issues there but mind," as he wrote at the end of *Clarel*, he betrayed his truly "metaphysical anguish," his thirst for conclusiveness. The summing up, however, was in East Twenty-sixth Street, where this wanderer in thought was hidden by the frantic busyness of New York.

Melville retreating to New York regarded himself as a private thinker, nearly anonymous. The anonymity was parallel to the theme at the heart of all his work. Was there a home for thought, unavailing, unending thought, in this world of indifference? Ahab's assault on the white whale was not more dogged than Melville's on the looming nothingness that invades his style with endless play on words ending in "less"—*homeless, landless, formless, speechless*—on images of extreme personal will—*furious*—on different names for blockage—*verge, wall, pyramid.* The beast always in view is emptiness, the deception inherent in the mere appearance of things. The harpooner rising to "strike" gets caught from "behind," is snagged and twisted in the rope whose coiled force catapults him into the sea. Dream and electric bitterness, strength and abjection, give us the polarities of Melville's life and work. No other "isolato" (he made up the word) in American writing communicates so fervently a writer's looking for a place to put his mind.

Emptiness! In the New York of the Gilded Age and the Brown Decades, the landlocked sailor was more than ever alone with himself. It was his nature to rebound on himself as the desperate quest. But his strangest association with New York was that living *there* did not matter.*

---

*Melville had taken the measure of "society" in *The Confidence Man* (1857), unmistakably the work of an extraordinary mind obsessed with the falsity of appearances. As a satire on a trickster's society, it repeats itself claustrophobically—Melville's depression is all over the book like fog. This ship of fools never takes off; is not intended to. Melville rings so many changes on his single idea that for all the intellectual ferocity of the book, the shifting appearances of the trickster in his "masquerade" make heavy going. There is no conflict, no crisis, no development. Man here is entirely static—not a comfortable stance for Melville's natural energy.

Still, Melville did have his roots, and more besides, in this "Babylonish brick-kiln." New York from the 1860s to Melville's death in 1891 was the money city that the expatriate Edith Wharton would return to in her last, unfinished novel, *The Buccaneers*. It would soon be the city that another New Yorker, Henry James, would confront in 1904 as the most "extravagant" of international cities. To think of Melville back in New York is to remember Edith Wharton's complaint that "he was qualified by birth to figure in the best society," for he was a cousin of the Van Rensselaers. Alas, she "never heard his name mentioned."

We can imagine what the rich and bossy Edith Wharton (Henry James complained that she regularly "swooped" down on him even when he welcomed the discovery of the world from her "motor") would have made of a descendant of the best society working as a customs inspector at three dollars and sixty cents a day. Bright prophetic Britishers and Canadians wrote Melville of their admiration for him and their inability to procure all his books. They wanted to see him. Robert Buchanan in New York complained that "no one seemed to know anything of the one great imaginative writer fit to stand shoulder to shoulder with Whitman on that continent." All that the reigning literary mediocrity of the day, the stockbroker-poet Edmund Clarence Stedman, could tell him was that "Melville is dwelling somewhere in New York."

Melville had no assurance of tenure in his "political" job. He was so much in danger of losing it that his brother-in-law John Hoadley wrote to the secretary of the treasury

> to ask you, if you can, to do or say anything in the proper quarter to secure him permanently, or at present, the undisturbed enjoyment of his modest, hard-earned salary, as deputy inspector of the Customs in the City of New York,—Herman Melville. Proud, shy, sensitively honorable—he had much to overcome, and has much to endure; but he strives earnestly to so perform his duties as to make the slightest censure, reprimand, or even reminder,— impossible from any superior. Surrounded by low venality, he puts it all quietly aside, quietly returning money which has been thrust into his pockets behind his back, avoiding offence alike to the corrupting merchants and their clerks and runners, who think that all men can be bought, and to the corrupt swarms who shamelessly seek their price; quietly, steadfastly doing his duty, and happy in retaining his own self-respect.

This glimpse of Melville during the Iron Age (when New York became the great exchange place for money and money-making) can fascinate a New Yorker in search of Melville the New Yorker. He is still easy to imagine in old New York—the lower city. In the eighties, when he had retired from his nineteen years on the docks, he sometimes dropped in on John Anderson's bookstore in Nassau Street—and he is rumored to have bought copies of his books in the financial district, where Bartleby did his scrivening. His genially uncomprehending employer was a Wall Street lawyer:

> I placed his desk close up to a small side-window in that part of the room, a window which originally had afforded a lateral view of certain grimy backyards and bricks, but which, owing to subsequent erections, commanded at present no view at all, though it gave some light. Within three feet of the panes was a wall, and the light came down from far above, between two lofty buildings, as from a very small opening in a dome. Still further to a satisfactory arrangement, I procured a high green folding screen, which might entirely isolate Bartleby from my sight.

Melville himself flashes into animation when he can report "a ship on my district from Girgate—Where's that? Why, in Sicily—the ancient Agrigentum. . . . I have not succeeded in seeing the captain yet—have only seen the mate—but hear that he has in possession some stones from these magnificent Grecian ruins, and I am going to try to get a fragment, however small, if possible."

The altogether proper, nobly stoical resident on East Twenty-sixth Street returned each evening to the bust of Antinoüs on a stand in the hall, the little white sails in the Bay of Naples on the wall, the oversized desk in his bedroom. On Sundays he walked with his grandchildren in the park. "At my years, and with my disposition," he wrote to John Hoadley, "one gets to care less and less for everything except downright good feeling." Home he is and taken his wages. Surely his feelings were those he had confessed to Hawthorne in the exultation of finishing *Moby-Dick*—"Am I now not at peace? Is not my supper good?"

But if Melville was "peaceful" (the Melville family motto was Heaven at Last, and Melville may still have had longings in that direction), the resurrected Melville, the Melville who surfaced posthumously with *Billy Budd* (and much more besides), seemed anything but peaceful, was still endlessly dramatic. Melville may have been ditched by his own century; he became important to the next because he stood for the triumph of expression over the most cutting sense of disaster, negation, and even the most ferociously unfavorable view of modern society in classical American literature. Melville to many another "isolato" in the next century represented the triumph of a prisoner over his cell, of a desperado over his own philosophy. There is in Melville the peculiar bitterness of a man who has lost everything except the will to survive by writing—and who is acid yet clamorous in a style that reminds us more of Rimbaud and Beckett than of the stoic acceptances of Hardy and Conrad. Melville's protagonist and hero is thematically the deserter, the shipwrecked sailor, the castaway, the tramp, the mad author, the criminal—and most centrally, the iconoclast who does not escape retribution from society by becoming a murderer.

VII

On September 13, 1971, more than a thousand New York State troopers stormed the Attica State Correctional Facility, where 1,200 inmates held thirty-eight guards hostage, thereby ending a four-day rebellion in the maximum-security prison. Many of the troopers shouted "White Power!" as they broke into the prison yard. Nine hostages and twenty-eight convicts were killed. One of the dead was Sam Melville, known as the Mad Bomber, a leader of radical groups in the 1960s who had adopted his last name because of his total veneration of a writer he identified with revolution. Carl Oglesby, another radical leader in the sixties, said in an article on "Literature as Revolution":

> Our abiding contemporary Melville posed in effect the following question: "Given these historical origins and social sources, these current grounds of spirit and pathways of hope, how might we secure the faith that our imperial-minded republic, unlike its ancient homologues, will not commit its energies in immense genocidal gulps at the expense, one time or another, of all the major colors, types and varieties of mankind?"

Melville, eclipsing his idol Hawthorne, became a hero to all who found a mirror image in Melville's expansiveness and "ambiguities." "Call Me Ishmael," said the poet Charles Olson in an excited little book most important for documenting Melville's debt to Shakespeare. "Call me Billy Budd," thought many a young man fascinated by the beauty and pathos of Melville's last work. In the 1920s Melville fascinated Hart Crane, Lewis Mumford, Jean Giono; was soon to fascinate W. H. Auden, Cesare Pavese, E. M. Forster, Benjamin Britten. He became such an obsession for highbrow opinion that the best-selling novelist John Marquand jealously attacked him. In the postwar reaction against the Popular Front liberalism of the 1930s, Melville even became a totem to neoconservatives in academe. In death as in life, Melville was like no other American "classic"; he divided bitter political loyalties.

Which of his many books speaks for him *now?* Which had the last word? From *Billy Budd,* certainly his last work, the secret work of his old age, it is easy to assume that Melville had found a solution to his long search for truth past the chimera of this world. The solution is law, or authority. In the great debate over Billy Budd's fate, between Captain Vere and the young officers of the court martial trying Billy for the "accidental" killing of Claggart, Vere drives them to hang someone who is possibly his own son.

> "How can we adjudge to summary and shameful death a fellow creature innocent before God, and whom we feel to be so?—Does that state it aright? You sign sad assent. Well, I too feel that, the full force of that. It is Nature. But do these buttons that we wear attest that our allegiance is to Nature? No, to the King. Though the ocean, which is inviolate Nature primeval, though this be the element where we move and have our being as sailors, yet as the King's officers lies our duty in a sphere correspondingly natural? So little is that true, that in receiving our commissions we in the most important regards ceased to be natural free agents.... Our vowed responsibility is in this: That however pitilessly that law may operate in any instances, we nevertheless adhere to it and administer it."

Perhaps it was not "resignation" to which Melville gave "assent" at the end; it may have been "authority." This may have been his way out of the total anarchy of appearances in *The Confidence Man,* that nihilistic babel of voices from an unmoving ship on an unbelievable river. No one is going anywhere in that book. But in the ever-growing contempt for American professions of honesty, *The Confidence Man* became what one anxious scholar called "Melville as Scripture." So the drama of his many changes went on, as it had for so long gone on within Melville himself, each book seeming to cancel the one before.

It was Melville's capacious intellectual personality that drew so many people to the different images he now presents. But the tormented subjectivism behind all his work shows the same problem—to find truth that would not disappear from voyage to voyage, book to book.

> Where is the foundling's father hidden?

> Where do murderers go, man! Who's to doom, when the judge himself is dragged to the bar?

> By vast pains we mine into the pyramid; by horrible gropings we come to the central room; with joy we espy the sarcophagus; but we lift the lid—and no body is there!—appallingly vacant as vast is the soul of man.

Melville's "tales of terror told in words of mirth" were wonderful enough. But his assault on the "axis of reality," driven by the most consummate doubt of where reality finally lay, pointed to lustful contradictions that only the future would relish. And that the future would not untangle or replace.

7

Wrecked, Solitary, Here: Dickinson's Room of Her Own

Attentiveness without an aim is the supreme form
of prayer.

SIMONE WEIL, *Notebooks*

I

"I think I could write a poem to be called Concord," Thoreau wrote in his journal for 1841. "For argument I should have the River, the Woods, the Ponds, the Hills, the Fields, the Swamps and Meadows, the Streets and Buildings, and the Villagers."

The Villagers were the afterthought. Virtually every item in the list lacks a specific name. *Walden* is a hymn to salvation achieved. It is so beautifully arranged, made and remade, finished and stylized in every part, that its particular triumph is to put you into harmony with it. But the style is too deliberate and always exclusive of what does not suit Thoreau's fable of man totally at home with nature and himself. Hell, as Jean-Paul Sartre was to say in *No Exit*, is "other people." Thoreau called them "visitors." They interrupted his perfect solitude.

Thoreau did think that people were always too much. Like his epigrams, they were separate pronouncements, not necessary to his world. He stood at a sharp angle to every foreign object in his specimen book of nature. Man in nature must lead to Perfection, which is the aim of existence. This is understood only as man feels himself under the eye of God. Nature is another name for God's purpose. To this, other human beings can be an obstruction. In the "Village" chapter of *Walden* Thoreau explains:

Every day or two I strolled to the village to hear some of the gossip which is incessantly going on there, circulating either from mouth to mouth, or from newspaper to newspaper, and which, taken in homeopathic doses, was really as refreshing in its way as the rustle of leaves and the peeping of frogs. As I walked in the woods to see the birds and squirrels, so I walked in the village to see the men and boys; instead of the wind among the pines I heard the carts rattle. In one direction from my house there was a colony of muskrats in the river meadows; under the grove of elms and buttonwoods in the other horizon was a village of busy men, as curious to me as if they had been prairie-dogs, each sitting at the mouth of its burrow, or running over to a neighbor's to gossip.

Where in the world except transcendental New England—and this when the United States was exploding on the world scene—did solitude so contentedly approve of itself at the expense of the human species? Where else would so total a visionary have been content to write, "Not till we are lost, in other words not till we have lost the world, do we begin to find ourselves, and realize where we are and the infinite extent of our relations"? In *Walden*, the fish, the muskrats, the ants, and the fox are more generously characterized than the unfortunate "James Collins, an Irishman who worked on the Fitchburg Railroad." The vibrations binding us to phenomenal nature feature no one but Henry Thoreau.

Of course Thoreau's abiding solitariness is "religious." He is a perfect demonstration of Alfred North Whitehead's "religion is what we do with our solitariness." Thoreau's ideal was sainthood exerted on the emptiness around Concord. The altar was Nature, but Henry Thoreau's God was one of those faint radio signals that can still be detected from a stellar explosion that ceased millions of years ago. Emerson's God finally came to rest in "the infinitude of the private mind"; this God was a last-ditch personal claim without the church, despite the church, against the church. Thoreau's whole life depended on his preserving it through a style that was really the practice of happiness. There could be no doubts, no obvious anxiety, above all no opening to contradiction. His life in nature—his God—gave Thoreau a sense of importance he never had in Concord.

11

It was natural for Thoreau to idealize his experience; he earnestly believed that writing follows experience and can be an exact substitute for it. The writer is a fixed, self-fulfilling entity who makes an ideal version of his life; this becomes the authorized version.

Emily Dickinson, no romantic about an existence that was as endlessly various as it was difficult, was fascinated by words as starting points. Words were not transcriptions of experience; they often invented it. Words were roles. She demonstrated in almost 1,800 poems—and successive drafts of poems—that she was able to live by the incessant shift of roles that mind and nature, subject and object, life and death, "soul" and self, "woman" and "me," play—often *at* each other. Her aim is not Thoreau's conversion of Nature into her own mind; it is the minuteness, the exact shading, of an actual human cycle forever reenacting itself within a domestic setting. Everything in her life is in her poems—especially when she has to make it up. "Amherst," her outside world, receives the slightest physical detail in the cycle. The Civil War is not named, although in 1862–63 it led to her writing more than a poem a day—and some of her fiercest poems. But everything is there, including the people she loved and the family she saw most. She lives in the village, and it is *her* village. She is its great reflector, perhaps because she never intended to "do" Amherst itself. Amherst was the whole of America and the cycle of life.

> Some things that stay there be—
> Grief—Hills—Eternity—
> Nor this behooveth me.
>
> There are that resting, rise.
> Can I expound the skies?
> How still the Riddle lies!

We get the daily round as we do not get it from the symbolic use of the seasons in *Walden* or from Whitman's catalogues of Americans at work. The daily round was also the daily urgency to write poems (and hundreds of letters that are as antic in mood and swift in thought as her poems). They include some open hysteria, a ready sense of farce, deathbeds, sexual entreaty, playing the little girl or "Majesty," mockery of male pomp, "what soft cherubic creatures these gentlewomen are," the Connecticut Valley weather at play, plants and animals that positively imitate Victorian society. In many poems she says that she springs to the page from being pressed down. Thoreau, who found his life in words, believed that they replace an experience exactly. Emily Dickinson did not feel that she had replaced a day or an hour—and certainly not the people she loved—by writing. Poetry was not the equivalent of experience and certainly never a solution to anything. Least of all was poetry a sanctification of experience. Like God, whom she pleasantly missed, poetry was something else.

Emily Dickinson did not idealize the self; she was too close to it. She was well acquainted with idleness, reverie, blankness, despair.

> I'm Nobody! Who are you?
> Are you—Nobody—Too?

Least of all did she believe that the human soul was needed to complete the universe. Saturated in a theological tradition that still provided the language for everyday experience, she made this tradition her daily resource. Religion was the background of her life, but her quest for a living God was often humorous. She must have recognized herself (in addition to her other troubles) as a reluctant sceptic ahead of her time. She was the first modern writer to come out of New England.

Even in secluded little Amherst, the harsh Puritan vision of an all-seeing God had evaporated into propriety. The supernatural had been replaced by exemplary behavior. No one was allowed to forget that New England was still the American evangel—of reform movements. Yet Dickinson somehow managed to live the dialectic of the old religion—the minutely observing self under God's all-seeing eye. Every instant of life was morally of supreme importance. This made her incessantly expressive, a Puritan trait. But she never affirmed faith where there was only a longing for faith. Her view of life remained strenuous, problematic, a contest. Writing was a trial of strength. God, whatever else He was not, was still the greatest *weight* on her life. Death was the next stage of life but was such a break with everything known that it could just as easily be called Immortality as not. Thus she lived a more complex consciousness than most American writers knew anything of. The "eternities" for Dickinson, as for Melville, are not to be doubted. But where Melville gave them extended physical properties—the sea, the ominous whiteness of the whale, limitlessness, landlessness, frightfulness—for Dickinson they are names for her mental states. She alone supports them. Frail but persistent, as Freud said of the intelligence, she will prod and rotate them endlessly in her great cycle of 1,775 poems, 1,049 letters, 124 prose fragments.

The pressure of mind against circumambient "reality" left so persistent and even tumultuous a record of battle that Dickinson is above all unsettling. She unsettles, most obviously, by not being easily locatable. She initiates the terms on which her intimate universe is founded, then shifts without warning into recesses of privacy. Her most difficult poems are held together by an idiosyncrasy, her characteristic "slant," that is sharp to the point of violence:

> Tell all the Truth but tell it slant—
> Success in Circuit lies
> Too bright for our infirm Delight
> The Truth's superb surprise

Dickinson's style is private exclamation. When it is not experienced in its own terms, "wrecked, solitary, here," it bombards us without effect. The contractedness of her "breathing," phrasing, the undisclosed territory between her capitalized nouns, between the dashes as her abrupt punctuation— all this seems to mock the anxious expressiveness of Victorian America. The abstractions with which she orients herself are homemade. Emerson sought "dry light and hard expressions." Thoreau could never resist epigrams, puns, scornful little pellets of Yankee wit. They were practicing "economy." Dickinson respected Emerson but must have laughed at so much conscious rhetoric. She wrote out of turbulence, feeling now like "nobody," now like a "queen"; she wrote as a person bargaining for her life, line after line, not as an "infinite" soul. She often rushes at a poem, takes an immediate gulp of the situation in the first line—"There came a Day at Summer's full"; " 'Hope' is the thing with feathers." Sometimes she positively hurls the opening at us—"Heart! We will forget him!"; "Just lost, when I was saved!" There are great silences within her poems that are not withholdings from the reader but contractions of feeling ("a zero at the bone") that tighten sense almost to inaudibility in the pell-mell rush of her thinking to herself.

Above all, what is unsettling is her *closeness* to every emotion and event rather than the "littleness" of her world. The keenness is witty:

> The Grass divides as with a Comb—
> A spotted shaft is seen—
> And then it closes at your feet
> And opens further on—

full of foreboding:

> There's a certain Slant of light,
> Winter Afternoons—
> That oppresses, like the Heft
> Of Cathedral Tunes—
>
> Heavenly Hurt, it gives us—
> We can find no scar,

> But internal difference,
> Where the Meanings, are—

She can press her special names into a poem without indicating their connection; she certainly wrote more for herself than she did for strangers. But her many remarkable effects come from her suddenly veering off to *look* at what she has presented. Drawing to the seen object, she wraps herself up closely, as if she were hiding. Her famous terseness and breathless brevity derive from her persistence in seeing the world now on one surface, now on another; folding and refolding the object in her hands. Poetry is not always "the past that breaks out in our hearts" (Rilke). In Dickinson the present is entirely present. It makes a phenomenology of pure being.

III

> Almost every woman described to you by a woman
> presents a tragic idea, and not an idea of well-being.
>
> EMERSON, *Journal*, 1838

No one has ever drawn Emily Dickinson's real character except herself. We must accept her saying that the "I" in her poems is not herself but her "representative." But the "Years and Hours" recorded in her work present us with an overwhelming record of one person's most minute reactions to existence. Whatever the woman's actual relationship to the poet—obviously this poet is this woman thinking—we cannot help reading the tumultuous cycle as one of the fullest records ever left of a *life,* a life whose outlet more and more became poetry.

The poetry seems to come directly out of her saying "I": "I am afraid to own a Body—"; "I am alive—I guess—"; "I can wade Grief—"; "I cautious, scanned my little life—"; "I dwell in Possibility—." Almost one hundred fifty poems begin as intensely personal reaction to the seasons, to meticulous changes in the weather and the light, to the slightest leap and ebb in her morale, to the arrivals and departures of people, to death in a neighbor's house. There are poems of pure observation, poems so dominated by her zeal for capitalized abstractions that the freshest images turn into more "ideas," poems that read as if she had just run up to her corner room to write down something she could laugh at. She often wrote to exorcise black depression. Her life was not so regular as it looked, since two moments of thought were never the same for her. But living her life is what she dwelled on, and she was so conscious of what was missing, of what need not be said, that a sense of absence serves not only to condense her poems but as her best punctuation.

"I would eat evanescence slowly," she wrote in a letter. Nothing became so real as instances of change. These finally coalesced into the departures of people, life passing, the possible unreality of her favorite counters—Heart, Sky, Eternity, God. She moved them as if they were chess pieces. The sense of change formed her style, dictated its terseness. The spread of "moods," reactions, fantasies, impersonations, is very wide. The cycle contains so much elation, transfiguration through nature, desolation; her emotions represent so many marriages, death scenes, crises in the life of her family, friends, neighbors, that we become entangled in her life. This recluse involves us more than most poets do.

No one can read these poems over and again without experiencing the unrelieved pitch of crisis that sent them forth. To read her three volumes of letters is to learn how often she sent a poem with a letter; a letter in its abrupt use of images as absolutes served her as another "offering." Single lines and phrases show the same urgent sense of contraction—"A letter always feels to me like Immortality because it is the mind alone without corporeal friend." The letters are astonishing; she starts in the middle of the most private thought, sends a friend her most arcane images, with the same confidence that she brings to the gnomic self-sufficiency of a poem. She trusted her mind even when she had little confidence in her life. The act of writing was the excitement of entering a body of thought, of keeping in sight the "circumference" of her farthest idea. Writing was a "leap," following a trajectory different in kind from the self-consuming that threatened her.

> I can wade Grief—
> Whole Pools of it—
> I'm used to that—
> But the least push of Joy
> Breaks up my feet—
> And I tip—drunken—

The reader is startled first by her immediacy, the hurtling directness of her attack. One is even more startled by her ability to present separate words as physical sensations. Her lexicon replenished itself from dictionaries, farmers' almanacs, maps, and especially Shakespeare, her favorite. He had such a large vocabulary. She had a whole cupboard of place names, nature names, chemical names. *Yellow Sea, cochineal, mazarin, Caspian Choirs, Broadcloth Hearts, Saxon* finally belong to her alone, sit up in "Majesty," as she liked to say. There is a rushing eagerness about her appropriations that makes us remember Conrad Aiken's reference to "The Kid." She was skilled at posing, as brother Austin laughingly reminded people when her banter was taken seriously. She could play the "coquette," as her "dear preceptor," Thomas Wentworth Higginson, noticed to his alarm when that virtuous man called on her.

Higginson, an advanced liberal for his time and place, a courageous, decent, limited man, noticed the furtive surface of her personality.* Her "nervous force" exhausted him. One of his more objective biographers, Tilden Edelstein, notes that he was

> accustomed to confront aspiring woman writers directly and to bring such relationships down to the level of simple truth and everyday comradeship— as he had done with Harriet Prescott Spofford, Rose Terry and Helen Jackson. . . . He found [Dickinson's] views about poetic sensibility and the state of mankind "the very wantonness of over-statement." "I never was with anyone who drained my nerve power so much."

Higginson did not see that provocativeness had become necessary to her surprised contact with anyone. The range of impersonation in her poetry is so wide that it is easy to believe that she once made "a spectacle of herself,"

*Higginson, colonel of the First South Carolina Volunteers, the first black regiment in the Union army, was of course an ex-minister, an abolitionist, an early supporter of women's rights. He was the only one of Brown's secret backers who did not disown him after Harper's Ferry. He even procured a lawyer for Brown; after Brown was hanged, Higginson attempted to save his followers.

Higginson, representative conscience of his time and place, was for all his good deeds in war and peace as conventional a mind as the moral courage of New England put on the American stage. He was a popular lecturer in the Mark Twain era on "The Natural Aristocracy of the Dollar."

Higginson had the curiosity to seek Dickinson out (after she had responded to his "Letter to a Young Contributor" in the *Atlantic Monthly*). But his incomprehension of Dickinson's originality is clear in the rewriting perpetrated in the first edition of Dickinson's poems (1890), edited with Mabel Loomis Todd. It is amusing to read Higginson's smug little tract, *Common Sense About Women* (1881), which Higginson probably considered the bravest word on the subject:

". . . If [woman] has traits of her own, absolutely distinct from his, then [man] cannot represent her, and she must have a voice and a vote of her own.

"To this last body of believers I belong. I think that all legal or conventional obstacles should be removed, which debar woman from determining for herself, as freely as man determines, what the real limitations of sex are, and what the merely conventional restriction.

". . . It is better not to base any plea for woman on the ground of her angelic superiority. The argument proves too much. If she is already so perfect, there is every inducement to let well enough alone."

as they long remembered in Amherst, then closed herself up again after hearing from the sisterhood.

IV

Dickinson's poetry must be taken, initially, as a young woman's rebellion. There are obvious cries of frustration, a sexual kittenishness and bravado, from the round corner room (her first image of "circumference") in the house on Main Street. She was very late in accepting restrictions on her destiny; it was a game to make restrictions on herself when her brother, Austin, and Susan Gilbert were married and lived next door. Amherst was "old," sedate, churchly, assured. The Dickinsons were important people. The life of an unmarried young woman in the family setting was traditional. Whatever her often self-mocking cries of protest, she accepted the setting and the life that came with it. Amherst was a habit, like being a woman. But the narrowness of her outer experience shows in the repetition of her themes, her images of struggle, "her" seasons and birds. The deeper she sank into an altogether private destiny—to violate the "circumference" of a surrounding mind that had no room for hers—the more she depended on other people. Some she made up.

Of course there were great loves in her life and behind her poetry; there were almost too many. She loved by turning the arbitrary choice into the necessary predicament. Some of her letters and poems emit wild shrieks: connection must be kept up with *someone*. Her "Master," as she addressed one still unknown to us, was probably not just another broken link. She conferred authority on more than one man—ministers like Charles Wadsworth, editors like Samuel Bowles. Men of professional distinction were as much shadows of divinity as her favorite ideas. That was another Amherst tradition, like the Dickinsons themselves. But since she never harped even on this, her wit turned to banter—of her longing for some intercession.

She played the ingenue, the gamine, what Amherst called the "coquette." She is so light and springy in the cycle of her moods—so much the tease, acrobat, and willing clown of her many emotions—that even apart from the fact that she resembles no other writer, she is especially unlike the earnest souls who dominated writing by women soon after the Civil War. Her own intense admirations were for Emily Brontë, Elizabeth Barrett Browning, George Eliot. Helen Hunt Jackson, the author of *Ramona* and *Mercy Philbrick's Choice,* a stilted novel supposedly about Dickinson herself, was a loyal friend.* It would be interesting to know what Dickinson made of such evangelical fiction of the early industrial scene as Rebecca Harding Davis's "Life in the Iron Mills," which we know she read in the *Atlantic Monthly* for April 1861. But how much did she attribute her reluctance to publish to her being a woman? How much did she feel hampered, restricted, and even denied as a writer in her time because she was not a man?

Being a "woman writer" likened rebels otherwise as different as the prodigious George Sand and the perkily brilliant but self-symbolizing Margaret Fuller. They dramatized their rebellion in society; Hawthorne's enduring dislike of Fuller and Emerson's embarrassed efforts to accept her aggressive declarations of "friendship" show that provincial little Concord was rocked by Fuller's independence and incessant expressiveness.

Hawthorne, treated as the lord of creation by his Sophia, expressed himself violently about the "damned lot of scribbling women. . . . I wish they were forbidden to write on pain of having their faces deeply scarified with an oyster shell." What bothered him was the "lot," the club, the tribe of indistinguishably genteel and sentimental magazine writers of the period. After the Civil War, the popularity of fiction in the new "age of the magazine," when the dominating audience was one of women,† helped to launch so many women writers that Henry James, supposedly writing an appreciation of the novels of his friend Constance Fenimore Woolson (*Harper's Weekly,* 1887), confessed that "in America, at least, one feels tempted at moments to explain that they are in themselves the world of literature." His "feeling" about women writers was certainly complicated.

> The work of Miss Woolson is an excellent example of the way the door stands open between the personal life of American women and the immeasurable world of print, and what makes it so is the particular quality that this work happens to possess. It breathes a spirit singularly and essentially conservative—the sort of spirit which, but for a special indication pointing the other way, would in advance seem most to oppose itself to the introduction into the lot of new and complicating elements.

*If not a comprehending one. From *Mercy Philbrick's Choice* (1876): "Mrs. Hunter had showed him several of Mercy's poems, which had surprised him much by their beauty, and still more by their condensation of thought. They seemed to him almost more masculine than feminine; and he had unconsciously anticipated that in seeing Mercy he would not see a feminine type. He was greatly astonished. He could not associate this slight, fair girl, with a child's honesty and appeal in her eyes, with the forceful words he had read from her pen. He pursued his conversation with her eagerly, seeking to discover the secret of her style, to trace back the poetry from its flower to its root."
†The (majority) female reading audience was described by a contemporary as "the Iron Madonna who strangles in her fond embrace the American novelist."

James was relieved that poor Constance Woolson (who among her other troubles was in love with him) was not one for new and complicating elements. Even if James had been open to poetry (he was not) and the posthumous Dickinson had come his way, he would have been embarrassed by her. She was not in the "real" world, society. For James literature was a demonstration of society, while the heroic pathos of an Isabel Archer and the spunkiness of a Maggie Verver represented virtues missing in a society dominated by men. It was easy for him to feel the greatest sympathy for women; their quiet resistance and even martyrdom exposed the nature of the society, European as well as American, that fascinated him. But could rigid little Amherst be thought of as "society" when he had such contempt for *Boston?* "I don't even dislike it!" he wrote. Dickinson in all her *privacy* would have seemed to James as ineffectual as everything else he condescended to in the New England he had long put behind him.

Yet to be a "woman writer" was in nineteenth-century New England to be distinguished. In a Maine inn there long hung a group picture of "Our Female Authors." Some of them had not been photographed with the others but had been painted in. Standing together in their heavy black dresses and fencelike bustles, they clearly strengthened each other against anything one of them might disapprove of. There were Harriet Beecher Stowe and Julia Ward Howe, Louisa May Alcott and Louise Chandler Moulton, Elizabeth Stuart Phelps and Helen Hunt Jackson, Rebecca Harding Davis and Sarah Orne Jewett, Mary E. Wilkins Freeman and Rose Terry Cooke. Looking at that solid phalanx of "authoresses," most of them ministers' daughters and ministers' wives, one silently protested that Harriet Beecher Stowe was a big talent, Sarah Orne Jewett at least a genuine one, and that it was wrong to club them in with women who were merely earnest or merely clever—or merely women.

Henry Adams, who was married to the brightest woman in Washington, had no greater praise for a woman than that she was brighter than her husband. Why were the leading men in America—men in general—so lacking in color? Henry James was stirred to write *The Bostonians* by the "decline in the sentiment of sex." The men in his book are generally ineffectual, but woman's representative figure, Olive Chancellor, is positively military in her resistance to men. This did not save Olive from defeat at the hands of a reactionary ex-Confederate, no believer in women's equality with men, who took helpless Verena Tarrant away from Olive. Woman's brightness, as James could never forget about his old friend Marian Adams, somehow lent itself to tragedy. But was a "bright" woman more tragic than the "pure" woman—the wives of Mark Twain, Howells, Lincoln, McKinley, who were all neurasthenic in the fashion of the time and some of them erratic, like Mary Lincoln and Ida McKinley? "Bright" or not, all such suffering women—passive women—were left so by the absence from their lives of the great American drive for success. Dickinson in the midst of the Civil War:

> What Soft—Cherubic Creatures—
> These Gentlewomen are—
> One would as soon assault a Plush—
> Or violate a Star—

Meanwhile, the business class sacrificed itself to what William James would call the "bitch goddess." No wonder Henry Adams and Henry James thought American men usually less interesting than their women. Emily Dickinson's knowledge of men did not include the business class. The Dickinson men—grandfather, father, brother—were by profession trustees of a clerical tradition transferred to the education of young men, embodied in Amherst College. Thanks to the invaluable biography of Emily Dickinson by Richard B. Sewall, we know that brother Austin, though Amherst College's treasurer like his father before him, lacked his father's iron character. (He had an affair with the wife of the college astronomer, Mabel Loomis Todd.) The father was "Squire Dickinson," a natural leader, the college treasurer for thirty-eight years, a Whig congressman. His daughter said that on Sunday her father read only "lonely and rigorous books." Courting his future wife, Edward Dickinson told her that he looked forward not to pleasure but to a life of "rational happiness." When he died, his daughter wrote that "his heart is pure and terrible and I think no other like it exists."

New England after the Civil War was out of the running, which helps to account for the terrible purity of most Dickinsons—whose type of mind was still clinging to considerations of Immortality in the hoggish times of President Grant. Her being an anachronism was good for Emily Dickinson's poetry, if not for her rational happiness. The good New England writers left were the last leaves on the Puritan tree. Harriet Beecher Stowe was established as an eccentric; Sarah Orne Jewett was an exquisite but ultimately too fragile miniaturist of Maine villages and farms, of totally ignorable lives that did not seem to be part of the Age of Enterprise. The more New England became a tradition, like Cornwall and Brittany, the more its heavy sense of its own past, of its intellectual virtue and moral fractiousness, lent itself to subtle historical novels like Stowe's *The Minister's Wooing*. And this before the Civil War; after it, as James satirized it all in *The Bostonians,* the great tradition had become a cameo, a photograph album. The Yankee who founded the country's religious tradition had become a curiosity.

Emily Dickinson, however, had no other world to write about or to write from. The voice of her poetry is peculiarly immediate, exclamatory, anguished, and antic in its concern; it is the most concentrated cry for life we are to hear from an American in her time.

Not in this World to see his face—

> Papa above!
> Regard a Mouse
> O'erpowered by the Cat!

> For each ecstatic instant
> We must an anguish pay
> In keen and quivering ratio
> To the ecstasy.

> After great pain, a formal feeling comes—
> The Nerves sit ceremonious, like Tombs—
> The stiff Heart questions was it He, that bore,
> And Yesterday, or Centuries before?

> Dare you see a Soul *at the White Heat?*
> Then crouch within the door—
> Red—is the Fire's common tint—
> But when the vivid Ore
> Has vanquished Flame's conditions,
> It quivers from the Forge
> Without a color, but the light
> Of unanointed Blaze.

The concentration of person is "naked," forceful, goes straight to the issue, which is solitary existence in all its pain and illusion. But even the poems that begin as unrestrained exclamations proceed in a line of minute thought. They operate as syllogisms, riddles, dialectic exercises: the "I" and its enclosures, opposites, extensions, frightenings, fight each other for ascendency. There is a constant battle with unreality as with "reality," a need to lay the ghost.

> I felt a Funeral, in my Brain,
> And Mourners to and fro
> Kept treading—treading—till it seemed
> That Sense was breaking through—

And when they all were seated,
A Service, like a Drum—
Kept beating—beating—till I thought
My Mind was going numb—

And then I heard them lift a Box
And creak across my Soul
With those same Boots of Lead, again,
Then Space—began to toll,

As all the Heavens were a Bell,
And Being, but an Ear,
And I, and Silence, some strange Race
Wrecked, solitary, here—

And then a Plank in Reason, broke,
And I dropped down, and down—
And hit a World, at every plunge,
And Finished knowing—then—

The problem of life for the modern artist (and ultimately for everyone else) is that consciousness may exist for its own sake. To be "attentive," to be endlessly aware, even with no object or purpose in view, is in Emily Dickinson's view to be alive, to live a life fraught with danger. To be alive is to be alone with consciousness, and the only resolution is to "see" this to the end. This was a favorite thought of Henry James and, he liked to add, was all his religion. He was to write that the business of the artist was to carry "the field of consciousness further and further, making it lose itself in the ineffable . . . ; that is all my revelation or secret." Emerson, for whom the revolution of the times was to bring "man to consciousness," did not think that the business of consciousness was to struggle against death. Not even in the vicinity of death. "As for death, it has nothing to do with me." Dickinson's greatest poem, "Because I could not stop for Death," would carry consciousness to the very sight of the grave. Earlier she had not been afraid to record the slightest intimations of death in all their queerness, unexpectedness, marginal terror.

There's a certain Slant of light,
Winter Afternoons—
That oppresses, like the Heft
Of Cathedral Tunes—

She was not afraid to write "Heavenly Hurt, it gives us"—"Heavenly" had to do with distance, not grace; this particular poem is in fact an exploration of "Hurt," the impact from afar, the shudder of awe in itself. Even more than is usual with her, who is metaphysical *and* sceptical, she plainly says about what "oppresses" that

> None may teach it—Any—
> 'Tis the Seal Despair—
> An imperial affliction
> Sent us of the Air—

Of course this poem can be taken as just another moment of depression, or as a meticulous rendering of how winter twilight in the Connecticut Valley can sink the heart. But Dickinson never became depressed without raising an issue: "Heavenly Hurt, it gives us." There is no scar (a certain slight terror just passed us by), "But internal difference, / Where the Meanings, are." Everything is interior, personal, and just possibly of not the slightest reverberation for anyone else. The whole poem is so closeted in the deepest intimacy that it is also about anonymity. It is the projected "Landscape" that "listens"; it is "Shadows" that "hold their breath." And when that certain Slant of light finally goes, "'tis like the Distance / On the look of Death"—the dead person is visually alone and apart. The *us* struck by "Heavenly Hurt" has been all alone, but this poem of meticulous consciousness shows the "distance" indeed *between* us and death.

Whitman "praised" Death. Dickinson took on the last passage of life and thought before nullity took over. Victorian America made a ceremony of what has been called "the snug sofa"—the weepy, crowded, Victorian business of dying in company; this was supposed to provide consolation. There was a vast "consolation literature" that rose to expected heights in describing the serenity with which the faithful faced death: the dying had to do it right so as to assure the survivors. This was not always possible. Walt Whitman's brother Andrew was reported in the family to be "very desirous of having us around him when he died. The poor boy seemed to think that that would take nearly all the horror of it away." A violent death, such as Melville delighted to put into *Moby-Dick,* seemed hostile to the spirit of consolation so natural to the Christian Republic. The almost one million casualties in the Civil War could be treated sacramentally by noncombatants like Walt Whitman, but survivors like Ambrose Bierce and Oliver Wendell Holmes, Jr., were sardonic on the subject. The real view of soldiers, which young Stephen Crane absorbed thoroughly, is the lesson of *The Red Badge of Courage:* "He had been to touch the great death, and found that, after all, it was but the great death—for others."

Deathbeds were the peak of social experience in Amherst, just ahead of weddings and the college commencement. They afforded a break not entirely unwelcome in such a drowsy town.

> There's been a Death, in the Opposite House,
> As lately as Today—
> I know it, by the numb look
> Such Houses have—alway—
>
> The Neighbors rustle in and out—
> The Doctor—drives away—
> A Window opens like a Pod—
> Abrupt—mechanically—
>
> Somebody flings a Mattress out—
> The Children hurry by—
> They wonder if it died—on that—
> I used to—when a Boy—
>
> The Minister—goes stiffly in—
> As if the House were His—
> And He owned all the Mourners—now—
> And little Boys—besides—
>
> And then the Milliner—and the Man
> Of the Appalling Trade—
> To take the measure of the House—
>
> There'll be that Dark Parade—
>
> Of Tassels—and of Coaches—soon—
> It's easy as a Sign—
> The Intuition of the News—
> In just a Country Town—

Dickinson was to lose a particular friend, Frazar Stearns, in the war; in a letter to her cousin Louise Norcross about the deaths of two Amherst brothers, she wrote an apprehensive elegy over Stearns before his death.

> I hope that ruddy face won't be brought home frozen.
> Poor little widow's boy, riding tonight in the mad wind,
> back to the village burying-ground where he never
> dreamed of sleeping! Ah! the dreamless sleep!

Death was a public event. It was awful but an occasion. What fascinated Dickinson was the ebbing away that nothing could conceal, the private doubts and open terror that piety could not absorb. Something like amusement shows in Dickinson's ability to make death the worst possible shock.

But in the day-to-day struggle that made up her life and became her text, death was the great weakening, the most intimate diminution of the strength necessary to her frail body and uncertain morale. It raised every possible question about our destiny while providing minute omens of future dissolution. Death, starting with every thought of her own death, became her favorite topic as well as her chief connection to Eternity. For a woman always hanging on some precipice of consciousness, transfixed by the incessant eventfulness outside her door,

> These are the days when Birds come back—
> A very few—a Bird or two—
> To take a backward look.
>
> These are the days when skies resume
> The old—old sophistries of June—
> A blue and gold mistake.

Death was virtually "irresistible." No novelist could have been so fascinated with the ultimate *scene* as the poet who began,

> I heard a Fly buzz—when I died—
> The Stillness in the Room
> Was like the Stillness in the Air—
> Between the Heaves of Storm—

The dying person and our attentiveness become one and the same. The minute observation so long practiced on birds, snakes, the drift of clouds, now sees, in an ecstasy of plainness, whatever there is to see.

> The Eyes around—had wrung them dry—
> And Breaths were gathering firm
> For that last Onset—when the King
> Be witnessed—in the Room—

Who else, thinking as if from the deathbed, would have thought "last Onset"—and have made it "King" while granting Death nothing but effect? Death, the supreme power, makes the dying small indeed and even "cute."

> I willed my Keepsakes—Signed away
> What portion of me be
> Assignable—

But in the end consciousness, struggling with itself (as always) to endure, to keep *some* victory for itself against the superior universe, has its say, its last say.

and then it was
There interposed a Fly—

With Blue—uncertain stumbling Buzz—
Between the light—and me—
And then the Windows failed—and then
I could not see to see—

v

The Romantic transcendentalists found death no trouble. Thoreau was wonderfully haughty about its lack of connection with him. "How plain," he once wrote to Emerson, "that death is only the phenomenon of the individual or class. Nature does not recognize it, she finds her own again under new forms without loss. Yet death is beautiful when seen to be a law, & not an accident—It is as common as life."

When it finally came Thoreau's turn, the Concord sheriff Sam Staples said of Thoreau that he had never seen a man dying in such perfect peace. Even Melville's Ishmael could jauntily boast: "here goes for a cool, collected dive at death and destruction, and the devil fetch the hindmost." Thoreau ended his beautiful prose poem, the book of total aspiration that he identified with his life, on Spring and one other symbol of resurrection:

> Every one has heard the story which has gone the rounds of New England, of a strong and beautiful bug which came out of the dry leaf of an old table of apple-tree wood, which had stood in a farmer's kitchen for sixty years, first in Connecticut, and afterwards in Massachusetts,—from an egg deposited in the living tree many years earlier still. . . . Who does not feel his faith in a resurrection and immortality strengthened by hearing of this?

So *Walden* ends in rapture: "such is the character of that morrow which mere lapse of time can never make to dawn." Dickinson could never have written "mere lapse of time." Since "time" was something more to her than her one possession, it was not something to be "eclipsed." God, she wrote to Higginson, was an eclipse; she alone in her family was not in the habit of asking Him for anything. God was idea, not a person. He was the greatest longing. "God is the name of my desire," Tolstoy told Gorky. And if He was not always real, death was. Death turned life itself into an idea—it became the final idea as well as our idea of everything final.

Dickinson could not limit death to a "law"—or "praise" it, as Whitman did, because it was "fathomless." Living with death as a great event in her life, hearing of death every day in that Civil War year that saw her write more poems than there were days, she lived intimately with death, as people used to do in the nineteenth century. It was not something you could omit from the day's register. But neither was it with any claim to certainty the bridge to a "higher realm." But it was certainly a bridge. How, when you came to it, to approach and seize it for what it had to say to you as the *next* stage of consciousness that was still the task of life?

What fascinated Dickinson the poet was each detail of the dying consciousness. Her lifetime investment in the poem as miniature made her see that only the barest lyric could render so much finality, the purest personal fantasy of travelling into death with the mind radiantly poised for novelty. Prose fiction can include such a theme but soon passes over it. The poem and the journey into death would have to be identical in order to make the *humility* of the human state the real feature of the work.

There is nothing of its time and place so charming as the poem that begins

> Because I could not stop for Death—
> He kindly stopped for me—

yet by the time we come to the end,

> Since then—'tis Centuries—and yet
> Feels shorter than the Day
> I first surmised the Horses' Heads
> Were toward Eternity—

we can experience the shudder of awe that Goethe described as man's highest tribute to the universe. The great decorum of this courtly poem—on the surface so ironically demure—is that, binding us to that final "shudder," it leaves us with the perfect enigma, terse, irrefutable, incommunicable. The horses' heads were toward Eternity; there is no going back. The effect of the poem is "dying"—stanza by stanza we see less and less of what we are passing through, what is soon behind us.

> We passed the School, where Children strove
> At Recess—in the Ring—
> We passed the Fields of Gazing Grain—
> We passed the Setting Sun—

What that famous Eternity is we cannot say.

So much in Dickinson is "symbol," but the key word in the fourth line of the first stanza, Immortality, does not symbolize anything. It is a state of mind. She describes the journey into death (nothing was more familiar by

1863, with the news from the front). She suggests to the uttermost the dying of the light, the lengthening strangeness, then the stricken awareness of the irrevocable.

> We paused before a House that seemed
> A Swelling of the Ground—
> The Roof was scarcely visible—
> The Cornice—in the Ground—

The shock may be our strongest sense of death as long as we can be shocked. The frail Dickinson gives us a sudden sense of the most that we can know. We are with it, all the way. There is no blinking anything. We see the human soul stretched to the furthest, valor encompassing the total end of things. And she was alone with this. But "I would eat evanescence slowly."

8

Creatures of Circumstance:
Mark Twain

Only an American would have seen in a single lifetime
the growth of the whole tragedy of civilization from the
primitive forest clearing.

BERNARD SHAW TO HAMLIN GARLAND, 1904

I went right along, not fixing up any particular plan, but
just trusting to Providence to put the right words in my
mouth when the time came; for I'd noticed that Providence always did put the right words in my mouth, if I
left it alone.

MARK TWAIN, *Huckleberry Finn*

All I wanted was to go somewheres; all I wanted was a
change.

MARK TWAIN, *Huckleberry Finn*

I

He was a redhead five feet, eight inches tall, liked to make it five feet, eight
and a half, and he talked constantly. He had a professional drawl and a
resonant twang even in private that struck William James as perverse, his
brother Henry as wistful. But from the "lecture" platform on which he
performed for a lifetime he was the delight of audiences from Western
mining camps in the 1860s to Freud's Vienna in the 1890s. He would shuffle
out on the stage in slippers, hands in his pockets, stare impassively at the
eagerly waiting faces until the first giggles told him that he had them
thoroughly at his mercy. "His carefully studied effects," Howells wrote in
My Mark Twain, "would reach the first rows in the orchestra first, and ripple
in laughter back to the standees against the wall, and then with a fine

resurgence come again to the rear orchestra seats, and so rise from gallery to gallery till it fell back, a cataract of applause from the topmost rows of seats."

He had only to make some pleasantly derisive sounds to leave them "howling" with delight. "Howling," along with "astonishment," were among Samuel Langhorne Clemens's favorite words. They stood for the raw, total, unlimited gush of pleasure he expected to arouse by just talking. He was the champion funnyman, the smartest voice out of the West. When he was in his late sixties and lived on lower Fifth Avenue, people went into raptures at the sight of Mark Twain talking to a friend and followed him up the avenue for miles. "Howling" also stood for his scale of feeling; his scorn was equally extreme. The loud clarity and positiveness of his feelings explain the brightness of his style. Anything he said, because of the confidence with which he said it, sounded right. And all this arose not just from his love of talk, from his perfected and professional skill in writing as if he were still talking, but from his enjoyment of himself, which he exuded like the smoke from his ever-present cigar. There was a tradition in the South and on the frontier of "selling" oneself by talk. His father, a transplant from Virginia to Missouri who failed to make anything out of the "Tennessee land" he had once bought, talked his family into the dream that the land would yet make them rich. Talk would become the son's favorite show of power.

Long before he "astonished" all those drifters, prospectors, gamblers, and other stray journalists in Nevada, young Sam Clemens in Hannibal must have sounded like his Tom Sawyer—amazing the home folks by his inventiveness and spiel. His style was formed on his lifelong relish of himself as a performer. And forever pushing the performer into action was this perennial boy's awareness of being a favorite, a star. He expected people to hang on his words, and he always meant to "astonish" them, to take them over. The glow of his style would obscure the raw dread he got into *Huckleberry Finn*, the violence of *A Connecticut Yankee in King Arthur's Court*.

He was the favorite, the winner, the Jim Dandy all-American boy (and man: in old age his entourage spoke of him as "King"). Like many another "real live nephew of my Uncle Sam," he was always on stage; his delivery was sardonic and his message the wisecrack. All in the "American" style. And what was that style, now, but "irreligion," scepticism in all things, dissolution in any direction of the eternal verities? No one before the Civil War, no one not from the West, would ever have mustered the poker face to get away with "the calm confidence of a Christian with four aces." In Mark Twain everything went to express suspicion and to conceal hostility by laughing at something or someone established. He was a Southern Presbyterian scornful of sky-blue transcendental Yankee idealism, a poor boy from a family that still believed itself to be "quality," and he was kept hysterical by expecting wealth from the "Tennessee land." An overpowering egotist as well as an always vulnerable one, he had acquired in mining camps, saloons, and newspaper offices a bumptiousness, a special swagger. He was everlastingly the verbal winner, the fastest mouth in Virginia City, San Francisco, and Hawaii.

What formed Mark Twain's perennial "act" was the underplayed but unmistakable attack on belief and believers. No matter how friendly he remained to the end of his life with the Reverend Joe Twichell, no matter how often he assured "Livy" that he might yet be as content with church-going as others in their prosperous Hartford set, a preeminent object of his many dislikes was the church, churchgoers, prayer meetings, and the complacent banalities of established clerics. A profoundly middle-class soul himself for all his mischievousness, the very type of the boastful, loud, frantically unsure promoter, he used his "low" experiences to needle the "quality" without for a moment sacrificing the aggressiveness of the one and his respect for the other. His striking doubleness in so many American activities, his histrionic expressions of guilt at being a divided soul, were the predicament that he turned into his greatest feat. Mark Twain never ceased to be Mr. Clemens.

What rankled most (in a nature that luxuriated in irritations) was Christianity's assumption of unity, of a creation overseen by Providence. The truth was not in any organized body or systematic belief, for there was no single truth. It was certainly not in the mind alone, as Emerson had preached. There was nothing but the mixed-up pieces of our raw human nature. This realism was crucial to Mark Twain's enduring popularity; after Cooper, he was the first significant American writer to whom people turned just for pleasure, without thought of improving themselves. Just as his one great book is an example of what the French call *le roman fleuve,* the novel which carries life along like a river and is as wayward as the great river that flows through *Huckleberry Finn,* so his genius was always in some sense for the circumstantial, never the abstract formula. After Mark Twain, many an early American classic would seem too ardent. His large, ever-larger audience, in Europe as well as in America, made him the most loved and the best rewarded of American writers. His humor—always on the attack—was certainly not "ardent" about anything. He lacked the intellectual will to give life one dominating shape. His work required none of the training needed to meet Captain Ahab when the great man ranted, "Who's over me? Truth hath no confines!"

Mark Twain's famous "naturalness," his ability beyond anything else to give an episodic quality to life, spoke to a generation not altogether alarmed by the recognition that there was no necessary connection between man and the universe. His genius for improvisation was as important as his instinct for ridicule. Nothing he ever wrote—not even the determinism of *What Is Man?* and his other outcries in old age against the old American confidence and self-approval—was deliberated for a pilgrim race to make use of. His worst books were written as spontaneously as his best, and many of his projects resembled promoters' schemes in Western lands that came to nothing. He thought *Joan of Arc* his best book. *Huckleberry Finn* was dropped for six years on the principle that "as long as a book would write itself, I was a faithful and interested amanuensis and my industry did not flag, but the minute that the book tried to shift to *my* head the labor of contriving its situations and conducting its conversations, I put it away and dropped it out of my mind." When he picked it up again, he did not understand how much this novel-as-river had been moving in some deep channel of its own. Before he turned the last ten chapters over to Tom Sawyer, he established in the book's harshest scene, the murder of Boggs and the simplicity of the people in this "little one-horse town in a big bend," the hateful yet comic truth written entirely from inside Southern society.

Emerson dreamed that the earth revolving in space was an apple and that he ate it. By contrast with the Romantic will to absorb the world into oneself, Mark Twain made the world laugh as he exposed the rawness and deceitfulness of human nature. He softened the awful truth by enjoying his own performance so much. There was nothing to fear—not yet. Mark Twain darkened only as the century did. The performer kept a certain lordly air, like Colonel Sherburn in *Huckleberry Finn* deriding the mob come to lynch him, even as he paraded the new Western frontiersman. He flourished in all possible American worlds and was free to comment on anything in his own way. He was a dissolvent of the old ways while unmistakably keeping some privileged independence and, like a good Southerner, his ancestral place.

II

Henry James is supposed to have said that only primitive people could enjoy Mark Twain. Mark Twain was always more popular in England than James, who was not popular there at all. He was a favorite on the Continent, where James would never have an audience. Of course "delicious poor dear old M.T.," as James condescended after their one meeting, was no more "primitive" than James himself. He was intensely respectful—for himself—of all Victorian amenities. But growing up with the country, as James never did, absorbing its unrest, its extremes of poverty and wealth, its crudest lust for power and position, he naturally identified himself with the many Americans who were forever fighting it out, just barely keeping their heads above water. James gave primacy to his own impressions; this made Europe sacred as the favorite source of his impressions. Mark Twain's first book, *The Innocents Abroad* (1869), typically took him to Europe and other holy places as a destroyer, the "American vandal."

These two major storytelling talents, of a time and place when realistic fiction began to dominate our literature, did not feel that *they* were living in the same time or place. They could not read each other. Mark Twain said he would rather be "damned to John Bunyan's heaven" than have to read *The Bostonians,* conceivably the one James novel he might have attempted for its satire on respectable New England. But as he confessed to Kipling, he did not read fiction at all; he preferred biography and history, *fact* books. The genius of fiction and the waywardness of nineteenth-century America permitted James and Mark Twain to make contraries of storytelling, of form, of literature itself, while retaining their parity as individualists.

In the end both came to what James called "the imagination of disaster" —James because his conservative "tradition," sacred Europe, was as corrupt as anything else; Mark Twain because nothing failed him like success. But disasters were only the outer shell of capitalism, the great God of chance, the Balzac novel of grandeur and decline that every ambitious nineteenth-century soul lived through. James, who was to say that the starting point of all his work was "loneliness," tried to find in society imaginatively considered what he despaired of finding in lasting affection. Mark Twain came to say that "the greater the love, the greater the tragedy." Even the women in his family were too frail to support his demand for constant assurance; wife and daughters sickened, then died on him.

But James and Mark Twain were certainly Americans of their time and place. Both began life under the rule of overwhelmingly religious fathers: James became indifferent to organized religion, Mark Twain hostile. Both were wanderers from earliest age; both were significantly without the conventionalizing university stamp that our bravest speculative minds—Whitman, Melville, Dickinson—were also free of. Both became preeminent literary figures very early, always with *some* audience for James, an eager one for Mark Twain, and were indefatigable producers into their seventies. Both were star writers for the new magazines that made fiction a going concern in their time. Yet both were increasingly idiosyncratic and uneasy in relation to the mainstream of fiction in English; both felt in old age that their audiences had not kept up with their originality and independent force. Both, despite their great success in society, their attraction (Mark Twain's was magnetic) for the great and powerful, ended up American isolates like Hawthorne, Melville, Dickinson, Whitman.

Mark Twain's harshly Calvinist father died broke when his younger son was twelve, leaving with him a searing memory of having to look at his father's corpse—no doubt because it exposed the ultimate humiliation of the human body. He was a wandering printer in his teens, a newspaperman, a silver miner, an editor, a correspondent, a professional humorist, and finally, after a practical and respectable Victorian marriage, a newspaper owner, property owner, and best seller on the subscription system. This fabulous American career, representing America to itself, made Mark Twain the legendary example of what his friend William Dean Howells called the post–Civil War type—"the man who has risen." Unlike the general type, Mark Twain became the man who saw through the pretenses of society. The frontier, Howells said, made Mark Twain more "the creature of circumstances than the Anglo-American type." It broke up all cultural traditions even when it wanted to respect them; it was derisive of the consolations of religion even when it retained the church as an institution and a social control; it *lived* the survival of the fittest; it naturally venerated the profit motive, the predatory character, the rich strike, and the eventual domination by monopoly. It took violence as the proof of manhood, made a cult of woman, the "good" woman, at a time—as you never learn from Mark Twain —when whoring as well as boozing and gambling were the chief distractions from prospecting. The frontier, having no tradition, worked on images of the past like acid.

It also created the picturesque figure of the liar, the deceiving teller of tales, the professional hoodwinker of the innocents back East. The West became an idyll even when—sometimes because—its inescapable savagery could not be concealed. It became a fundamental article of romance for some new realists. His assiduously pleasing friend Howells, from the old Western Reserve (Ohio) but long since merged into Boston, adored "Clemens" (the two were always "Clemens" and "Howells" to each other) because the Western environment seemed to stick to him. Howells said he never tired, even when he wished to sleep, watching his friend lounge through hotel rooms in the long nightgown he preferred and telling the story of his life, "the inexhaustible, the fairy, the Arabian nights story, which I could never tire of even when it began to be told again."

As Howells told it in *My Mark Twain* after his friend's death in 1910, the man melted into the career, the career into the country, the country into a legend of endless advancement, freshness, gusto. Somehow the legend always came back to the idea of Mark Twain as the perfect American type, a Westerner, "more dramatically the creature of circumstances than the old Anglo-American type."

> He found himself placed in them and under them, so near to a world in which the natural and the primitive were obsolete, that while he could not escape them, neither could he help challenging them. The inventions, the appliances, the improvements of the modern world invaded the hoary eld of his rivers and forests and prairies, and, while he was still a pioneer, a hunter, a trapper, he found himself confronted with the financier, the scholar, the gentleman. They seemed to him, with the world they represented, at first very droll, and he laughed. They set him to thinking, and, as he was never afraid of anything, he thought over the whole field and demanded explanations of all his prepossessions—of equality, of humanity, of representative government and revealed religion. When they had not their answers ready, without accepting the conventions of the modern world as solutions or in any manner final, he laughed again, not mockingly, but patiently, compassionately. Such, or something like this, was the genesis and evolution of Mark Twain.

Howells, like Mark Twain a self-educated printer and reporter, had learned very early how to play up to Boston's good opinion when Boston was still authority. Charles Eliot Norton must have been thinking of the smoothly dutiful Howells when he described the writers *he* knew as "the best that the world has seen . . . the pleasantest to live with, the best-intentioned and honestest." Howells knew how to please—and to be pleased. Mark Twain was an endless surprise and delight to him, he was so "free." Howells constantly praised Mark Twain's freedom to Mark Twain even when, reading proof on *Tom Sawyer,* he sighed over Huck Finn's saying "they comb me all to hell" and had it changed to "they comb me all to thunder": "I'd have that swearing out in an instant. I suppose I didn't notice it because the locution was so familiar to my Western sense, and so exactly a thing that Huck would say. But it wont [*sic*] do for the children." Mark Twain's endless spoofs and explosive temper were prime contrasts to the fat little man who in one photograph of the two eminent authors is wearing spats while his famously temperamental friend looks as if he is about to tear into the photographer.

In *My Mark Twain* Howells purred over Mark Twain dead as he had purred over Mark Twain alive. Mark Twain was not really a pioneer and he was never a hunter or a trapper. At the end of his life he felt betrayed by many a financier, but he adored the Standard Oil Company's Henry Huddleston Rogers. "Hellcat Rogers," as he was known on Wall Street, helped rescue him from bankruptcy when the rich and successful Mark Twain lost almost everything trying to get still richer on the ill-fated Paige typesetting machine. While Mark Twain was a satirist of get-rich-quick schemes as early as *The Gilded Age* (1873), "the genesis and evolution of Mark Twain" can hardly be credited to his demanding "explanations of all his prepossessions —of equality, of humanity, of representative government and revealed religion." He ended up an angry and rebellious critic of many American beliefs, but only after he had come to feel that they had betrayed *him*.

Howells ended *My Mark Twain*: "Emerson, Longfellow, Lowell, Holmes—I knew them all and all the rest of our sages, poets, seers, critics, humorists; they were like one another and like other literary men; but Clemens was sole, incomparable, the Lincoln of our literature." The highest tribute from Howells is "Western sense." And it is true that Mark Twain, like Lincoln, was a Westerner, a type which, as late as 1925, F. Scott Fitzgerald could hymn at the end of *The Great Gatsby* as the soul of honesty fated to be corrupted by the East.

Like Lincoln, Mark Twain was restless and ambitious for the main chance before he knew what it was. Growing up in America's border country, a drifter in a generation of drifters, Mark Twain could have said, as Lincoln did during the Civil War, that he was never really in command of events. And if he seemed to have sprung out of the American ground, as Lincoln did, he also knew a hidden America of emptiness and secret terror. The celebrated funnyman was "often crazy in the night" and, like Lincoln, suffered the melancholy and unrest that deprecated self and told jokes. Unlike Lincoln, Mark Twain was a booster, believed for the longest time that success was his destiny, and was enraged by the slightest failure. Until he was old and it was almost too late, he did not know what it was like to stand apart from the circumstances of his life. He could describe them dynamically, picturesquely, but until life took him by the throat and amazed him by frightening him, he saw no alternative to the American epic of progress. His genius, his special luck, was to offer himself up as a new environment.

Turning his friend into "the Lincoln of our literature," Howells slighted an important aspect of Lincoln: his rationalism, objectivity, fixity of purpose. Lincoln never had a personal God; as he admitted in his greatest public utterance, the Second Inaugural, "the Almighty has His own purposes." This represented to Lincoln not chance but a divinity which he humbly recognized as beyond personal desire; it filled him with awe and made him feel that it was worthwhile living in a universe in which could be detected some mysterious tendency toward justice.

Mark Twain's world was all personal, disjointed, accidental. He was indeed, as Howells said, the "creature of circumstances." And so were his characters, which made them creatures of chance in a world more sceptical than had been seen before in the literature of "God's own country." "Circumstances" made Mark Twain, and the shock and fascination of them in succession gave the airy tone to his work. His genius lay in accumulating episodes; he turned life into a stream of facts and pictures—comic, unpredictable, exaggerated, wild—without overall meaning, without ideology, without religion.

From the beginning, Mark Twain's real subject—against a landscape of unlimited expectations and constant humbling—was the human being as animal nature, human cussedness taken raw, single traits magnified as fun, pretense, burlesque, spectacle, and violence. He took from the blatant demonstrativeness of frontier humor its central image of man undomesticated, removed from his traditional surroundings—a stranger wandering into a thin and shifting settlement of other strangers, then plunging into a dizzying succession of experiences always "new."

Mark Twain is the ancestor of all that twentieth-century fiction of Southern poverty, meanness, and estrangement that was out of step with American moralism and pious abstractionism. The characters are generally low, and there is no attempt to make them less so. Southern characters just *lived*, without ostensible purpose, sometimes in mud everlasting, as do the "Arkansaw" characters in that "little one-horse town in a big bend"—chapter 21 of *Huckleberry Finn*—where Colonel Sherburn will shoot down poor, miserable Boggs. This is the poor white's South before (and after) the Civil War, not the plantation house from which Colonel Sherburn scorned the mob.

All the streets and lanes was just mud; they warn't nothing else *but* mud—mud as black as tar, and nigh about a foot deep in some places; and two or three inches deep in *all* the places. The hogs loafed and grunted around, everywheres. You'd see a muddy sow and a litter of pigs come lazying along the street and whollop herself down in the way, where folks had to walk around her, and she'd stretch out, and shut her eyes, and wave her ears, whilst the pigs was milking her, and look as happy as if she was on salary. And pretty soon you'd hear a loafer sing out, "hi! *so* boy! sick him, Tige!" and away the sow would go, squealing most horrible, with a dog or two swinging to each ear, and three or four dozen more a-coming; and then you would see all the loafers get up and watch the thing out of sight, and laugh at the fun and look grateful for the noise. Then they'd settle back again till there was a dog-fight. There couldn't anything wake them up all over, and make them happy all over, like a dog-fight—unless it might be putting turpentine on a stray dog and setting fire to him, or tying a tin pan to his tail and see him run himself to death.

Mark Twain, as he could have said, "sort of specialized" in characters who "just lived"—who perhaps lived to talk. They talked all the time, performing for each other in a world relieved from emptiness only by the comic imagination in talk. What other writers always noticed about Mark Twain was how professional he was with them, tailoring himself to a particular audience. He talked as he wrote, wrote as he talked, to the point of developing the most "lifelike" "right" rhythm in sentence after sentence of just the right length, with always the telling emphasis in just the right place. He talked and talked so inexhaustibly at any audience that in his regular changes of mood he felt sheepish and even guilty for making such demands on everyone within earshot. But talk was the way he lived and in a sense what he lived for. As he said in his account of his brief and inglorious time as a Confederate volunteer, "The Private History of a Campaign That Failed," he was "an experienced, industrious, ambitious, and often quite picturesque liar." Everything came out of the "perversest twang and drawl," that endless flow of words, sweet and right in its rhythm for all occasions.

His always appreciative friend Howells, who was never picturesque but became a dainty and unerring Victorian stylist, had also learned the right use of words at the type fount and the newspaper desk. Those once self-educated, literature-mad American writers and speechifiers! Howells knew that his friend's extraordinary power to write as cleverly as he talked represented a tapping of the half-conscious mind in its most relaxed rhythm. It seemed to Howells that no other writer had ever captured the elusive spontaneity of the human mind.

Near the end of his life Mark Twain dictated from bed the fragmentary, supposedly daring passel of unrelated reminiscences and anecdotes he called his *Autobiography*. There he spoke of his instinctive method.

With the pen in one's hand, narrative is a difficult art; narrative should flow *as* flows the brook down through the hills and the leafy woodlands, its course changed by every boulder it comes across and by every grass-clad gravelly spur that projects into its path; . . . a book that never goes straight for a minute, but *goes*, and goes briskly, sometimes ungrammatically, and sometimes fetching a horseshoe three-quarter of a mile around . . . but always going, and always following at least one law, always loyal to that law, the law of *narrative*, which *has no law.* Nothing to do but make the trip, the how of it is not important, so that the trip is made.*

III

Where did Mark Twain learn to write like that? To catch on paper, as he did in speech, the exact cadence of words as they fall within the mind? Of course the South produced great talkers, and like so many of its vehement personalities up to and including Lyndon Johnson, they knew how to apply pressure on people.† Mark Twain must have learned very early that the mouth must always be ready. The celebrated funnyman began as a bookish, sensitive, undersized, violently moody youngster who learned how to defend himself, then—like Tom Sawyer—to command a situation by throwing in occult references, interspersing a string of words between himself and every bit of trouble at hand.

The special "trick," the infallible trigger-quick snap and emphasis on the right word, was something more distinct, and purer, than the traditional gift of gab. Mark Twain's instinct is for the sentence, the thunderclap of surprise essential to the monologist—an effect usually more suited to the short poem, which must be all style, than to prose fiction. He knew, as Robert Frost was boastfully to put it, that "a sentence is a sound on which other sounds called words may be strung." A sentence in Mark Twain, as in Frost, is above all a right sound. Hemingway, for all his homage to *Huckleberry Finn* as the initiator of modern American writing, was a rhetorician who brought an ironic and brutal simplicity to a style not "natural" like Mark Twain's but ostentatiously reduced. Hemingway (like Thoreau) does not try to capture the spoken sound of a sentence. You can sense him checking his own spontaneity as he writes. He is a painter, a whittler, not a listener. Henry James, carrying his wholly mental English to the farthest periphery of conscious-

*The *Autobiography* was to be published only after his death, for "only dead men tell the truth." In a footnote to the "Aldrich Memorial," his description of the reluctant journey he and Howells made to the memorial for that eminently forgettable man Thomas Bailey Aldrich, Mark Twain was so alarmed that readers would learn that he disliked Mrs. Aldrich that he footnoted: "At this point I desire to give notice to my literary heirs, assigns and executors, that they are to suppress, for seventy-five years, what I am now about to say about that curious function. It is not that I am expecting to say anything that shall really need suppressing, but that I want to talk without embarrassment and speak with freedom—freedom, comfort, appetite, relish."

†"You have to be able to dominate the existence that you characterize. That is why I write about people who are more or less primitive." (Flannery O'Connor to a friend, September 30, 1966)

ness, somehow managed not to stumble even when he composed in rhythms that were not only removed from ordinary speech but were inconceivable from anyone but Henry James. Frost could have been speaking for Mark Twain when he wrote in a letter, "The vital thing, then, to consider in all composition is the ACTION of the voice,—sound—posturing, gesture. . . . Why was a friend so much more effective than a piece of paper in drawing the living sentences out of me? . . . I can't keep up any interest in sentences that don't SHAPE *on some speaking tone* of voice."

Some speaking tone of voice became the everyday voice of Mark Twain as he wrote. And what he heard in himself was often mimicry. The *edge* in people's voices, their littlest emphases and explosions, was something he could never resist putting down. They were the little "snags," in the mouth as on the river, the clots natural to speech before it floods on. Of course he knew from steamboat days, having had to memorize everything on the Mississippi, how to make words reproduce the river—"and by and by you could see a streak on the water which you know by the look of the streak that there's a snag there in a swift current which breaks on it and makes that streak look that way." But much of the line in a character's mouth is mimicry of every quantity of sound Mark Twain got down from someone's speech. "The streets was full, and everybody was excited." "The place to buy canoes is off of rafts laying up at shore. But we didn't see no rafts laying up so we went along during three hours and more." Mark Twain's often shrewish voice can be heard in Colonel Sherburn's scorn of the mob flocking up to his gate to lynch him after he has contemptuously murdered Boggs. The all-assertive inflections, the complacent self-reference, the unsparing *absoluteness* of every ad-hominem shot, is straight from the repertoire of Southern vocal duelling, public insult: "The idea of *you* lynching anybody! It's amusing. The idea of you thinking you had pluck enough to lynch a *man!* . . . Do I know you? I know you clear through. I was born and raised in the South, and I've lived in the North; so I know the average all around. The average man's a coward."

The pleasure we share in all this assertiveness is the pleasure of command —to command attention, to command the crowd. Mark Twain was sometimes "radical" when things went against him; he was no egalitarian. It is the eternal ego power of Tom Sawyer, that nonstop performer, that the old Mark Twain came to recognize in another show-off, Theodore Roosevelt, and heartily detested. No doubt with something of a twinge, for in old age, when he resembled King Lear more than he did Tom Sawyer, he called himself "an old derelict" and "God's fool." But the everlasting type, the genius of the ever-ready verbal topping, is Tom Sawyer. Tom, so prompt to trick and direct others, is clearly one version of what saved his alter ego, Mark Twain; the boy makes his way and always has his way by words alone. What pleasured Mark Twain most about youth—and this is the genius of Huck Finn, who is also no mean talker and a ready deceiver—is its capacity for first impressions, the aspect of discovery. Mark Twain's fellow Missourian T. S. Eliot, reading *Huckleberry Finn* in late middle age for the first time, noticed that the adult in Mark Twain was boyish, "and only the boyish side adult." The boy seems to have learned very early in life how to "handle" adults as well as the boy gang with words. His "angelic," decidedly mature, easily suffering wife sighingly called him "Youth."

I V

"It is a pity we cannot escape from life when we are young," Mark Twain wrote when he was seventy-one. His two most famous creations, Tom Sawyer and Huckleberry Finn, never had to grow up.* They remain eternally boys—*the* American boys of legend. More than any other characters in our literature, they convey a fabled freedom. Now virtually enshrined in time and place, the "old" Southwest frontier on the edge of the Mississippi, they seem to represent forever the newness of a new country.

Although no other writing in America has made boyhood seem so idyllic, a state sufficient unto itself, Mark Twain's own boyhood in Hannibal was secretly contradictory in feeling, often touched with dread. *The Adventures of Tom Sawyer* (the ingratiatingly offhand title) is for the most part, but not entirely, an equally chummy portrait of boyhood against a setting almost mythic in its selective use of the past. Mark Twain said that the book was "simply a hymn, put into prose to give it a worldly air." But when Howells, who counselled that the book be directed to children, allowed himself to wonder "why we hate the past so," his friend responded from the depths, "It's so humiliating."

The forty-year-old who composed *Tom Sawyer* in 1875–76 was far from his boyhood poverty and the old Southwest but not from the vehement uncertainties that were as much a mark of his character as his aggressive humor. The author of that "hymn" had become perhaps the most commercially successful author in America; his books were sold by a network of

---

*Though it is impossible to imagine Tom Sawyer as anything but a boy, Mark Twain's sassy brat, imagination in America has often indulged itself in the fantasy of Huck Finn grown old and not a bit less derelict as he haunts contemporary scenes of progress.

subscription agents who were hard to turn away from the door. He was one of the most public characters in America; somehow everyone knew how happy and prosperous Mark Twain was as he doted on his wife and four children and "humorously" complained of what it cost him to keep up in Hartford the large, overdecorated, ornately stuffed Victorian mansion. The house was another one of Mark Twain's many fantasies come to life. It had everything that the genteel tradition required of a successful man, but like Mark Twain himself for all his heartburnings, it was also defiantly up-to-date. It was the first house in Hartford with a telephone; Mark Twain was the first eminent American writer to possess a typewriter. There was a large staff; their flamboyant employer alternately boasted and cringed at what his servants cost him when he compared his laundry woman's wages with what his family in Hannibal had lived on. The Hartford enclave, Nook Farm, was literary, prosperous, clerical—"the quality" to the life. For a poor and once "shiftless" boy who at thirteen had been apprenticed to the local newspapers, and at eighteen had started his wandering career as a printer in St. Louis, New York, Philadelphia, Muscatine, Keokuk, and Cincinnati, Mark Twain at forty was certainly that post–Civil War type, "the man who has risen."

And he had done it all through *words*—which at times made him feel that everything he had gained by quicksilver cleverness, the stage drawl and the platform manner, was unreal. His life resembled a work of fiction made by works of fiction. He already had a disposition to think of his life as a "dream" —the American dream, of course, but one that also revealed a writer's tendency to wonder whether the thoughts and projects that occupied him day and night had any existence outside himself. At the end of his "wonderful century" whose many wonders he personified to his countrymen, he was to write in *The Mysterious Stranger* that the universe itself was a dream, thus rounding out a century of American solipsism.

In Nook Farm, Hannibal itself became a dream. The proud, opulent, but endlessly reminiscent Mark Twain was writing *Tom Sawyer* in the smug atmosphere of postwar Republicanism; the ragged Confederate volunteer was now a favorite orator at reunions of the Grand Army of the Republic.* He could not help touching up the past, to the point where it would all come

---

*No one in the North became so publicly admiring of General Grant, "who cannot deliver himself of even the simplest sentence," as the sprightliest of word-men, Mark Twain. He never tired of elevating Grant as the greatest but most modest of warriors. He would clearly have liked to put words into Grant's mouth. He did the next best thing by publishing Grant's memoirs when the great man, defrauded by those near him, went bankrupt. After the Paige typesetting machine had brought about his financial collapse, his rescue of Grant proved Mark Twain a resourceful man of business.

back less humiliating. But he now invented the past more than he renovated it. After all, *Tom Sawyer* was his first real novel.

Postwar America was already looking to the "old West" for a golden age. Our now-celebrated author had revisited Hannibal on a sentimental journey; he had gone up and down the great river to write his utterly sunshot pieces for the *Atlantic Monthly* on learning to be a steamboat pilot, *Old Times on the Mississippi*. The undestroyed vividness of his old associations amazed him. Had he ever left Hannibal?

> The things about me and before me made me feel like a boy again—convinced me that I was a boy again, and that I had been simply dreaming an unusually long dream. . . . During my three days' stay in the town, I woke up every morning with the impression that I was a boy—for in my dreams the faces were all young again, and looked as they had looked in the old times.

He recognized the melancholy limitations of his old life—how remote and isolated a village like "St. Petersburg" in *Tom Sawyer* could be, and how it forced "good" people together. (The "good" people furnish the authority figures in the town, and Tom Sawyer knows how to overcome them from time to time without displacing their authority, which he needs more than anything else to keep him perpetually in adventures.) The sunny togetherness of the town is really everyone's similarity; it excludes people different in "blood," like Injun Joe, the villain of *Tom Sawyer*, who is only half Indian but like a good citizen knows "the Injun blood ain't in me for nothing." Hannibal was bounded by the always mysterious and changeable river, by creepy stretches of forest and uninhabited river islands. Although the whole town seems to have spent Sunday going to church and getting recalcitrant boys and girls to Sunday school, anxiety and superstition came down to children from their elders, along with the rituals and superstitious oaths (Nature was still the Great Adversary) passed on by one generation of children to another.

v

Mark Twain had great trouble deciding whether *Tom Sawyer* was for children or for adults. In 1876, when he finally decided that it was a "children's book," the contrast between the respectable life he led and the untiring devotion of his hero to fun and games made it necessary for him to be arch —to keep a proper distance from his brat. Archness is all over *Tom Sawyer*. He may have had to return to the past in *Old Times on the Mississippi* and

Tom Sawyer in order to make Nook Farm real. There may have been some obscure guilt as he hobnobbed with the genially prosperous literati, preachers, and businessmen. With *Tom Sawyer*—the first of his books to show him entirely as objective storyteller—he capitalized on his early life. Before *Huckleberry Finn*, he had no greater story to tell than one about an irrepressibly imaginative boy who could make other boys submit to his (book-learned) fantasies.

It was a story to be told at a comfortable remove. The archness fitted the benevolence of middle-aged successes toward their younger selves, of urban leaders toward the old farm and the rustic village. Heavily Victorian Americans could feel that America was still young. Now that the dire Calvinist suspicions that children were as damnable as everyone else were done away with, boys and girls emerged sweet and cute, lovable and cherishable—as nice and as good, in short, as grownup Americans.

The growing comfort and self-satisfaction of middle-class life made happy families dote on their children as never before. There was little religious consolation when they died—Mark Twain was to lose three, and the death of one particularly beloved daughter at twenty-four was a shock he never got over. Anxiety in prosperity made the now-lovable American child as significant a type as the "shrewd" self-respecting Yankee. The child in popular American literature becomes a dear little fellow, the lovable urchin and "scamp," the professional "bad boy." These were milksops turned inside out, future leaders of American enterprise, from Thomas Bailey Aldrich's Tom Bailey to Booth Tarkington's Penrod.

One began to miss the clairvoyant Pearl in *The Scarlet Letter*. That child of sin had a cool and deadly Puritan eye for concealment. What simpleminded "rascals" barefoot American boys become in the illustrations to children's books, as they skip off to the ole fishing hole in a frayed straw hat and with one gallus trailing down their torn pants. What little darlings girls become in their yellow curls and starched ruffles—what "spirit" they show in the face of adversity!

Henry James in the last, unfinished volume of his autobiography, *The Middle Years*, described the passing of youth as a raid on "the enemy country, the country of the general lost freshness." Perhaps nowhere as in New England, with its race pride making up for its loss of moral authority, were so many children's books manufactured for magazines like *Youth's Companion*, *St. Nicholas*, *Riverside Magazine for Young People*, *Wide Awake*, *Our Young Folks*. No wonder that Mark Twain, at ease in Hartford, got into the game. Nowhere else did comfortableness with one's racial, social, religious, and financial well-being get itself complacently expressed in so many images of the *manly, sturdy, bright,* and *cheery* Protestant boy. Thomas Bailey Aldrich in *The Story of a Bad Boy:* "an amiable, impulsive lad, blessed with fine digestive powers, and no hypocrite . . . in short, I was a real human boy, such as you may meet anywhere in New England, and no more like the impossible boy in a storybook than a sound orange is like one that has been sucked dry."

No wonder that Mark Twain in Connecticut remembered the raw Missouri of the 1850s so fondly in *Tom Sawyer* as a place where children had no life but play. Of course he could not decide until the last moment whether this idyll, this hymn put into prose to give it a worldly air, was for children or adults. Howells, who knew the middle road in all things (until in the darkening nineties he grew weary of the Establishment and moved to New York), persuaded his friend to call *Tom Sawyer* a children's book. And it was Howells who had him remove innocent bits of real life from the novel (Becky sneaking a look at a naked body in teacher's anatomy text) as "awful good but too dirty." Howells always knew what the public would take, and he wrote straight *to* this public, whose inquiring photographer in fiction he was for so long that he felt he had been created by the reading public.

Nowhere as in America after the Civil War were there so many books for adults about children having fun. If the prosperous middle class in the United States already impressed European visitors as a society somehow geared to children, that was because it showed how prosperous, easy, and self-indulgent, how happy, prodigal, and *young,* adults could remain in America. The young had become the real Americans. This was a society that children could love without question. A child's high expectation of life, his high spirits and his general air of having a surplus vitality that, like surplus cash, had to be spent, proved the extraordinary good fortune that so many Americans were experiencing. The splendor of children in American literature of the time! Obviously some Americans felt as protected as only children ever do.

In *Tom Sawyer* Mark Twain was not yet ready to disclose the deep as well as the bright side of a Mississippi River boyhood. He celebrated boyhood as a state sufficient unto itself, almost entirely removed from the contingencies of the adult world. It is removed even from the looming sexuality of childhood and adolescence.

VI

When he revisited Hannibal and climbed Holiday's Hill to get a comprehensive view, Mark Twain felt himself back "in the midst of a time when the happenings of life were not the natural and logical results of great general laws, but of special orders, and were freighted with very precise and distinct purposes—partly punitive in intent, partly admonitory, and usually local in application." (Mark Twain could become self-consciously elevated when he was among the "quality" and writing *down*.) The world of *Tom Sawyer* is indeed under "special orders"—not only from adult to boy but from boy to boy. In imagination it is limited so generously to the wishes of boyhood that from one point of view it is unreal, which explains why Tom Sawyer himself, as well as his adventures, has become legendary. This boyhood will seem forever special to itself, privileged, a sport. There is no real family life in the book—Tom's mother is dead, he is being raised by his Aunt Polly; the father is never mentioned; nor do we ever find out why Sid is only Tom's half-brother or why cousin Mary seems to live in the same household. Joe Harper and other boys in the gang do have families—at least they have mothers, and thus God-fearing homes.

Huck Finn is the exception to all this. His father is the town drunk, and Huck has no home at all.

> Huckleberry came and went, at his own free will. He slept on doorsteps in fine weather and in empty hogsheads in wet; he did not have to go to school or to church, or call any being master or obey anybody; he could go fishing or swimming when and where he chose, and stay as long as it suited him; nobody forbade him to fight; he could sit up as late as he pleased; he was always the first boy that went barefoot in the spring and the last to resume leather in the fall; he never had to wash, nor put on clean clothes; he could swear wonderfully. In a word, everything that goes to make life precious, that boy had. So thought every harassed, hampered, respectable boy in St. Petersburg.

But Huck as exception to the respectable world of St. Petersburg is of only slight importance in *Tom Sawyer*. Tom is the driving force of the gang. Tom the "bad" boy—the supposedly bad boy, the predictably good boy—is not so much "bad" as he is impossibly romantic and even visionary. He is what he is because he reads "pirate" books and such, then tries to make his pranks (and those of the gang) live up to them.

Mark Twain as a famous author confessed that he did not care to read fiction. The young Sam Clemens in Hannibal must have read himself sick on stories of pirates, Robin Hood, medieval knights and ladies. (He was always romantic about the Middle Ages.) Tom Sawyer represents the future author's greatest fantasy: to turn life into a book. Of course there is a good deal of routine, boys-will-be-boys mischief. "And when she closed with a happy Scriptural flourish, he 'hooked' a doughnut." Tom must get the best of every encounter, confrontation, negotiation. Sceptics may see a future corporation type in Tom's ability to swap his inferior store of boy's goods —"twelve marbles, part of a jew's harp, a piece of blue bottle-glass to look through . . . a dog-collar but no dog"—for stuff slightly less inferior. His chief trait, which leads to his many (sometimes unbearable) intrigues, is his unquestioned sense of himself as guide and leader to every other boy in town. He is a born dominator, for he is totally—as young Sam Clemens must have been—at the mercy of his imagination. Whatever he has read of that world beyond the village, in which pirates and Robin Hood and medieval knights act out some "gorgeous" code, Tom himself must act out. Other boys follow him because they can no more resist Tom's wild fancy than we can resist Mark Twain's.

The most famous episode in *Tom Sawyer*—Tom's persuading his friends to pay him for the "privilege" of whitewashing Aunt Polly's fence—can be believed only if you recognize what a power of fantasy drives this mighty spieler. Tom can talk people into anything because no one else really shares, much less understands, his determination to live by the book. This gives him a power over them that reminds us of an author's power.

From his guardian, Aunt Polly, on down, the adults in St. Petersburg must also participate in the book Tom is acting out; they are the chorus, plaintive but unavailing, as Tom goes through his adventures. Near the opening of the book Aunt Polly laments the fact that Tom has just (again) escaped her control. "He's full of the Old Scratch, but laws-at-me! he's my own dead sister's boy, poor thing, and I ain't got the heart to lash him, somehow. I've *got* to do some of my duty by him, or I'll be the ruination of the child." So Tom can persuade even "hard-eyed" Joe Harper into sailing off with him as pirates to Jackson's Island. (Huck Finn "joined them promptly, for all careers were one to him; he was indifferent.") Tom can cajole the other boys into staying on the island when they are homesick; a great storm seems to bring the end of the world. In the book's most astonishing scene, a cold-blooded Tom can secretly revisit his home and stay mum while Aunt Polly and Mrs. Harper are lamenting the boys' death. Tom manages the shattering appearance of the boys at their own "funeral." As everyone says, you never did see a boy like him.

This writer has never found Tom "lovable." Tom is so bent on having life live up to his favorite stories that he takes over people's lives. But like the townspeople of St. Petersburg, one is impressed and even abashed by

Tom's power. That is the fascination of the book: Tom believes himself irresistible. A main consequence of *Tom Sawyer*'s being told in the third person is that Tom becomes a direct creation of Mark Twain's own arbitrary power to make this boy seem forever "special." Mark Twain keeps him a professional boy, incessantly a boy, nothing but a boy.

Tom is so special a boy that even though there are contradictions in his makeup, we can hardly bear to notice them—so compelling is the overpowering role he has to play throughout as the young prince behind all mischief. When asked in Sunday school for the names of the first two disciples, he at last comes up with "David and Goliath!" This gets its laugh. But how is it possible for a boy who reads so much, and is forever hearing the New Testament being read at him in school, in church, at home, not to know better? It is possible because Tom (like everyone else in the book, even Huckleberry Finn) is all of one piece, limited to a few traits. As in all true comedy, these traits are trotted out over and again; the fun depends on the power of repetition.

Tom does "grow" in the story from a bad boy into a hero. When Muff Potter is put on trial for murdering Dr. Robinson in the cemetery at night, Tom overcomes his fear and gets himself to court to nail the real murderer, the villainous half-breed Injun Joe. When his adored Becky Thatcher cannot keep away from the anatomy book that the schoolmaster secretly keeps in the closet and then accidentally tears the page showing a "human figure, stark naked," our Tom takes the blame, bears the punishment—and wins Becky's "love." At the end Tom nobly safeguards Becky when they stray away from their friends and cannot easily find their way out of the cave. The stolen treasure bestowed on Tom and Huck is their reward for behaving well in a crisis. To conclude the book, Tom even accommodates himself to the adult values he has hitherto defied; Huck must go back to the Widow Douglas if he wants to be accepted into the gang. (This proves conclusively that the activity of the gang is really playacting by respectable people. It is necessarily where *The Adventures of Huckleberry Finn* will begin, for Huck is not middle-class and respectable, so he must escape the "Widder.")

In *Tom Sawyer* all the shenanigans at the end denote the happy ending and spirit of reconciliation natural to comedy. By writing Tom's adventures in the third person, Mark Twain could "handle" Tom any way he liked. He admitted that there was no real plot to the book.

In his original preface to *Tom Sawyer*, from Hartford in 1876, when he was living in such grand style, he wrote: "part of my plan has been to try to pleasantly remind adults of what they once were themselves, and of how they felt and thought and talked, and what queer enterprises they sometimes engaged in."

This was not and could not have been all that the floodgates of memory opened up. Tom and his friends are superstitious about many things in a way that shows their dread of the unknown powers behind nature as well as their childish ignorance. Why do they visit a tumbledown cemetery *at night* just in time to see a grave robbery and murder? Why does Huck carry a dead cat with him? Why is a recurrent image in the book that of the moon dropping behind a cloud? All these people are alone with natural forces that, as in the scene of the terrible thunderstorm, seem to sport with the tiny settlement on the mysterious great river. Tom and Huck, being boys, think they can control the occult forces of darkness, dread, and violence by laying spells on them. But evil in the background is necessary to comedy, for evil is defeated. Wickedness in the person of Injun Joe dies of starvation in the cave; the fears of the cave are overcome by Tom and Becky; our prankster is a hero. He has really been a hero all along—a hero disguised as a mischievous and disobedient boy. This adds folklore to comedy. Everything works out for the best in this best of all possible Americas. Successful, benevolent Mark Twain is looking back on his own boyhood so sweetly, so archly! The prose in which Tom is put through his paces could not be more heavily facetious: "he uncovered an ambuscade, in the person of his aunt; and when she saw the state his clothes were in, her resolution to turn his Saturday holiday into captivity at hard labor became adamantine in its firmness."

This is far from being the easy, "natural" first-person style of *Huckleberry Finn.* Mark Twain had to put a certain distance between himself and his famous boys before he could enter more deeply and *recklessly* into a boy's life with *Huckleberry Finn.* There is a lot of carefulness and anxious propriety behind the writing of *Tom Sawyer.* It now seems absurd for a near-adolescent like Tom to ask Becky for a kiss only because that is the ritual he has read about in books when people get "engaged." "Now, Becky, it's all done—all over but the kiss. Don't you be afraid of that—it ain't anything at all. Please, Becky." In the closing pages Huck bitterly complains how unbearable he finds life with the Widow Douglas: "She makes me git up just at the same time every morning; she makes me wash . . . them ways comb me all to thunder." Since Mark Twain had persuaded himself (prodded by his wife and Howells) that the book was really "a boy's and a girl's book," he was glad enough to change "hell" to "thunder." The naked human figure Becky Thatcher steals a glance at in the schoolmaster's anatomy book apparently belongs to neither sex and contains no sexual interest for Becky.

All this marks the gentility from which Mark Twain looked down on his boyhood. So much propriety and prudent respectability were perhaps necessary to describe boyhood under "special orders." Adulthood and boyhood are absolutely divided here between authority figures and escapees from authority. Tom is the immortal boy because there is no chance of his growing up—of ever becoming anything more than a boy. Tom is everlastingly the type and legend of the American boy because his youthful sense of freedom still represents the youthfulness of the United States—before Mark Twain settled down. Tom is legendary because he is an adult's fantasy of defying the many adults we cannot defy so lightly when we become adults. Above all, Tom is "immortal" because he always wins.

Huckleberry Finn is not middle-class like Tom, and he will never be rewarded for his propriety by the proper people in town. Huck says at one point, "You see, I'm kind of a hard lot—least everybody says so, and I don't see nothing against it." Tom has the whole town to defy, for he is securely a part of it. Huck does not even have a home. Everyone disapproves of him in this book, even Tom Sawyer. He is "low company," the kind of character that stretched Mark Twain's imagination to the uttermost and became his genius. Still, it had been genius for Mark Twain to put Huck into the company of Tom. Each is so necessary to the other that it was perfect instinct for Mark Twain, once he came to the end of *The Adventures of Tom Sawyer*, to write *The Adventures of Huckleberry Finn*. Huck says at the beginning of the new book, "You don't know about me, without you have read a book by the name of *The Adventures of Tom Sawyer.*"

VII

When Mark Twain turned to *The Adventures of Huckleberry Finn* after finishing *The Adventures of Tom Sawyer* in 1876, he clearly meant to write another "boy's book" in the light comic tone that for the most part had carried Tom and his friends in St. Petersburg from one escapade to another. Despite the dread, the fear-soaked superstitions, and the violent deaths described in *Tom Sawyer*, the book is a comedy and in tone benign and more than a shade condescending to boys who, when all is said and done, are merely boys. Mark Twain had become a wealthy and ultrarespectable member of the best society in Hartford by the time he sat down to recreate his own boyhood in *Tom Sawyer*—minus his own religious fear and loneliness.

His benevolence toward childhood and boyhood is a little smug. Mark Twain undertook more than he anticipated when he turned to *Huckleberry Finn*. By an instinct that opened the book to greatness, he wrote Huck's story in the first person and so at many crucial places in the book *became* Huck. Yet the facetious "Notice" facing the opening page is only one of many indications that *Huckleberry Finn* was intended to be just a sequel to *Tom Sawyer:*

> Persons attempting to find a motive in this narrative will be prosecuted; persons attempting to find a moral in it will be banished; persons attempting to find a plot in it will be shot.

From the moment Mark Twain began to describe things as Huck would see them, and to make of Huck's vernacular a language resource of the most captivating shrewdness, realism, and stoical humor, Mark Twain was almost against his will forced to go deeper into his own imaginative sense than he had ever gone before. Odd as it may seem, he was compelled—in this one book—to become a master novelist.

He had not been a novelist at all before writing *Tom Sawyer;* obviously everything having to do with his early life in Hannibal recharged him and opened not only the gates of memory and imagination but also his unexpected ability to write close, sustained narrative. Writing in the first person became the deliverance of Mark Twain. Still, given his training in one vernacular style after another during his days as a frontier humorist, it was not in itself exceptional for him to impersonate a fourteen-year-old vagabond, the son of the town drunk, who hates being "adopted": "The Widow Douglas, she took me for her son, and allowed she would sivilize me; but it was rough living in the house all the time, considering how dismal regular and decent the widow was in all her ways."

What made the difference between this and just another humorous "oral delivery" was that Mark Twain had fallen completely into Huck's style and Huck's soul. (There were to be passages in which Huck became Mark Twain.) Smart-alecky and sometimes mechanically facetious as Mark Twain was when he first assumed Huck's voice, winking at the reader as he presented Huck's ignorance of religion, of polite language, of "sivilized" ways, Mark Twain would soon be committed to a great subject—Huck the runaway from his father and Jim the slave running away from Miss Watson, going down the river, hoping to enter the Ohio River and freedom. Freedom from respectable ways for Huck, freedom from slavery for Jim: the quest is eternal even though they miss the Ohio River in the dark and keep going South. In the last third of the book they return to the purely boyish world of *Tom Sawyer,* with Tom the everlasting kid, prankster, brat, forcing a Jim who was really free all the time (as only Tom knows) to be a "prisoner" on the Phelps farm.

The quest for freedom is eternal because Huck and Jim have nothing in this world but that quest. Mark Twain the ultrasuccess in Hartford had returned to what he once knew, most feared, and what always excited his imagination most—the Mississippi Valley world at its human bottom, the world of the totally powerless and unsettled. He, too, remained something of a vagrant, a drifter; in old age he called himself a "derelict." He would never, despite appearances, be content with his celebrated position in life; like Huck at the end of this book, he wanted "to light out for the Territory ahead of the rest."

Huckleberry Finn is above all a novel of low company—of people who are so far down in the social scale that they can get along only by their wits. In 1885 the Concord Public Library excluded *Huckleberry Finn*. It was not altogether mistaken when it complained that the humor was "coarse" and that the substance was "rough, coarse and inelegant, dealing with a series of experiences not elevating, the whole book being more suited to the slums than to intelligent, respectable people." The wonderful satire in chapter 17 on the genteel way of life in the Grangerford family would not be possible without Huck's unpreparedness for such a way of life; the hilarious Victorian sentimentality is put into true perspective by Huck, the anguished observer of the murderous feud between the Grangerfords and the Shepherdsons.

Huck has *nothing* but his wits. As he says about himself, "I go a good deal by instinct." The society along the river is class-conscious, but the classes cannot help knowing each other and entering into each other's lives. In chapters 24–29 the awful Duke and Dauphin enter into the family of the dead Peter Wilks, pretending to be its English branch, and the fact that they do not talk "educated," but make the most ridiculous mistakes, does not alert the family until it is almost too late. From time to time Huck temporarily attaches himself to plain middle-class folks like Mrs. Judith Loftus; in chapter 11, when he disguises himself as a girl, it is his sex rather than his low speech that gives him away.

Huck certainly gets around. He can be pals with Tom Sawyer and be taken in hand by Judge Thatcher, the Widow Douglas, and Miss Watson; he convinces Mrs. Judith Loftus that he *did* grow up in the country; in chapter 13, he steals the canoe attached to the foundering *Walter Scott* and so helps to send the robbers caught on the boat to their deaths; he can play the servant to professional con men like the Duke and Dauphin, who at successive times masquerade as actors, medicine men, and Englishmen.

In a great novel of society—which *Huckleberry Finn* so acidly turns out to be whenever Huck and Jim go ashore—what counts is the reality behind the appearance. That reality, though sometimes naively misinterpreted by

Huck (but only for a self-deluded moment), depends always on Huck's inexperience. Nothing could be more devastating as social satire than the Victorian gingerbread and sentimental mourning described absolutely "straight" by the homeless and admiring Huck. All this turns into a hideous bloodbath as a consequence of Huck's ingenuous help to the lovelorn couple from feuding families. To go from the Grangerford parlor to the riverbank where Huck covers the heads of the Grangerford boys slain in the insane feud is to travel a social epic. Only the classic "poor white," Huck, goes the whole route—as the onlooker that Mark Twain remained in his heart.

The riverbank scene ends on one of those recurrent escapes that make up the story line of *Huckleberry Finn*—"I tramped off in a hurry for the crick, and crowded through the willows, red-hot to jump aboard and get out of that awful country." Huck *has* to keep running from "quality" folks like the Grangerfords, the Wilkses, the murdering "awful proud" Colonel Sherburn. He "weren't particular"; he just wants to go "somewheres." He chooses to *stay* low company, as his father does. Vagrancy is his first freedom. He does not even choose to go traipsing down the Mississippi with Jim, who just happens to be on Jackson's Island when Huck gets there. The novel is one happening after another; Huck *happens* to fall in with a runaway slave instead of living by the book with Tom Sawyer. As Pap Finn chooses the mud, so Huck chooses the river. Or did the river in fact choose him?

Thanks to the everlasting river, the "monstrous big river," the always unpredictable river, Huck and Jim on their raft float into a tough American world. It is full of hard characters, crooks, confidence men, kindly widows and starchy spinsters who in good Mark Twain fashion never seem to be sexually involved with anyone; slaveowners and slave hunters who can never be expected to regard Jim as anything but a piece of property; pretty young girls for whom Huck's highest accolade is that they have "the most sand" —grit and courage, the power to disbelieve and defy the lying elders around them. The church is fundamental to these people, but their religion emphasizes duty to God rather than brotherhood for the outcast and the slave. They are hard without knowing it, for they are hysterically self-protective. They are a human island in the midst of a great emptiness.

So Huck, not yet fourteen, has to struggle for a knowledge of adult society without which he will not survive. In *Tom Sawyer* children and adults lived in parallel worlds without menacing each other; in *Huckleberry Finn*, as in real life, children and their elders are in conflict. A middle-class boy like Tom Sawyer has to "win" a game in order to triumph over his inevitable defeats in later life. Huck has to survive now. He has to win over Pap Finn's meanness and the Widow Douglas's strictness; over Tom Sawyer's boyish silliness and Jim's constant terror that he may be caught; over the murderous robbers on the *Walter Scott* and even the protectiveness of Mrs. Judith Loftus; over the horrible arrogance of Colonel Sherburn and the lynch mob foolishly crowding Colonel Sherburn's door; over the greediness of the "King" and the cool cynicism of the Duke.

Huck on the river, becoming a part of the river, making the river one of the principal characters, reminds us of the genesis of *Tom Sawyer* and *Huckleberry Finn.* Mark Twain recalled in *Old Times on the Mississippi* that he had had to learn the *whole* river in order to become a pilot. Huck has to be the unresting pilot of his life and Jim's; he must become the American Ulysses in order to survive. This is why from time to time he can lie back and take in the beauty and wonder of the scene, as in the glorious description of sunrise on the Mississippi that opens chapter 19. This chapter significantly has the book's meanest characters, the Duke and Dauphin, coming aboard. Think of a boy Huck's age struggling against a father who wants to keep him down, who tries to rob him, and who beats him and keeps him locked up. Whereupon *our* Ulysses contrives his own "death" and gets away with it after making as many preparations for his deception and escape as a spy going into enemy country. No wonder he is always on "thin ice," or as he says in one of his best descriptions of flight, "I was kind of a hub of a wheel."

There, in the struggle of a boy to establish himself over hostile powers, in the discovery of menace when confronting life on one's own terms—there is the true meaning of a "boy's book"; it explains why boys can read *The Adventures of Huckleberry Finn* as boys and then grow up to read it as an epic of life that adults can identify with. The great epic, the tale of the wandering hero triumphing over circumstances—this is the stuff of literature that a boy is nearest to, since every initiation into the manhood he seeks must take the form of triumphing over an obstacle. Whether he is planning to deceive his father into thinking he is dead, scaring off slave hunters with stories of smallpox on their raft, or (in the last ten chapters) submitting to Tom Sawyer's games and thus subjecting poor Jim to real imprisonment, the hero of this book is still only a boy. This proximity to both real danger and made-up danger is how life appears to a boy, who must steal from the adult world the power, but also the fun, that he needs in order to keep feeling like a boy. Even though he must trick this world, lie to it, outwit it, he is a boy in his conventional attitudes. The Wilks girl had "the most sand" you ever did see in a girl, and the Grangerford house was the splendidest.

Huck does not have the easy out of pretending to despise a middle-class world whose love comes his way without his seeking it. Nor does love from people he has just met mean as much to him as his own measure of people.

He is attachable, but not for long; adoptable, but he will not admit liking this. You remember his boyish inexperience when you see how much he values, in the sunrise along the river and in the circus into which he has sneaked, the beauty and "splendidness" the world has kept in store for him. The nature of the life experience, as the story of a boy always brings out, is that we just pass through and are soon different from what we thought we were; are soon gone. Life is a series of incommensurable moments, and it is wise to enjoy them; one minute the Grangerford boys are bloody dead along the river, and the next morning or so, "two or three days and nights went by; I reckon I might say they swum by, they slid along so quiet and smooth and lovely."

Pap Finn in delirium tremens cries out to the Angel of Death, "Oh, let a poor devil alone!" This expresses the real struggle, against underlying despair, that Mark Twain admitted for the first time in *Huckleberry Finn*, before he savagely settled into the despair of his old age. The river that "holds" the book in its grasp is full of menace as well as an unreal floating peace. For the most part travelling the river is a struggle, a wariness, even when Huck is temporarily on land. In the marvellous and somehow central scene in which Huck methodically arranges his "death" and then, worn out, prepares to catch a few "winks," he is still a river rat who feels himself pursued at every turn.

From the very beginning of their flight, Huck and Jim are in ecstasies whenever they are safe for a while. Early in the book, when Huck watches the townspeople shooting off a cannon to raise his "body" from the bottom, he says with an audible easing of his breath, "I knowed I was all right now. Nobody else would come a-hunting after me." Just treading on a stick and breaking it "made me feel like a person had cut one of my breaths in two and I only got half, and the short half, too." A boy is up against forces bigger than himself, the greatest of which can be his inexperience. So he has to play "smart." But the smarter the boy, the more fatalistic he is; he knows who runs things. Wary of people, Huck weaves his way in and out of so many hazards and dangers that we love him for the dangers he has passed. He *is* our Ulysses, he *has* come through. Yet coming up from the bottom, he has none of Tom Sawyer's foolish pride; the "going" for this boy has become life itself, and eventually there is no place for him to go except back to Tom Sawyer's fun and games.

The sense of danger is the living context of the book's famous style, the matchless ease and directness of Huck's language. Huck and Jim are forever warding off trouble, escaping from trouble, resting from trouble—then, by words, putting a "spell" on trouble. Jim is always getting lost and always being found; Huck is always inventing stories and playing imaginary people in order to get out of scrapes before they occur. As Jim in his ignorance is made to play the fool, so Huck in the full power of his cleverness is made to play the con man. They need all the parts they can get. They live at the edge of a society that is not prepared to accept either one of them; they are constantly in trouble, and it is real trouble, not "prejudice," that menaces Jim. Although Mark Twain often plays to the gallery when he mocks the iniquity of slavery from the complacent perspective of Connecticut in the 1880s, the feeling that Huck and Jim attain for each other is now deservedly the most famous side of the book. For once, black and white actually love each other because they are in the same fix. "Dah you goes, de ole true Huck; de on'y white gentleman dat ever kep' his promise to old Jim."

But we never forget what the hard American world around them is like and why they are both in flight. For people who are penniless, harried, in real danger of death, vigilance alone gives a kind of magical power to a life over which "mudsills" and slaves have no power. The superstitions Huck and Jim share are all they have to call on against the alien forces of nature. Equally effective, a kind of superstition as well, is the spell they put on things by arranging them in strict order. Although Huck sometimes becomes Mark Twain when Mark wants to satirize old-time property "rights" in slaves, Mark sinks into Huck when, in the crucial scene preparing his getaway, Huck doggedly lists everything he has, everything he is taking with him, everything he *knows*—in order to shore himself against danger.

It must have been this scene in chapter 7 of *Huckleberry Finn* that so deeply drew Ernest Hemingway to the book. All modern American writing, he said in *Green Hills of Africa*, comes out of *Huckleberry Finn*. He called the much-disputed end of the book "cheating," but he recognized his affinity with the book as a whole. Hemingway surely came to his famous "plain" style through his compulsion to say about certain objects, *only this is real; this is real; and my emotion connects them.* In Hemingway's great and perhaps most revealing story, "Big Two-Hearted River," the suffering mind of the war veteran Nick Adams seeks an accustomed sense of familiarity from the stream he fished before the war. He then puts his catch away between ferns, layer by layer, with a frantic deliberateness. So Huck preparing his getaway in chapter 7 tells us:

> I took the sack of corn meal and took it to where the canoe was hid, and shoved the vines and branches apart and put it in; then I done the same with the side of bacon; then the whisky jug; I took all the coffee and sugar there was, and all the ammunition; I took the wadding; I took the bucket and

gourd, I took a dipper and a tin cup, and my own saw and two blankets, and the skillet and the coffee-pot. I took fish-lines and matches and other things —everything that was worth a cent. I cleaned out the place. I wanted an axe, but there wasn't any, only the one out at the wood pile, and I knowed why I was going to leave that. I fetched out the gun, and now I was done.

The boy without anything to his name finally has something to carry away. Taking the full inventory of his possessions is a ritual that Huck goes through whenever he is in danger and about to hunt up a new place to "hide." This element of necessity can be the most moving side of the book. It "explains" the unique freshness of the style as much as anything can. A writer finds his needed style, his true style, in the discovery of a book's hidden subject, its "figure in the carpet." Here is a book which is an absolute marvel of style, but in which, by a greater marvel, life is not reduced to style and is certainly not confused with style. Huck Finn's voice has many sides, but fundamentally it is the voice of a boy-man up to his ears in life, tumbling from danger to danger, negotiating with people, and fighting back at things as necessity commands. The sense of necessity that only bottom dogs know is what gives such unmediated, unintellectualized beauty to the style. Mark Twain, fully for the first time, knew how to let life carry out its own rhythm.

The interesting thing is that he did not particularly intend to do this. When he took the book up again several years after he had written chapter 16, planning to describe the comedy and horror of the Grangerfords' existence, he was tougher on the society along the river than he had ever expected to be. For starting with chapter 17 he had to describe the folly of "quality" folk like the Grangerfords, the inhuman arrogance of Colonel Sherburn, and the stupidity and loutishness of "ordinary" plain people.

Mark Twain's fascinated loathing extends to the whiskey-sodden townspeople who egg on poor old Boggs as he stumbles about, foolishly threatening Colonel Sherburn. Because that imperious man murders Boggs, Mark Twain can disgorge himself of his own exasperation with "ordinary" Americans by describing the crowd around the dying man.

> There was considerable jawing back, so I slid out, thinking maybe there was going to be trouble. The streets was full, and everybody was excited. Everybody that seen the shooting was telling how it happened, and there was a big crowd packed around each one of these fellows, stretching their necks and listening. One long lanky man, with long hair and a big white fur stove-pipe hat on the back of his head, and a crooked-handled cane, marked out the places on the ground where Boggs stood, and where Sherburn stood, and the people following him around from one place t'other and watching everything he done, and bobbing their heads to show they understood, and

stooping a little and resting their hands on their thighs to watch him mark the places on the ground with his cane; and then he stood up straight and stiff where Sherburn had stood, frowning and having his hat-brim down over his eyes, and sung out, "Boggs!" and then fetched his cane down slow to a level, and says "Bang!" staggered backwards, says "Bang!" again, and fell down flat on his back. The people that had seen the thing said he done it perfect; said it was just exactly the way it all happened. Then as much as a dozen people got out their bottles and treated him.

The famous speech by Colonel Sherburn after the murder ridicules the crowd that has come to lynch him. The speech is wonderful in its lordly contempt for the townspeople, but of course it is not Sherburn but Mark Twain who is telling the crowd off. The crowd admiringly watching the man in the "big white fur stove-pipe hat" act out the killing is Mark Twain at his best. In this pitiless scene, one of the most powerful blows ever directed at the complacency of democracy in America, life becomes farce without ceasing to be horror. The grotesqueness of the human animal has put life to the final test of our acceptance. And we accept it. The absurdity and savagery that Mark Twain captured in this scene proved more difficult to accept when, no longer young and now humiliated by near-bankruptcy, he found himself face to face with a driving, imperial America that was harsher than anything he had known on the frontier.

9

The James Country

How can places that speak *in general* to the imagination
not give it, at the moment, the particular thing it wants?

JAMES, *The Portrait of a Lady*, Preface

I

These Americans never saw Europe: Abraham Lincoln, Henry David Thoreau, Walt Whitman, Emily Dickinson. Whitman, who fascinated the English (Mrs. Anne Gilchrist settled here for a season in the hope of getting him
to marry her), might have enjoyed some preposterous celebrity there, as
Oscar Wilde did in Western mining camps. It is hard to imagine what
Europe would have done for Lincoln or Thoreau. Mark Twain was forever
in Europe, and while Europe enjoyed him more than he did Europe, it
contributed to his fund of anecdotes, but added nothing to his imagination.
Stephen Crane settled in a moldy, drafty English manor house in order to
escape his creditors and to live openly with Cora Stewart; he died in Germany.

Margaret Fuller, a restless soul and in intention a revolutionary, escaped
her priggish male society (heavy with second-string transcendentalists) in
Italy. She participated in some epic days of the Risorgimento, became a
friend of Mazzini, married the unlettered young Marchese Ossoli, and had
a child. All three perished in a shipwreck off Fire Island as Margaret was
returning to America. Emerson, who sent Thoreau to look for her effects,
was condescending to her in death; Hawthorne was hostile. Henry James
mocked her as "finally Italianised and shipwrecked." Margaret Fuller, unap-
peasably critical of male mediocrity in Boston and Concord (there was as yet
no other kind to notice), had proved herself unforgivably peculiar. She had
gone to Europe on her own terms, the most vivid of our romantic exiles—
as a personality, not as a writer. After the Civil War, for the first time in the
history of Americans, Europe became not merely an experience but, to use

one of Henry James's essential terms, an "opportunity." Europe was news, and American writers and artists were still explorers—like Melville from the South Seas—bringing home tales of strange places. Scholars of modern languages from George Ticknor to Longfellow and Lowell prepared themselves in Europe for their Harvard professorships. Longfellow, ambitious to bring back to Cambridge everything he could learn, worshipfully saw Europe as the great world. America, for all its freedom and prosperity, soon had almost as many distinguished exiles as czarist Russia. Most of them were pitifully conventional sculptors and artists from notable families—Henry James was to write their history, with ironic deference, in *William Wetmore Story and His Friends.*

William Dean Howells had never been abroad before he earned the Venice consulate by writing Abraham Lincoln's campaign biography in 1860. Sitting out the Civil War in Europe gave the self-educated former printer and reporter the background he needed for the fine travel books he was to produce and the smoothness and poise he brought to his fictional reportage of American society. Europe, Howells's only university, turned out to be his Harvard Business School, his training in literary management. The tactful, assiduous autodidact was to make it big in Boston by way of Venice. In Howells's easy, graceful *Venetian Life* and his essays on Goldoni and Italian comedy, the reader back home is exposed not only to the benefits of foreign travel but to a conscious savor of superiority. He was to decline Longfellow's and Lowell's Harvard chair in modern languages.

Europe for Howells was his lucky chance to step up from Ohio. For Henry James it was the familiar repository of tradition, art, manners, civilization. It was equivalent to literature itself, and it made possible his career. And his career was his life. It was of course easier for Henry James, with a father airily dissociated from the usual American concerns with business, a "hotel childhood" in Europe, early schooling in Geneva, London, Paris, Boulogne, and Bonn, to think of Europe as a second home. It was easy for him, always, to think of America as *not* being home. (And only an American, then and now, has had purely temperamental reasons for thinking so.) William James said that his brother was an inhabitant of the James family and had no other country.* There was a heightened mental existence to daily life in that country, an abnormal removal from the "vulgar," that made them strange to

*Henry James kept a certain fondness for his birthplace, or at least for his early associations with it. He named the collected edition of his works the New York edition. He remembered "his" New York in his first volume of autobiography, *A Small Boy and Others*, with special fervor; in *The American Scene* with disdain at what it had become. But even his first fifteen years in New York were punctuated by visits to Europe. He did not think of New York as "home."

others and exceptional to themselves. It radiated all too evidently from Henry James, Senior, a belligerently independent religious philosopher and Swedenborgian, a utopian socialist with a private income. He had lost one leg as a boy trying to put out a fire and, being the most uxorious of husbands and the most dedicated of fathers, was happy to be in constant supervision of his family from his writing table. He was described by Ellery Channing as "a little fat, rosy Swedenborgian amateur, with the look of a broker, and the brains and heart of a Pascal."

With his vehement and "vascular" temperament, his contempt for most other American thinkers, his income from an Irish Protestant father who had become rich on Albany and Syracuse real estate after arriving in America a penniless boy wild to see Revolutionary War battlefields, his pride that *he* and *his* children were never "guilty" of doing "a stroke of American business," the father of Henry and William James was known to be independent to the point of eccentricity. He was also generally considered unreadable. William Dean Howells, whose father was a Swedenborgian, wrote that "Mr. Henry James has written a book called *The Secret of Swedenborg* and has kept it."

The elder James's problem, which descended on all five of his children (even the ungifted but equally unstable two youngest boys, Robertson and Garth Wilkinson), was spiritual homelessness, a fervid need not easily understood by others to make attachments to a higher consciousness than his own. He was a natural believer who assured his son William that he had never known a sceptical moment. But his God was in no sense an external spirit; it was the divine principle working itself out in humanity. To know that saved us from being "sick souls," from falling into the abyss that awaits all unaided human effort, all attempts to escape the "nothingness" of mere self, "the abyss of evil over whom even the best men hover."

That evil expressed itself as despair. There could be no heaven without a hell, as long as the individual insisted in good American style on regarding himself as self-sufficient. Empirically we *know* we are creatures with a lack, a destitution, a death in us. Real selfhood comes from God—and God is the redemption of man in society. This is the "divine humanity" in our "natural humanity"; it is founded on the solidarity of the race, the "social rebirth of the individual." Our seeking perfection will "give ourselves no rest until we put on the lineaments of an infinite or perfect man, in attaining to the proportions of a regenerate society, fellowship, and new brotherhood of all mankind."

It was typical of the elder James to say that Genesis was too optimistic.

The "void" did not vanish when the creation was completed; we feel it still in our aloneness. Bernard Shaw thought the father was the most gifted member of his remarkable family. He was certainly the most influential, for he passed on even his neuroses. The Jameses experienced challenge to their innate beliefs as illness. Their recurrent illnesses seem to have been ideas—in revolt against authority—and the benevolently pervading, all-too-loving father who was always at home was the children's authority.

They were all exceedingly mental beings, sometimes so far removed from actual society that certain of Henry James's final works, like the unfinished *The Sense of the Past*, take place in an England that is nothing but a mental elaboration. William James, actually less worldly than his brother for all his "pragmatism," innocently equated pragmatism with the "cash-value" of an idea. What he was really after was correlation, the human action and effect that should follow from *having* an idea. They lived in words. For all of them there was an emotional necessity to every particle of expression. It is seen first in the father's amazing projection of temperament into his wordy pursuit of the divine. He managed to sound excited even when he was most ponderous.

Dr. William James's recorded oscillations, depressions, physical uncertainties (he was his only patient) were to prove almost suicidal until the Personnalisme of the French philosopher Charles Renouvier gave him the confidence to assert his natural belief in moral liberty and freedom of choice. He was like a character in a Dostoevsky novel—his psyche staged violent ups and downs as he looked to new ideas for his salvation.* Alice James, the youngest child and the only girl, was all her life a prodigal sufferer and medical mystery; her diary and letters show her struggling against ideas not her own. The youngest brothers, otherwise undistin-

---

*Only William James among modern philosophers was to use the "passional" as a positive direction for the human mind. His theory of the emotions in his *Psychology* (1890):

". . . bodily changes follow directly the perception of the exciting fact . . . our feeling of the same changes as they occur *is* the emotion.

". . . the entire organism may be called a sounding board, which every change of consciousness, however slight, may make reverberate. . . .

"Every one of the bodily changes, whatsoever it be, is FELT, acutely or obscurely, the moment it occurs."

This pioneer text of modern laboratory psychology reverberates with the personal charm (and dilemma) of being William James. No one but James, at the height of positivism, could have counselled "the Will to Believe" as a guide to the perplexed. And only James, lecturing to future professors of philosophy, would have granted religion the status of a "hypothesis" and have then gone on to clinch it with, "deadness and liveness in an hypothesis are not intrinsic properties, but relations to the individual thinker. They are measured by his willingness to act. The maximum of liveliness in an hypothesis means willingness to act irrevocably."

guished, were self-sacrificing pro-black idealists in the South after hard service in the Civil War.

In William and Henry James every particle of intellectual faith became a living and, happily, a restorative experience. Their mental life—so intense that it became in truth a spiritual world—was the root of their being. This was *their* self, not like anyone else's; so much inner life was their despair and their vocation. "Self" isolated them. It became their main subject matter. William James, taking a medical degree between nervous collapses, was to work his way through psychology and academic philosophy to achieve his own doctrine and message—as if, while airily competent in both science and philosophy, he was all the while thinking of curing his own "sick soul." Henry gave his life to the novel because, above all other forms of literature, it appropriated the endless subtlety of human relationships.

I I

"We work in the dark," the dying writer was to say in Henry James's story "The Middle Years," "we do what we can—we give what we have. Our doubt is our passion, and our passion is our task. The rest is the madness of art."

Henry James never wrote a story around this theme that was not a story about lonely, fundamentally unrewarded devotion to art, the craving to reach "perfection," the contempt for the novel-devouring public content with the usual commodities.

The "passion" of Henry James—and how consistently he insisted on it in stories, criticism, notebooks, letters—was to bring the modern novel into a literature whose founding sage, Emerson, could not read fiction. Eventually, with growing isolation even in England, James's "passion" was to achieve the novel as the form most suited to his consciousness. Unlike the novelists he admired most—George Eliot, Balzac, Turgenev—he certainly lacked "saturation" in the life of his native society. He just wanted to be a novelist and read other people's novels, not only with oversharp eyes but as his main intellectual diet. Even poetry soon bored him. With the precocious sophistication acquired through a childhood in Europe, and his detachment from the commercial cares and interests that dominated his generation after the Civil War, his early work dramatized the tritest love story from the outside, easily worked up a "situation." Brother William the physician and psychologist emphasized the individual case; brother Henry, the drama, the plot. In some mysterious way which he came to equate with accomplishment in the novel, Henry James was intellectually disengaged, free of "ideas," forever on his own and left to his own devices.*

He turned out to have a great many. From early childhood, absorbed in the bound volumes of *Punch* and every possible "story book" when the family still lived on Fourteenth Street in New York, James collected images of England, social chronicles and memoirs of the country that most represented a "high civilization." He practiced his future trade by writing brilliant travel sketches about Saratoga and Newport. Even Emerson was properly impressed by the vividness of his "pictures." (James's extraordinary capacity for images was to exfoliate in his "major" novels of the early 1900s until they resembled the superplush, madly overdecorated hotel parlors of the period he satirized in *The American Scene*.) The young man began at twenty-one, in the midst of the Civil War, a smooth professional before he had anything very pressing to write about.

The "magazine era" after the war gave James his great opportunity as a reporter and practitioner of the new European-style fiction of manners. Old or new, magazines like the *Atlantic Monthly, Scribner's Monthly, Harper's Weekly, Harper's Monthly,* the *Century,* now had a distinct middle-class audience whose moral standards and literary tastes editors busily anticipated. Never before had native periodicals been able to count on a body of readers so contained, so full of prosperous self-satisfaction, and so receptive to social fiction—which brought this class news of itself. The feminine component was described as an "Iron Madonna" chaining writers to women in "society," their snobberies and inhibitions. James was to lose much of his original popularity when *Daisy Miller* offended the proprieties; no "decent" American girl would go about Rome unchaperoned, with a mere Italian. Daisy had betrayed her class, not her sex. But the magazines had early welcomed James's unique knowledge of "foreign parts," his special ability to write "transatlantic sketches."

When James died in the midst of the Great War, leaving two novels and a third volume of autobiography incomplete, he had published twenty-two novels, one hundred twelve "tales," volume on volume of travel, biography, criticism. No other novelist in the great age of the novel wrote so much about his own fiction and was so mindful of everyone else's fiction. He was clamorously to describe his aims for the novel as the great form, to confide secrets

---

*Grimly as James came to admire Zola, for example, he could not understand Zola's leaving his desk to take up the cause of Dreyfus. George Eliot's evangelical youth he saw as a stage she had to outgrow. The political (as well as personal) instincts that made Turgenev flee Russia escaped Turgenev's admirer.

of the workshop. The archbishop of Canterbury himself, at a dinner party, had given him the anecdote that became the "germ" of "The Turn of the Screw"! For the New York edition (1907–09) of his collected works, James rewrote his earlier novels in his elaborate later style (itself a form of critical commentary) and composed prefaces to each of his principal works and to many of his best stories. With his overflowing articulateness and the flutteriness of his last period, he recounted how the "situation" came to him, where he walked thinking it out, where he sat down to write it, and how this specific work fitted into his master strategy of the high art of fiction. In the end, he confided to Grace Norton, he even thought of writing a preface to his prefaces. His collected letters are as full of his professional avidity as his notebooks, where in his "sacred struggles" he often addressed his writing self, his "genius," as his only recourse in life. "Without thee, for me, the world would be, indeed, a howling desert."

Late in life James confessed in a letter: "The port from which I set out was . . . that of the essential loneliness of my life, and it seems to be the port also, in sooth, to which my course again finally directs itself. This loneliness [is] deeper than my 'genius,' deeper than my 'discipline,' deeper than my pride, deeper, above all, than the deep counterminings of art."

The reader has an instinct of this in the familyness of James's protagonists. As late as the "major" novels, Lambert Strether in *The Ambassadors* is a widower who has lost his only son; Milly Theale in *The Wings of the Dove* is an orphan; and Maggie Verver, marrying an Italian prince with all too many relatives, has to explain that "they hadn't natural relations, she and her father." Why not? Obviously James identified his better characters, especially his favorite ones, with his own solitariness. Hence their mental precautions (sometimes it is positive fright) before other people, their frustrated interchanges, the desperate conjectures which the "witty" dialogue brushes over. The voyeur is prominent among James's characters as outsider, gossiper, prurient innocent. A tribute to James's power, his underground conduit of feeling, is that he was able to get so much interest and even suspense out of characters shut up in their own minds.

Henry's "loneliness" and William's unstable psyche were to lead them to pursue the mystery of personality to every hiding place. And long before James confessed it, it was out of "essential loneliness" that he sprang into furious productivity with such nervous force and cultivated "relationships" as his prime interest in life and art. If he worried that his experience even of New York life was "downtown" with the "pastry cooks," never uptown in the business world, it was because he wanted to succeed in a "big" American way. His dogged industry and constant anxiety about his career remind one of the tireless American entrepreneurs of his generation. He was always conscious of the public for whom his fiction was serialized on both sides of the Atlantic, and he certainly *meant* to satisfy it. He had nothing of Flaubert's horror of the modern audience and gladly tried to educate up to his own standards readers who asked him to explain what he was up to. To flourish in his chosen field, never to give up in the face of mockery and failure, was his manliness.

Henry Adams was proud of not being known to the general public. Mark Twain courted the public endlessly. William James, shifting from field to field before finding himself in middle age, drove himself to document his mature philosophy in one great book but died feeling that he had not fully justified his faith in his own originality.

Henry usually justified himself. He had poor digestion and in his early letters from Europe sounds bereft as he moves from one hotel room to another. But he escaped the unsettling illnesses and the even more unsettling political idealism that was marked in his father, his sister, *all* his brothers. He wrote, he wrote, he wrote. Even when he was dying, he kept chanting sentences aloud, like the dying Emerson. We do not know what Emerson was saying; James's secretary did take down those amazing "letters" from James in which he thinks himself Napoleon. They are mysterious, but they throb with the familiar sonorousness of James's sentences.

Napoleon, Leon Edel has shown in the five-volume biography whose total sympathy reveals James's fascination for our generation, was a model for James, as he was for many unsoldierly pen pushers. Napoleon was France and France was James's Olympus, his classical world. James, too, was a "colonial" drawn to the mother country, another ambitious provincial with a great design. His career was one long deliberation of his art and a determination to show himself sui generis; he meant to be such a novelist as his own country had never conceived, as even "old England" in his time could not match for total devotion, accomplishment, form.

James was to become a great original, a powerful critic, the unique portraitist of society on two continents. This was conceded even when, at the height of his powers, he was a problem to such brilliant writers and intimates as Edith Wharton ("Don't ask me what I think of *The Wings of the Dove!*" she said to a Scribner's editor), H. G. Wells, Stephen Crane, André Gide. When James died in 1916, T. S. Eliot admitted that James had been dead for some time. In his last years the "Master" was something of a joke, so isolated that he scorned every popular fiction and "fictionalist." He became the great dissenter from the disorderly tradition of the English novel, invoked "form" and "composition" at every turn, found Tolstoy and Dostoevsky "loose baggy monsters," referred to some of his own productions as "almost perfect."

James certainly did not begin with this self-magnification and haughtiness toward other novelists. Like his always obliging friend Howells, with whom he was at first allied in producing the new fiction of manners for the magazines, James adopted a deliberate strategy. His early fiction duplicates Howells's studied equanimity, his easy irony and delightfully slow pace, everything deliberated as if he were preparing clever remarks at a dinner party. Howells's gift was for impersonating social tone. He leaves you slightly anxious, of course; each sentence is such a conscious preparation for the next. He lacks James's *edge*. James understood and (for a time) even relished his need to please the audience on whom he drew for his material. If "there is something voluptuous in meaning well," as Henry Adams said, that was certainly Henry James's voluptuousness. His collected letters wear the reader down with what James admitted was the "twaddle of mere graciousness."

James at the beginning was identified with the new market for fiction, and as he came into his maturity he took it on himself to defend fiction from the suspicion of not having a clear moral purpose. His 1884 essay, "The Art of Fiction," resonantly invoked freedom for the novelist: "The only reason for the existence of a novel is that it does attempt to represent life. . . . Enjoy [the novelist's freedom] as it deserves; take possession of it, explore it to its utmost extent, publish it, rejoice in it. All life belongs to you."

James called fiction the most human form of art—it caught "the look of things, the look that conveys their meaning, to catch the color, the relief, the expression, the surface, the substance of the human spectacle." The rising market as well as a more professional aptitude for fiction helped to mute the standard objection that fiction had no clear purpose. The modern system of royalty payments took hold about 1880. The cost of printing fell with the introduction of machine-made pulp paper, the rotary press, steam power, and the linotype machine. National magazines bid eagerly for the rights to new fiction when James was popular on both sides of the Atlantic. Even in Russia the fiction vogue forced novelists to start serializing their novels before they had thought them all out. Dostoevsky complained that he had to write with the copyboy at his shoulder. James T. Fields, owner of the *Atlantic Monthly*, told contributors that they were tied to the pace of industrial production.

James could afford to give up a share of the family income to his invalid sister, Alice. But he could never hope to make such a business of letters as Howells did. Howells, forever grinding away (of course he had an invalid wife), ran his own fiction in the *Atlantic* when he was editor. By 1885 he was able to make this arrangement with *Harper's:* "For a yearly 300-page novel he was to receive $10,000 in salary for the serial rights, and a 12½ percent royalty on the finished book. Whatever he wrote for *Harper's Monthly* would bring $50 per thousand words, and for *Harper's Weekly,* $30 per thousand." Howells also conducted for six years the "Editor's Study" column in *Harper's Monthly.* He was a steady producer of fiction, essays, travel books, and reviews who complained to his mother and sister back in Columbus that he could not afford to leave his desk. During his prime years Howells made the current equivalent of $150,000 a year. His literary tone of voice satisfied —though a shade of irony proclaimed his intellectual independence—the conscious propriety of Beacon Hill. Always working up social topics* (the businessman, the police station, divorce), Howells managed to retain the benevolence of the Brahmins, to inform and edify the largely feminine reading audience, to earn the plaudits of Mark Twain, who obviously found him harmless ("you are my only novelist"), and the polite interest of Henry James. (Howells was James's loyal admirer. His admission that he had "never lived" led to the character of Lambert Strether in *The Ambassadors.*) Howells, though he soon bored the elite like Henry Adams and exasperated the socially pretentious by his insistence on the ordinary ("that is the right American stuff"), managed dangerous topics as he managed his relations with publishers, the reading audience, and society in Boston. He was a friend to both Mark Twain and Henry James, and who else could have managed that?

In the early nineties Howells, outraged by the legal lynching of some immigrant anarchists in the Haymarket affair and the increasingly brutal influence of American business, rebelled against the self-satisfaction of Boston, moved to New York, and for a time regarded himself as a socialist and wrote with more bite. But "the question of the opportunities," as Henry James liked to put it, was always on Howells's mind. One feels about How-

---

*Ford to Egeria Boynton in *The Undiscovered Country* (1880):

" 'I'm serious enough, but I don't respect my writing as it goes on. It's as good as most; but it ought to be as good as the least.'

" 'What are social topics?' she asked presently.

" 'I suppose I'm treating a social topic now. I'm writing about some traits of New England country life. . . . I couldn't help noticing some things on the way; my ten years in town had made me a sort of foreigner in the country, and I noticed the people and their way of living; and after I got here I sent a letter to the newspaper about it. You might think that would end it; but you don't know the economies of a hack-writer, I've taken my letter for a text, and I'm working it over into an article for a magazine. If I were a real literary man I should turn it into a lecture afterwards, and then expand it into a little book.' "

ells that he trained himself to become a novelist at a time when the novel had become synonymous with magazines as a way of disseminating to the new middle class information about itself. If Howells had been brought up in the eighteenth century, he would have been a party pamphleteer in America, in Europe a librettist for Mozart's operas. He was a literary jack-of-all-trades who before the Civil War wrote imitations of Heine and after it social novels based on reportage—he had come to Boston in 1860 as a reporter investigating the shoe trade. He was a literary factotum who knew he could pass muster at every kind of writing. Thanks to his being in Europe during the Civil War, he was able to launch the novel of manners in America.

Howells's concern with the strategy of success would not have been possible without his "literary passions." He was crazy about writers as well as about books. James always buttered Howells up with faint praise. He appreciated what Howells had done for this newfangled business of describing "society" for itself alone, what Howells's vogue had opened up for James himself, and how much and in the end how little all this had done for Howells himself. With his head always turned to Europe, James of course thought Howells suburban. As he said in reviewing a routine Howells production, *A Foregone Conclusion* (1875), "Civilization with us is monotonous, and in the way of contrasts, of salient points, of chiaroscuro, we have to take what we can get."

Howells's characters come out of the same American pot. They are essentially mild civil beings, even genuinely resemble one another in their American good faith—a recipe not likely to make for excitement. What was monotonous about "my dear native land," as even Hawthorne had grumbled, was its atmosphere of "commonplace prosperity." James when twenty-four, lamenting that America was not sufficiently available to fiction, patriotically added: "We must of course have something of our own—something distinctive and homogeneous—and I take it that we shall find it in our moral consciousness, our unprecedented moral vigor."

The domestic kind of moral consciousness soon added to James's vexation about America. As he showed in *The Bostonians* (1886), it could turn cranky, sterile, hard. What James needed were contrasts that could enliven the tame scene and fill up a certain emptiness. In his early biography of Hawthorne, James took up and developed with a flourish what he thought was Hawthorne's failure to develop. It was proof "that the flower of art blooms only where the soil is deep, that it takes a great deal of history to produce a little literature, that it needs a complex social machinery to set a writer in motion."

Why did James not see a subject in the aggressiveness of American society? Why, fourteen years after the federal government crushed the most massive "rebellion" in history, could James write in his Hawthorne study that there was "no State, in the European sense of the word"? Why, in the midst of a society already feared by James's adored Britain as its imminent rival, did James suffer for the "very lack of air to breathe"?

James never had to say this, he did not even have to think this until he satirized in *The Bostonians* the cranks who now represented New England's religious idealism. He himself had no more respect for church religion than his father did and far less belief in a spiritual world detached from human society. His only faith was in the private consciousness—not Emerson's correlation of this with some shadow divinity but consciousness pushed steadily back on the individual himself, as in brother William—consciousness seeking an outlet and finding it in the inner world of other personalities. The "soul" was now a synonym for the individual, not an organ of perception receiving flashes of the divine. There was in fact a great blank where Emerson's "soul" had so confidently labored. But many Americans were very sure of what James had called their "spiritual lightness and vigor." "Genuine belief," Whitman had said in *Democratic Vistas,* "has left us"; religion had become sterile, small-minded, and was often faked in the travesty of Emersonianism that became Mary Baker Eddy's "spirit world." But Americans, precisely because they were humdrum, middle-middle in the tame bourgeois style that gave James no stimulus to imagination, and socially innocent, were purer than other peoples. This was a drawback to such a "grasping imagination" as James early declared himself to be, by contrast with Howells. The England lacking to poor Hawthorne was a fantasy that would never quite wear out for James even when he lived there:

> No sovereign, no court, no personal loyalty, no country gentlemen, no palaces, no castles, nor manors; nor old country houses, nor parsonages, nor thatched cottages, nor ivied ruins; no cathedrals, nor abbeys, nor little Norman churches; no great universities nor public schools—no Oxford, no Eton, nor Harrow; no literature, no novels, no museums, no pictures, no political activity, no sporting class—no Epsom nor Ascot!

V. S. Naipaul, another brilliant novelist from the Western hemisphere to settle in England, says that the novel is the product of "highly organized societies." James's England was even more "organized" than Naipaul's is today. When James revisited his native land in the early 1900s to write *The American Scene,* he found it not only rather too unorganized for his comfort but resoundingly vulgar. Victorian society made possible this crucial dialogue from *The Portrait of a Lady* (1881)—impossible to imagine in any country but James's dreamland, upper-class England, yet true to American virtuousness, it is spoken by an American to his father and unwittingly prepares the American heroine's doom:

> "I want to make her rich."
> "What do you mean by rich?"
> "I call people rich when they're able to meet the requirements of their imagination."

III

What James's first judges among the Brahmins would not have credited in such a pleasing young man was his secret avidity. To have "perception at the pitch of passion," to be "saturated," to "conquer," "appropriate," "triumph"—the intensity of his personal vocabulary becomes as routine in his writing as his hieratic settings. The settings were bestowed on him by tradition, were capable of "transmission," radiated the "tone of time." The ever more eloquent and echoing pressure James put into his renderings of Europe reflect an intoxication that even the refrain in his early letters—"At last I live"—does not fully convey. "The great thing is to be *saturated* with something, and I choose the form of my saturation."

What James demanded for himself, and eventually thought he had found in England, was a class, a style of life, the presentation of which would produce its effect. Its complexity, he assured himself, would answer to his deepest need as an artist: to bring out the *hiddenness* of personality. A leisured, upper-class society provided not only the surface that made for contrast with the secret soul but the intrigue that exposed it. James was a snob with a great purpose. Only superior society made possible what he thought of as the necessity and difficulty of discernment. Only the formal routine of "high civilization" made possible the arduousness (to do a work that would show "the most doing") that became his essence of art. So he narrowed himself. Not that he had a choice. In one of the late prefaces he wrote for his New York edition (of *Lady Barberina*), he admitted that

> nothing appeals to me more, I confess, as a "critic of life" in any sense worthy of the name, than the conquests of civilization, the multiplied symptoms among educated people, from wherever drawn, of a common intelligence and a social fusion tending to abridge old rigors of separation. . . . Behind all the small comedies and tragedies of the international, in a word, has exquisitely lurked for me the idea of some eventual sublime consensus of the

educated. . . . There . . . in the dauntless fusions to come—is the personal drama of the future.

James's "discovery of Europe" was that its *virtù*, its preciousness, was enough to frame a character, to release a story. By contrast, the bareness of American settings had been a special irritant to him. In *The Europeans* (1878) the Baroness Munster looks around her Boston hotel room with a grimace at its "vulgar nudity." In *The Bostonians* James emphasized "the general hard, cold void of the prospect" overlooking Back Bay. "There was something inexorable in the poverty of the scene, shameful in the meanness of its details, which gave a collective impression of boards and tin and frozen earth, sheds and rotting piles." The "glare" of gaslight is prominent in James's America but oddly missing in Europe. Like the lone tourist in so many nineteenth-century photographs of Italy, James seems to have had Europe all to himself. No wonder he was to fix on a character's "point of view" as the structure of a novel, and that what had begun as a limitation of experience he was to turn into a base of operations.

This was a Europe of imagination indeed, all tradition and background for the starved American senses that could now find in the touch of history, in any street, long-sought opulence for the mind. James's style grew prodigal whenever he drew a European setting. It shows a mind perfectly pleased, Virgilian in its silky *pietas* toward the cherished object. There is a purring effect to the opening of *The Portrait of a Lady*—James describing the great lawn at Gardencourt at tea time, that most delectable of ceremonies—that certainly contrasts with Newport before the Vanderbilts built their marble summer palaces: "The plain gray nudity of these little warped and shingled boxes seems to make it a hopeless task on their part to present any positive appearance at all."

A particularly happy example of how Europe will make possible "composition as positive beauty" occurs in part six of *The Ambassadors*. The puritan Strether, duly forewarned against the European temptress, calls on Mme. de Vionnet only to find himself charmed by her against the background of the old house in the Rue de Bellechasse. The "spell of transmission" is in full force. Strether warms to the lady under the spell of what is really a picture. As in an Italian Renaissance painting where the landscape positively hovers over the sitter, her house becomes the vibration of Mme. de Vionnet herself.

The house, the court "large and open, full of revelations, for our friend, of the habit of privacy, the peace of intervals," "the immemorial polish of the wide waxed staircase"—these, with so many more exquisitely right and revealing details, cause Strether "at the very outset to see her in the midst of possessions not vulgarly numerous, but hereditary, cherished, charming." (The anxious good taste of this in a novelist who adored Balzac would have amused Balzac, who loved to emphasize possessions vulgarly numerous.) Strether has his first "revelation" because of this delicately beautiful woman. Mme. de Vionnet and her house are so beautifully fused that Strether is soon released from his suspicions.

What wins us, too, is the typical Jamesian idyll of Europe as feminine, passive, unmoving, a picture:

> By a turn of the hand she had somehow made their encounter a relation. And the relation profited by a mass of things that were not, strictly, in it or of it; by the very air in which they sat, by the high, cold, delicate room, by the world outside and the little plash in the court, by the first Empire and the relics in the stiff cabinets, by matters as far off as those and by others as near as the unbroken clasp of her hands in her lap and the look her expression had of being most natural when her eyes were most fixed.

Mme. de Vionnet will be sacrificed by her lover, Chad Newsome. As early as *The American* (1877) Claire de Cintre was finished off for life by her feudal family. James returning to *The American* for the New York edition was surprised to see how "romantic" it was, how arbitrary and unsupported he had made the tragedy of his American hero and French heroine. "Europe" as setting had been enough to supply him with motivation. By contrast, James's American heroines, though they could be as high-mindedly duped as Isabel Archer in *The Portrait of a Lady*, as sweetly victimized as Milly Theale in *The Wings of the Dove*, as patiently long-suffering as Maggie Verver in *The Golden Bowl*, all showed an edge, an American strength, because they prevailed "morally." The American girl, his "princess," the "heiress of all ages," was always a more dominating figure in James's fiction than his pale, indecisive males.

She makes her triumphant and still most memorable entry striding into *The Portrait of a Lady* as bouncy American independence in all things—a Katharine Hepburn in her prime. Nothing so illustrates the roles of America and Europe in James's mind as the contrast between Isabel's health, her innocent self-assurance, and the Europeanized Americans around her. Withered Mr. Touchett, sickly Ralph Touchett, corrupted Madame Merle, and daemonically selfish Gilbert Osmond, all enlivened by her, virtually seduce her by their subtlety and their conscious charm. It was to be caught up like this that Isabel waited through dark lonely days in Albany. Although her attachment to her American-born "Europeans" almost destroys her, Isabel conveys all the "spell" of Americans entering upon Europe that was James's own.

Isabel embodies the note of "relation" that made society real. Women—certainly James's women—do not stand outside society. What James would have made of the tragedy of his friend Mrs. Henry Adams is fascinating to imagine. He would not have isolated her as a psychological case, in effect dropped her as everyone else did; he was a novelist. But of course Isabel, who shares with Marian Adams the famous spiritedness of the upper-class "American girl," really had spirit, and this was her eventual triumph. Marian went under.

Daisy Miller was no more than a type for a magazine story, "the innocently adventuring, unconsciously periculant American maiden," as Howells put it.* "Never was any civilization offered a more precious tribute than that which a great artist paid ours in the character of Daisy Miller. . . . But the American woman would have none of Daisy Miller . . . because she was too jealous of her own perfection to allow that innocence might be reckless." Was this idealization sincere, or was it just flattery of the "Iron Madonna" by the man who said that "the man of letters must make up his mind that in the United States the fate of a book is in the hands of the women"? In James's "Pandora," another early study of an American girl who is startlingly direct and uncomplicated, a married woman modelled on Marian Adams the Washington hostess reflects: "The type's new and the case under consideration. We haven't had time yet for complete consideration."

To "consider" other people is the morality of manners; to keep someone unrelentingly under consideration is the chief occupation of James's characters; finally to reflect and "consider," endlessly, is what the moral life comes to. Isabel's rashness in marrying Gilbert (precisely because his considerateness seems to ask nothing for himself) is the one *act* in the book—an act that requires her to spend the rest of her time considering its folly. So the whole book asks us to join in consideration of Isabel's case.

Reflectiveness becomes the norm in this world. But the betrayal it considers, terrible enough in view of the aching good faith with which Isabel entered upon it, is enlarged by the attentiveness, molding, shaping, that James brings to our unrelieved consideration of Isabel's plight.

. The concentration is wonderful, giving us point by point knowledge of the heroine as well as sympathy for her. We do not know so much of the poor, ill, palely loitering Milly Theale in *The Wings of the Dove*. We would not want to know this much of the relatively unsympathetic Maggie Verver

---

*Even in the rough commercial Chicago that Dreiser described in *Sister Carrie* (1900) a "Daisy Miller" was a term of reproach for a girl too forward for her own good.

in *The Golden Bowl;* Maggie is altogether too practical and too spoiled, her father's little princess even before she gets herself a real "prince." Isabel's plight engages us because she is not ambiguous like Maggie and is no wraith like Milly. She is altogether healthy in life, alone only because of her natural independence and honesty. There are no secrets to her—and this in a world where those who betray her have nothing to them but dirty little secrets. Ralph Touchett, who loves her but exposes her to evil by making her rich, is too sickly, and therefore complicated. The Jamesian male, usually a wall-flower, gets Isabel's compassion but not ours.

Isabel, launched on her perilous European career by millionaire Americans, open to exploitation by corrupt Americans, is led and misled every inch of the way by considerations that depend on European beauty, European ritual. The great lawn at Gardencourt dazzles her; Lord Warburton courts her by walking her past his family portraits; though the English nobleman attracts her, the false Gilbert Osmond wins her by seeming to speak for the esthetic soul of Europe itself—all consideration of the right art, the right values, the right setting. Isabel is the fairy-tale princess in the dark wood, out of her depth; but this being Europe, it is the sacred wood. Rich, picturesquely rich, tradition-rich Europe shines like a portrait indeed as the reflection of all the worshipful glances directed at it. And Gilbert thinks he represents it better than anyone else. He is the "first gentleman of Europe." After Isabel's honest American soul, Europe is virtually the main feature of the novel.

Isabel is vaguely unsettled by the sight of Madame Merle standing while Gilbert is all too comfortably seated. She has no reason to suspect that they are anything but "friends." Between friends, this would have been a breach of manners in Boston. In Boston the sight would not have weighed so heavily on our heroine's mind. The intrigue, the unsuspected intimacy that the scene imparts, helps to build up the increasing suspicion that the surface of "consideration" (a term Gilbert applies equally to social standards and esthetic matters) is false. We sense in this world something contrived and *wrong*, not just narrow and snobbish. We are beset by the dominating image of a "portrait," both as *virtù* and as the deception inherent in social appearance.

Wickedness in James is duplicity, usually sexual. An eye is always at the peephole, and being nothing but an eye, it sees the worst. Lambert Strether will recognize quite late in *The Ambassadors* that Chad and Mme. de Vionnet, who are always in each other's company, are in fact lovers. Maggie Verver will get the point about her prince and Charlotte Stant as a kind of triumphal crisis, the richest experience yet of her already distinguished life. Milly Theale, for all her pressing mortality, seems to have understood about Merton Densher and Kate Croy, and in death she exerts this knowledge around them as the supreme act of her life. The "criminal," and James uses the word, is a conspirator. There was nothing in James's world to conspire about but the secret love to which money is attached.

The bystanders, the onlookers, are mainly virtuous; action and sin are synonymous. James's central fixation on the "ruminant," the observer in all things (like Strether in *The Ambassadors*, he will want nothing for himself), helps to explain why coupling is arranged in bad faith and is vaguely dirty. Madame Merle wickedly gets Isabel married to Osmond; Kate Croy and Merton Densher get Milly Theale to love Densher; Charlotte Stant, Prince Amerigo's mistress, gets Maggie Verver married to the prince. What moral inflexibility it took on the part of Henry James to overlook the cynical mores of English country weekends in favor of standards acceptable to—Henry James. What genius it took on his part to carry this off, to make it all acceptable *now* as well as then. So Milly Theale's legacy to her would-be betrayers shames them into not being able to add it to any satisfactory life together. So Maggie wins back her husband by her "character." Naturally, this makes possible endless interpretation of Maggie's "real" character, though James would seem to have had no doubt—in his more innocent time —that she was a real American girl (and the daughter of a billionaire) and able to get her husband back if she wanted to.

James's unredeemed characters, like Gilbert Osmond, are villains through inflexibility. They are addicts of the wholly mental life, which is secrecy. Gilbert Osmond is one of his great creations because Gilbert (who forces Madame Merle to do the same) never stops thinking and planning. By nature they are spies. Not only does Madame Merle get Isabel married to Osmond as stealthily as she conceals her past relations with Osmond; we also feel, as the book begins to heat up after the long, languorous opening, that Madame Merle and Osmond are never thinking of anything but Isabel. It is true that everyone in the book has an eye on Isabel and that this steady focus draws us into James's own fascination with her. Lord Warburton, whom she rejected, seriously considers marrying Gilbert's infantile daughter—so that he can remain in the company of Isabel? The dying Ralph Touchett comes to Rome so that he can hover over her. Caspar Goodwood seems to have nothing to do but to run over periodically to Europe to persuade a married woman that she is beauty in distress. Henrietta Stackpole functions only as the comic maid in attendance on the queen.

But Madame Merle and Gilbert are *obsessed* with Isabel. They seem to have no interest in life apart from her. Madame Merle claims to be forever dashing about Europe, but she has not been travelling at all; she has been watching at the keyhole, waiting to get at poor Isabel again. All this watching and waiting works on us because we recognize a compulsion. Isabel's marriage to Osmond has become a conspiracy against her. Even the staple of Victorian melodrama—Madame Merle's inability to declare herself to her own daughter (who dislikes her anyway)—becomes intrinsic to Madame Merle's stealthy nature.

James's scene-drama succeeds because he, too, is unrelenting in his attention. Everything must point, point all the time. James bears down hard on a scene. We feel his excitement. The book leads us from scene to scene as if it were a play. James never discovered how characters should talk in a play, for his dialogues are founded on mistrustful people who are always picking each other up on words, as in a quarrel. But the drama is in the disclosure of the evil in those closest to us. The nearness of Osmond to Isabel is stifling, while she is surrounded by great English country houses, Tuscan villas, Roman streets. In the great dark palazzo this girl, so surrounded by things, will sit alone by the fire, recognizing at last that she has been violated to the very soul.

The moral crisis Isabel comes to in chapter 42 is James's classical moment, his tie with the virtuous tradition he left in America. Isabel recognizes that "the first gentleman of Europe," as he believes himself to be, the man with inhumanly perfect taste, is outraged by her freedom of mind and is trying to destroy it. Since the *Portrait* in its beauty of surface and scene, its investiture of old Europe as civilization, is in great part a "consecration" of the esthetic ideal, James's association of spiritual wickedness with a total esthete shows how "native" his sense of good and evil remained.

The sharpest portrait in James's international gallery is Gilbert Osmond. Gilbert illustrates James's ability to "do" Americans who have been set free in Europe to think of nothing but their good taste. Only minor, comic characters like Henrietta Stackpole have jobs (and James had a particular aversion to the woman writer as journalist). Business hardly comes into his world; the Newsome family in *The Ambassadors* manufacture "an object of domestic utility," no doubt because James could not think of an actual object. In *The Golden Bowl* the superrich Adam Verver from "American City" is entirely free to saunter about his great English estate, "Fawns," reviewing his relation to his daughter. But how many fine consciences there are, how many quivering sensibilities, how many people anxious only to keep each other under review! James's world is truly imagined—a world in which people keep imagining each other, in which (usually) every possible allowance is made for the merely sensitive, in which the merely sensitive have come to think of themselves as the "fine." "O Gilbert!" Isabel cries out when he has broken her heart, "you who were so fine!"

IV

James adored the "educated class" but did not idealize it. The connoisseur, the dilettante, the well-bred man who seemed to have been bred to no purpose but the savoring of his own distinction, could be the end product of so much leisure and civilization. Gilbert Osmond as the epitome of this type provoked all his horror of the evil hiding in the house of art. That prodigal artist Henry James could not have been more scornful of the type —especially where it represented the passive side of so much "civilization" and hence something of himself.

Osmond is one of James's finest creations. This decadent and shallow-hearted man lives only for what he is pleased to call culture, has equated society entirely with culture, yet wants the world to notice his every effect. James in a passionate aside notes that no man is more the slave of conventional opinion. Osmond's cultivated powerlessness makes him conformist, and his conformity *is* wickedness. His exaggerated respect for society makes him destructive in his relations with other people. Osmond carries out to its final logic, by trying to destroy all independence in his wife, that weakness of being a mere spectator that James illustrated in the character of Ralph Touchett, who protects himself against women by being constantly ill. The elder Touchett's own early withdrawal from love may be responsible for the eccentricity of his wife. James knew enough of fastidious withdrawal and anxious self-protection to see an alter ego in a type which even in its generosity does harm, as Ralph Touchett does by making Isabel rich.

Gilbert is the ultimate refinement beyond which James did not care to go. Ralph Touchett, dangling from the tree of his father's millions like a withered apple about to fall, can fulfill himself only in misguided fantasy. Wanting to make Isabel "rich," he gets his father to leave her three hundred fifty thousand pounds. People who meet the requirements of their imagination can be called rich. This double use of the word "rich" is unbearable; Ralph knows nothing of how riches are acquired. But Gilbert is not so removed. His haughty estheticism, his obsessive fastidiousness in all things, are soon turned against his wife, whom he hates for her independence, as he hates everything and everyone he cannot control.

In this gallery hung with so many gleaming surfaces and fine portraits, Gilbert is the dilettante who would kill. He betrays the society of fine surfaces by showing the black heart beneath. Everything that prides itself on "taste" as a social task, on the epicurean and the epicene, is incarnated in

Gilbert Osmond's lethal conformism—what surprises and shocks his wife most about him. Despite so much adoration of the fine surface, Gilbert wants just to know what the powerful think. The real threat to the soul—to Isabel's, for Gilbert is past saving—arises from an excessive worship of the fine surface.

Yet in *The Golden Bowl,* the greatest, richest novel of his triumphant last period, in the twentieth century, James showed that it was indeed the world of fine surfaces, civilization in excelsis, that inspired him to transcend himself as the great novelist of manners. He positively shone in the reflection of the "great world" given him by imperial England, the second Roman Empire —and with a Roman "prince" at the center of the action!

The Wings of the Dove depends for its dominant image of "mortal" beauty on the figure of a dying girl, the intended dupe of a plot to acquire her fortune conceived by the man she loves and his mistress. Milly Theale's thoughts and actions are not seen directly; her effect on others, especially after her death, makes the book. So her pale, merely outlined self needs the contrast with resplendent, moneyed London, with the hard-pressed Kate Croy and her "devouring" Aunt Maud—with the Swiss mountaintop on which we see the dying Milly ironically perched as the "heiress of all the ages," with Lord Mark dreaming of fortune in the Piazza San Marco, "the drawing room of Europe." In *The Ambassadors* the virtuous and self-denying figure of Lambert Strether becomes vivid against the Paris setting, the "Babylon, bright and hard." Lunching along the Seine with the supposed femme fatale, Mme. de Vionnet, whom he has come to Europe to separate from the son of his patroness, he cannot tell the perfection of the lady from the perfection of the moment. The most famous scene in *The Ambassadors* has Strether, the yearning, life-impoverished puritan in the garden of the great sculptor Gloriani, crying out that he has never "lived." *The Ambassadors* ends on Strether's denying himself the love offered by Maria Gostrey; *The Wings of the Dove,* on Milly's power after death to "elevate" those who planned to use her in the most shameless way.

All this privation and nobility impresses us less than the power that Europe had to make people *shine.* In *The Golden Bowl,* the last novel James completed, all his dreams of the great world, the favorite landscape of his imagination, were fulfilled by a set of characters who are made to *seem* perfectly matched to James's enduring love of Europe itself. Nowhere else in James are such greedy and crooked people so constantly ennobled in conversation with people who are distrustful and distrusted but regularly come out with "You're wonderful"—because of a social status that on all sides compels respect, especially from Henry James. Even William James, disliking "the method of narration by interminable elaboration of suggestive reference (I don't know what to call it, but you know what I mean)," admitted that "in spite of it all, there is a brilliancy and cleanness of effect, and in this book especially a high-toned social atmosphere that are unique and extraordinary."

Only James would have thought up an impoverished Roman "prince" who is always ceremoniously referred to as "the Prince." He enters the book, on the eve of his marriage to the daughter of an American billionaire, in an understandably somber mood; even a prince in need of a fortune, and mildly in love with an American billionaire's daughter, must have some conflict within himself about laying his head on the marriage block. He could not afford to marry his real love, Charlotte Stant; she could not afford to marry him. So she returns from a hurried, distasteful sojourn in her native America to help celebrate the marriage of her lover to her dearest friend, Maggie Verver. The duplicity, the many second thoughts felt like the famous flaw in the flawed and gilded crystal bowl that Maggie eventually buys herself as a wedding present, do not keep the prince from enjoying both Charlotte and his wife's money. Status in *The Golden Bowl* is everything, it resolves with magic force an existence that consists entirely of the most measured affections and reflections.

Adam Verver, the American billionaire whose only tie to his origins and presumable enterprise in "American City" is the planned donation of a museum, spends all his time on his English estate looking after his daughter—when he is not depositing art as if it were bullion. "There are things," Maggie tells her prince on the eve of their marriage, "that father puts away—the bigger and more cumbrous, of course, which he stores, has already stored in masses, here and in Paris, in Italy, in Spain, in warehouses, vaults, banks, safes, wonderful secret places. . . . But there's nothing, however tiny, that we've missed." Still, Adam is so far removed from the usual earthiness of the American superrich that "it was all, at bottom, in him, the aesthetic principle, planted where it could burn with a cold, still flame; where it fed almost wholly on the material directly involved, on the idea (followed by appropriation) of plastic beauty, of the thing visibly perfect in its kind."

"The surfaces ring." Of course this world is "flawed" by adultery, secret and dishonest because of sex. Sex has nothing to do with the way Adam Verver, that good man if all-too-loving father, made his money. (Like his namesake in Eden, Adam is troubled only by the trouble that women get him into.) It would be sentimental to suppose that James's great fairy tale turns not on his adoration of these highly placed and privileged characters but on the moral imperative (or a natural sense of possession) that leads Maggie to reclaim her prince and her father to take his wife, Charlotte, in self-sacrificing exile back to their native land. Nowhere else does one feel that James has at last met up with the ideal personages of his English dream world. James was right to call *The Golden Bowl* the best and richest of his novels. Nowhere else does he seem so totally at ease in the happy spilling over of his images for mental states; nowhere else does he so obviously luxuriate in the duration of his characters' endless fascination with their own status and with each other.

James's great achievement in this last novel was to make "personality" triumph over the accumulation of experience. With this he demonstrated a distinctness of and fascination for personality that became increasingly dim in twentieth-century fiction after him, as a clinical psychology replaced every traditional sense of uniqueness. For James the individual soul is still the product of the most finespun relationships, can be put into motion only by a civilization that values persons in the most delicate assortments and combinations. Adultery, though "criminal," was fundamental to James's novelistic sense of drama. *The Golden Bowl* really has only four characters spinning each other out over almost eight hundred pages. Without the total involvement of each member of the quadrille with all the others, there would be no joy to the book at all. Given the involvement in all its suspense, we get such a feast of implications and recognitions as James most wanted to write—and finally achieved.

What if all this was not "civilization" as the wisest Europeans knew it? What if it was so perfectly composed, every nuance linked, that the very perfection declared its necessary fragility? James would not have tolerated the objection, much less have understood it. This was his country, his only country. No other novelist of the new century—not Proust, not Kafka, not Joyce—would in *his* country have been so secure as Henry James was when he completed *The Golden Bowl.* He exultantly told Scribner's that it was "the most *done* of my productions . . . a shaft sunk to the real basis of the subject —a real feat of engineering."

It was his supreme moment. The terror of August 1914 was still inconceivable. His own proficiency in technique, in the logic of art, in nuance, he felt to be tribute to the civilization that had made him less of an exile. He even felt the book to be an accomplishment of that civilization. It was "rich" in every suggestion, able to meet the requirements of Henry James's imagination. And it was secure, a book like an imperium of sorts, and one that would surely last. One of the high moments of *The Golden Bowl* is a ball at which royalty makes an appearance. There is even a field marshal. The lovers, intoxicated by their nearness at the ball, are borne up by a passion greater than their passion for each other. It was James's finest hour. There are societies, he gravely tells us in *The Golden Bowl*, "subject to the greatest personages possible."

10

Chicago and "the East": Dreiser, Adams, Mark Twain

> Sometimes I see myself as a hoop in an arc reaching over from one phase of existence to another.
>
> THEODORE DREISER

I

One day in 1889, eighteen-year-old Caroline Meeber from Columbia City, Wisconsin—"Sister Carrie as she was half affectionately termed by her family"—boarded a train for Chicago that was to take her (and the surprisingly but never dependably gifted newspaper reporter from Terre Haute who had imagined her for his first novel) into world literature. The twenty-eight-year-old Theodore Dreiser, who had been raised in an immigrant German Catholic home and was largely self-educated, having hungrily absorbed in public libraries harsh doctrine from Balzac and Herbert Spencer, was never to forget his first glimpse of Chicago in the 1880s. To the boy just off the Indiana train, the raw and muddy city was an "Aladdin's view" from *The Arabian Nights*. "Had I one gift to offer the world, it would be the delight of sensing the world as I then saw it." The Aladdin's lamp became the "giant magnet" in *Sister Carrie*. Chicago's population on the eve of the 1890s was

> not so much thriving upon established commerce as upon the industries which prepared for the arrival of others. The sound of the hammer engaged upon the erection of new structures was everywhere heard. Great industries were moving in. The huge railroad corporations which had long before recognized the prospects of the place had seized upon vast tracts of land for transfer and shipping purposes. Streetcar lines had been extended far out into the open country in anticipation of rapid growth. The city had laid miles and miles of streets and sewers through regions where, perhaps, one solitary

house stood out alone—a pioneer of the populous ways to be. There were regions open to the sweeping winds and rain, which were yet lighted throughout the night with long, blinking lines of gas-lamps, fluttering in the wind. Narrow board walks extended out, passing here a house, and there a store, at far intervals, eventually ending on the open prairie.

Carrie was eighteen in 1889 because Dreiser, born in the year of the Great Fire, was then eighteen. The Chicago that Carrie first saw was the Chicago rebuilt as steel after the 1871 fire had almost completely wiped out the old wooden ramshackle Chicago. Still clinging to the lake, and backed up by the empty prairie, the city with its eye on the future was by 1893 to transcend itself. Suddenly a center and showplace of American "energies," as Henry Adams was surprised to note, it grabbed for itself the World's Columbian Exposition in honor of the four hundredth anniversary of Columbus's unintended discovery.

No one who was there ever forgot what was to become the most celebrated fair and exposition in American history. It marked the symbolic end of their rustic and small-town world for many Middle Western Americans. It saw the greatest outpouring of crowds since the Civil War, proudly exhibited American industrial processes and the latest technology at a time when the United States was eclipsing Great Britain, and inspired a brash new style in mass entertainment, the era of Coney Island amusement parks. Whitman, who had died the year before, would have gloried in what he called democratic "ensemble"—the urban mass he called the counterpart of *Leaves of Grass*.

"Theo" Dreiser had special reason to remember the fair. He met his future wife, Sara Osborne White (familiarly known as Jug), in the summer of 1893 when the twenty-one-year-old star reporter on the *St. Louis Republic* "shepherded" to the fair a group of Missouri schoolteachers who had won a contest sponsored by the newspaper. Dreiser, with just one year at the University of Indiana paid for by a high school teacher, was self-conscious about his lack of a degree and of middle-class refinement. German had been spoken in Dreiser's home, even by his native-born Mennonite mother, in deference to his immigrant father. The fact that Jug the schoolteacher had a firmer hold on grammar than Dreiser did had helped to make her desirable. In the course of a madly erotic life he often managed to combine a love affair with editorial help. At his urging after their marriage, Jug went through the manuscript of *Sister Carrie* and made many genteel revisions. Dreiser was anxious to tone down the sexual matter that was central to the book, in the belief that this would make the book more acceptable to a publisher. It did not. Dreiser never suffered long from objections to his style; he unconsciously relied on narrative force to carry him through. The firmness of Jug's character, once a welcome contrast to his "dissolute" sisters (models for Carrie and Jennie Gerhardt), was eventually to prove too much for the moody Dreiser, who could never remain interested for very long in any one woman—and who liked from time to time to torment himself about this failing.

Chicago in the nineties, the most disturbed period in American life after the Civil War, was Dreiser's destined subject, as it was for other Midwestern writers. He did not choose it, as Henry James chose so many things to write about. Chicago seemed to choose him—which was what Dreiser felt about every circumstance in his life, every plot in his fiction. He was the first American novelist to invest the big city with such a hungry, avid sense of power. No one after him has yet rendered the physical discovery of a city in such haunting detail, with so much feeling brought up from the depths of the old small-town experience. As a foreigner of sorts, the first major American writer who was not a Protestant, and a "barbarian" by accepted standards, he could not help challenging the pieties of a society unable to anticipate their loss.

Dreiser's images of the city have a lasting hold because he described the most familiar objects in a great city as if they were foreign to him. The pathos of distance became his fictional perspective, the medium in which his most affecting characters move. Every appearance of the modern city became single, hallucinatory, painfully distinct with that first impression of a new world. Carrie comes to Chicago to live with her sister, finds herself unwelcome, and walks about, looking for work. The frightened but impressionable eighteen-year-old girl from Columbia City matched the newness of Chicago. Dreiser identified the stupor and loneliness in Carrie's heart with the unfinished landscape and the brutal unconcern surrounding it. The force with which Chicago had been built up from the prairie fascinated its own intellectuals. In *With the Procession,* a satire by Chicago's "patrician" Henry Blake Fuller, a character pointing to the "new" Chicago says that the town

> labors under one disadvantage: it is the only great city in the world to which all its citizens have come for the one common, avowed object of making money. There you have its genesis, its growth, its end and object. . . . In this Garden City of ours every man cultivates his own little bed and his neighbor his; but who looks after the paths between?

Chicago was halfway between the wilderness and the stock exchange. Every human aggression was closer to the writer's eye. Chicago was a concentrated force accessible enough to become a favorite subject of social criticism on the part of early realists like Fuller and Robert Herrick, transplanted Harvard poets and scholars at the new University of Chicago like William Vaughn Moody and Robert Morss Lovett, tough-talking "literary" reporters from Carl Sandburg to Ben Hecht. Much of Thorstein Veblen's *The Theory of the Leisure Class* (1899), with key terms for the appetites of the new-rich like "conspicuous consumption," was documented from Chicago. The new science of sociology, often based on the immigrants' settling into their separate ethnic wards, found brilliant exponents at the university founded on Rockefeller money. The sardonic criticism of American wealth and its manners that was to fill early-twentieth-century fiction also found its grim material in the Haymarket affair, the stockyards, the meat-processing jungle, the terrible winters and sometimes even more terrible police. Nowhere but in Chicago would a millionaire (Levi Leiter) have offered to buy the Great Wall of China.

The obvious thing about Chicago was that it was forever making itself, as it was remaking the Polish and Slavic immigrants and the children of farms and small towns who streamed into it. As a subject, it was easier to get hold of than New York, was present all compact to a writer's eye; the transformation from the old provincial life to the magnificent views from Lake Shore Drive was the work of one short, violent period in history. Chicago incarnated the big change that so many young people were making in their lives. And Dreiser, in the literalness of his fascination with the city, the obsession with fact that he developed as a skilled reporter and effective writer of "tragedy and heartbreak" stories for the Sunday supplements, identified totally with the "lure" of the city.

In the original version of *Sister Carrie* Dreiser reproduced the names of Chicago saloons, restaurants, business establishments. He carefully listed "Chicago windows" as the "large plates of window glass . . . then rapidly coming into use." He did not have to invent anything that Carrie saw when she first made the rounds of Chicago looking for work, or the "gorgeous" and "truly swell" saloon where Hurstwood was manager. Not the overhead curved marble oscillating fans above the bar, the ceramic tile floor, and the top-hatted ward heelers, actors, merchants, politicians, "the general run of successful characters about town, a goodly company of rotund, rosy figures, silk-hatted, starchy-bosomed, be-ringed and be-scarf pinned to the queen's taste." Not Hurstwood himself, who enters *Sister Carrie* "dressed in excellent, tailored suits of imported goods, several rings upon his fingers, a fine blue diamond in his necktie, a striking vest of some new pattern and a watch chain of solid gold which held a charm of rich design and a watch of the latest make and engraving."

I I

The twenty-eight-year-old Dreiser began his first novel in the fall of 1899 by suddenly writing on a half sheet of yellow copy paper "Sister Carrie." He had never thought of writing a novel until pressed to try his hand by Arthur Henry, his managing editor on the *Toledo Blade* and his most intimate friend. Henry was a glibly conventional writer of fiction, but he gave an appearance of flair, which Dreiser certainly lacked. He was an "emancipated" husband and assertive thinker in the ironic style favored by such end-of-the-century newspapermen as Stephen Crane—their representative man and attested genius. Like Dreiser's future friend and pugnacious supporter, H. L. Mencken, Henry provided a figure of authority to Dreiser, who was to demonstrate awesome force as a social novelist but little personal self-confidence.

Dreiser had been scarred by the poverty and shiftlessness of his large family, the rigidity of his German Catholic father, his Mennonite mother's seeming helplessness, and his own lack of formal education. To the end of his life, when he managed to die a member of the Communist Party and a communicant of one church after another, he was easily lulled by other people's ideas. Henry, remembered today for his influence on the composition, editing, and publishing of *Sister Carrie* in 1900, made himself important to Dreiser. He prodded "his" reporter to write his first short stories when Dreiser wanted to write plays; he cut a good many sentences and paragraphs out of the manuscript of *Sister Carrie*, largely on the ground that Dreiser's philosophizing over the fate of his characters was not necessary to the remorseless tread of the novel. He pushed Dreiser to hold Doubleday, Page and Company to its agreement when Frank Doubleday, shocked by Carrie's failure to suffer appropriately after living with two men (he was also prodded by Mrs. Doubleday's displeasure), tried to get out of publishing the novel.

Henry may also have been a model to the Dreiser who, after marrying the pretty redheaded schoolteacher he had fallen in love with at the fair, became as restless as Drouet and Hurstwood in *Sister Carrie*. Henry had with great aplomb left his wife for Anna T. Mallon, who was also to have an effect on the published version of *Sister Carrie*. She ran a typing agency and had the manuscript typed up by a succession of her "girls" as a favor to Dreiser; they also found things to correct in the always "correctable" Dreiser.

"My mind was a blank except for the name. I had no idea who or what she was to be. . . . There was something mystic about it, as if I were being used, like a medium." When Dreiser, "as if in a trance," began his novel, he was thinking of his sister Emma, who had run off to New York with a married man, L. A. Hopkins, a cashier in Chapin and Gore's tavern in Chicago. Hopkins had panicked when his wife learned of his affair with Emma and had absconded with thirty-five hundred dollars. This rash act provided the basis for the central scene in *Sister Carrie* (duplicated for the power of "accident" only by the boating "accident" in *An American Tragedy*) in which Hurstwood takes ten thousand dollars from his employer's safe quite without meaning to. In *An American Tragedy* Clyde Griffiths, who wants to be rid of his pregnant mistress, Roberta Alden, watches her drown without technically killing her. In both novels—and this is Dreiser's lasting achievement—"accidental" crime forcibly illustrates Dreiser's belief that we do what a "voice" within us tells us to do. That voice is the criminal, thief, and murderer in us that everything in our laborious upbringing and officially moral civilization tries to suppress. The true source and inspiration of our actions is always unexpected. Civilization is an ordeal. Inwardly, we are always in flight.

Hurstwood is unable to put the money back in the locked safe and, suddenly released by the fact that he cannot put it back, persuades Carrie to run off with him, first to Montreal, where they have a mock wedding ceremony, then to New York. In New York Hurstwood soon goes through what money he has left after returning most of the stolen funds, and after a series of catastrophes in business he falls apart. Carrie leaves him and becomes a successful actress. Hurstwood gasses himself in a flophouse.

Hurstwood is the active center of the novel, not Carrie. The most celebrated feature of the novel is Hurstwood's collapse in New York; he changes rapidly and shockingly from a smoothly self-assured saloon manager into a derelict. When William Heinemann published *Sister Carrie* in England, he thought the novel so much Hurstwood's story that he had the opening two hundred pages, before Hurstwood appears, cut to eighty-four. Dreiser was right, of course, to keep the original title when Frank Doubleday, reluctantly publishing the novel in 1900, wanted to call it *The Flesh and the Spirit*. Dreiser not only saw Carrie as a catalyst of Hurstwood's startling collapse; he saw her, in all her early timidity and lasting silence, as the deepest possible force, the role he naturally assigned to women. To the always alienated and radical Dreiser, Carrie represents the power of transformation, the woman as catalyst. At the same time, he identified with her—in this respect she was truly his "sister"—as a wondering, brooding center of perception.

If Carrie is the precipitant, Hurstwood is the stage on which Dreiser's first American tragedy is unrolled. The tragedy is that Americans may have nothing to live for but the "bitch-goddess." Dreiser, far outside the area of James's moral concern, knew that for such a man as Hurstwood, success included the acquisition of Carrie at any risk. So much sexual greed, shocking as it may have been to those who would not admit lust as a counterpart of the general acquisitiveness, was inherent in Dreiser himself. It gave force to his novel. His own furious sexuality he interpreted as a protest against American hypocrisy in all things. In the unforeseen creation of Hurstwood (he bore no resemblance to the forgettable embezzler with whom sister Emma had run off—they had ended up in New York placidly renting out rooms for "immoral purposes") Dreiser revealed the deepest traces in his own soul not only of Hurstwood's passion but of Hurstwood's failure of nerve. After *Sister Carrie* was killed by its own publisher, Dreiser actually went through a nervous collapse amazingly like Hurstwood's and was himself on the point of suicide when he was rescued by his brother Paul, the successful songwriter and man of the theater with whom "Theo" had written "On the Banks of the Wabash."

Dreiser was no sooner recovered than he began to write fawning portraits of business leaders for a magazine called *Success*. As editor of *Butterick's*, he carefully kept out of that ladies' magazine examples of the new realistic fiction. But Dreiser identified with Hurstwood's pursuit of woman and of the "bitch-goddess," and he knew all too well the panic that is always the underside of that pursuit. He incarnated in Carrie the unconscious force of sex that Henry James never allowed his heroines, who were triumphantly moral in life (Isabel Archer, Maggie Verver) or in death (Milly Theale). Henry Adams, in the famous meditation "The Dynamo and the Virgin," "asking himself whether he knew of any American artist who had ever insisted on the power of sex," could come up only with Whitman. Adams certainly liked to see woman as goddess. He would have resisted the "lure" of Carrie even if the book had come to his attention. She was lower-class and too much trouble.

Carrie and Hurstwood were both aspects of Dreiser himself. They represented the underside of American life, which was all too familiar to him. When he was eleven, the distressed Dreiser family made a new home in Evansville, Indiana, thanks to Annie Brace, the madame of a local brothel who was his brother Paul's mistress. His "Carrie" sister ran off with an embezzler; his "Jennie Gerhardt" sister, as the novel relates, became the mistress of a politician. Dreiser as a young laundry-wagon driver in Chicago kept back some of the collections from his employer. To the end of his life he never lost a sense of his own insignificance, of the ambition necessary to savage new forces. But it was his sense of force, desperately as he tried to locate this in the conventional determinism of his generation, that gave him his startling grasp of human drift and accident in all things. Only Dreiser would have been stopped in the writing of the most powerful scene in *Sister Carrie*, Hurstwood's deteriorioration, because "Somehow, I felt unworthy to write all that. It seemed too big, too baffling."

The artist in Dreiser was always stronger than the man. Few writers with Dreiser's power had such crude verbal habits, such rudimentary instincts about life. A writer brought up with the "proper" English of a middle-class family in the Midwest would not have introduced Carrie as possessing "four dollars in money." We learn at the outset that "she could scarcely toss her head gracefully," just as we are told on meeting Hurstwood that "Fitzgerald and Moy's Adams Street place" was "really a gorgeous saloon from a Chicago standpoint. . . . It was a truly swell saloon."

Dreiser's unimpeachable sense of social fact led him to report that Hurstwood spent all of one dollar and fifty cents for dinner, that Carrie at the shoe factory earned three dollars and fifty cents a week, and that for her first day at work she "dressed herself in a worn shirt-waist of dotted blue percale, a skirt of light brown serge rather faded, and a small straw hat which she had worn all summer at Columbia City." At the shoe factory "the whole atmosphere was one of hard contract." Dreiser occasionally interrupted his own story to sigh and "philosophize" over the irreversible actions of his characters; he was swept up by the process he was recounting, item by item, with such hard logic. Despite these clumsy interventions, no other "reportorial realist" could have led his heroine so convincingly into Carrie's crisis.* She becomes ill and loses her job before Drouet takes her over. Her numbness, shyness, and outward submissiveness are powerfully contrasted with the compulsions of the market system and the ravages of a Chicago winter.

Unable to understand, much less to resist, the "forces" that surround this "waif," and virtually forced out of her sister's dreary flat when she loses her job, Carrie allows herself to be bought by Drouet, the flashy drummer whom she had met on the train that first brought her to Chicago. We see how right Dreiser was to warn us, at the opening of Carrie's journey to the big city,

---

*"Reportorial realist" was the phrase used by the reader for Harper and Brothers who turned down *Sister Carrie*. "I cannot conceive of the book arousing the interest or inviting the attention, after the opening chapters, of the feminine readers who control the destinies of so many novels."

that "self-interest with her was high, but not strong. It was, nevertheless, her guiding characteristic." In the chapters following Carrie's fall from virtue, we see that while there is nothing heroic about her, her submission is also natural to the highly limited person she is. It will not take her long to see how shallow Drouet is, but her own automatism is not really clear to her.

Carrie—this is Dreiser's "modern" insight—is a construction of society. Her assets are a certain prettiness and a "dawning" sensibility rather than a trained intelligence—a sensibility in which Dreiser portrayed his own conscious makeup. Carrie's success (not Hurstwood's collapse) makes her increasingly "ponder" her life and, near the end of the book, "dream such happiness as you may never feel." She will never lose her essential passivity, her "wondering," the unconscious cruelty of being able to captivate Drouet, to infatuate and ruin Hurstwood, without herself coming to any realization about them. In some cardinal meaning of the word, Carrie is innocent—in the sense that she is *lacking.* Naively wrapped up in her own life, she is unable to imagine another's. This may be the fate of "modern" people whose personalities are constructed for them by "want" and fulfilled by "society." There were to be more and more people with nothing of their own but a desire for "happiness." This, as much as the selfishness sanctioned by the market system, Dreiser may have had in mind when he said that the whole atmosphere of Carrie's first factory was one of hard contract. We finally see Carrie in her famous rocking chair; she broods and broods over the mystery of it all without seeing anything more clearly than she did on the day she set out for Chicago.

I I I

How did a character so passive and composed of so much inert "wondering" come to have a strong and altogether compelling novel written around her? Carrie is hardly a designing femme fatale, and *The Flesh and the Spirit* would have been an irrelevant as well as a meretricious title for a book that turns as much on Carrie's passivity as on Hurstwood's lust. Carrie haunts the novel that bears her name because she represents the force of sex, the challenge to the established mores, that can make even a wistful and ignorant young girl irresistible to men who are wrapped up in the daily pursuit of profit. Her original helplessness when confronted with Chicago, her sliding into a life with Drouet and Hurstwood that she hardly anticipated, the stage success she never planned or even understood, convey Dreiser's view of the modern soul's merging into a situation from which mind and affection remain detached. Classical tragedy was based on human limitation—the larger struggle with the universe was always in view. Modern tragedy is unreflectiveness, apartness in our hearts from the lives we actually live and drive others to live. The first chapter title in *Sister Carrie* is "The Magnet Attracting: A Waif Amid Forces." This "waif" will never really know what is happening to her. Her sexuality is as incomprehensible to Carrie, as fatal to Hurstwood, as nature was to primitive man. This sexuality accomplishes a revolution in people's lives, however, and in 1900 it was recognized as a threat to the established order.

Dreiser did not altogether see this himself. Like Whitman, the stranger "to our ways" disturbed the secularized Protestant elect who had replaced religion with morality and morality with propriety. Unlike Whitman, he attempted to construct no new world of the spirit, no *personal* world. Always feeling himself rejectable, he did not understand the challenge he represented. What he did understand was that Carrie and Hurstwood are caught up in a situation beyond their power of reflection (and beyond Dreiser's), though he would struggle all his life with "science" and Spencer's "The Unknowable," and with his ultimate wistfulness would confess, "Sometimes I see myself as a hoop in an arc reaching over from one phase of existence to another." From which it followed that what a writer had to do was not only to narrate the sequence of force, to develop the inevitability of the plot, but also—as the Greek chorus did in the face of the destiny inflicted on human beings—to cry out in fragmented and sometimes helpless speech.

All his life Dreiser was told how inadequate a writer he was; he must also have been aware of how unconventional a first novel he had written, for to assure its publication some thirty-six thousand words were cut out of the manuscript by Arthur Henry, Dreiser's wife, and Dreiser himself. The original manuscript is more explicit about the sexual illegitimacy that is so important to the book. In it Carrie struggles with herself about moving in with Drouet and about leaving Drouet for Hurstwood (to whom she is deeply attracted). At the same time it is made clear that Drouet went on philandering even after he had coaxed Carrie into his bed, and that Hurstwood frequented prostitutes after he had lured Carrie to New York. The atmosphere of the original is steamier and more truthful to the characters of birds of passage like Drouet and Hurstwood. Carrie and Hurstwood make love in their Montreal hotel room before they go through the bigamous wedding ceremony. We are more aware than ever of Hurstwood's desperate character. He hated his wife but stayed with her as long as "she loved him vigorously."

Arthur Henry, who did most of the cutting, did not always understand what Dreiser was after. In eliminating Dreiser's pointed judgment of Hurstwood—"He saw a trifle more clearly the necessities of our social organization, but he was more unscrupulous in the matter of sinning against it"—Henry eliminated our own need to anticipate Hurstwood's actual subtlety. Although nothing in the original version prepares us for Hurstwood's disintegration, we still need to know more about the hidden forces in this strange man. His real secret is his essential despair over those things he can barely hold on to. Dreiser originally ended the book with Hurstwood's suicide, which confirms our premonition of his desperate nature.

To end the book with Hurstwood's death was more in keeping with the social logic of *Sister Carrie* than Carrie's stage musings from her rocking chair ("Oh, the tangle of human life"). But Hurstwood, as always, made Dreiser uneasy. Dreiser wandered off to the Palisades one day (the book was largely written on the upper West Side of New York) and finished off the story with the generalized meditation that ends, "Oh, Carrie! Carrie! Oh, blind strivings of the human heart!" He had begun by writing "Sister Carrie" as if in a trance; he had to return to Carrie in the end. She duplicated the young Dreiser, who was full of feeling and, in the person of Carrie, not beyond pitying himself. He had to carry her to this rhetorical finale in order to deliver her from the conventional world. That defiance was what he cared about most; it was the secret message of the novel. His publisher in New York, Frank Doubleday, understood this well enough when he did his best to kill the book.

IV

Mark Twain was in Chicago several times in 1893, the summer of the fair, but was so entangled in business affairs that he never got to see it. Nor did Henry Adams's black butler, who had come out with Adams and his friends in the private railway carriage of Senator Don Cameron, Pennsylvania's political boss, in order to cook for them. Adams, benevolently inquiring what his butler thought of the fair, was surprised to hear that he had been too busy looking after the Adams party.

Mark Twain, always the showman with his eye on the dollar, originally thought that it would be suitable for the four hundredth anniversary of the discovery to dig up Columbus's bones and exhibit them in Chicago.

No other writer made so much of the fair, was more impressed with the symbol of American "unity" that Chicago provided, than that constant traveller and increasingly bitter observer, Henry Adams. For the opening in

May, Adams was usually with Elizabeth Cameron, the elderly Senator Cameron's much younger wife. No one will ever know just how intimate Adams was with her or how intimate he would have liked to be. Adams always wrote to her as though he were in love with her, and since Senator Cameron (who was even older than Adams) was never far away, it is probable that with his usual delight in women of his class who possessed Elizabeth Cameron's charm and intelligence, the widower Adams was able without risk to enjoy the delight (and mischief) of public courtship. He managed, as usual, to make literature out of his passionate wistfulness toward Mrs. Cameron—his letters to her are as wonderful as anything this publicly frigid man ever wrote.

Adams soon left Chicago for his summer in France and the enraptured study of the medieval. Then the Panic of 1893, which was to launch the worst depression in American history, brought Adams home to save the family investments. Henry in the 1870s had documented the machinations on Wall Street of Jay Gould and Jim Fiske; his meticulous scholarship extended to all matters of finance. He handled the Panic so well that by September, he relates in the "Chicago (1893)" chapter of the *Education*, "the storm having partly blown over, life had taken on a new face, and one so interesting that he set off to Chicago to study the Exposition again, and stayed there a fortnight absorbed in it. He found matter of study to fill a hundred years, and his education spread over chaos."

The coolness of this, the surface air of personal intactness and detached curiosity, were in Adams's most practiced Mandarin manner. In the *Education*, that masterpiece representing the "unity" of Henry Adams without a hint of the cracks, he managed to gloss over the inclusive despair and political hatred that erupted in his letters. But his letters are his autobiography; the *Education* is a book about the nineteenth century—whose transformations, making the United States a great power, Adams thought he could measure. His personal sense of powerlessness and "failure"—the wrong people taking over—coincided with his increasing determination to quantify the new technology, to apply science to history. He was sure that the staggering new power would eventually break down from the "entropy" that operated in all closed systems. But the more his vision of "chaos" excited him, the more he grandly assumed the air of the objective historian.

Adams "professed the religion of World's Fairs." He liked a panoramic view in everything, for this promised "education"; he was particularly impressed by exhibitions of the latest technology.

The new American ... was the child of steam and the brother of the dynamo, and already, within less than thirty years, this mass of mixed humanities,

brought together by steam, was squeezed and welded into approach to shape;
a product of so much mechanical power, and bearing no distinctive marks
but that of pressure. The new American like the new European was the
servant of the power-house, as the European of the twelfth century was the
servant of the Church.

Adams saw the new technology, as he saw everything else, as an index
of change. Unable to forget how his own class had panicked with the stock
market—his brother John Quincy was in a few months to die of the strain
—he saw determinism behind every panorama. "Blindly, some very powerful energy was at work, doing something that nobody wanted." What a
contrast the brilliant new technology on exhibition at Chicago made with the
faltering American economy! With the condescension that had now become
second nature to him, Adams "admitted" the exposition "to be a sort of
industrial, speculative growth and product of the Beaux Arts artistically
induced to pass the summer on the shore of Lake Michigan." What impressed him was the ability of American energy to concentrate itself equally
on the dynamo and on the neoclassic Beaux-Arts style that dominated the
fair. He sneered that the exposition "seemed to have leaped directly from
Corinth and Syracuse and Venice, over the heads of London and New York,
to impose classical standards on plastic Chicago."

Adams, a traditionalist in everything except the application of "science"
to history, of course had no complaint against the Beaux-Arts style's temporarily taking over Chicago. Perhaps he guessed that the marble-white façades
were "staff," plaster of paris. The fair was the first no-expense-barred movie
set. With his synoptic gift for reading history at a glance, Adams reminded
those pained by Chicago's incongruous classicism that "all trading cities had
always shown trader's taste, and, to the stern purist of religious faith, no art
was thinner than Venetian Gothic. All trader's taste smelt of bric-à-brac;
Chicago tried at least to give her taste a look of unity."*

"Unity" was one of Adams's central themes, along with "chaos" and
"entropy," which represented the opposite. "Unity" was an obsessive metaphor for any glorious past (like the Middle Ages he was to celebrate as a
museum with walls—not for everybody—in *Mont-Saint-Michel and Chartres*). "Unity" stood for everything that had once been glorious, intact—
and was now multiplying, dissipating into the randomness of a market

---

*In 1904, sniffily disapproving of the "hard" prosperity he saw in New York's Central Park, Henry
James yet consoled himself. "It was not, certainly, for general style, pride and colour, a Paul Veronese
company . . . my vision has a kind of analogy; for what were the Venetians, after all, but the children
of a Republic and of trade?"

economy and mass society. The center of Adams's thought, the inescapable background of his personal "failure," was by the nineties the unlimited acceleration of change. The modern world was rushing madly to an explosion of its uncontrollable energy. How much his wife's suicide in 1885 had to do with Adams's insistence on world catastrophe Adams never confided to anyone. He hardly knew himself. Like some leading nonfailures of the new industrial era—Mark Twain, Andrew Carnegie, Henry James—Adams saw himself as the elegist of an innocent America obliterated by forces beyond control. "His world was dead," he claimed to have felt as early as 1868, when he returned to America after spending the Civil War in England as private secretary to his father, the American minister.

> Not a Polish Jew fresh from Warsaw or Cracow—not a furtive Yacoob or Ysaac still reeking of the Ghetto, snarling a weird Yiddish to the officers of the customs—but had a keener instinct, an intenser energy, and a freer hand than he—American of Americans, with Heaven knew how many Puritans and Patriots behind him, and an education that had cost a civil war. . . . He was no worse off than the Indians or the buffalo who had been ejected from their heritage by his own people; but he vehemently insisted that . . . the defeat was not due to him, nor yet to any superiority of his rivals. He had been unfairly forced out of the track, and must get back into it as best he could.

Adams was a strenuously gifted man with the deepest possible instinct for showing his life as history. At the New York pier he could make a historical drama of his favorite hate, the East European Jews, though in 1868 they had not yet begun to arrive. At Chicago he had only to sit on the steps beneath Richard Morris Hunt's Administration Building, the center of the exposition (a golden dome, astonishing to still-rustic Midwesterners, was meant to recall the Duomo in Florence and St. Peter's in Rome), for Adams "to ponder . . . almost as deeply as on the steps of Ara Coeli"—where Gibbon in 1754 conceived *The Decline and Fall of the Roman Empire*. Hunt, the favorite neoclassic architect to industrial magnates, had obviously reversed Chicago's natural trend by his classicism. Adams, as conservative in the arts as he was unbounded in historical speculation, wrote as if Chicago's pseudoclassicism would elevate the dumb masses.

> If the rupture was real and the new American world could take this sharp and conscious twist towards ideals, one's personal friends would come in, at last, as winners in the great American chariot-race for fame. If the people of the Northwest actually knew what was good when they saw it, they would some day talk about Hunt and Richardson, La Farge and St. Gaudens,

Burnham and McKim, and Stanford White when their politicians and millionaires were otherwise forgotten.

The derision, as usual, was for both sides. Adams wrote that "art, to the Western people, was a state decoration; a diamond shirt-stud; a paper collar." Easterners dominated the construction of the exposition as if by natural right. Chicago money wanted the tried and true, not pioneer functionalists like Louis Henri Sullivan. If the Chicago architect John Wellborn Root had not suddenly died just as the planning for the exposition began, it is possible that the stately white façade imposed on the lakefront, and interrupted only by Louis Sullivan's Transportation Building, would not have had Root's support. Harriet Monroe wrote in her biography of her brother-in-law that Root

> wished to admit frankly in the architectural scheme the temporary character
> of the fair: it should be a great, joyous, luxuriant midsummer efflorescence
> . . . a splendid buoyant thing, flaunting its gay colors between the shifting
> blues of sky and lake exultantly, prodigally. . . . Edifices . . . should not give
> the illusion of a weight and permanence; they should be lighter, gayer, more
> decorative than the solid structures along our streets.

Louis Sullivan—"Form ever follows function"—said in bitterness that the money behind the exposition allowed the East to "win" artistically. Daniel Burnham, the chief of construction, hailed the third greatest event in American history—after the Revolution and the Civil War. Augustus Saint-Gaudens, who did the hooded figure over Marian Adams's grave, excitedly told Burnham, "Look here, old fellow, do you realize that this is the greatest meeting of artists alone since the fifteenth century?" Adams noted that the famous artists brought from the East had no interest in Chicago—"to them the Northwest refused to look artistic. They talked as though they worked only for themselves." Louis Sullivan's hopes for a distinct regional style would have meant as little to them as it did to Adams, who was to celebrate Chartres Cathedral as the only refuge from his scepticism.

Adams never mentioned Frederick Law Olmsted, the creator of the first public parks in America and a pioneer landscape architect, who laid out the grounds for the exposition. Olmsted distrusted its grandiosity. His ambition for Central Park, hard as that is to recall today, was to provide refreshment in nature for the contemplative individual. He did not wish to see great spectacles in his park or to encourage mass activity. Since the fair was synonymous with crowds, this most practical of democratic visionaries was attentive to the look of easily abashed people. Not McKim, Mead & White, not Richard Morris Hunt, not Augustus Saint-Gaudens, and certainly not

Henry Adams, could have uttered Olmsted's admonition to Daniel Burn-ham: "More incidents of vital human gaiety wanted. Expression of the crowd too business-like, common, dull, anxious and care-worn."

v

Olmsted might have been describing Mark Twain in his time of troubles. That harried speculator had no time for the fair when he arrived in Chicago, a month before the grand opening, to salvage something from the ill-fated Paige typesetting machine. Instead of making him a millionaire, it had bank-rupted him. Henry Adams, who *was* a millionaire and wrote that "life wore a new face" because he had saved the family investments, may have been indifferent to the depression that followed the Panic, but he hardly ignored it. It was another historical phenomenon. He "wanted to know what was wrong with the world that it should suddenly go smash without visible cause or possible advantage?" This was a question many people were asking as the imminent close of the century somehow coincided with the ebbing promise of American life. The members of the American Historical Association at the exposition heard Professor Frederick Jackson Turner explain that the fron-tier had provided the momentum of American history but was now closed. An era was over. Adams, pondering the sudden arrest of American energies, knew that "the young, rich continent was capable of supporting three times its population with ease."

Still, Adams saw all American sorrows with detachment. As the century rushed to its end in a flurry of great-power rivalries, Adams would be more interested in world conflict than in the social misery filling up realism from Chicago. The Adamses had been diplomats in the service of the young republic before they had been anything else; Henry in his speculative way was more interested in world strategy than in the general welfare. He coolly ignored Turner's "The Significance of the Frontier in American History"; Turner, who never confronted anything besides the topic that made him famous, would soon attack Adams for not possessing a mind as provincial as his own. But Adams also bypassed Thorstein Veblen's sardonic observa-tions of the leisure class. Adams was more at ease with the Turkish ambassa-dor in Washington, a cynic whose exposition of American corruption he had put into his novel *Democracy*.

The depression was so damaging to the exposition that fire in the build-ings was attributed by Chicago's chief of police to deputy United States marshals "who hoped to retain their positions by keeping up a semblance of disorder." In 1894 *Harper's Weekly* ran drawings of the unemployed sleeping in the stone corridors of office buildings. A hundred thousand men in the city were out of work. Jobless men from all over the country had collected in Chicago in hope of getting something at the "Great Fair." While Governor William McKinley of Ohio hailed the fair as "the world spread out before us . . . something which the people of the United States, above all others, should feel it an imperative duty to see," Chicago itself, with its often helpless mass of immigrants, was focussing the attention of settlement workers and photographers of "social conscience" like Lewis Hine. Pioneer sociologists thought the city a human disaster. The eleventh edition of the *Encyclopaedia Britannica*, in its article "Chicago," would explain early in the next century how institutions in the city differentiated "the good from the bad" among the poor, the "economically inefficient" from the "viciously pauper." Henry Adams studying the new technology was interested not in how machines worked but in projecting theories of developing social chaos. Chicago was the great laboratory of social fact at the end of the century. It was the "wickedest city," and not entirely because more than three-quarters of its people were foreign born or the children of immigrants. Florence Kelley at Hull House was showing that census figures could not be trusted. More than ten percent of the labor force in thousands of Chicago establishments were children under sixteen—bootblacks, newsboys, domestics, street peddlers, cash messengers in department stores.

In the depression of the mid-nineties more than seventy of the great railroads failed; five hundred banks and nearly sixteen thousand businesses soon collapsed. Mark Twain, losing everything in the failure of the Paige typesetting machine, wailed that "the billows of hell have been rolling over me." He was not alone. In 1894 the Pullman Palace Car Company, which had accumulated twenty-five million dollars in surplus profits and had distributed in the past year two and one-half million dollars in dividends on its thirty-six-million-dollar capital, cut wages by a fourth but did not reduce rents in the company-owned houses of its "model community" in Pullman, Illinois. The workers went out on strike when Pullman refused to discuss their grievances. Eugene V. Debs's American Railway Union took up their cause, and transportation was paralyzed throughout the North when the union boycotted all Pullman cars. President Grover Cleveland's attorney general, Richard Olney, obtained an injunction against the union—under the Sherman Anti-Trust Law. Debs defied it and went to jail, where he became a socialist. Governor John Peter Altgeld of Illinois bitterly protested Cleveland's sending in federal troops to break the strike. Since Altgeld had already outraged respectable opinion by freeing three anarchists arrested in connection with the Haymarket affair, he was defeated for reelection.* The effulgence of the World's Columbian Exposition, never to be forgotten by those who had seen the great central Court of Honor under floodlights, was nevertheless a thing of the past.

V I

The Mark Twain who never got to see the fair, tormented by business worries, more the victim of money lust than the Wild West promoters, prospectors, and failures in his books, lived the nineteenth century to the full. He should have exhibited himself at the fair; Mark Twain was a greater testimonial to the Columbian Exposition than any of its industrial exhibits. He had grown up along the frontier, moved west with it, turned himself into its representative character even when he mocked its legend of endless promise. No other American writer suggested so much of its brawling energy, its background of violence, its readiness for make-believe. No other, as the "Great Century" rushed to its end on the usual American roller coaster of ups and downs, "flush times" and panic, national brag and breadlines, hunger marches and empire, was to feel himself both America's favorite and "God's fool."

Emerson had once thought that nature in America was too much for man. Industrial man, thinking he could supplant nature, had become too much for himself and could find no friendly echo or support in the universe. The human critter, "the damned human race," as Mark Twain liked to thunder, was the root of all evil. As his affairs failed, as his wife and most of his children died, as the sweet old roughness of the frontier became a lost world to pursue, Mark Twain was faced, Lear-like, with his own hyper-trophic ego dominating everything except his native terror. In the last years of his century, this all-too-representative American, the old derelict, God's fool, experienced a savage homelessness in the good old United States in its new world of empire.

He was to live it all—early hardship, the gush of dollars from the time

*As an anarchist meeting in Chicago's Haymarket Square was breaking up, an unknown person threw a bomb that killed several policemen and wounded several more. Although no proof of their responsibility was given, four leading anarchists were charged with inciting the assassin and hanged; three more were imprisoned for life.

he gaily announced that his first book, *The Innocents Abroad*, "sells along just like the Bible," the return in imagination to Hannibal while he was living the opulent life in Hartford, the inveterate gambler's need to put everything he had on the fatal typesetting machine, the demonstrative family love of which he said, "the greater the love the greater the tragedy." There was his constant thought and talk of money, the frantic moving about, and the sudden flights to Europe—as many surges of prosperity and panic as the country itself experienced. He was not the Lincoln of our literature, but he was certainly Lincoln's countryman. His weariness and disgust with the "race" found their correlation in his country. He was shocked by the "United States of Lyncherdom," driven back into himself and his earliest fears of religion by the oily virtuousness behind which Americans hid their propensity to violence. The nineteenth century, expiring to the noisy Wagnerian trumpet calls of blood lust, war, racial savagery, imperialism, did not overlook God's own country. But Mark Twain, more than most, was still shockable. He reacted furiously—though mostly in private—to the brazenness with which his beloved frontier democracy was pushing itself forward as an American empire after coolly knocking down Spain and brutally suppressing native protests against its de-facto acquisition of the Philippines.

It was typical of Mark Twain "in eruption," so proud of brandishing "a pen warmed-up in hell," to leave so much of his protest in manuscript. He had never written so much as he did in his last years, and never before had he been afraid of getting published. He not only confided his bitterest thoughts to a rambling autobiography, to notebooks and letters, but somehow he made sure that his sharpest shafts from the grave against orthodox Christianity, like *The Mysterious Stranger*, would be found in so many versions that only near the end of the next century would his real intentions be exposed. One volume of posthumous papers, sketches, and diatribes, edited by Bernard De Voto as *Letters from the Earth*, was ready in 1939 but was not published until 1962 because Mark Twain's only surviving child, Clara, refused permission to publish material that "distorted" her father's "real ideas."

Yet if anything is clear about Samuel Langhorne Clemens in the last twenty years of his life, it is that his exasperation with "man" was founded on a need to reverse the biblical account of God's providence and man's moral responsibility. In these years Mark Twain played the village atheist with a vengeance, and even though he unwittingly kept to the determinism of his Presbyterian upbringing, he turned it into a grimly assertive denial of God's grace and man's possibility of salvation. He was of the Devil's party now, and he knew it. His first instinct was to attempt to roll back the biblical account of sin; his own proverbs of hell were meant to show that God, by insisting on the "moral sense," was really evil. The Satanic visitor to the world of men in *The Mysterious Stranger* showed by his neutrality and indifference to their affairs that he alone could assist man in freeing himself from his greatest burden—guilt.

Success had not made Mark Twain feel "guilty"; it just established what William James called the religion of chronic anxiety. But success like Mark Twain's bred the expectancy of failure, a personal conviction of wrongdoing, that reproduced "panic" in the business cycle. It turned the world to ashes and intensified Mark Twain's readiness to feel that his magic journey from West to East was really a dream after all. Nothing was what it seemed, so perhaps nothing had really happened. Why did he now always wear white? To be the "only clean man in a dirty world."

Innocence was of the West, it was childhood, newness, the great legend of American beginnings. It was real things. But destiny was in the East, where abstractions took over and broke the innocent heart that was trying to enlist them to the human order.

"That's my Middle West," F. Scott Fitzgerald was to write fifteen years after Mark Twain died, "not the wheat or prairies or the lost Swede towns. . . . I see now that this has been a story of the West, after all—Tom and Gatsby, Daisy and Jordan and I, were all Westerners, and perhaps we possessed some deficiency in common which made us subtly unadaptable to Eastern life." Yet Mark Twain, taking that for granted as the bitter sum of his life, was still of his own century and so had a quarrel with God. The "drifter" had always been proud of letting his mind go where it liked. That was the one constant in the American succession, the Emersonian legacy: the unconscious mind as oracle. Howells thought of his friend as the embodiment of what William James in 1890 first called the stream of consciousness. Howells was amazed by Mark Twain's perfect naturalness. This of course was Mark Twain's own opinion, and in his (largely dictated) *Autobiography* he was proud of writing "a book that never goes straight for a minute, but *goes,* and goes briskly, sometimes ungrammatically . . . but always *going.* . . . Nothing to do but make the trip; the how of it is not important, so that the trip is made."

Mark Twain had not counted on being locked up in his own spontaneity. He could not withstand his own deepest reactions to the Wall Street plunderers who were nevertheless of the class that put him together again when he was financially ruined. He hated the Spanish-American War, hated missionaries in China paving the way for commercial concessions, hated professional patriots, hated Theodore Roosevelt. But these were all popular passions, and he was out of step. So, much as he now liked to think of himself as a spoilsport and a wicked fellow, it did not suit him to be outside the consensus.

The "moral sentiment" was at fault; it was supposed to be innate, and Mark Twain believed in nothing that was not. His guilt was so crushing that he could escape it only by wishing the damned human race away. That was the real message of *The Mysterious Stranger* and of his cocky essays in determinism like *What Is Man?* Since man's greatest folly is to assume that he makes a difference for good because God invested him with His own importance and dignity, the only way out of such a conceit, which tolerates the corruption of society and the poisoning of the earth, is to blot the whole thing out. Speeding back to the mysterious beginnings of things in the Bible, lampooning the Bible's self-centered view of man, Mark Twain (always a romantic rebel at heart, if not in his books) made Satan his God, his charge against humanity.

Satan was a relief after Jehovah: he was indifferently benign, contemptuous of man's preposterous belief in his own importance.

It is true that which I have revealed to you: there is no God, no universe, no human race, no earthly life, no heaven, no hell. It is all a dream—a grotesque and foolish dream. Nothing exists but you. And you are but a *thought*—a vagrant thought, a useless thought, a homeless thought, wandering forlorn among the empty eternities!

Speeding all the way back to the creation, which now he annulled, Mark Twain said that it all came to a dream because *he* was alone with his own consciousness. The writer's old glory in his own mind had become an island consciousness, man alone with his own mind, a solipsism all too familiar in the scepticism that marked the end of the century. Of course there was a contradiction in Mark Twain's reversals of the Bible, for he never ceased to assail the God who had instilled the "moral sense." No God but the God who had created guilt! In the end Mark Twain's incisive hope, his only paradise, was that he alone would in imagination rewrite the world. If ever a man lived a dream, it was Mark Twain when he came to the end of his dream.

11

The Youth: Stephen Crane

> I told a seemingly sane man that I got my artistic education on the Bowery, and he said "Oh, really? So they have a school of fine arts there?"
>
> STEPHEN CRANE TO JAMES HUNEKER

I

Stephen Crane, a young reporter of very good family from Newark—his father was a Methodist minister, his mother was a bulwark of the Women's Christian Temperance Union, and he liked to boast that during the American Revolution "the Cranes were pretty hot people"—discovered in New York that "the sense of a city is *war.*" Of course he was carrying the sentiment of his class a bit further than it would have liked. This was his style. In his short life—he was not yet twenty-nine when he died in 1900—he saw much of war in the nineties, that decade of many wars, and he even entertained the brazen conviction that the city of New York behaved in a warlike manner toward many of its citizens. But to old-stock Americans, New York *was* the shocker. Henry Adams would concentrate all his brilliance in his attempt to describe New York in the new century.

> As he came up the bay again, November 5, 1904, . . . he found the approach more striking than ever—wonderful—unlike anything man had ever seen— and like nothing he had ever much cared to see. The outline of the city became frantic in its effort to explain something that defied meaning. Power seemed to have outgrown its servitude and to have asserted its freedom. The cylinder had exploded, and thrown great masses of stone and steam against the sky. The city had the air and movement of hysteria, and the citizens were

crying, in every accent of anger and alarm, that the new forces must at any cost be brought under control. Prosperity never before imagined, power never yet wielded by man, speed never reached by anything but a meteor, had made the world irritable, nervous, querulous, unreasonable and afraid.

Henry James, revisiting his native city after an absence of nearly a quarter of a century, was affronted by its democratic vulgarity. He responded eagerly to the vigor of the great harbor—"the restless freedom of the bay . . . 'coming' at you, so to speak, bearing down on you with the full force of a thousand prows of steamers seen exactly on the line of their longitudinal axis." In *The American Scene,* the record of his visit, New York was more exciting to write about than it had been in the pale days of "old" New York and *Washington Square.* "The subject was everywhere—that was the beauty, that was the advantage; it was thrilling, really, to find oneself in the presence of a theme to which everything directly contributed, leaving no touch of experience irrelevant." But the excitement—to which every old association contributed —would also be harder to get into fiction, as James showed in the thin and even meretricious stories of the "new" New York, like "A Round of Visits." James was floridly, impressionistically at his best as he described himself in *The American Scene* reeling about New York in alarm at people eating in the street, Jewish immigrants crowding the lower East Side, everywhere "the inconceivable alien" as "the agency of future ravage." The organ tones of his late late style sounded out with sonority and wit when he described himself as, really, helpless before the air of "hard prosperity" that the new-comers showed in Central Park, and in the very streets "the consummate monotonous commonness of the pushing male crowd, moving in its dense mass—with the confusion carried to chaos for any intelligence, any percep-tion; a welter of objects and sounds in which relief, detachment, dignity, meaning, perished utterly and lost all rights."

The impact of New York on his prodigious sensibility made *The Ameri-can Scene* a "travel book" like no other. But it was not the novel he had come too late to write. He had missed a whole chapter of American life. And since he had long given up any desire to be a "native" novelist—even of England!—it no longer matters that the author of *The Golden Bowl* would have found *Sister Carrie* too crude for comment. But since James as critic was all his life spellbound by the possibilities of fiction, there is a certain wistfulness in "The Lesson of Balzac," which he read to lecture audiences on his American tour.

"Things" for him are francs and centimes more than any others, and I give up as inscrutable, unfathomable, the nature, the peculiar avidity of his interest in them. . . . The imagination, as we all know, may be employed up to a certain point in inventing uses for money; but its office beyond that point is surely to make us forget that anything so odious exists. This is what Balzac never forgot; his universe goes on expressing itself for him, to its furthest reaches, on its finest side, in terms of the market.

Nothing James said, or would have liked to say in the face of America's money-mindedness, so revealed his predicament. In the preface to *The Ambassadors* for his collected New York edition, he bravely said of his pride in the book: "there is an ideal *beauty* of goodness the invoked action of which is to raise the artistic faith to its maximum. . . . *The Ambassadors*, I confess, wore this glow for me from the beginning to the end."

I I

The "cylinder" had indeed exploded in New York. New York was now the "environment"—a big new word for writers in the nineties, and one that young Stephen Crane virtually adopted as a talisman. William Dean Howells, who had been settled in New York since 1891 and was among the first to recognize that the professionally casual author of *Maggie* was a genius— he told his friends that Crane had "sprung into literature fully armed"—said that New York was Crane's only inspiration.

New York was Crane's introduction to "real life"—to the "angry class," as Henry Adams's distinguished friend John Hay called it. Unlike Dreiser in every respect but their common fascination with the social war, Crane *chose* to be negative about whatever his class took as gospel—especially the Gospels. He was a thoroughly well bred man, a natural sceptic and iconoclast, who as a reporter on the lower East Side quickly understood the misery and violence and then turned them, with many a colorful adjective, into exemplary tales of the tough new wisdom. "Environment is a tremendous thing in the world and frequently shapes lives regardless," he wrote, inscribing *Maggie* to Hamlin Garland. He relished the picturesque colors of the great city as he did the stylistic swagger of the "clever school in literature" made famous by Kipling. He was to renounce this influence, but its irony and knowingness are all over his work. Just as he continually went slumming in order to alarm the summer crowd along the Jersey coast, so he liked above all things to look "bad" in the eyes of his class, to satirize authority, to defend prostitutes in New York's Tenderloin district against persecution by the police.* As a novelist, he leaned just a little too heavily on the picturesque. As he said, the Bowery gave him his "artistic education."

Mere sympathy for the miserable did not interest Crane, and certainly not the alternating roles of "success" and "failure" that dominated the uneasy soul of Theodore Dreiser. Crane's perspective on the immigrant masses festering in New York was from the top looking down. Dreiser's characters in *Sister Carrie*, all too much like Dreiser himself, may have reflected the distance stretching from their inarticulate selves to the towers that seemingly contained all the wealth, position, and "romance" in the world. Crane had the easy detachment of young men of good family growing up in the solidly comfortable worlds that once dominated Newark, Port Jervis, Asbury Park. No one else in his turbulent decade would alarm so many elders by his precocity, would to the end seem so irreverently young. At seventeen he was already mildly satiric in reporting "shore news" from the Jersey coast. He naturally saw things at a slant, life as an "episode," people as humorous constructions. He was a prodigy who rushed through the disorder of his generation too quickly to make out its historic outlines.

The slums of New York announced the perpetual conflict that as a correspondent he pursued on the battlefields of Greece and Cuba. War would be the great news of "his" decade, promoted by press lords like Hearst and Pulitzer. But to the end his heart lay in the small towns (their serenity a façade) that with his sense of mortality he put into his *Whilomville Stories*, one of them the searing tale of a town's moral collapse, "The Monster." There were the porch-lined streets, the maples, the wistful street lamps. Whilomville is, in appearance, the dear little American town from which all decent people come, the overgrown village, leisurely and easy, on which all fables of innocence in America rest.

Crane did not particularly value the experience that led to his making his early reputation with sketches of the Bowery, "An Experiment in Misery," *Maggie*, and *George's Mother*. "Experiment" was indeed to be the key word to his New York sketches and stories, "episode" to the battle of Chancellorsville in *The Red Badge of Courage*—a book he thought slight by contrast with

*The district between Twenty-fourth and Fortieth streets, from Fifth Avenue to Seventh Avenue, was known as the Tenderloin after Captain (later Inspector) Alexander C. Williams, newly transferred there, was quoted as saying: "I've had nothing but chuck steak for a long time, and now I'm going to get a little of the tenderloin."

his "lines," the poems he considered wholly innovative and which presented his totally agnostic outlook. The early works about New York were tryouts for a man who was always in a hurry to get down *all* "the pictures of his time." Fortunately, he had a genius for rendering the intense succession of moods and effects, for the underlying logic of narrative. So little was he in sympathy with his slum characters that he emphasized their most lurid traits. *Maggie* displays his gift for spasmodic scenes and effects, but it is as much a cartoon as it is a story. Crane explained in a letter that "the root of Bowery life is a sort of cowardice. Perhaps I mean a lack of ambition or to be willingly knocked flat and accept the licking."

Good Americans with Crane's upbringing were unwilling to be knocked flat and accept a licking. Crane did not lend himself to the standard run of Asbury Park comfortableness, to the self-righteousness of the Methodist parsonage and the Women's Christian Temperance Union conclaves of his childhood. He took a scornful pleasure in saying no. He was always young, for he was convinced that he would die young. He was even more of a fatalist about himself than he was about the misery and violence that he was paid by Pulitzer and Hearst to report. But unlike "the youth" of his most famous work, *The Red Badge of Courage*, Crane did not regard himself as a man things just happened to. He pitted his own youth against an America grown fat, hypocritical, and self-righteous, and he never doubted that the contest would go against him. He was "smart," a young daredevil, smilingly defiant in the style of the nineties. He liked to remind people that he was a preacher's son. Crane's scorn for the American gods is awesome, for he had no urgent reason to disbelieve them. He just did. His career is the best possible proof that the 1890s—now so easy to prettify—had running through them simultaneous currents of irreverence toward God and the established order. Crane was more sensitive to secret disorder than he was to anything else. H. G. Wells, who bothered to understand Crane all the way as Crane's solicitous country-man Henry James did not, said at Crane's death, "He was the expression in literary art of certain enormous repudiations. . . . It is as if the racial thought and tradition had been razed from his mind and its site plowed and salted."

Crane recognized the effect of "environment" on himself as well as on East Side paupers. But his real environment was the fin de siècle. Crane embodied its fascination with social breakdown, its naive scientism and belief in mechanism, and its scorn for sexual taboos, especially when intoned by politicians and enforced by corrupt policemen in New York's Tenderloin district. Without being a willing part of bohemia in New York, he learned from the artists and newspaper illustrators who dominated the "artistic quarters" in New York's Chelsea district. He was at home with independent-minded writers and illustrators (as he was not with newspaper stars of the period like Richard Harding Davis) who favored the "picturesque" side of city life.

Unlike most bohemians of his generation, unlike the pioneer realists Howells and Hamlin Garland, who befriended him in New York when he had to publish *Maggie* under a pseudonym and at his own expense, Crane was exceptional. He saw the tempest of his time in a fashion different from everyone else, and he stuck to the evidence of his eyes. He used his stabbing, colorful, thoroughly ironic and cool style as the primary element in which he thought and through which he saw anything at all. Style was primary with him, as it was to be with the Hemingway he often anticipates; Crane is the first of the American modernists in texture as well as thought. (He would have been approaching fifty as the 1920s began.) His self-reliance was absolute, cocky in the proverbial American style, but lightly expressed a sense of doom. He could not adjust himself to official views.

His genius was for dissidence. He naturally saw everything in contradiction to what he was supposed to say. "Of course I am admittedly a savage. I have been known as docile from time to time but only under great social pressure." He enjoyed his singularity. In 1898 he wrote to a friend:

> When I was the mark for every humorist in the country I went ahead; now, when I am the mark for only 50% of the humorists of the country, I go ahead, for I understand that a man is born into this world with his own pair of eyes, and that he is not at all responsible for his vision—he is merely responsible for his quality of personal honesty. To keep close to this personal honesty is my supreme ambition.

III

"Realism," whether in eighteenth-century England or nineteenth-century America, was sure of its access to the matter-of-fact. The novel is the bright book of life, D. H. Lawrence was to say, the form nearest our broad human experience. The method is meticulous description of the external world. Dreiser certainly believed this. Crane parodied the "real" world; he did not ape it. He took it seriously only as an occasion for rebuttal. His mind was mordant, fatalistic, with a sense of the ominous running through his everyday perceptions that suggests not the realist's usual interest in social truth—and sometimes social alleviation—but the difference between Stephen Crane and what the world is supposed to mean. Long before the next century's chain of wars would prompt a mounting sense that the human will is absurd, Crane, rushing about *his* little world of war—bestial New York, primitive Mexico, oppressed Cuba, and rebellious Greece—felt a total sense of incongruity between himself and official assurances by state and church that all was well.

Crane was as independent an imagination as the first cubists in painting; he delighted in the conscious "distortion" of the external scene. The distortion was never aimed at correcting other people's views; Crane sought a pattern harmonious with his instinct for the moment, the breakdown of life into clusters of colored sensations. The 1890s were full of social dissolution and "stormy" with anticipations of greater storms to come. When we consider how much less "free" they were than the 1920s, Crane's insistence on total independence is all the more remarkable. Crane was the only major American in his time who was part of the symbolist movement, and this without knowing it. He constantly used symbols as absolutes representing the human state, not as merely descriptive terms. He was not even a "realist" in the conventional sense, for he did not credit anything outside himself with objective truth, and he acknowledged as necessity only the need to stick to his own memory. "An artist, I think, is nothing but a powerful memory that can move itself at will through certain experiences sideways and every artist must be in some things powerless as a dead snake."

Yet Crane's outlook was instinctively, above all biologically, what others speculatively played with as "determinism." The old Henry Adams and Mark Twain, the young Theodore Dreiser, thought that their personal disenchantments were sanctioned by the mechanistic theories of the fin de siècle. Crane was more interested in behavior for its own sake. War fascinated him because it released energy, "demonstrated" the unpredictable and crazy-seeming correlation of the human animal to extreme situations. A routine word—or scene—is "altercation." Behavior (he might have been reading William James's epochal *The Principles of Psychology* [1890], but Crane never learned anything from *books*) is discontinuous. We may be caught like rats in a trap, but *in* the trap we do not think of ourselves as rats; the will to survive is as interesting to the man "caught" as it is to the storyteller because the human will is continuous with thought and rich in devices. We may be programmed; we do not act as if we were. To think is to imagine oneself free. Every wave in what William James called the stream of consciousness aims at a goal that we identify with ourselves.

Crane, distant from conventional America in everything else, was removed from ordinary realism as he was from the genteel tradition. He said in a letter, "There is nothing to respect in art save one's own opinion of it." He said, "I always want to be unmistakable. That to my mind is good writing." By "unmistakable" he meant *physical:* "Art is a child of pain." The writer is rooted in some mysterious disjunction and, basing himself entirely on the truth of his psychic impressions, renders experience in flashes. The subversion of all existing conventions is found first in oneself. Style is a form of subversion, and Crane's style is as self-consciously personal and defiant as a style can be.

IV

Dreiser was not yet thirty when he published *Sister Carrie,* but no one could have thought of him as a "young writer." By the 1890s Henry Adams and Mark Twain were in their sixties, exhausted by family tragedy and every year growing steadily more embittered by the great change in America and the eclipse of what they aggrievedly mourned as *their* republic. A year after Crane died in the Black Forest, Mark Twain, outraged by the crushing of the Filipino revolt, bitterly wrote "To the Person Sitting in Darkness."

> Everything is prosperous now; everything is just as we should wish it. We have got the Archipelago, and we shall never give it up.... And as for a flag for the Philippine Province, it is easily managed. We can have a special one —our States do it: we can just have our usual flag, with the white stripes painted black and the stars replaced by the skull and cross-bones.

Mentally, Mark Twain had always merged into the American environment, and he was never easy criticizing it. His most despairing shots were reserved for the future to discover. Dreiser was not capable of separating himself from the system he protested.

Crane really stood outside. He went to all the wars, he lived the strenuous life that one of his many enemies, Theodore Roosevelt, preached with his usual bluster, but he laughed at every pretense of an American consensus.* One of his greatest stories, "The Monster," was to show in the coolest

---

*As police commissioner of New York, 1895–97, Roosevelt defended a corrupt and brutal policeman, Charles Becker (he was to be electrocuted in 1912 for instigating the murder of a gambler), whom Crane accused of persecuting a prostitute. Crane so angered the Police Department that an attempt was made to "bar" him from New York. Roosevelt the war lover of course admired *The Red Badge of Courage.* In 1896 he wrote Crane in reference to one of his Western stories, "A Man and Some Others," "Some day I want you to write another story of the frontiersman and the Mexican Greaser in which the frontiersman shall come out on top; it is more normal that way!" But Roosevelt never forgave Crane for exposing police corruption, and of course the Rough Rider could not like what Crane as a reporter sent back from the Cuban fighting. "I did not see any sign among the fighting men, whether wounded or unwounded, of the very complicated emotions assigned to their kind by some of the realistic modern novelists who have written about battles."

possible terms the moral collapse of a small American town in the face of an extreme situation. Needless to say, the collapse, like the flight under fire he described in *The Red Badge,* interested him not as a fall from virtue but as mere behavior. So it was with the dangerous life he lived in Florida, where he attached himself to the remarkable woman who kept the "Hotel de Dream," then joined the filibustering expedition that ended in shipwreck and the ordeal he described in "The Open Boat." In Florida, in the Cuban fighting, in the Graeco-Turkish War, in England with the remarkable woman to whom he was not married, he was never remotely like anyone else. Dying at twenty-eight, worn out by the excessive turbulence of "his" decade, he was befriended by Henry James as a brilliant, ailing young countryman. Conrad and Wells recognized that the nature of his gift was as singular as his mental independence. He was a prodigy.

Crane's achievement began so early—he was a reporter at seventeen—that he now seems an adolescent of genius. If in his more florid moments and his fascination with the military life he now reminds one of the young Winston Churchill (three years his junior and a soldier-correspondent in England's imperial wars), he bears comparison in other respects with an adventurer and desperado of the intellect like Rimbaud. Crane was not so much against established authority as he was just in excess of it. One of his distinguishing traits was his impersonal intellect. His constant air of indifference covered a profound fatalism about the death awaiting not him but present civilization. His telegraphic little poems are syllogisms "demonstrating" over and again that God is really missing. Even his relaxed, surprisingly good-humored Western stories carry the refrain that everything in nature bears "a message—the inconsequence of individual tragedy."

> If I should cast off this tattered coat,
> And go free into the mighty sky;
> If I should find nothing there
> But a vast blue,
> Echoless, ignorant—
> What then?

V

It was called the "clever" decade because clever journalists-turned-storytellers, like Kipling, favored a nervy, bantering, vaguely insolent way of calling attention to themselves. Crane wrote with the swagger that was Richard Harding Davis's only distinction. Kipling the journalist in India always came up with exotic stories but carefully separated the novelties from the eternal verities. The latter were somehow incarnated in the stoicism and loyalty of the military. The English in India were a standing army; they were always fighting or preparing to fight.

Despite the Civil War and the many skirmishes with Indians in Crane's brief lifetime, America lacked such military presence and tradition. It never confused the military with lasting authority. The middle nineties saw a period of war consciousness and war preparation that led straight to 1914–18 and the chain of wars that has crazed the twentieth century. There was a quarter-century's peace after 1870–71, but the nineties and after saw nothing but war and preparations for war. Having nearly brought off a war with Great Britain over Venezuela, the United States made war on Spain and on the Filipinos. Greece and Italy fought Turkey, China fought Japan, Japan fought Russia, and the century ended with the British still fighting the Boers.

Crane as a correspondent in the Far West and Mexico observed force at first hand. He was never heard to protest America's maneuverings against Spain in the name of Cuban "freedom." He was just a reporter covering a story. What happened to him when he accompanied a filibustering expedition to Cuba at the end of 1896 went into his greatest story, "The Open Boat"; after his ship sank he spent thirty hours in that boat struggling with the waves. "Many a man ought to have a bathtub larger than the boat which here rode upon the sea." Nothing in Washington's pious professions about the war in Cuba, which Crane in a state of exhaustion half-heartedly covered less than two years before his death, could have surprised him. Crane's formal bitterness was always directed at the self-righteousness in which he had been brought up. He would have laughed his head off when President McKinley justified the seizure of the Philippines:

> I am not ashamed to tell you, gentlemen, that I went down on my knees and prayed Almighty God for light and guidance that one night. And one night late it came to me this way. . . . There was nothing left for us to do but to take them all and to educate the Filipinos and uplift and civilize and Christianize them, and by God's grace do the very best we could by them, as our fellow men for whom Christ also died.

Crane would not have been overcome with surprise if he had read Henry Cabot Lodge's exultation over the Spanish-American War: "What a wonderful war it has been. What a Navy we have got & what good fighters our soldiers are. Nothing but victory & at such small cost." He would have been enchanted with John Hay's letter from the American embassy in London on July 27, 1898, congratulating Theodore Roosevelt on the war that Roosevelt, as assistant secretary of the Navy, had helped to start: "It has been a splendid little war; begun with the highest motives, carried on with magnificent intelligence and spirit, favored by that Fortune which loves the brave. It is now to be concluded, I hope, with that fine good nature, which is, after all, the distinguishing trait of the American character."

Distinguished intellectuals led by William James formed an Anti-Imperialist League when America in the Philippines conducted what has been called "the bloodiest colonial war (in proportion to population) ever fought by a white power in Asia." The league charged that "the real firing line is not in the suburbs of Manila. The foe is of our own household. The attempt of 1861 was to divide the country. That of 1899 is to destroy its fundamental principles and noblest ideals." But James in a private letter admitted of the war against Spain that "the *great* passion undeniably now is the passion for *adventure*. We are in so little danger from Spain, that our interest in the war can only be called that in a peculiarly exciting kind of sport."

Crane certainly believed this, just as he believed with Mark Twain that America, like any other great power, was playing "the great game." He would have enjoyed Whistler's flippancy from London: it was "a wonderful and beautiful war. The Spanish were gentlemen." Although *The Red Badge of Courage* was published in 1895, before Crane saw war in Cuba and Greece, his novel could not have been written outside the warlike atmosphere and constant rumors of war in the nineties. The "long peace" of the nineteenth century, as it was to be called from the vantage point of the twentieth century, was felt to be over when Crane in ten nights composed his clinical and mocking succession of scenes reporting the responses to war of one youth.

Of course the Civil War was still fiercely remembered and debated when Crane wrote. He owed many details to the Century Company's *Battles and Leaders of the Civil War;* a brother owned a set. But he was so objective about his undertaking that after observing action in Greece, he exclaimed that "*The Red Badge* is all right." He had been worried enough. "I have spent ten nights writing a story of the war on my own responsibility but I am not sure that my facts are real and the books won't tell me what I want to know so I must do it all over again, I guess." Nothing so delighted him as the assurance of old soldiers that Stephen Crane had been in the Civil War himself.

VI

No veteran could have been so coldly removed from the spirit in which Justice Oliver Wendell Holmes addressed a soldier's reunion. "Our hearts were touched with fire." Crane's heart was touched by war as "the peculiarly exciting kind of sport" that William James called "our interest in the war. . . . But excitement! Shall we not worship excitement? And after all, what is life for, except for opportunities of excitement?" Although he surely never looked at James's *The Principles of Psychology*, Crane submitted "the youth" to war as if war was another example of the scientific psychology just coming in during the nineties. "I got my sense of the rage of conflict on the football field," he said. Some of the most graphic surprises in *The Red Badge* are images of war as athletic contest. "The two bodies of troops exchanged blows in the manner of a pair of boxers." At another point the "contest" becomes a "scrimmage."

The very title of the novel is a jeer. "He wished that he, too, had a wound, a red badge of courage." "The youth," as he is usually named, is neither better nor worse than any other green soldier exposed to the boredom, the uncertainty, and (suddenly) the extreme peril of war. Henry Fleming enlists as hundreds of thousands of other farm boys enlisted, in order to see a war; he is wept over and prayed over by a mother of standard piety who would like to believe that her son is an exception (a standard mistake). Until he is caught up in hard fighting, the youth sees nothing and says nothing that is outside the general wisdom of the group. He is silly, boastful, ignorant like his mates, *knows* nothing except what is passed along by them. In his greenness and youthful ignorance he exists as a mockery of the hopes and delusions common to soldiers before battle.

"The youth" is paralleled by "a certain tall soldier"; in the opening pages there is remembered "a certain light-haired girl," "another and darker girl." These first epithets rob the characters of personality; they come at the reader as a sequence of dissociated traits. The style is vaguely unsettling. "She had had certain ways of expression that told that her statements on the subject came from a deep conviction." "At last, however, he had made firm rebellion against this yellow light thrown upon the color of his ambitions." What can Crane the nimble ironist be up to? The style has the same patronizing emphasis on ignorance, awkwardness, helplessness that one found in *Maggie* and *George's Mother*. Does Crane mean to "position" his characters from such a distance? Does he see nothing more in these fighters for freedom and union than he saw in the wretches of the lower East Side? The answer is that Crane's passion as an artist is to set up a "situation," seemingly any situation, that can show people responding to it.

It is the intensity of the response that fascinates Crane; life is an explosion of movement quickly consumed. This requires the most patient and even stolid enumeration, an excruciating absorption in the moment fleeting by. The response to their "environment" on the part of Maggie's parents, her brother, and her seducer is simply more of the same. Maggie is ultimately a form of pathos ending in suicide. But as the youth in *The Red Badge* is finally relieved of being part of a "blue demonstration" and thrown into the "furnace" of battle, his responses are alarmingly brought to scale. There is a crescendo of "effects." The youth is hammered by blows that seem never to cease, and the key to this madness between men of the same country, of the same race, probably of the same opinions, is that everything seems specifically aimed at the youth. Understandably feeling himself guiltless, he cannot understand why the universe onto which he projects all his sensations seems indifferent to him.

The only lapse in Crane's astonishingly sustained sequence of sensations in *The Red Badge* is a tendency to smirk at the youth for being astonished by this. But no one ever mimicked the pathetic fallacy with such witty understanding of a soldier's frantic projections. "Tattered and eternally hungry men" fire "despondent powders"; guns are "surly"; the "battled flag . . . seemed to be struggling to free itself from an agony"; "the guns squatted in a row like savage chiefs. They argued with abrupt violence. It was a grim pow-wow." "He could not conciliate the forest."

Men in battle do transfer their emotions to the guns, the weather, the surrounding landscape. Stephen Crane seems to have been born with the awareness that Henry Adams and Mark Twain bitterly came to near the end of the century. Power has passed from men to their instruments. Of the hundreds of brilliantly unsettling sentences in *The Red Badge*, none is more characteristic of the 1890s than Crane's observation in chapter 6 that "the slaves toiling in the temple of this god began to feel rebellion at his harsh tasks." But of course this is a wholly literary observation, and one made not only in Crane's highly stylized narrative voice but as a personal reflection. Henry Fleming would not have thought that, and he could not have said it. Crane's knowing style dominates the novel, and there are only a few snatches of folksy dialogue in which the soldiers speak for themselves (invariably betraying their fear and ignorance). Once the fighting breaks out and the youth realizes to his horror that he is entirely on his own, the sense of fear and entrapment is so graphic, mounts so cruelly, that the youth in his sensations clearly speaks for Crane as much as Crane does for him. Fear not only maddens Henry Fleming, it *occupies* him. Everything else is blotted out as "bullets began to whistle among the branches and nip at the trees. . . . It was as if a thousand axes, wee and invisible, were being wielded." "The fight was lost. The dragons were coming with invincible strides. The army, helpless in the matted thickets and blinded by the overhanging night, was going to be swallowed. War, the red animal, war, the blood-swollen god, would have bloated fill."

What was Crane's own "fear"? We know only that it was expressed in a certain militancy; he would never be at a loss for a retort to circumstances, and this, a persistent angle of dissidence, took the form of style. Never as in the nineties was style so obtrusive, so "clever," so emphatic in marking the fatal distance between men's concern for their lives and the universe.

> From across the river the red eyes were still peering. In the eastern sky there was a yellow patch like a rug laid for the feet of the coming sun; and against it, black and patternlike, loomed the gigantic figure of the colonel on a gigantic horse.
>
> The youth turned, with sudden, livid rage, toward the battlefield. He shook his fist. He seemed about to deliver a philippic.
> "Hell—"
> The red sun was pasted in the sky like a wafer.

Crane obviously drew from painting. His admirer Conrad was no doubt right to see Crane as an impressionist and "only an impressionist." The reflex thinking behind Crane's elaborate style is that war is just another situation in which human beings display themselves as objects to *literary* inquiry. What goes on in *The Red Badge* is a classic end-of-the-century behaviorism. Crane is genially "objective," persistent in his irony. The youth is put through every possible test. In actual fighting he is shown, like his fellows, to have no control over his actions, and runs away. But he is finally able to rejoin his outfit, to have the minor head wound he receives in a scuffle with a retreating soldier of his own army accepted as a battle wound. He is convulsively brave at the side of his comrades and seizes the enemy's flag in the final charge. His most significant experiences are of seeing other men dead or dying. His friend the "tall soldier" becomes the "spectral soldier" when, fatally wounded, he staggers in a spasmodic dance before he falls. In the forest "where the high, arching boughs made a chapel," he stops, "horror-stricken at the sight of a thing."

He was being looked at by a dead man who was seated with his back against a columnlike tree. The corpse was dressed in a uniform that once had been blue, but was now faded to a melancholy shade of green. The eyes, staring at the youth, had changed to the dull hue to be seen on the side of a dead fish. The mouth was open. Its red had changed to an appalling yellow. Over the gray skin of the face ran little ants. One was trundling some sort of a bundle along the upper lip.

The youth gave a shriek as he confronted the thing.

Every detail piled on the youth's helpless soul anticipates what Wyndham Lewis said of the Hemingway hero. He is "the man things are done to." But the youth has no personality, no history, no career outside his reflex responses. He is not only the subject of Crane's mocking inquiry; he is all too much what Crane had come to think of as the average man caught up in a situation. Of course Crane, tossing the book off in ten nights, called it "an episode," protesting that it did not express his total view of things as his poems did. He allowed the newspaper and book editor Ripley Hitchcock to cut the book. It was a "situation," not the Civil War, that enlisted all his attention; although Chancellorsville has been established as the battle in the book, its name is never mentioned. Would historic references have taken *The Red Badge* out of Crane's control? Control, in the form of his most picturesque and dominating prose, is clearly Crane's own passion behind the book.

If the youth is "the man things are done to," Crane is the man who knows what is being done. Even when the youth "felt carried along by a mob," he found no support in others but was "exhausted and ill from the monotony of his suffering." Crane's similes likening the enraged contestants to reptiles and dragons mock the youth's fear as much as Crane's many clinical details pin him down. The individual caught up in the melee is credited with "the acute exasperation of a pestered animal, a well-meaning cow worried by dogs . . . the swirling battle phantoms . . . were choking him, stuffing their smoke robes down his parched throat." Crane's driving style alone lifts, in the unnerving crescendo of battle, the totally isolated and fear-maddened youth into primitive connection with his surroundings. And Crane's language in the ecstasy of his genius takes over completely when, exactly halfway through the book, the battle goes mad.

He became aware that the furnace roar of the battle was growing louder.

The youth began to imagine that he had got into the center of the tremendous quarrel, and he could perceive no way out of it. From the mouths of the fleeing men came a thousand wild questions, but no one made answers.

The bugles called to each other like brazen gamecocks.

The orderly sergeant . . . made attempts to cry out. In his endeavor there was a dreadful earnestness, as if he conceived that one great shriek would make him well.

Crane's grip on his "hero" does not relent in the famous passage in which the regiment's charge has reestablished its reputation and the youth finds that he has survived to triumph over his great fear. "He had been to touch the great death, and found that, after all, it was but the great death." We know now that Crane originally wrote "it was but the great death—for others." His coolness about the youth, not unsympathetic but hardly respectful, persists to the end. It is not the youth but what happens to him that engrosses Crane, and we identify with the youth only when the terror of battle becomes our own. We can see why Crane thought of his novel as an "experiment," since the seeming trivialization of death can only be provisional, a shock effect in Crane's bantering style. As a novelist he did not have to say, as Crane the poet did, that war is man's fate, that war is the great negative of freedom and hope. The American army in Cuba astonished Crane by its resemblance to "a well-oiled machine." To Crane, any self at war, its possibilities mocked by war, *must* be a clinical experience, an ordeal, a subject for "inquiry." War "the red animal, the blood-swollen god," is in the exact nature of things, *and just now,* man's definitive experience.

VII

Crane, saying that a writer's only duty was to "leave pictures of his time," was a great anticipator. The omens of annihilation are everywhere in another masterpiece, "The Open Boat." Though it is founded on an actual experience and retains some of the professional jocularity Crane put into his report to a New York newspaper, the story menaces all our easygoing ways by turning the discomfort and anxiety of four men in a ten-foot dinghy, and finally their terror in having to make it to the beach in the heavy surf, into something as concentrated as thirty hours in the dinghy itself. There is humor and fellowship between the oiler and the correspondent as they row together and, with desperate weariness, spell each other at the oars; the injured captain with his arm in a sling gives orders to the cook, who just as routinely repeats the order to bail. But, retaining traditional order even in a dinghy, the men are mocked at every moment by the waves, the birds, the land looming up before them—on which, until the very end, nothing and no one can be seen.

The usual burden of Crane's poems is that man has nothing and no one in this baffling universe supposedly created and administered by an all-powerful deity. Man runs round and round the world, howling his defiance and despair at the empty sky. But Crane's "lines," as he called his poems, are just that; they breathe an air of satisfaction, they seem too easily satisfied with their contemptuous brevity. In "The Open Boat" the universe is not that easily dismissed. It surrounds the four men in the most annihilating expanse of indifference.

Not even in *The Red Badge*, where the adjectives are piled on to point up the contrast between the soldier's terror and the unresponsiveness of "nature," did Crane project so sharply onto surroundings the protest of man's ultimate helplessness and loneliness in mortal situations.

> There was a terrible grace in the move of the waves, and they came in silence, save for the snarling of the crests.

> The crest of each of these waves was a hill, from the top of which the men surveyed for a moment a broad tumultuous expanse, shining and wind-riven. It was probably splendid, it was probably glorious, this play of the free sea, wild with lights of emerald and white and amber.

> This tower was a giant, standing with its back to the plight of the ants.

The sequence of such "ultimate"-sounding sentences is pitiless, crushing. Between sea and sky man knows only this enclosure and is *caught*. The friendliness between the men in the dinghy could not be more touching— and ultimately more useless. When they are finally pulled to the beach by the one man able and willing to come to their rescue, the rescuer cries, "What's that?" The correspondent says, "Go."

> In the shallows, face downward, lay the oiler. His forehead touched sand that was periodically, between each wave, clear of the sea.

VIII

In his last years, far from home in the Brede Place manor in England where he could live with "Mrs. Stephen Crane" as he could not in God's own country, Crane went back for material to the small American town, the once-upon-a-time world of the *Whilomville Stories*. Whilomville was not what we thought it was when we lived in it. The surface of the town (Port Jervis mostly, with a touch of Crane's old Jersey hangouts) is the legendary routine and rightness of Tom Sawyer's St. Petersburg and Tom Bailey's Rivermouth. Although

> Whilomville was in no sense a summer resort, the advent of the warm season meant much to it, for then came visitors from the city—people of considerable confidence—alighting upon their country cousins. . . . The town . . . drawled and drowsed through long months during which nothing was worse than the white dust which arose behind every vehicle at blinding noon, and nothing was finer than the cool sheen of the hose sprays over the cropped lawns under the many maples in the twilight.

In Whilomville, little Jimmie Trescott knows no greater sorrow than to discover that the Presbyterian Sunday school has decided not to have a tree this Christmas but will spend the money on the poor Chinese. He transfers to another Sunday school and discovers that the Christmas tree will be skipped there, too. How kind and protective are small-town Americans, the salt of the earth, to their less fortunate brothers! It is also made abundantly clear in the *Whilomville Stories,* and in a story that has no parallel in that collection, "The Monster," that the dark-skinned people of the earth, who function only as handymen and stealers of watermelons, are charming but absurd. They are irresponsible, like children. But black Henry Johnson bursts into Dr. Trescott's burning house to save little Jimmie, falls under a rain of chemicals exploding in Dr. Trescott's laboratory, and loses his face. He becomes a "monster" whom no one would keep, whom everyone is afraid of—except Dr. Trescott, who stolidly repeats to the town's elders urging him to jettison Henry that "he saved my boy's life."

The people in town finally boycott Dr. Trescott and will not come to Mrs. Trescott's tea party. Once in the lovely summer evening they were a "crowd"; now they are a mob. As Mark Twain said in "The United States of Lyncherdom" (of course he had said it better, playing Colonel Sherburn facing down the mob), "O kind missionary, leave China! come home and convert these Christians!"

All this takes place not on the Bowery, with Maggie's awful family, but in the perfect American small town, our old home, where once we lived with Tom and Huck. In Whilomville the newfangled electric arc lights throw ominous shadows. Crane the mighty wielder of epithets knows enough to describe the light for its own sake. Everything in this world on the verge of the new century is lighted brilliantly, but this light can show too much.

> The wind waved the leaves of the maples, and, high in the air, the blue-burning globes of the arc lights caused the wonderful traceries of leaf shad-

ows on the ground. When the light fell upon the upturned face of a girl, it caused it to glow with a wonderful pallor. . . . In the shivering light, which gave to the park an effect like a great vaulted hall, the throng swarmed, with a gentle murmur of dresses switching the turf, and with a steady hum of voices.

In this severe and terrible story, a child plays a classic role. A child is the human creature that must be saved at all costs. Henry Johnson, who on his day off strutted the town in lavender trousers, pays the cost and becomes a "monster." The very word intones Crane's posthumous world. The people thronging the park on gay summer nights under the electric arc lights look exactly alike. And they are. One Martha alone holds out against the gossip and the fear.

"They say he is perfectly terrible."
"Oh, I don't care what everybody says," said Martha.
"Well, you can't go against the whole town," answered Carrie, in sudden sharp defiance.

PART THREE

Ruling by Style:

History and the Moderns

1900–1929

"Where do murderers go, man! Who's to doom, when the judge himself is dragged to the bar?"

MELVILLE, *Moby-Dick*, "The Symphony"

"I hear the ruin of all space, shattered glass and toppling masonry, and time one livid final flame. What's left us then?"

JOYCE, *Ulysses*

12

A Postponed Power: Henry Adams

... the secret isolated joy of the thinker, who knows that, a hundred years after he is dead and forgotten, men who never heard of him will be moving to the measure of his thought—the subtle rapture of a postponed power, which the world knows not because it has no external trappings, but which to his prophetic vision is more real than that which commands an army ...

OLIVER WENDELL HOLMES, JR., 1886

I find it such a mistake to have lived on—when like other saner and safer persons, I might perfectly have not—into this unspeakable give-away of the whole fool's paradise of our past.

HENRY JAMES, 1914

I

Eleven years after he completed it and had it privately published in an edition of one hundred copies which he sent "to the persons interested, for their assent, correction, or suggestion," *The Education of Henry Adams* was finally released to the public in November 1918. The author had died in March. It was an auspicious time for the world and for the astonishing emergence of Henry Adams. A self-declared "failure" after his wife's death in 1885, a brilliant misanthrope respected and feared by his illustrious friends in the American governing class, and outside Washington confused with many another Adams, a historian easily slighted by more prosaic historians, he suddenly became a great example, a prize winner, and even a best seller. The *Education* would become an American classic, and just as if he were Thoreau, Poe, Whitman, Melville, or any other notoriously complex and difficult writer, this most imaginative and far-ranging of American historians would continue in death to baffle his admirers and to fascinate his detractors.

Unlike other great men in the American story, he never acknowledged being a problem to himself. He did not subtitle the *Education* "an autobiography"; his publisher did. He had burned most of his diaries and his letters to his wife after her suicide, and he did not mention her name in the *Education*. History was the problem to which he addressed himself in the *Education*—History in relation to one "Adams" who was saturated in a family history that was easily identified with the national history. He had lived through the most eventful century recorded by man, had seen the classical republic of his great-grandfather John Adams and grandfather John Quincy Adams turn into the "powerhouse" now commanded by greedy little men. Adams wrote as if personal hesitation to claim a public role in his time proved the decline of the republic. His brother Brooks would call it "the degradation of the democratic dogma."

The *Education* was in a sense special to Henry Adams, who said that his autobiography began with *Mont-Saint-Michel and Chartres*. The medieval and the modern in perfect antithesis explained the life of Henry Adams! But the *Education* was certainly a most personal document to come from a historian so aloof from the passions of his time that he ended his book with eleven chapters demonstrating history as "science." The connection between Henry Adams and history was not mysterious, just special. He thought of himself *as* history. Even his theories of history were to become history. And this in a century when the sense of change was overpowering, having excited and alarmed the keenest minds. Never before were men so conscious of the replacement of epochs and the succession of human destinies, so time-minded, so process-minded, so spellbound by incessant change. And never since, at least in the West, have men so innocently believed that development itself is the climax and the "meaning" of History.

The history of how the Bible came to be organized became the critical tool, the higher criticism, with which the Bible's sacredness was displaced. Personal salvation was replaced by some ultimate point to be reached by History itself. Marx, that powerful man of letters, and Engels, his appealing simplifier, were to drive into millions of heads the conviction that socialism was not merely necessary but the inevitable next stage in history. The adversaries of the established order personified history as a birth process, a new society wrested from the old—and one that fulfilled, on a social basis, primitive Christianity's own revolutionary dream of human purposiveness and rebirth.

The nineteenth century began with the French Revolution: many liberal ideologues felt and hoped that the revolution would continue. The "century of hope," of secular progress and unlimited freedom, was now exposed as a liberal illusion: so many conservative and neo-Catholic minds felt this after the Great War. The century itself seemed to many of its writers *the* drama of dramas. Rebels like Emerson, contemptuous of mere institutions, were too conscious of their personal influence to be impressed by the divinity of History as it was summoned by Hegel and Marx. Carlyle had remonstrated with Emerson for not taking events seriously enough. But even Emerson came to recognize Napoleon as the representative man of the nineteenth century, the apostle of the emancipated and aggressive middle class rather than a classical conqueror like Caesar and Alexander.

Literature felt itself equal to transformation on such a scale. It was an age of history *because* literature was still the queen of the arts, the sacred record. It was an age of revolutions whose leaders wrote in the impassioned tones of the prophets, an age of science when a Darwin as well as a Marx reported straight to the general public his most detailed investigations. Nietzsche fearlessly wrote his speculations as if he were closer to Dante than to the subdivided and self-dividing philosophers of the future. Literature was still all-inclusive. History—all or any of it—was the most natural subject for its epic ambition. In writing the *Education* at the top of his form, in the isolation of the twentieth century, in the concentrated reflectiveness of old age, Henry Adams was no more a "popularizer" than his idols Gibbon and Tocqueville, his mentor John Stuart Mill. He was conscious of having a great story to tell and, as a historian in the great tradition, of being an artist equal to it.

He was lucky, posthumously, in finding the right audience for his sweep, his subtlety, and his malice. The ending of the Great War opened up a grand inquest into the nineteenth century, into "eminent Victorians" and "liberal illusions" that Adams's cronies in Washington and among the great capitalists would have been too stuffy to understand and enjoy. Since Adams steadfastly accused the nineteenth century of being the wrong one for his "eighteenth-century" type, Adams's book landed him in the right century at last. He outdistanced John Hay and William McKinley to become a contemporary of T. S. Eliot and Ezra Pound. Like Whitman, Melville, Dickinson, like Henry James and the great realist painter Thomas Eakins, Adams was to seem a sacrifice to one century but a glory to the next.

How many anticipations he had made of American power and technological supremacy in the twentieth century, of the inevitable collision with Russia, of the discoveries of prehistoric painting to be made in the caves of the Dordogne, of the wealth of beauty in the South Seas and the art of the Orient! Dying when his book was known only to fellow clubmen in the

American elite, Adams had aimed his bombshell and the moment of his triumph straight at an America he had predicted but would never see. Of course he had not assumed *identity* with the postwar world. On the contrary, he was sure only of its future deadliness. He had had an instinct since the Civil War that modern technology could endanger the planet. The twentieth century welcomed Henry Adams as the nineteenth did not, for it was only in 1918—and in 1945—that limitless power betrayed its cost.

There was another reason for Adams's new fame. The *Education* was the product of a period that more and more had come to be expressed by social fiction. Adams's remarkable but singular book, a personal epic of society, illustrates the dilemma as well as the brilliance of a literary artist who was not a novelist.

I I

Adams was an unusually subtle writer; among the American historians who still regarded history as a branch of literature, he stands out as the last and the best. Although he was to close the *Education* on eleven chapters offering a "scientific" approach to history, it will be seen that he wrote "science," as he had always written history, from a confident, magisterial, even arrogant literary instinct. As he admitted, "images are not arguments," and his images dealt with the fall of History, not with the fall of a single weight. He was an extraordinarily accomplished writer, but by the time he came to write *Mont-Saint-Michel and Chartres* at the beginning of the century and then to complete the *Education* in 1907, he was to show himself to the friends for whom he privately printed these books, as he had already shown himself in his letters, to be an original writer. William James told Adams that "from beginning to end *Mont-Saint-Michel and Chartres* reads as from a man in the fresh morning of life, with a frolic power unusual to historic literature." Henry James was amazed by the amount of personal revelation in the *Education* and the artist Adams revealed. Adams's literary virtuosity was in fact to make casualties of his much-vaunted science of history and his sense of historical truth.

Still, of all the interesting American historians, Adams had the largest intellectual ambition and the surest literary gift. So it is natural to think of him as a great historian—and not merely because we recognize him as an artist. A "great historian" is not the most *immediately* influential writer of history, not the most painstaking specialist in history, but the writer who, within the discipline of scholarship, has more than any other created our image of History, who in fact shapes an idea as "History."* The great historians, the great dramatists and analysts of history, are closest to what history means to us. Since History, as an intellectual order in the mind, is the creation of historical *writers,* it follows that it is such writers who have made history.

More than any other American writer devoting himself to history, Adams has made us see the transition to the modern age in his terms. Yet not many Americans have read Adams's most important professional effort, his nine-volume *History of the United States of America During the Administrations of Thomas Jefferson and James Madison* (1889–91),† or such specialties as his *Chapters of Erie* (1871), *Essays in Anglo-Saxon Law* (1876), *Documents Relating to New England Federalism* (1878), *The Life of Albert Gallatin* (1879), and *John Randolph* (1882). Most of Adams's works, including his two novels, *Democracy* (1880) and *Esther* (1884), are virtually unread even by the literary public, and this is true of Adams's *Life of George Cabot Lodge* (1911) and the essays toward a science of history, *The Degradation of the Democratic Dogma,* collected by his brother Brooks and published in 1919, the year after Henry's death. Most of his works are not in print, and their circulation has always been limited. He published one novel anonymously and another under a feminine pseudonym. Even his letters (the gayest, most brilliant private chronicle of politics and manners ever composed by an American) are largely known only to scholars. So the claim of his influence may seem strange, and the nature of it needs some explaining.

No one who has read the *History of the United States of America During the Administrations of Thomas Jefferson and James Madison,* who admires it as a fully achieved construction of history in the grand manner, studded with brilliantly memorable portraits and graphically documented episodes of life in the great worlds of diplomacy and war, would claim that Adams's importance as an image maker of history is due wholly to the literary skill and architectural grandeur of this enormous work. History must be felt by many people, not just admired by individual connoisseurs. History exerts its power as literature not because a book has literary distinction, but because the magisterial pattern it weaves is felt to shape us, to change us, to embody our idea and image of collective experience. History then becomes a memory of the race.

*In his biography of Henry James, Leon Edel notes that after some English readers complained of James's criticizing the European nobility, James "had the sense at last of his own power, of the writer whose image of society becomes the mirror in which society looks at itself."

†The complete work was last reprinted in 1930.

What turns history into literature is a literary power so great that we come to think of it as historical truth. Even the historical work most famous for its fine writing and its conscious sense of style, Gibbon's *Decline and Fall of the Roman Empire,* has prevailed because the grandeur of its conception and the unbroken confidence behind it make Gibbon's picture of the late-classical world the supreme image we have of that subject. Yet if Gibbon's work did not, on the whole, still stand up as historical fact, it would seem as unreliable as Carlyle's *French Revolution,* which is "literature" now because it is not history. Carlyle's book lives as historical play, but there have been too many other books on the revolution, more committed ones, for us to take Carlyle's wordplay for reality. The historical thinkers we read over and again, because their books *are* the history we have, are those whom we believe even if we do not accept their argument. Our image of history is not even obtained directly from their books; it is passed from mind to mind in the excited discovery that this is how history "works," how it moves. It is only the version of certain writers that has made history believable, that has given us a belief in history. This alone makes them artists in their line. They convince us not by single new facts, but by the logic of the pattern, by the new order they give to fact.

Henry Adams was such an artist. The *Education* is a work of such high art, is so accomplished, subtle, and persuasive in its own way, that it has taken under its wing, as it were, Adams's other books. It has gathered his life, his works, his celebrated family, into a single document of the great transformation of American life after the Civil War, a document that also offers itself as the single key to that transformation. Adams's account of his education has become the great fable of the period. Since 1945, even more than after 1918, every humanist's effort to make his way through twentieth-century science and technology has corroborated Adams's fear that literature and history are not enough. "The history of an epoch," said Einstein, "is the history of its instruments." Adams came to believe that. Since he guessed that the instruments would be decisive but did not know how they worked, the "failure" of his education assured him triumph as an example. His book made the most of his effort to understand. The age was getting beyond him—beyond everyone! He anticipated this with a precision and fury that turned his failure as an education into his conviction that he was a seismograph of history, an advance guard of the race.

No other American historian took in so much, has had such a triumph; few American intellectuals have left this much connection in our minds between a single personality and history. Henry Adams, who despised the masses, despaired of progress, declared himself a failure, and drew the last drop of bitterness from his experience, has turned out to be one of the ruling myth makers of American history.

It was an extraordinary subtlety that set all this in motion—a prodigious ability to persuade that is the way of the man behind the scenes, the courtier and wary observer who leaves court memoirs, inside stories of power. The *Education,* though it insinuates his "failure" to become a great political figure in the Adams tradition and declares him an "eighteenth-century" type thrust into the savage world of modern American capitalism and technology, succeeds as a work of history because Adams can present the actors of history while turning his *not* being one of them into a philosopher's disinterested virtue. Adams as a writer triumphed through his ability to suggest both the greatest possible intimacy with history and his own disdainful removal from it. His book, nominally written for his friends, is a patrician's inside story of a dominant group, a leading class, an elite. Once you become aware of the book as a practiced monologue spoken to the few who are capable of grasping his nuances of feeling and references to fact, you find nothing strange in thinking of Adams as the master of his literary trade and the willing tool of his own imagination. How crafty Adams is, in the driving spirit of his monologue, in editing the facts of his life! How much he leaves out, how much he glosses over! How archly, cynically, and self-hallucinatingly he retouches material he had reported very differently in his letters! In the full freedom of talk that no one can interrupt, he plays his life over, plays at facts, often arranges a whole period to a motif as if it were a piece of music. He seeks to create impressions, to prove a case by so thoroughly being one. Everything in the life of this man, his country, his ancestors, his generation, and his particular subject—the predicament of the human mind trying to calculate, but constantly being outdone by, the mighty new forces it has raised up—finally arranges itself as a pattern to produce a particular effect. Modern society is flying apart through its own madly self-multiplying energies. A world is going to hell in explanation of the worldly "failure" of this prophetic nature, Henry Adams.

III

Henry Adams had a literary imagination so insistent that it was to prove mystifying even to itself. But into whatever his mind moved, his purpose was always to write history. "The Irish gardener once said to the child: 'You'll be thinkin' you'll be President too!' " He was to create his first memorable effect in the *Education* by contrasting the Adamses as the fathers of American history with himself as the dilettante son, the spectator of history. Of course he was too much the intellectual to have accepted office if it had been offered. There are rumors that he could have been minister to Guatemala.

Closeness to power is so fundamental to Adams's self-confidence in writing history that he finally adopted intimacy with power as his literary strategy for writing *anything*. Of course he was not abashed by Washington when he resigned his Harvard professorship in 1877 to take up residence just across Lafayette Park from the White House. "The fact is, I gravitate to a capital by a primary law of nature," he wrote in one of his jaunty, gossipy, brilliant society letters that report every event and rumor in the citadels of power as an experience of Henry Adams. "This is the only place in America where society amuses me, or where life offers variety." "Cambridge is a social desert that would starve a polar bear." He was in Washington in order to write his *History of the United States;* he had the free run of the archives and was even given a desk in the State Department. Adams's literary mind so naturally sought unspoken authority from his family's and his own relationship to power that he was able to turn his position into his best material.

Marcel Proust was to pay the highest compliment to a fellow artist by parodying the Duc de Saint-Simon's *Mémoires* in his early work. (The court of Louis XIV was in fact to become one of the "invisible presences" within *A la recherche du temps perdu*.) Saint-Simon did not consciously see himself as an "artist"; he wrote in order to settle accounts, to satisfy some grudges, and above all to show that he knew what was going on. "Thus, apart from my other concerns, my curiosity was satisfied, and you must admit, whether you be somebody or nobody, that this is the only nourishment to be found at Courts, and that without it you would die of boredom." Adams's brilliantly gossipy letters show all these motives to be his own; yet he would not have admitted them into or about the *Education,* where his literary "doubles" are Augustine, Gibbon, and Rousseau.

In the *Education* he cleverly turned himself into a character, not Henry Adams but "Adams," "a manikin on which the toilet of education is to be draped in order to show the fit or misfit of the clothes." "Adams" became even more elusive a character than the author suggested in the preface, where he invoked analogies with Rousseau's *Confessions* (this made his brother Charles Francis laugh his head off). No doubt Rousseau was brought in to give the possibly bewildered reader a literary tradition within which to place this strange book. But Adams, who so easily dominated the narrative of his life, could not dominate the pressures of his own imagination. He became, inextricably and winningly, first a witness to history, then a symbol of history, and finally the embodiment of history trying to understand itself. So the *Education* draws always on history in order to portray Henry Adams as a type. He is by turns an example of the human species in the nineteenth century, Harvard College, and New England, the young American in his *Wanderjahre* in Europe, the discreet private secretary in an American embassy, the sensitive intellectual too fine for the Gilded Age. He finally becomes the savant trying to understand the century's acceleration of history, the very personification of all intellectual exhaustion in the fin de siècle, of the startling failure of the "best people." A "type *bourgeois-bostonien*" he listed himself among other representative men in his 1903 letter to Henry James about *William Wetmore Story and His Friends.* The "type" was Adams's fiction; it made the *Education* a work of art.

The pleasure of reading the *Education* is the pleasure of reading a work of literature made up, literally, from historical facts: History—the world of record—is recast as individual experience and speculation. It is the pleasure of seeing history come alive, of seeing it move, of seeing behind history to the actions and actors. It is the pleasure of seeing revealed the humanity so often concealed in history; the humanity, as we like to think, that explains history; the humanity that at least embodies history and often is all that can believably document history.

To achieve this pleasure the reader must have enough interest in the past to enable him to enter the one setting after another that underlie the *Education.* Place names *become* the landscape of Adams's journey through memory —Quincy, Boston, Washington, Harvard, Germany, England during the Civil War, Washington after it, the West, Chicago in 1893 (the Columbian Exposition), Paris in 1900 (another Great Fair), the White House under Roosevelt, the State Department under John Hay, the twin houses opposite the White House built for Hay and Adams by Richardson, the Bois de Boulogne in that moment when the book ends, one warm evening in early July 1905, when Adams learned as he "was strolling down to dine under the trees at Armenonville" that Hay was dead. But what is far more difficult now even among those who are interested enough in the past to "know" it, the reader of the *Education* must suspend disbelief—must agree for the moment that history is written because it composes a moral order, a definite progression, a Journey to the Holy City or a Decline and Fall.

To write history in the nineteenth century was to create a design. The most famous chapter of the *Education,* "The Dynamo and the Virgin (1900)," is an iconography of history in its two most starkly concentrated periods, the age of "unity" versus the age of mechanical energy and its dispersion. Adams explains here that

> historians undertake to arrange sequences,—called stories, or histories—assuming in silence a relation of cause and effect. These assumptions . . . have been astounding, but commonly unconscious and childlike. . . . Historians . . . had never supposed themselves required to know what they were talking about. Adams, for one, had toiled in vain to find out what he meant. He had even published a dozen volumes of American history for no other purpose than to satisfy himself whether, by the severest process of stating, with the least possible comment, such facts as seemed sure, in such order as seemed rigorously consequent, he could fix for a familiar moment a necessary sequence of human movement. The result had satisfied him as little as at Harvard College. . . . But he insisted on a relation of sequence, and if he could not reach it by one method, he would try as many methods as science knew. Satisfied that the sequence of men led to nothing and that the sequence of their society could lead no further, while the mere sequence of time was artificial, and the sequence of thought was chaos, he turned at last to the sequence of force; and thus it happened that, after ten years' pursuit, he found himself lying in the Gallery of Machines at the Great Exposition of 1900, his historical neck broken by the sudden irruption of forces totally new.

Obviously "sequence" was of primary importance to Adams. He said of the scheme that joined *Mont-Saint-Michel and Chartres* to the *Education* as twin parts of an "autobiography" that he was interested in the century of Amiens Cathedral and the works of St. Thomas Aquinas "as the unit from which he might measure motion down to his own time, without assuming anything as true or untrue, except relation." His examples of historical causation often show the freewheeling irony that is so much a part of his manner in the *Education*, but his feeling for "sequence" is fundamental. There is a good deal of his life that he omits, contracts, or smooths over in order to keep the "sequence." That is how the reader, in spite of Adams's aloofness, gets so close to his mind. The enjoyment of history lies in our ability fully to take in a particular historical design. To experience design can do more for us than to agree with the argument that supports it. As Adams says, the argument may not really be known to the historian himself.

Adams was an extraordinary historian because he naturally and constantly saw all life moving into history. What he created in the *Education* above all was, for him, *his* writing on the face of time, his effort to "fix for a familiar moment a necessary sequence of human movement." History was moving into the totally unfamiliar. The stranger it became, the more anxiety it brought to his mind, the more maledictions he poured out on it. But "sequence" remained history in its most concrete—and esthetic—manifestation; it was the satisfaction beyond all others that the mind could obtain from the dizzying impact of unlimited force. Sequence was form, and form alone was meaning.

I V

Before Adams—the first self-declared "scientific" historian of his own country—the prominent historian George Bancroft had described the evolution of this country as fulfilling, from the age of discovery, the will of a beneficent Providence. In the first volume of his *History of the United States,* Bancroft noted in his easy and confident way of the Plymouth Company Council Charter that "the results, which grew out of the concession of this charter, form a new proof, if any were wanting, of that mysterious connection of events, by which Providence leads to ends, that human councils had not conceived." Although Providence in its particular concern for the United States is missing from Adams's own *History of the United States,* the most striking literary characteristic of this book is also its easiness, its intellectual address, that magisterial command over the materials that is associated with the historian's natural confidence in himself as a judge of history. Adams said that he wrote his *History* to show that the peaceful and orderly evolution of society under favorable conditions was a subject for scientific history. At the end of his long work, discussing this task in his pivotal chapter, "American Character," he said that

> the scientific interest of American history centered in national character, and in the workings of a society destined to become vast, in which individuals were important chiefly as types. . . . Should history ever become a true science, it must expect to establish its laws, not from the complicated story of rival European nationalities, but from the economical evolution of a great democracy. . . . North America was the most favorable field on the globe for the spread of a society so large, uniform and isolated as to answer the purposes of science. There a single homogeneous society could easily attain proportions of three or four hundred million persons, under conditions of undisturbed growth.

Although Adams distinguished scientific history from old-fashioned nationalistic history, he was closer to Bancroft in his positiveness about the nature of history than he was to the cautious professional historians of the

future. Adams called himself a scientific historian because he lived in a
positivist age and was much influenced by scientific theorists who still wrote
for the general public. But in a sense he had taken all history for his province
before he embarked on his *History*. Within this book his conception of
science was one that, far from restraining him, encouraged his tendency
toward speculation. He was not in any sense a scientist; he was a freewheeling intellectual fascinated by science as a force working on the mind of man.
Adams thought that history was so different, because it was without heroes,
that it could become objective. His own *History* was not objective, for Adams
was just as much concerned with political leaders as his predecessors had
been. His own subtle purpose was to show how all of them—with Jefferson,
the chief victim of his illusions, at their head—were swept by a force, national
destiny, that they could not control. It was not science but force that was
already, in Adams's *History*, the great motif and interest of his work. And
with that touch of apocalypse that was to fascinate him in all his future
excursions up and down human history, he was to say that

> in American history the scientific interest was greater than the human. Else-
> where the student could study under better conditions the evolution of the
> individual, but nowhere could he study so well the evolution of a race. The
> interest of such a subject exceeded that of any other branch of science, for
> it brought mankind within sight of its own end.

Comparing American history to the Rhine, which starting from its gla-
cier in Switzerland first flows among medieval towns and feudal ruins, then
becomes a highway for modern industry, and at last arrives at a permanent
equilibrium in the ocean, Adams said that with historic glaciers and medieval
feudalism American History had little to do, "but from the moment it came
within sight of the ocean it acquired interest almost painful."

The pressure of this painful interest is felt whenever Adams touches on
his family. Adams wrote as a prophet of the national power which Jefferson
fostered against his will but which John Quincy Adams had dreamed of as
the destined opportunity for a philosopher-president to direct from Washington. Henry Adams wrote his book not as a self-limiting "scientific"
analyst of his subject but in the proud spirit of the intellectual—like Tocqueville in his *Recollections* of the 1848 Revolution and Trotsky in his *History of
the Russian Revolution*—who has been excluded from office. Adams never
held office, but he was writing for his grandfather and great-grandfather,
each of whom had been president of the United States, each of whom had

been vehement in his principles, and each of whom had left the White House, after one term, as a victim of what he considered the wickedness of popular opinion.

Henry Adams, who tacitly described himself in the great closing chapters of his *History* as a detached student of process, tracing the evolution of American society from a rivulet to the ocean, was no spectator. He satisfied his dominating instinct for form, his need to show himself in perfect control of his material, by retracing Jefferson's hopeless entanglement with England from an administrative point of view. Only the privileged man behind the scenes, with full access to the diplomatic files, could have done this.

The theme of Adams's *History* is the submission of principle to power. In everything that Adams wrote, the underlying theme is in fact the ineluctability of power. (Marian Adams's death by her own hand was to become the supreme instance in his life of the power that can be exerted by a personal compulsion. She bowed under this yoke and he bowed to the force of her necessity.) He is first the student and then the prophet of power—the national power, the power of concentrated force, the power exerted by certain powerful minds or leading political personalities. Of course he believed, as every reader of the *Education* knows, that American politicians were too naive to understand the power they held in their hands, that the scientists were too specialized to know what they had wrought, that the masses were too far from the head of the procession, "its few score of leaders," to know what was going on. Only the historian, with the whole scale of development open to him, could do justice to the gradually overwhelming concentration of power in modern times—and above all in America, *the* "modern" country. Only the historian kept all the lines of history clear and could see the full dimensions of this unprecedented situation. In the full consciousness of so much growth and change, the historian became equal to history. The historian's was the only instinct equal to man's stupefying extensions of himself in each generation. On April 11, 1862, writing from London to his brother Charles Francis in the field, Henry noted the end of England's wooden navy and said of the English:

> To me, they seem to be bewildered by all this. I don't think as yet they have dared to look their position in the face. People begin to talk vaguely about the end of war, and eternal peace; just as though human nature was changed by the fact that Great Britain's sea-power is knocked in the head. But for my private part, I think I see a thing or two. . . . Our good country the United States is left to a career that is positively unlimited except by the powers of the imagination. . . .
>
> You may think all this nonsense, but I tell you these are great times. Man

has mounted science, and is now run away with. I firmly believe that before many centuries more, science will be master of man. The engines he will have invented will be beyond his strength to control. Some day science may have the existence of mankind in its power, and the human race commit suicide, by blowing up the world. Not only shall we be able to cruize [*sic*] in space, but I'll be hanged if I see any reason why some future generation shouldn't walk off like a beetle with the world on its back, or give it another rotary motion so that every zone should receive in turn its due portion of heat and light.

Adams was never to worry too much over the social effects of what his intuition discerned. He claimed Mill and Tocqueville as his models, but unlike Mill he was not an intellectual reformer, and he did not share Tocqueville's profound sense of political responsibility for the future. He admired Marx (at least he liked to provoke his millionaire friends by citing Marx), but he had none of Marx's passionate insistence on changing history, society, the individual, the "world." Adams called history his "personal universe." What interested Adams was his own personal consciousness of history—and this consciousness was as elastic in its judgment of individuals, as undependable in its sympathy, as his extraordinary dexterity would make it.

Beyond this personal absorption in history, Adams did feel, and was sometimes overwhelmed by, an intellectual loyalty to the Adams family that was to be the strongest tradition in his life. An Adams was an intellectual statesman who might be a failure in the White House but was really the keenest prophet of the whole political mission in America. Henry always had before him the eighteenth-century philosopher-president whose intellectual capacities brought him many offices but whose "disinterestedness," combined with the touchiness that was also a family trait, made him fall to popular revolutions—John Adams in 1800 to Thomas Jefferson, John Quincy Adams in 1828 to Andrew Jackson. Yet everything that Henry wrote about John Quincy Adams shows a harshly critical view of the old man's rigidity of character, and of the Adams character in general, famous for its bleakness and its inability to meet people halfway. Henry in fact combined a Puritan distrust of human nature with a specific mistrust of his own Adams character. This surely played some role in the tragedy of his marriage, if only in the exaggeration of his responsibility.

"Our" Adams had the singular problem of being both an Adams and an artist. John Adams had anticipated something like this when he wrote to his beloved Abigail from Paris in 1780.

I must study politics and war that my sons may have liberty to study mathematics and philosophy. My sons ought to study mathematics and philosophy, geography, natural history and naval architecture, navigation, commerce and agriculture, in order to give their children a right to study painting, poetry, music, architecture, statuary, tapestry, and porcelain.

Henry Adams may not even have wanted the offices that two presidents took as the privilege of their revolutionary generation, but he could not help feeling marked down by his mundane contemporaries. At the same time, like all his family before and after him, Henry Adams regarded the Adams forebears, especially John Quincy Adams, as tragic figures. He thought they exemplified the tragedy of leadership in a democracy agitated by false expectations. They were too *serious,* a consequence of the specialization in political imagination that had lifted a humble cordwainer's descendants, for four generations, to national significance. Like all the Adamses, Henry still thought of politics as leadership; he would always identify himself with the governors, the minds at the center. It was from this central point that his books took their design; it was to this center that his fascination with power always returned.

But in his history of himself, this instinct for design, for the different shapes that power can assume, begins with an ironic celebration of the Adams family tradition to which Henry felt himself inadequate. The most famous theme of the *Education* is that those who should lead by force of intellect, culture, and tradition are no longer in charge. But before he comes to this, Adams makes it clear that the exalted offices identified with the family were too much for him, a born artist in his response to color, architecture, and music and in his inordinate emotion—an undersized *sensitif* unable to compete in the coming race of the century.

v

Henry Adams's famous sense of "failure" began not in 1868, when he sat in the Senate gallery and heard announced the rich men in Grant's cabinet; it began in the fact that, starting with John Quincy Adams, the Adamses had a strong sense of failure. They were so proud that they could never live up to their own legend, and they were such intellectuals as to be always frustrated and maddened by ordinary political reality. Henry's youngest brother, Brooks, was to say of their grandfather that he was disappointed because he was not supernatural. Henry had no such hopes. Long before he came to feel himself an eighteenth-century man forced to contend with a twentieth-century world, he knew himself to be a lover of summer in a world of winter, a young man dominated by memorials to old men, a possible stray bent to the service and history of the Adamses. This was a family so conscious of itself that the self-mortification necessary to Puritan pride and the stiffness of a New England temperament that *was* pride strengthened Henry's conviction that he could not live up to their name.

Henry Adams suffered, as it were, only on the heights, in grand style, in the grandest possible rooms, from his great library in Washington to his white-and-gold living room at the Continentale in Paris. But we cannot doubt that he suffered the penalties of what he felt to be the family grandeur. The legend of impossibly high beginnings is announced in the famous opening of the *Education:* "Had he been born in Jerusalem under the shadow of the Temple and circumcised in the Synagogue by his uncle the high priest, under the name of Israel Cohen, he would scarcely have been more distinctly branded, and not much more heavily handicapped in the races of the coming century, in running for such stakes as the century was to offer."

This is the myth of the ruling elite, the intellectual priesthood, that is so essential to the *Education.* Great expectations are associated with a son of the New England Temple. From the moment we open the book and take in those wryly boastful first lines, we are expected to understand that a new baby boy in the Adams family stood out like a prince. We have been brought inside the web of history as the history of its leaders; we have been introduced to one of the great intellectual families that have been the aristocracy of this country. Even the "Editor's Preface" for the first public edition in 1918, artfully written by Adams himself, to be signed by his ex-student and halberd bearer, Henry Cabot Lodge, prepares us for the *grand geste* associated with a book first privately printed in 1907 to the number of one hundred copies. Under the signature of Henry Cabot Lodge, Adams speaks to us from a preface dated six months after Adams's death—so great is the hold he wants to keep on the reader, so calculated is the effect he prepares. Historical fatality is one effect he wants—a decline and fall, a twilight of the gods—and he prepares for it like a storyteller watching the faces of his listeners. Only in the relaxed dogmatism of private conversation would so carefully trained a mind say, "Any schoolboy could see that man as a force must be measured by motion from a fixed point," then swing from one century to another—from one millennium to another!—"without assuming anything as true or untrue, except relation."

But this concern for effect on a few immediate listeners is the psychological driving power of the *Education*. During his life Henry Adams did not have a large audience and could not have wanted one. He turned this lack —even the fact that he paid Scribner's to publish his great *History*—into a way of imposing himself on his own distinguished circle, dominating his "inside ring" with the speculative freedom of his talk as he dominated the adoring young ladies he called his nieces.

Adams liked to work behind the scenes, from the wings, to make his effect, which was often devastatingly personal, with the greatest possible show of indirection and impersonality. Surely he valued history, as he did the anonymous documentary article in a magazine, for all the opportunities it gave him to express his complication of intellectual and personal passions with the authority of scholarly objectivity. He always knew how to retain his "position," his special social edge, his aura of learning. Both his anonymous novels are full of thinly disguised portraits of his friends and other notables of the day. Adams valued the effect of these novels on his own group more than he did creating the slightest stir as a novelist. Neither as a writer nor as a political thinker was Adams ever concerned with the public; he liked being anonymous and refusing all honors for the power refusal gave him. But in everything that Adams wrote—history, biography, fiction, autobiography, letters—he showed an extraordinary intuition for the effect that a particular form can produce.

In that sense all his writings are "political"—they are meant to influence. Nowhere else in his writings is his writing to an immediate audience so plain as it is in the *Education*. He exploited the slipperiness of autobiography to the full. But it was also, for him, a way of making history by writing it. Probably one of the strongest motives behind the *Education* is the need to confess, but when Adams got down to it he had less to say about his dead wife than he did about history as vertiginous change. He fulfilled this personal passion and so imposed his images of history on the next generation.

The pious journals kept by Adams's Puritan ancestors were account books of the soul rendered up to an all-seeing God. Even the great diary of grandfather John Quincy Adams, which was sustained for over sixty-five years and is probably the longest public record by a single man, was written for the eye of God and for posterity, as a vindication of self. The old man has many faults to complain of in himself, but his conscience is the only courtroom that can impress him, and this conscience is his proof that God lives and is daily preoccupied with the virtues and faults of John Quincy Adams. So one of the most famous political personalities in the Western world, who knew all the rest, who could describe in his daily record the most complex negotiations for the Treaty of Ghent and his conversations with Alexander I as they paced along the Neva, who was in Russia when Napoleon invaded, who was a minister to many European countries, a United States senator, secretary of state, president of the United States, and finally a congressman fighting the attempt of Southerners to gag all discussion of slavery in the House—this man reported to an Invisible Court.

It is the appeal to some secret authority or tribunal that gives such a mysterious imperative to the great diaries, confessions, autobiographies of one's *éducation sentimentale* (and even Henry Adams pronounced no education more significant than that). But now the inner group to whom Henry Adams is recounting all that he is willing to tell of *his* education has replaced the good opinion of the public, which Adams never solicited, and that of his grandfather's God, who has entirely lost personality and no longer addresses the creation in human words. Adams's book reveals in the self-checking balance of his sentences his need to polish up every experience—to be always in control, amused and detached, to make a history which would smooth out all the silent disorder of one's real life.

This powerful compulsion is not merely to show order in one's life but to show one's life *as* order. In the setting of Adams's larger compulsion to show American history as the decline and fall of his class, the patricians made so by their intellectual dedication, we can see why, by the time we get to the exciting but pretentious latter chapters of the book, on the future of history, Adams had to put this complicated drama of the self and history into the smoothly impersonal rhetoric of an all-encompassing determinism. The historian's compulsion "to arrange sequences, called stories or histories"— his tendency to "assume in silence a relation of cause and effect"—has become the servant of the most concentrated historical imagination this country has produced. The subject was overwhelming—history rushing to its end as the historian wearily descends to his. The egotism of this is monumental, historic, creative. Only an American could have felt it. Unlike Oswald Spengler and similar catastrophists, Adams could identify himself with what was noblest and grandest in his national history. It was the proprietary attitude he took to American history (with some reason) that made his vision so intense and his ideas so pertinent. To the great European writers "history" began so far back that any intervention in it was a matter of stepping right into the middle of things. In the nineteenth century any American writer with a comprehensive imagination, but especially an Adams, could show where history began and who made it. A European could naturally be more diffident about asking: "Was Europe a Success?" A European was likely to see the tragedy of history not as violated idealism but as the cycle of aimless recurrence that is typified by so many human sacrifices —a subject that does not often break through Henry Adams's Brahmin chill. Adams was so bitterly conscious of what the political will in America had aimed at, and where it had failed, that he silently buttressed his vision by his personal tragedy. "Woman" finally stood for "force"—but so, finally, did everything else. Without the Puritan God, yet all too conscious of his own mistrustful character, Adams had somehow come back to the belief—for him irrational—that a man's private character is somehow betrayed by his good or bad fortune in life. Everything for him had become part of history and showed its significance.

VI

"Adams, you reason too much!" his friend John La Farge the painter said to him. Mind, restlessly devouring, unsatisfiable mind, mind helplessly descending through the cosmos in search of itself, "the man-meteor," was to become his obsession. To "reason" up and down the stream of time, and in his many travels, was to become Henry Adams's assertion in the face of what he saw everywhere as "chaos"; "reason" was to become his style in life. But how should he not reason, and reason inextricably, like all those Protestant heroes of thought in the nineteenth century condemned in a faithless world to argue themselves into some historical certitude? How should he not reason when Lyell and Darwin, Marx and Comte, held out to his eager mind a law of development that always stopped short of his own experience, so that one had to reason beyond the known confines of history? How should he not continue to reason from history and to make history seem reasonable even in its "chaos" when the compulsion to reason from sequence was in his pride as an Adams, in his training as a historian, in his cautions as a millionaire, in his physical timidities as an undersized man, in his loneliness and guilt as a husband?

What is characteristic is that all these urges and torments were invariably translated into history as law. Marian Adams died in 1885. For thirty years after, until he positively gloated in Wilson's declaration of war as the confirmation of all his predictions of a world made a single event, Adams sought the secret, the almost daemonic unity of history that he was determined would not escape *him* who had so long tired of mere historical actors. History was moving too fast to reveal itself to its leaders, but it would not refuse its subtleties to him. The law that he had sought in the money markets, in the materialistic physics so soon to dissolve after Adams's death, made up the web in his tortured mind, with its unlimited sense of "acceleration," from which he did not wish to flee. Nemesis would justify him.

No wonder that in this typically modern absence of objective certitude, riddled with desperate guesses which only his own science of history could confirm, haunted by the "absurdity" of his own speculations, Adams, writing the *Education* in his late sixties, made of the dilemmas of the historian the new content of history itself. But before he came openly to this point, he had found, in the symbolic decline of his family and of his class, material for a presiding character: "Adams," truly a third person, as if this narrative device could found literature on the dilemmas of the historian himself.

Never before had an American historian loomed so large in his own picture of history. Never before had an American historian been so much the subject of history. Not Henry Adams but "Adams" becomes a character in history.

And so does the family. Adams never lets us forget why the pioneer eugenicist, Francis Galton, was to include the Adamses in his *Hereditary Study of Genius* (1869). They are the only Americans there. To Henry Adams they would always be the fathers of American history as well as of his own. Before office, in office, and out of office John and John Quincy Adams had been intellectual sages of the young republic—and a mere congressman for twenty years after leaving the presidency, John Quincy Adams became, at least in Washington, the antislavery conscience of a distraught country. It was a family noted for its diplomats, its scholars, its literary distinction, its political firmness, its knowledge of Europe, and for the maddening but impressive tendency of Adamses to identify themselves with absolute political virtue. Henry Adams had grown up in the midst of the Free Soil Party in Massachusetts. He had been at Harvard when it was still a college, he had known Germany as a student, he had thoroughly studied England during the Civil War; he had virtually founded the modern school of history at Harvard; he had written what was undoubtedly the most distinguished work of history by any living American. He and his clever wife, Marian, provided the center of the most brilliant society in Washington, he was the closest friend of the secretary of state, and he called himself a "stable companion to statesmen." He was as rich as he was cultivated, he was as worldly and well travelled, ripely urbane, and polished, as he was intellectually independent.

If any writer in America knew "society" to its fingertips, knew it for its manners and vanities, knew it as a spectacle, knew it as so many American novelists merely hoped to know it, it was Henry Adams, who had been with Charles Sumner in antislavery meetings and Swinburne in English country houses, who had been at Stafford House in London when "Garibaldi, in his gray capote over his red shirt, received all London, and three duchesses literally worshipped at his feet," and had watched his father, the American minister, stand up to arrogant British enemies of the Union cause like Gladstone and Lord John Russell.

More than any American social novelist of his generation or later, more than James, and even more than the rich and cosmopolitan Edith Wharton, Adams was intimate with the ripe and distinguished social world on both sides of the Atlantic that was close to the centers of power. He knew all the prime observation posts, from Mount Vernon Street in Boston to American embassies, from country houses in Yorkshire to the special enclaves of millionaire senators. As only an American could, he enjoyed the friendship of figures in the English governing classes who could not abide each other. Whatever the personal confidences he enjoyed, whatever his special instinct for history as diplomatic intelligence—negotiations between the highest—he insinuated being in the know, having the authority of the insider that molds every line in the *Education*. In style and manner it is more an English than an American book. To anyone who has observed the place that intellectuals hold in the English Establishment, and how attentive they are to the grace that can come with power, the *Education* is a lasting reminder of how little the style of the elite has changed within itself.

Perhaps it is the English surface of the *Education* that explains why the book has received comparatively little notice in America as a literary account of society. The tone is altogether too casual (even if the prose is not), too easy in its mock diffidence, for us to recognize what a very large claim Adams is making to the knowledge of society. By writing in so allusive a tone, even when he is alluding to his own failure, by writing to so restricted a circle as his selected one hundred readers, he is subtly advancing his own importance. He disparages the intellectual leaders of New England as a type, Harvard as a place of learning, Washington as a capital. Above all he disparages himself. His lack of knowledge is insisted on throughout—he was a conventional student and a failure as a professor; he failed to appreciate music, he failed to assimilate German civil law, he failed to master the mathematics necessary to an educated man in his generation. How gleefully Adams ticks off his failures. But the pride is unmistakable; no one else knew enough to recognize the insufficiency of *his* education. No one else was in a position to fail so grandly, to fail so much expectation, to fail in so many distinguished fields and important places.

Adams was in fact at the center of the ruling American elite. Even during the Gilded Age, when the Adamses lost so much influence in their native Quincy that Henry's oldest brother, John Quincy, ran for governor of Massachusetts as a Democrat, Henry was the protégé of Hayes's secretary of state, wrote a famous exposé of corrupt railroad financing, was a dominating figure at Harvard, and was soon to become an important figure behind the Washington scene, while his brother Charles Francis, the hearty elder brother who distinguished himself in the Civil War and later mastered the science of railroading, became head of the Union Pacific.

This Establishment is still the symbol of disinterested professional intelligence, scholarship, and tradition in a commercial society; it embodies a standard even if it no longer rules as a power. Henry Adams could afford to look down on presidents, on all the presidents he had a chance to observe, from Zachary Taylor to Theodore Roosevelt; in his family alone, as he felt, had the peculiar moral responsibility attached to the presidency been used as a form of intellectual power and as an expression of intellectual virtue. All other presidents under his eye, he manages to suggest, were biological sports. Look attentively at their portraits in the *Education*, and you will see that under Adams's always caustic eye and withering touch, each is shown in the White House as awkward, too small for the power that he directs and is *unaccountably* in charge of.* Zachary Taylor he remembers receiving callers as simply as if he were "in the paddock"; Lincoln at his inaugural ball is "a long, awkward figure . . . evidently worried by kid gloves"; Grant is the unattractive, unpromising American of the "inarticulate" classes—so awkward that although his force as a general is

*A White House reception in *Democracy* (1880): "Madeline found herself before two seemingly mechanical figures, which might be wood or wax, for any sign they showed of life. These two figures were the President and his wife; they stood stiff and awkward by the door, both their faces stripped of every sign of intelligence, while the right hands of both extended themselves to the column of visitors with the mechanical action of toy dolls. . . . To the President and his wife this was clearly no laughing matter. There they stood, automata, representatives of the society which streamed past them. . . . What a strange and solemn spectacle it was. . . . She felt a sudden conviction that this was to be the end of American society; its realization and its dream at once. She groaned in spirit."

admitted, this force is somehow mere automatic instinct, a fact in biology. Even if we did not know from Adams's letters that he regarded Theodore Roosevelt in office as a maniac, the stealthy references in the *Education* would be enough to tell us that he thought T.R. *de trop* even at his own table in the White House.

By contrast, however, Charles Francis Adams, Henry's father, was a man whose mind was "singularly in balance." The besetting quality of the American male was a lack of fine consciousness, of virtually all intellectual consciousness—a type sodden with whiskey and work, "his two stimulants." But so marked was the Adams quality that the *Education* confers it on the brothers-in-law of Charles Francis Adams, Edward Everett and Dr. Nathaniel Frothingham; on Charles Francis Adams's associates in the Free Soil Party, Dr. John G. Palfrey, Richard Henry Dana, and Charles Sumner; on Henry's cronies in England, Charles Milnes Gaskell and Francis Palgrave; on the particular Adams friends at home, John Hay and Clarence King; and even on the right financier, like William C. Whitney, and the right editor, like Whitelaw Reid.

In his preface to a new edition of the *Education,* Denis Brogan points out that Adams's friend Richard Monckton Milnes, Lord Houghton, who is an important presence in the book, possessed the greatest pornographic library of modern times, and Brogan says that "it is impossible to believe that Adams knew nothing of this side of Lord Houghton or that it excited no curiosity in him." But whether he knew of the collection that first introduced Swinburne to the Marquis de Sade, it is a point of Adams's social chronicle that all his friends and associates are described as the friends of his *ideas*—lonely spars and relics of the intellectual Establishment in a world overrun by bankers and Jews.

It is not from the *Education* that you learn that his much-lamented friend Clarence King, the brilliant geologist, was married to a Negro woman; that as their friend the British diplomat Cecil Spring-Rice pointed out, neither Hay nor Adams, so deeply concerned with politics, bothered to retain his legal residence in a state to which he could go home to vote. King's failure to exploit his discovery of valuable mining properties is laid entirely to his easy freedom in an age of grasping yahoos; John Hay, secretary of state to both McKinley and Roosevelt, is somehow too fine for his job. Adams, who typically scored Harvard College for not telling him about *Das Kapital* (published nine years after his graduation), managed even in this to suggest that Karl Marx was distinguished rather than dangerous.

Yet it is exactly this passion of friendship, this quality of intellectual sympathy and protection attached to *his* relatives, associates, and friends, this conscious vantage point from which the elect judge the world, that gives the *Education* its brilliance. As for the many he just as brilliantly ignores, it is no doubt in the American disposition—it was certainly in Adams's own— to judge the world severely. Adams cannot forgive the great new bustling, vulgar American world for the loss of his "eighteenth-century" world. The subtle bitterness of the *Education*—where he puts everything more ironically than he does in the often histrionic rages of his personal letters—can be construed as another of those self-dramatizations by which Adams's generation condemned history at large for the loss of its innocent hopefulness.

Despite the urbane and even silky surface of the *Education*, no social chronicle could be more obviously lacking in exactly that sense of human limitation which forms, and is, the charm of character in novels of manners. No one in the *Education*, least of all Henry Adams, is described for himself alone, as in a novel; each one is carried along by the historical process—of which Adams feels himself to be both the particular victim and the expert observer. We miss the element of play which is behind all invented situations, that delight in character and action as pure demonstration; we miss the unassimilable human fact; we miss that sense of comedy which is unpanicked by candid weakness and open vice.

Adams gives us an autobiographical excursus into history, and this has the quality of anecdote: we are less conscious of the story than of the man telling it. Adams is the center, and more particularly it is his style, his way of staying at the center. Adams's closest friends, here described to readers who thus become his other friends, are those other selves of Henry Adams who convey his discriminations and accomplishments. He says in the chapter "Twenty Years After (1892)" that with John Hay's multivolume *Life* of Lincoln and his own *History*, "between them they had written nearly all the American history there was to write." So there was nothing left to write, just as in the slack of American history there was now nothing *worth* doing. Adams and Hay addressed each other in letters as "Dearly Beloved," "Apple of Mine Eye," "My Own & Only One—Tres Cher"; in his book Adams makes one feel that in a society of idiotic congressmen, bumbling presidents, vicious bankers, and indescribable vulgarians, "Hay" and "Adams" had become the few points around which collected the honor that might be left in American life.

Of course the disproportions in Adams's chronicle would be comic if he did not usually make us overlook them. So much caressing sympathy and understanding for poor John Hay, who as secretary of state is shown wearing himself out in the service of this vulgar democracy—and so little regard for Grant, who as general helped to save the great democracy which alone had given this ambitious young climber out of the Ohio Valley, John Hay, his chance to serve presidents, to marry money, to rise in the newly powerful American world. The closest friends of Henry Adams—Clarence King died in 1901, Hay in 1905—are portrayed as the leading victims of a world that soon, in the last chapters of the *Education*, will be shown literally racing to chaos. Once Adams has suggested, in chapter 21, that his personal life has come to an end with the death of his wife, his book turns from a chronicle of history into a philosophy of history that will substantiate his "failure."

Yet with all these examples of a constricting intellectual egotism, the *Education* is a unique social chronicle and a great history of an intellectual caste, precisely because it takes this "Establishment" as the center of value and at every point strikes that essential love and admiration for a particular group that makes the literature of "society" possible. This is the positive side of his book. No matter how slyly Adams may undermine his friends for lacking the historical intelligence on which he prided himself, this love of his own is the exuberant side of the book. He was always more agreeable than he meant to be. For he loves "society," which means the leading group that furnishes the records of a society, as only the true novelists of manners, the true historians, courtiers, and gossips of power do. This was the greatest advantage he derived from being an Adams, an intimate of power.

He loved as social fact what his complicated mind could not accept as excellence. He never felt the romance of wealth and power in England as Henry James did, but he could suggest the political influence that was at work in English country houses, the blunt force of the Yorkshire personality, the charm of so many aristocratic intellectuals, as easily as he could the cynical bark of Lord Palmerston and Swinburne's total recall of everything he had read. The *Education* is even richer in its portraits of American "notables," so many of whom were Adams's friends that the book seems to be linked together by names. But though the book finally becomes the most brilliant suggestion of the hidden force moving American society, no connection is shown between these friends and the society which in fact they led. It is this failure to show the connection that explains why Adams, in spite of the facility with which he wrote his novels *Democracy* and *Esther*, never thought as a novelist does and could not have turned his memories into a novel.

Cecil Spring-Rice, the British ambassador and a member of the Hay-Adams circle, noted that rich Americans fled from the soil on which they had been raised and from their own people. Unlike the British, whose wealth was related to the land, the American rich were rootless and disoriented; Spring-Rice found "something rather melancholy about the talk of educated people here." To Adams the American elite represents its own memories. But for just this reason Adams's grief over the powerlessness of his old idols in New England leads him to invoke, as the shape of his own youth, the "eighteenth-century" world—by which he means John Adams and John Quincy Adams. It is an astonishing historical creation. And even though the account of his personal life breaks off in the middle, to suggest the impact of his wife's death, he manages still, in the theory of history that makes up the rest of the book, to show his struggle with the society created by the Civil War. Thus his book is strangely two books—the first the history of a self, the other a philosophy of history.

Did his life end so soon? Did Henry Adams also merge wholly into the "ocean" of history? Any European historian, brought up on society as tradition *and* revolution, would have seen in Adams's polarities fresh proof of the innocent self-indulgence that was possible to rich Americans. A man who could have struggled on the highest level, in the open political arena, had turned himself into a malicious and secretive recluse—and this just across Lafayette Square from the White House! What a Saint-Simon, what a Horace Walpole, what a Tocqueville or Mill or Comte this is! Where *is* society in this book after 1885? Where *are* the public issues and the real actors who correspond to the fight against slavery—to Sumner and Lincoln—to the years in Britain during the Civil War—to Palmerston and Russell? Where above all is Henry Adams as we find him in his letters, brilliantly describing to his adored friends the social texture of every country in the world he roamed so obsessively? It is easy to imagine his English friends in particular turning away from the book after "Twenty Years After (1892)" and saying in justified irritation, What a sentimentalist and fraud! What pretensions to the intellectual secret of the universe when he cannot face the truths of his own heart!*

---

*Adams's English friend Moreton Frewen said of the *Education* that it was a very stone of Sisyphus which "defies all analysis."

No "autobiography," we may readily admit, tries so hard to withhold the secret that the author himself would have liked to discover. In its style alone, the book is an inimitable case of what Adams called form—"the instinct of exclusion." It is so brightly enamelled, finished, sealed off, so wary in its irony, so entirely formal in its effect, that by its side the pompous rhythms of Gibbon's autobiography seem spontaneous; Gibbon's book is certainly more direct. But then Gibbon wrote as a success, Adams as a "failure."

Yet Adams's instinct for style, which reminds us of his extraordinary compulsion to style itself on every side of life—his elegantly oval handwriting was as exquisite and *made* as any script could ever be—is surely the real secret of Henry Adams, which could only be, in so tensely ordered a mind, his intellectual passion, the fixation of the born artist on the material in which he divines the final pattern that alone interests him.

The Education of Henry Adams is the story not of a man born out of his time, who lacked the science he needed to understand the nineteenth century; it is the story of an artist deprived of having around him the sense of tradition that makes the art of history, and who then found himself unable to express the terms of his isolation or to believe that anyone, even this made-up "Henry Adams," could say just what his interest in history was. This, I believe, was style: the style in which so many aspects of the past came to him, from the Virgin at Chartres to the dynamo at the Paris Exposition of 1900. Style was the look of the historical process as it was appropriated by the savant as connoisseur. Style was development, panorama, the emblems of change that constitute our sense of time. It was the perfect detachment, with "all history" for subject, that perhaps only an American could feel about all "their" history, that only a millionaire scholar, luxuriating voluptuously in inaction, could adopt as his portion: the almighty spectator.

> Life [he wrote to his brother Brooks in 1899] becomes at last a mere piece of acting. One goes on by habit, playing more or less clumsily that one is alive. It is ludicrous and at times humiliating, but there is a certain style in it which youth has not. We become all, more or less, gentlemen; we are *ancien régime;* we learn to smile while gout racks us. One lives in constant company with diseased hearts, livers, kidneys and lungs; one shakes hands with certain death at closer embrace every day; one sees paralysis in every feature and feels it in every muscle; all one's functions relax their action day by day; and, what is worse, one's grasp on the interests of life relaxes with the physical relaxation; and, through it all, we improve . . . we should almost get to respect

ourselves if we knew of anything human to respect; so we affect to respect
the conventions, and ask only to be classed as a style.

This is Adams happily spreading himself to his most adoring audience,
the younger brother who thought him the most powerful mind he knew; this
was the bitterness of the surface, the mere *look* of things that a vindictive,
unhappy man could seize on. Life had become entirely a matter of playacting
for the actor who no longer knew what he was hiding from others. The man
who went around the world not talking to anyone saw everyone as appearance—slightly foolish. Yet Adams's letters are profound in their observation
as well as snobbish. The superb eye that saw that "positively everything in
Japan laughs" began his great book on the Middle Ages: "The Archangel
loved heights."

Adams saw social forms as style, he saw power as style, he could even
see American presidents as the wrong style. This intense personal appropriation of the past as style could come only to the man who had the unity
of history always on his mind, so that the government buildings that he
saw at twelve, on his first visit to Washington, became in chapter 3 of the
Education "the white marble columns and fronts of the Post Office and
Patent Office which faced each other in the distance, like white Greek
temples in the abandoned gravel-pits of a deserted Syrian city." To see
history as style, one must begin with the sense of command: apart from the
troops, who are lost in the mud of actual living and fighting and cannot so
easily see "the whole picture." But to see history as style also means to see
history as a book that one is writing. Style divines the kinship between
different sets of material (and who will challenge this creative urge?),
knows what naturally belongs together in a book that makes that book, is
rooted in some instinct for affinity.

Henry Adams commanded his knowledge so well that his intense, astonishing sense of perspective became a way of drawing in historical images. A historical episode became what an object in space is to a painter: it made a setting. "Had he been born in Jerusalem under the shadow of the Temple . . ."
"This passage from Gibbon's *Autobiography* . . . led Adams more than once
to sit at sunset on the steps of the Church of Santa Maria di Ara Coeli. . . ."
"Concord, in the dark days of 1856, glowed with pure light . . . a Gothic
cathedral." The Adamses, dropped off at a New York pier, return from
England in 1868 as strange to the country as if they "had been Tyrian traders
of the year B.C. 1000, landing from a galley fresh from Gibraltar. . . ." "Society

offered the profile of a long, straggling caravan, stretching loosely towards the prairies, its few score of leaders far in advance and its millions of immigrants, negroes and Indians far in the rear, somewhere in archaic time."

For Adams these memories become images compressed by the intensity of his overview. In the ecstatic acceleration of Adams's mind through time —time past, time recovered, time relived—the titles of great books, the thinkers of primary theories, the names of ancient cities in the Roman Empire evoked from the steps of Ara Coeli—Karnak, Ephesus, Delphi, Mycenae, Constantinople, Syracuse—the great place-names in Adams's personal history—London in 1861, Washington in 1868, Chicago in 1893, Paris as the site of the dynamo in 1900—all become colors and sounds in the vibration of the historian's consciousness. Without the search for the total design, such references would be frivolous. But in the *Education* these cities, churches, books, these sacred names of thinkers, represent the effort to make the whole force of the past live in a single line. Only *The Waste Land* among later works has this intention, and Eliot seeks it in virtually every line. But Adams, in his less concentrated prose, does not view the past as a mirage.

> What is the city over the mountains
> Cracks and reforms and bursts in the violet air
> Falling towers
> Jerusalem Athens Alexandria
> Vienna London
> Unreal

The past is still real to an American's "education."

When Adams wants to describe the full grip on his imagination of the *Origin of Species,* he describes himself lying on the slope of Wenlock Edge in Shropshire, daydreaming of the different items that form the mysterious stream of human development.

> The triumph of all was to look south along the Edge to the abode of one's earliest ancestor and nearest relative, the ganoid fish.... Life began and ended there. Behind that horizon lay only the Cambrian, without vertebrates or any organism except a few shell-fish. On the further verge of the Cambrian rose the crystalline rocks from which every trace of organic existence had been erased.
>
> That here, on the Wenlock Edge of time, a young American, seeking only frivolous amusement, should find a legitimate parentage as modern as

though just caught in the Severn below, astonished him as much as though he had found Darwin himself. In the scale of evolution, one vertebrate was as good as another.

In this typical play of Adams's historical sense, the items are merely sounded, not explained. But no general idea in the nineteenth century meant so much to Adams and his friends as evolution, and Adams has only to sound *Darwin,* as at different times he sounds *Ara Coeli, Washington, Byzantium,* for the passion of the design to carry the theme along. History may not give meaning but, as history, it *is* meaning. This is its dependable interest. History is what we possess in common—this is its consolation as experience, and as literature, its ability to delight. Why should names alone, *Wenlock Edge* and the *Severn,* which denote places I may never have seen and which Adams does not bother to describe, delight me? It is because names are traditions. Each of these names has been sounded repeatedly in the culture that I share with Adams; *Severn* and *Wenlock Edge* are familiar to me from English poems that Adams does not have to mention for me to think of them. Without knowing exactly what the landscape over the Severn looks like, I possess the association as I might possess a character in a novel. The landscape that was put into depth for Henry Adams by Darwin is one that the reader can now possess as his intellectual landscape; Darwin and the ganoid fish and Henry Adams are his world, too.

"Community of thought" is what Adams meant by society, and this he tried to create with the friends for whom the *Education* was privately printed. To enjoy the *Education,* later readers must feel that such a society exists, as literature, and that one belongs to it as one belongs to the society of *Pride and Prejudice, The Golden Bowl, A la recherche du temps perdu.* Not to enjoy the *Education* as a visit to that society is of course to undervalue Adams—he rather looked forward to that—and to misunderstand his book, which he expected and in a sense even desired, so that what did exist as community of thought would form more closely around him. Society for Henry Adams, as for all traditionalists who identify it with their real or ideal memories, is the union of those who share a culture—not always at the same time, perhaps, but they recognize it in each other when they do share it. We now see what happens to the "novel of society" in revolutionary times, when whole classes and races hitherto not regarded as being fully human suddenly assert themselves, and the famous "community of thought" on which society has so long prided itself turns out to be the ideal of a tiny elite, one that it has possessed only in forms of ritual.

The community that Adams could not *depend* on in life he tried to create through the *Education,* which, like all the classic autobiographies, was written in order to help the author contend with his life. What Adams could not find in his own culture he found only in the imagination of time past and of society-as-friendship that he so brilliantly sustained by his autobiography and letters. So the form in which he tried to create *his* society was at least his very own. It is exactly the subtly insinuating approval of what is acceptable and the extraordinary insolence toward what is not that explains the lasting qualities of the *Education* as a social chronicle.

At the expense of a civil war, Adams got a very great deal out of England. By adopting the casual knowingness of the English upper classes, the inability to be surprised—or to praise anything clearly—he forged the authority of the intelligent, the cultivated, the just. As in a novel of manners, the *Education* makes you identify with the author's irony the standard of values by which to judge everybody else. This is always a triumph of style, whether in *Pride and Prejudice* or in *The Great Gatsby.* Civilization has a center at last, and you know where it is—with the author's control.

It is this ability to persuade lesser breeds that values are given from Oxford or Cambridge as time is told from Greenwich that has been the charm of the English intellectual Establishment. Anyone who has observed at high table a normally fluent Englishman sending the talk back with the port will recognize the style that Adams learned in English country houses. It is a style in which people expect familiarity with books the others have not read for the same reason that they take for granted a consideration that the others may never demonstrate. To gentlemen of this class, books and ideas are social facts, not the pedantries of solitary men. It is because Adams is writing in this style to his hundred ideal readers, his hundred perfect friends, that he pays the highest possible compliment to them by assuming what in the order of things they will assume.

Style as a development from manners—a style of personal cultivation and conversation; a style of behavior; a style that embodies one's deepest habits as a man—became Adams's way of writing. In the chapters of the *Education* that recount the attempt of the British cabal in office—Palmerston, Russell, and Gladstone—to strengthen the Confederacy, Adams triumphantly manages to make the reader feel that Gladstone was a fool, Russell a villain, and that Palmerston, though prime minister, could be let off only for not knowing all that Russell was up to. The major issue, the survival of the American republic, is never once explicitly justified. The Civil War, seen from London, has come down to a controversy between rival British sets—Russell and

Gladstone in one; John Bright and William E. Forster in the other. A would-be biographer of John Hay was astonished, on interviewing Adams, to hear him put down his former best friend. But who cares to remember this rather than the pity for the dying Hay on which the *Education* closes. Adams called himself a "stable companion" to statesmen. All this suggests his shiftiness as well as the power in the hands of his friends.

In the *Education* all friends are flattered by being put into the book; enemies, like personal conflicts, are just left out. Neither Justice Oliver Wendell Holmes, who found Adams's acidulousness impossible to take after a hard day's work, nor Owen Wister, who after an interview with Adams recorded the man's baleful no to all things, has suggested much charity by Adams toward his friends. But within the charmed circle of the *Education,* everything past had style, and even one's cronies fitted in—as style. This was the embittered historian's one triumph. In a culture that could hardly share his concern with time past, that positively gloried in obliterating the past, Adams came to believe, as Proust would, that language was the mold into which the past would fit.

Of course he did not have the psychological curiosity that gave Proust the courage to confront his disordered life. But then, as his greatest book shows, Adams was not a novelist. The subject of his autobiography—which he disclaimed as being one—is not personality, not even his own. Characteristically, it is history. And history deals with public, not private worlds. That is why, unlike fiction, history often seems to write itself, to follow the pattern seemingly implicit in public records. History lets us off as private individuals, and in reading history *we* are let off. As Adams said in the last chapter of his *History of the United States of America During the Administrations of Thomas Jefferson and John Adams,*

> history had its scientific as well as its human side, and in American history the scientific interest was greater than the human. Elsewhere the student could study under better conditions the evolution of the individual, but nowhere could he study so well the evolution of a race. The interest of such a subject exceeded that of any other branch of science, for it brought mankind within sight of its own end.

He was a man much preoccupied with ends. No one can doubt the delight that "the sense of an ending" brought to him, for the total design it could suggest. Within the spacious and even cosmic vistas of history that now engrossed him, there was no need to speak of the tortured historian himself. He broke off in the middle of his book and assumed the airs of a scientist—though no one quite knew what the subject of inquiry was. He played with magnets at his dinner table. He liked to surprise ordinary scientists by asking unanswerable questions. The world was running down, and he was going to show why—in prose that would have to do for mathematics, but would be as elegant. Science was the new language. Like his own *History*, his *nuova scienza* would show that necessity unrolls in set quantities and therefore could be fixed in the rhythms of his own prose. Science was even more comfortably impersonal than History, and the catastrophes it might visit on the human race could be discussed as easily as we discuss the Bomb at our dinner tables. It was another example of History's rushing to its end, with man "the meteor mind" (Adams's great metaphor) falling with History through infinite space.

No physicist, since Adams made use of a docile government scientist or two in the nineties, has claimed to know what he was talking about in the "scientific" chapters of the *Education*.* Yet physicists feel that they have no business with Adams anyway. For the future was compellingly real to Adams because the past was. If you think history naturally falls into a design, then you must anticipate how the story may end.

For Adams history was not just the past; it was the rhythm of "order rigorously consequent." He saw human thought in a cosmic setting of impersonal forces driving thought into a corner and threatening it with a subject too great for its powers. So large was the sweep of Adams's historical imagination that he wanted to see the whole shape, history as one great form, stretching from the past to a possibly calculable future. He wanted to determine the whole story at once—to carry the rhythm of his studies out to its final term—to catch the last reverberations as the meteor fell through world space. This intention belongs not to science but to art. So forceful a sense of style needed the future to complete the past.

---

*The most painstaking study of Adams's effort to create a "science of history," William H. Jordy's *Henry Adams, Scientific Historian* (Yale, 1952), concludes that Adams indulged himself and was perhaps ultimately a tourist in these countries of thought.

13

Going to Europe:
Eliot and Pound

Falling towers
Jerusalem Athens Alexandria
Vienna London
Unreal

ELIOT, *The Waste Land*

It is quite obvious that we do not all of us inhabit
the same time.

POUND, *Make It New*

I

When Thomas Stearns Eliot sailed for Germany in 1914 on a Harvard
fellowship (the war soon drove him to Oxford) he no more wished to become
an expatriate than did Henry Adams. By 1914 Adams was spending a large
part of every year in France, but he sailed for home as soon as war was
declared in August. Henry James came down from Rye to see him off. Both
men knew it would be their last meeting, and they talked together on
shipboard most of the night.

It was no great thing for American writers to live and work in Europe.
Even Mark Twain had done it for years at a time. Still in England when
America went to war in 1917, the twenty-nine-year-old Eliot tried to join the
United States navy, was rejected for health reasons, and when he obstinately
tried again, became ensnarled in red tape. An American civilian, he was fated
to make London his home and to find in wartime London the purgatory—
with the merest hope of salvation—that led to his most famous poem, *The
Waste Land* (1922). Read for decades as "criticism of the contemporary world
. . . as an important bit of social criticism," it was actually, Eliot ruefully

admitted in later years, "to me . . . only the relief of a personal and wholly insignificant grouse against life; it is just a piece of rhythmical grumbling."

The Waste Land was all of that. It was vibrantly so much more that the relaxed and mellow Eliot of the midcentury, the mystic of the *Four Quartets*, now shielded by his immense fame and happy second marriage, understandably had no desire to descend from the delectable mountain he had finally reached.

He had married in 1915 Vivien Haigh-Wood, an Englishwoman of unstable temperament. Defying his businessman father in St. Louis, who had expected him to return home and receive his Harvard doctorate, Eliot stuck it out in London as a schoolteacher, reviewer, bank clerk, assistant editor of *The Egoist*. For three years he regularly journeyed out of London to conduct workmen's evening classes in Southall. "I settled over here," he wrote after the war, "in the face of strong family opposition, on the claim that I found the environment more favorable to the production of literature." Eliot's claim was not good enough for his father, who died in 1919 believing that his son had made a mess of his life, and in his will he discriminated against this youngest of his seven children. Eliot broke down after the war while working on *The Waste Land* and had to be sent off to Switzerland; he felt that he suffered from "an aboulie" (abulia), a now old-fashioned psychiatric term for "absence of will-power or wish-power."* The highly unsettling Vivien had proved to be more of a stimulus than he expected when he married her.

Whatever Eliot's reasons for staying on in wartime London, his defiance of his family in St. Louis seems to have surprised him. This was the first significant *act* of his bookish life and highly introverted character. Though Eliot turned out to be more traditionalist than his family, a great believer in institutions as long as they were British, his move to England was a rebellious American act that parallels the "infidel" Emerson's leaving the church.

Still, it was perhaps only the more conservative Americans, like Henry James, who could live out their lives in England. Even in his twenties, Thomas Stearns Eliot was definitely conservative. Ralph Waldo Emerson had gloried in America as the promised country that would release the freeborn individual from all unnecessary ties. The American scholar could make it to God on his own. The young Eliot from St. Louis, the Harvard

---

*"The term implies that the individual has a desire to do something but the desire is without power or energy. Abulia itself is rare and with few exceptions occurs only in the schizophrenias. The more frequent disturbance in the will is a reduction or impairment . . . rather than a complete absence. . . .

"Inactivity, focal or diffuse, of an individual toward the environment, due to inability to settle on a plan of action. There may be a desire to contact the environment, but the desire has no power of action." (Campbell, *Psychiatric Dictionary*, fourth edition.)

major in philosophy who barely tolerated the influence of William James in favor of Irving Babbitt's hatred of romanticism, would turn out to be a traditionalist *à outrance*. One of his many traditions was the Eliot family. As Ezra Pound was to say of his own family, American history was virtually a family connection. Even the first Eliot in New England, Andrew Eliot, is rumored to have been less a radical Protestant than his fellow Puritans. He may have been a judge in the Salem witchcraft trials.

The Eliots in St. Louis looked upon the West as a colony of New England. The Reverend William Greenleaf Eliot had settled in backward St. Louis to spread the Unitarian gospel. He had founded Washington University, which he had refused to have named after him. In 1852, lecturing in St. Louis, Emerson had nothing but admiration for this "Saint of the West" but was certain that "no thinking or reading man" was to be found "in the 95000 souls." The Reverend Eliot's grandson was to complain that he had been brought up "outside the Christian fold." Christianity was the Incarnation. But too shallowly liberal as Unitarianism may have been for T. S. Eliot, he respected his family as New England personified, as missionaries engaged in good works. The Eliots supplied lasting images of authority to a poet who certainly believed in authority.

This youngest of seven children was a sickly, much-protected boy whom Lyndall Gordon, documenting Eliot's early years, describes as having been "fortified by a guard of grown-up sisters." His father considered public instruction in sex "tantamount to giving children a letter of introduction to the Devil. Syphilis was God's punishment and [the father] hoped that a cure would never be found. Otherwise, it might be necessary to emasculate our children to keep them clean." Other Eliots had less restrictive views of society. The poet's eldest sister, Ada, wrote case histories and worked in New York's Tombs prison. Marian enrolled at a school for social service in Boston. His cousin Martha became a physician specializing in child care and public health. Cousin Abigail's school in Roxbury became the precursor of all "head-start" programs for underprivileged children. Eliot's Harvard poems mildly lampooning the genteel tradition in Boston, the *Boston Evening Transcript*, "Cousin Harriet," "Aunt Helen," "Cousin Nancy," were mild satires understandably concerned with a fear of experience outside the tradition. He was to experience this fear at a depth not familiar to his sisters, his cousins, and his aunts.

Eliot in his beatific period after World War II genially let it be known in a lecture at his grandfather's university that he was "very glad to have been born in St. Louis." He never put St. Louis into his poems. He had been sheltered from a city notorious for the corruption of its businessmen, its inadequate sewers, its sulphurous fumes. Dreiser as a reporter in St. Louis and Lincoln Steffens, the muckraker touring "hell with the lid lifted," had noted its degenerate prosperity. The German enclave and what Eliot in England was to call its "nigger" cast encouraged his Puritan race pride. When he lectured in Virginia in the 1930s he emphasized that "race" as well as "religion" promoted a wholly Christian society. The model for Augustus Saint-Gaudens's famous statue *The Puritan* in Springfield was one of Eliot's maternal ancestors. Eliot's mother was a derivative poet-dramatist who described certain "figures" as saints of culture. When Eliot in the 1920s became a public seer as well as the dominant poet in the English-speaking world, he easily fell into the family tone when alluding to cultural inferiors.

Marrying in England and braving out the war as an American civilian, the unknown and isolated Eliot was making his protest not only against family and background but against America itself. More than he then realized, it was America's essential secularism and uplift that he was rejecting. (Secular America was to become his most avid audience; although Eliot's conversion did not convert many admirers, the complexity and allusiveness of his poems gave them the sense of a tradition.) After meeting Eliot in London and reading the now-famous early poems which no one had been willing to publish, Pound, urging them upon *Poetry* in Chicago, excitedly wrote Harriet Monroe that Eliot "has actually trained himself *and* modernized himself *on his own.*" Apparently it was only in the Old World that Eliot could prolong and develop his "modernization." His innate sense of style, as mimicry and provocation, would not have suited the importance of being a Harvard Ph.D. In 1916, when Eliot moved from High Wycombe Grammar School (salary one hundred forty pounds per annum, with dinner) to Highgate Junior School (salary one hundred sixty pounds, with dinner and tea), he admitted that although his wife had been very ill, his great friend Jean Verdenal had been killed, and he had been so "taken up with worries of finance and Vivien's health" that he had "written nothing lately," "I am having a wonderful time nevertheless. I have *lived* through material for a score of long poems in the last six months. An entirely different life from that I looked forward to two years ago. Cambridge seems to me a dull nightmare now."

At this moment, however, "Europe" visibly destroying itself became an embodiment of his personal trial—one he would link to the "universal cataclysm" and for which he would find the needed style. He and his wife were often ill, evidently making each other ill. The marriage was a constant trial. Eliot was apparently a virgin when he married, and his sexual difficulties were a shock to both of them. Although he had not even been sure at first that he liked England, he had been glad to be free of Harvard and "the college bell." Now hard pressed by his marriage, overworked and exhausted as he tried to keep up his writing after a day at the bank, Eliot in the midst of the war experienced a breakdown that left him with the deep conviction of the existence of a personal hell. It was somehow too late for him to go home. The difficulties of obtaining a passage in wartime, his reluctance to introduce his wife into the family circle, were convenient excuses. London itself was a constant test, like his marriage, and like his marriage it hypnotized him. To his father in 1917 he could write:

> Everyone's individual lives are so swallowed up in the one great tragedy that one almost ceases to have personal experiences or emotions, and such as one has seem so unimportant. . . . It's only very dull people who feel they have more in their lives now—other people have too much. I have a lot of things to write about if the time ever comes when people will attend to them.

He was gasping for time, for the freedom that he would find only when he broke down after the war and had to be sent off to Switzerland. Pound, who from the first days in London had been Eliot's mainstay, would after the war raise the money for Eliot's rest cure. And of course it was Pound who turned a mass of incongruous fragments into the brilliant mosaic of *The Waste Land*. But London even during Eliot's worst moments through the war contributed to his future poem by bombarding him with sensations that derived from the history around him. London gave him "the tone of time," the "pitch of association," as Henry James called them with the special appeal of England to an American of Eliot's background and temper. Eliot made even his assiduous, old-fashioned learning a form of sensation. There was in him an extraordinary conjunction of the sufferer and the scholar—each finding its voice in the other—that made of London the perfect state for personal expression. Any walk summoned back the most wonderful lines in English poetry and supplied the ironic retort.

> Sweet Thames, run softly till I end my song,
> Sweet Thames, run softly, for I speak not loud or long.
> But at my back in a cold blast I hear
> The rattle of the bones, and chuckle spread from ear to ear.

Wartime London, its crowds, monuments, and war profiteers, its constant reminder of the crumbling past, its trembling before the terrible casualty lists, did even more for Eliot than the violence of the Italian front did for Hemingway, the "enormous room" for Cummings. Those writers who stayed at home during the war and were easily indifferent to it missed its world significance as Eliot did not. The unredeemed wasteland of the century began with 1914, that onset of all our woe.

The tremulous noncombatant Eliot had some unexpected advantages over those who "saw action." He could identify his intense anxieties with a "fallen" world that provided a framework and myth—religious thirst—for his perturbations. Not even Henry Adams, with his unequalled sense of history, made such a "personal universe" out of the world's running down. For Eliot orchestrated the highs and lows of some irresistible personal emotion, as Stravinsky did in *Le Sacre du printemps.* This use of anxiety was to be grasped by many readers without their knowing why they were moved by *The Waste Land* as by no other poem of the period. A city has many voices. Eliot assembled them in echoes, fragments, and parodies because he heard them first in his own fear and trembling:

> Unreal City,
> Under the brown fog of a winter dawn,
> A crowd flowed over London Bridge, so many,
> I had not thought death had undone so many.
> . . .
>
> Unreal City
> Under the brown fog of a winter noon
> . . .
>
> O City city, I can sometimes hear

Each motif was particular; each, as the residue of strong emotion, would be carefully discriminated from another, and artfully repeated. Eliot always insisted on a *specific* emotion. This, his strong point as a poet, probably saved his sanity in the storm of his many troubles. Eliot buttressed his tale of a man blindly wandering a city with a fertility myth, carefully laid out in his notes, of desiccation and hope, of a dying land and rebirth by at least a *thirst* for faith. But as he cheerfully admitted much, much later, *The Waste Land* was forced out of so much personal urgency that he did not always know what he was saying. He did not always have to know. Armies of scholiasts, reading the poem from the top down as a myth, by the light of the references so grandly suggested in Eliot's notes, furthered not their artistic education but their (perhaps envious) image of Eliot's orthodoxy. The modern world was fallen, all fallen. But it was not Eliot's learned allusions that took many readers where they did not expect to go—the real effect of *The Waste Land.* What made the effect was Eliot's skill in combining "precision of emotion" with the "auditory imagination." He appreciated the moral genius of Catholicism for construing certain emotions as grand occasions when the soul really listens to itself.

Now line after line, whether as observation, quotation, or lament, expressed a separate movement of the soul and nothing else. Line after line, whether observation, quotation, or lament, expressed a specific turbulence and pressure. Each line took over from printed sources, half-forgotten reading still ringing in the mind, classical personages, to express the sensation of having to carry so much in the mind. Eliot's framework, the breaking up of the modern world, was no more haunting than the spread and variation of these many voices. What was most beautiful was their spacing, alternation, and eventual harmonization in a playful rhythm seemingly offhand. Eliot had learned a certain derisive style from the jeering, throwaway humor of *des âmes damnées* like Corbière, Laforgue, and of course Baudelaire. But he was no longer making grisly fun of himself, as in "Prufrock"; he was trying to put into one framework the desperate voices of a war-torn civilization.

This was a journey within the city of man and the mind of a single man, a haunted journey hovering on the edge of the past, such as is possible to a modern man only in an ancient city like London. It was a journey with ghosts that in Eliot's antic bitterness descended to the routine of domestic life, pub talk, the moment of release from the bank.

> At the violet hour, when the eyes and back
> Turn upward from the desk, when the human engine waits
> Like a taxi throbbing waiting . . .

A city is the junction of so many irreconcilable experiences! And each in *The Waste Land* was to leave its clanging reverberation.

> "My nerves are bad to-night. Yes, bad. Stay with me.
> "Speak to me. Why do you never speak. Speak.
> "What are you thinking of? What thinking? What?
> "I never know what you are thinking. Think."

And crossing the ever-present sense of deprivation, the "dryness" that reaches some shuddering hope of relief only in the closing din of thunder, we keep butting up against the strangest voices from the classic past, prophets and accusers:

> I Tiresias, though blind, throbbing between two lives,
> Old man with wrinkled female breasts, can see
> . . .
>
> I Tiresias, old man with wrinkled dugs
> Perceived the scene, and foretold the rest . . .

11

Every significant writer-participant—Barbusse, Graves, Céline, Ernst Junger, David Jones, Hemingway—was able by the 1920s to describe the war as a moral landslide. The terror of the war was generally left to the novelists and memoirists. Not many poets, and certainly none with a noncombatant's diffidence and such exhausting personal problems, was able to put into personal epic what Eliot did. This was the sense of being trapped between an almost vanished tradition and an eroding present. Salvation was a distant hope, but for Eliot it was somehow more urgent than for anyone else of his generation. What "saved" him—as an artist—was the obsessive particularity that comes with sickness. What he was to insist on as "precision of emotion" turned the war into a metaphor of the whole modern period. This emotion equalled a devaluation of the life principle, a desert, a rubbish heap indeed.

> A rat crept softly through the vegetation
> Dragging its slimy belly on the bank
> . . .
>
> White bodies naked on the low damp ground
> And bones cast in a little low dry garret . . .

The voice within the poem lamented a sense of restriction.

> Here is no water but only rock
> Rock and no water and the sandy road
> The road winding above among the mountains
> Which are mountains of rock without water
> If there were water we should stop and drink
> Amongst the rock one cannot stop or think

The disparity of past and present, the seeming profanation that *was* the present, were cleverly assembled and even appeared brilliantly jocular in relation to each other. But as Eliot admitted to Bertrand Russell, only part V of *The Waste Land*, "What the Thunder Said," seemed to him really successful. For there the sense of dread of which the poem is composed emerged into the light. The apprehension Eliot had expressed through repetition,

> And no rock
> If there were rock
> And also water

> And water
> A spring
> A pool among the rock

became extraordinary in its urgency, its felt suffering—and swept self and history into the tide joining the reader to Eliot's anguish:

> What is that sound high in the air
> Murmur of maternal lamentation
> Who are those hooded hordes swarming
> Over endless plains, stumbling in cracked earth
> Ringed by the flat horizon only
> What is the city over the mountains
> Cracks and reforms and bursts in the violet air
> Falling towers
> Jerusalem Athens Alexandria
> Vienna London
> Unreal

III

The Waste Land, formally resting on myth, became the favorite myth of one postwar generation after another. Eliot quoted Hermann Hesse in his notes: "Already half Europe, at least half of East Europe, is on the way to chaos, stumbles drunkenly in a holy delusion toward the abyss." "Chaos," one of Henry Adams's prime terms for what he saw in modern civilization, was what the modernist had to dispel in the secret, subtle unity of his work of art. Yet just as Eliot wrote *The Waste Land* "without always knowing what I was saying," the reader could be moved by it without always understanding it. Eliot as a boy was able to experience poetry in a foreign language he could barely read. Many a reader's emotional and instinctive experience of *The Waste Land* was a matter of experiencing the primitive emotions that had guided Eliot in writing it. His gift for relating his total experience to the reader was one that colder poets never possessed. Eliot's gift was more in keeping with Whitman's instinct for making personal epic out of a city's "ensemble" and "paradoxical unity" than with the ambiguous return to "classicism" that Eliot invoked in his criticism. Ezra Pound, who cut and edited *The Waste Land* so brilliantly that he became a virtual collaborator, was to say that "epic is a poem including history." History calls for a lot of skilled representation; one of Eliot's signal feats in *The Waste Land* was to represent himself struggling *with* the age. The age paid Eliot the compliment of seeing itself in the poem. This was another reason why it was able to absorb the poem without fully understanding it. Decade after decade *The Waste Land* represented "an attitude toward history" that went deeper than Hemingway's *In Our Time,* Spengler's *The Decline of the West,* Robert Graves's *Goodbye to All That.* More and more fashionably, Eliot's modernist poem came to represent the human failure of modern civilization.

For Eliot in England, surrounded by associations with the Establishment, the failure was really America. It was a failure of the isolated, supposedly "self-reliant" American self on which Emerson had rested his faith. In the 1930s Virginia Woolf was to note of Eliot in her diary: "How he suffers! . . . He seemed to have got so little joy or satisfaction out of being Tom . . . he revealed his passion, as he seldom does. A religious soul: an unhappy man: a lonely very sensitive man, all wrapt up in fibres of self torture, doubt, conceit, desire for warmth & intimacy."

The sense of fright within *The Waste Land,* its haunting ability to pull in the reader, explains the way it works on us as some irresistible discord. This sense of discord became, in Eliot's rebuttal of "self-reliance" and "the inner light," a succession of fragments that is really a mysterious striving within ourselves to eliminate fragmentation. We aspire to reach a unity that in the same breath we despair of.

Eliot was writing about the hope of God, "waiting for God," as one of his future admirations, Simone Weil, was to put it. But for many readers who were irredeemably sceptical, Eliot's fear and trembling were to emerge as a longing for authority, a contempt for democracy, a disdain for the "bugs," the "swarming creatures," as he called them in the original draft of *The Waste Land.* What Eliot could never admit about his own unhappiness in his many self-accusations in London, even when he was lecturing to workers' classes, was his lack of sympathy for the masses. He was made just as solitary by his politics as he was by his priggishness. In the street, as his Harvard poems stressing the "sordid" aspects of Boston made clear, he was a prickly Brahmin, the perennial outsider. He absorbed what Emerson praised as "the language of the street" without enjoying it. He never responded to the sense of possibility recurrent in democracy, the buoyancy that Whitman gained from living in a great city.

Eliot, born five years after Emerson died, sometimes wrote as if he had come into the world to roll back Emerson's work. This was not why he had come into the world, and in the end he was Emerson's double just as much as he was Emerson's adversary. For Eliot, too, made the perilous journey to faith all on his own. He, too, was a natural "isolato," an American. But unlike Emerson, Eliot could not trust his isolation and selfhood. Needing God, he settled for authority. "Authority" was what Europe alone could supply—in the form of culture.

IV

Emerson in 1837 had confidently assured the American scholar that "our day of dependence, our long apprenticeship to the learning of other lands, draws to a close. The millions that around us are rushing into life, cannot always be fed on the sere remains of foreign harvests."

Eliot in "Tradition and the Individual Talent" (1919), the essay that made him as celebrated a traditionalist as *The Waste Land* made him a poet, was not talking to scholars. He felt he was reconstituting war-broken Europe (and no doubt himself). His principal edict involved not self-trust, not oneself at all: "The progress of an artist is a continual self-sacrifice, a continual extinction of personality." The appeal was not to the soul's hidden powers but to the manifest sacredness of tradition. In Sophocles's *Oedipus at Colonus* the self-tortured hero found peace only in the sacred wood embodying divine powers. The sacred wood could be reached only by returning to tradition, but nowadays this demanded "great labour." And, what surely could not be left to labor alone, it demanded "the historical sense," which

> involves a perception, not only of the pastness of the past, but of its presence; the historical sense compels a man to write not merely with his own generation in his bones, but with a feeling that the whole of the literature of Europe from Homer and within it the whole of the literature of his own country has a simultaneous existence and composes a simultaneous order.

No European, no seasoned Catholic intelligence, could have delivered such a paean to the past. No one inheriting Europe's religious wars and its many cultural divisions could have believed for a moment that "the whole of the literature of his own country has a simultaneous existence and composes a simultaneous order." It was an American who was to ask: "Was Europe a Success?" It was an American who wrote that America's entrance into the Great War "made the world a single event." It was an American who now wrote in "Tradition and the Individual Talent" that "the existing order is complete before the new work arrives; for order to persist after the supervention of novelty, the *whole* existing order must be, if ever so slightly, altered; . . . and this is conformity between the old and the new."

This was the language not of Europe but of a visitor. Only an American —and this in 1919—could have wished any "existing order" to be "complete." Religion now was less a matter of God than of culture. Emerson's direct experience of divinity had indeed been replaced by the sacred wood. But only the visitor, the outsider, importuning the sacred wood for refuge, would have sensed so well that this ground was shaking and its towers were about to fall.

v

> The Gods have not returned.
> They have never left us.
> They have never returned.
>
> POUND, Canto CXIII

> but at least she saw damn all Europe.
>
> POUND, *The Pisan Cantos*

Nineteen hundred eight was the year (more or less), as Virginia Woolf was to remember with the authority of the modernists, when "human nature changed." Ezra Pound from Wyncote, Pennsylvania (though born in Idaho), is in Venice, sitting on the steps of the customs house. In Canto III, written sometime in the 1920s, he says he was sitting on the steps

> For the gondolas cost too much, that year,
> And there were not "those girls," there was one face,
> And the Buccentoro twenty yards off, howling "Stretti,"
>
> And the lit cross-beams, that year, in the Morosini,
> And peacocks in Koré's house, or there may have been.
>   Gods float in the azure air,
> Bright gods and Tuscan, back before dew were shed.
> Light: and the first light, before ever dew was fallen.
> Panisks, and from the oak, dryas,
> And from the apple, maelid,
> Through all the wood, and the leaves are full of voices,
> A whisper, and the clouds bow over the lake,
> And there are gods upon them,
> And in the water, the almond-white swimmers,
> The silvery water glazes the upturned nipple,
>   As Poggio has remarked.
> Green veins in the turquoise,
> Or, the gray steps lead up under the cedars.

These lines are so exquisite that even if we do not get all the Venetian references, or understand why the scene will suddenly shift from Venice (where there are surely no almond-white swimmers in the Grand Canal, for the water is notoriously not silvery) to Spain, we are aware of the poet's rapture in Mediterranean Europe. There have been many rapturous travel passages in our literature, but this one is different. Poor puritanical Lambert Strether in *The Ambassadors* discovered at a splendid garden party in Paris how little he had "lived." He had come to Europe to take Chad Newsome back to America, but there was "that striking truth about Chad of which he had been so often moved to take note: the truth that everything came happily back with him to his knowing how to live." Hemingway's passion for French-Italian-Spanish landscape was to express itself through Jake Barnes in *The Sun Also Rises*.

> Looking back we saw Buerguete, white houses and red roofs, and the white road with a truck going along it. . . . Ahead the road came out of the forest and went along the shoulder of the ridge of hills. The hills ahead were not wooded, and there were great fields of yellow gorse. Way off we saw the steep bluffs dark with trees and jutting with gray stone, that marked the course of the Irati River.

Pound's velvety, silky tone reminds us of James and Hemingway. His language describes pleasures: we are at a celebration. But even when we link Pound's and Hemingway's very inventory of Europe, we can see that the opening of Pound's Canto III is not exclusively concerned with the pleasures of the eye. In Pound, gods float in the azure air before the Grand Canal, Bright gods and Tuscan, back before the dew was shed. We have been shuttled in Pound's abruptly moving mind from Venice to Tuscany, from Tuscany to Greece, where little Pans and wood nymphs issue from the trees, and where the leaves are full of voices. The invocation is less of the Mediterranean than of its paganism. This is solemn stuff. This American poet, for all his love of medieval Romance, is intellectually outside Christianity, like the Fascists he will come to admire. Distinctly nonreligious, unlike his great friend the "Reverend Eliot," as he liked in varying tones of admiration and condescension to call that vulnerable—because so highly personal—poet, Pound will show a poetic sensibility bewilderingly impersonal, slashing, hard. His subject is not the Romantic Ego, as you might think from his passion for word association, but History as the warnings imparted by one great mind after another. Everything about the herd, the "bullet-headed many," passes like so much dirt. What the great mind dwells on is what will last. Literature is news "that stays news." Art alone offers some hint of immortality. The Judaeo-Christian God never sufficed Pound. Paganism is certainly closer, he thought, to the original sources of poetry.

Paganism, polytheism, culture fastening on culture to seek some common root: Greek, Chinese, Latin, even American! The key word in Pound's code became *paideuma*, the energy pattern of a particular culture. Pound was anything but the usual American literary tourist seeking something more restful than his own commercial civilization. His was the intoxication of returning to the roots of poetry, to an ancient world in Asia even more than to pagan Greece and Rome. Paganism: the living out of roles *in* nature, first by the gods and then by men. Paganism: an identification with the energy patterns in nature, not the modern habit of seeking to study nature by dominating it. Pound easily separated himself from America, for he did not regard nature as inherently different from oneself, as something to manipulate. He would not suffer from the bourgeois ignorance of the sources of vital energy, from the recurrent mental fatigue ultimately due to the split between subject and object.

The twenty-three-year-old poet was to publish a first volume in Venice, *A lume spento,* in that year he travelled via Gibraltar, Spain, and Southern France to Venice—1908. When it was reprinted in 1964, the poet recently returned to Italy from thirteen years in a Washington madhouse called it "a collection of stale creampuffs." There is indeed something flaky, very 1890-ish—as Wallace Stevens was to complain of Pound's total output—in many of these poems. But Pound, who at fifteen had announced himself a poet and in many respects never outgrew his view of the poet as public adversary, began by practicing every kind of poetry he could find. The early poems of his 1909 collection, *Personae,* astonish us by the absolutely faultless ear that will remain with Pound even in the most discursive sections of the *Cantos* and in his unaccountable intimacy with poetry in every language and of every period. The *fluency* with which Pound assimilates other poets, other languages, every "alien" sound somehow made friendly and absorbable by Pound's ear, was to give us that exquisite love poem "The River Merchant's Wife: A Letter" and such doubles of Anglo-Saxon verse as "The Seafarer."

> Bitter breast-cares have I abided,
> Known on my keel many a care's hold,
> And dire sea-surge, and there I oft spent
> Narrow nightwatch nigh the ship's head
> While she tossed close to cliffs. Coldly afflicted,
> My feet were by frost benumbed.

This is certainly the polar world of the Anglo-Saxons in all the harsh stormy alliterative stresses of a world with little human relief. By contrast, the silky shy tenderness of the young Chinese wife writing to her absent husband the river merchant, a poem Pound tells us is "by Rihaku," eighth century:

> While my hair was still cut straight across my forehead
> I played about the front gate, pulling flowers.
> You came by on bamboo stilts, playing horse,
> You walked about my seat, playing with blue plums.
> And we went on living in the village of Chokan:
> Two small people, without dislike or suspicion.

Pound the "translator" does what the gifted poet alone can do: he "imitates" the sounds and rhythm of a poem in a language otherwise foreign to him. Pound very early extracted an extraordinary but delusional sense of authority from his ability to reproduce other men's styles. *Personae* he called one collection of his poems outside the *Cantos;* they were all his roles. As a critic he was of course determined, like Eliot, to clear the ground for his own kind of poetry. But that kind was never so narrowly characteristic as Eliot's poetry. Pound's startling empathy with other men's work, his genius as a critic, is shown as much in his wildly linked poetry as in his often distracted essays. He was an assimilationist of genius, a ventriloquist able to reproduce alien and ancient voices, cadences, styles—often in wilful ignorance of the actual substance. Only an American, someone perpetually dreaming "Europe" as a whole, could have performed Pound's series of metamorphoses. From book to book, sometimes from line to line, Pound became in turn every poet he admired. He was to admit that he did not always know what he was doing as sound, quotation, fantasy, real dreams, and irrepressible pastiche moved ungraspably in metaphoric relation to each other.

Poetry, said Jean Cocteau, is a separate language. This must be so, since poets often reproduce each other's subtlest effects without knowing what instinct leads them to it. Eliot as a young man wondered that he could respond to poetry in a language he did not know. Pound never wondered. He knew the "language" in all its subtle strength as no other American poet has ever known it. He had an extraordinary natural endowment: perfect adaptability to other poets anywhere. He was the early supporter in England of Frost; the providential editor and "better artificer" behind *The Waste Land.* He never doubted that he could teach a whole generation the art of poetry by darting from moment to moment of insight. His instinct vis-à-vis poetry was so complete that poetry possessed him to the point of autointoxication. Pound did not need drugs or alcohol; poetry drugged him, blurred the distinction between poetry and the active world. It was just as much other people's lines as his own that drugged him—he was past the point of being able to distinguish between the beauty of a line from Provençal, a Chinese ideogram, and poetry's application to the economic distress of the 1930s. He could be almost unconscious of the slashing, domineering self-confidence that his absorption of poetry gave him. Shelley said that poets are the unacknowledged legislators of the world; Pound would have said not *unacknowledged* but *unread*—by the multitude.

Pound was to become an amazing seismograph of the force hidden in language, a kind of early warning system: he was to link his gift to tremors he sensed in the body politic. A poet born in Idaho emerged from a historical America to live and write in Europe as if Europe's poetry were its true history. Since poetry is not older than prose but stands in the same relation to it as the origins of life stand to the emergence of man on the planet, Pound detected in himself powers of divination, attributes of the shaman, the medium through which he touched a great mystery.

The mystery Pound touched was the secret of style—not, as he eventually thought, the damnable tendency of history to lapse from some great tradition or model furnished by Confucius, Dante, John Adams. Pound became the great exemplar and teacher of modernism by restricting it (whether he knew this or not) to a matter of style. And he was on safe ground as long as he insisted on its energy, its physicality. The physician and poet Oliver Wendell Holmes heard meter in the binary rhythm of the heart. Poetry can have such an effect on us as to seem *expected* by the body.

The authority of poetry over us does in fact rest on physical signs—of stresses and the intermittent relief from stresses. Emerson said of Dante that his verse was the nearest thing to hands and feet. When we look at the characteristic cross-rhythms of long lines and upspringing half lines that Pound developed into such concentration of emotion as visual *fact* on the page—poetry as sculpture, Donald Davie called it—we recognize an energy at work in the typographical arrangement of the lines, an energy that can become the theme of a poem. The spaces, the sudden springing, the iconic letters in Chinese and Greek—all this is like the art of the dance to which Nietzsche, that other totally spontaneous lyric thinker, compared his own style as poet-philosopher. Thus, from *Ripostes* (1912), "The Return":

> See, they return; ah, see the tentative
> > Movements, and the slow feet,
> > The trouble in the pace and the uncertain
> > Wavering!
>
> . . .
>
> Haie! Haie!
> > These were the swift to harry;
> These the keen-scented;
> These were the souls of blood.
>
> Slow on the leash,
> > pallid the leash-men!

Pound the restless instigator of modernism was not afraid of using obsolete words; his innate tie with the language materials of poetry in any language he encountered, even when he depended on a crib, as with Chinese, or when his own knowledge of it, as with Greek, was not so much imperfect as impatient, persuaded him that words in themselves, as Emerson said, were fossil poetry.

The romantic theory of poetry as being germane to the race, its unconscious resources already lying in the mind like separate pieces of type waiting to be put into rightly organized lines by means of the highest possible art, is one from which we have never really departed. What Pound added to this —or brought out of it—was the belief that the language of poetry is not primitive emotion but secret knowledge. The shaman was more important to Pound than the bard. "Poet" equals maker; *how* the poem is made denotes such an extraordinary amount of contraction, condensation, acceleration of human experience within a single context, that Pound came to believe that the highly contracted words were occult. So the function of the poet was to teach the way back to this arcane knowledge—as poet, by displaying all the verbal shimmer he could line up in his words and all the force he could reproduce in the structure of his verse.

The real Muse is History—but History buried in words: History as an excavation made possible only to those who know the lay of the land and where the old wisdom is hidden.

Pound's most famous work outside the 117 Cantos is his monument, *Hugh Selwyn Mauberley*, sculptured indeed in memory of the artist Gaudier-Brzeska, dead in the war. *Mauberley* is dear to the modernist public created by Pound and Eliot, which learned from them to accept nothing not in their image, because it displays Pound's total disdain "For an old bitch gone in the teeth, / For a botched civilization." *Mauberley*, like all of Pound's key works, is an experiment in style, detached and technical to maximum chilliness.

> Christ follows Dionysus,
> Phallic and ambrosial
> Made way for macerations;
> Caliban casts out Ariel.
>
> All things are a flowing,
> Sage Heracleitus says;
> But a tawdry cheapness
> Shall outlast our days.
> . . .
> There died a myriad,
> And of the best, among them,
> For an old bitch gone in the teeth,
> For a botched civilization,
>
> Charm, smiling at the good mouth,
> Quick eyes gone under earth's lid,
>
> For two gross of broken statues,
> For a few thousand battered books.

Here is the familiar post-trenches theme: contempt for Christianity, lament over forgotten ideals, fury at the pointless obliteration of a whole generation. Then the expatriate elite saluting itself, exasperated for having "been born / In a half-savage country, out of date." The most exact art alone will suffice.

> His true Penelope was Flaubert,
> He fished by obstinate isles;
> Observed the elegance of Circe's hair
> Rather than the mottoes on sun-dials.
>
> Unaffected by "the march of events,"
> He passed from men's memory in *l'an trentuniesme*
> *De son eage;* the case presents
> No adjunct to the Muses' diadem.

Oh but it does! What Pound added to the Muses' diadem was the interweaving of Greek and Latin with English, just as in his first lyric poems he "imitated" Anglo-Saxon, Provençal, Chinese, Dante, and Dante's friend Guido Cavalcanti. All this was to have an intimidating and even comic effect on an audience without those languages. This interflow of languages represented one thing in the mind of Ezra Pound, who dreamed in languages, for the languages came. It represented a totally fictitious authority in the minds of the audience.

Eliot's sense of tradition, he told us in the tumultuously experimental twenties, was Anglo-Catholic, classical, royalist. Eliot, who took his time admitting that *The Waste Land* was a poem about his personal sterility, and that he might have turned Buddhist as easily as Christian, nevertheless acquired a greater authority over literature in English than anyone since Dr. Johnson. Pound, who did far more for other poets than anyone else, and was forever pushing poets, prodding poets, and instructing everyone at large in books typically entitled *Instigations, Make It New, How to Read, ABC of Reading, Guide to Kulchur,* scattered his forces in London, Paris, Rapallo, was soon too heated an agitator for Social Credit and other favorite nostrums, and was never to achieve the same lofty dignity as the Possum. The great work of his life, the *Cantos,* turned out for some of us to be the great failure as the epic it proclaimed itself to be—and ultimately a work of such obscene hatred as to make one weep over the manic flaw in Pound, his overbearing illusion that through his innate tie to poetry he could instruct a disordered world.

Edgar Allan Poe said that a long poem could not sustain itself; especially, he might have added, at the hands of lyricists like himself and Ezra Pound, with an ideal vision not only of the classical world but of their own intellectual powers. The *Cantos* are full of miraculously beautiful lyrics; the work as a whole, if you can call it a whole, proceeds from Pound's inner ecstasy at poetry in all languages rushing out of each other into a mind driven to frenzy by the acceleration of words and images within it. What you find in the *Cantos,* above everything else, is this inner vortex of sounds and associations, all these buried quotations and anecdotes, these pages and pages lifted without discernible order from Renaissance history, American political documents, the conversation of Benito Mussolini, newspaper articles, economic lore, etc.

If an epic "is a poem including history," we had better remember that as we drift through the *Cantos.* History turns out to be anything that interests Ezra Pound, that he suddenly thinks of in connection with something else, that he has read, that he can quote, that he can in fact *repeat.* But this total recall and assemblage is the reverse of arbitrary; it is as natural to Pound as eating drinking copulating defecating, and it slides onto a page as if he were doing just that.

The great epic—the *Odyssey,* the *Aeneid,* the *Divine Comedy, Paradise*

Lost—is the poem of a whole civilization. Pound assumes the authority behind such an epic, and although the *Cantos* are at times not so much written as accumulated, Pound does take on more than one civilization. Which is not why he fails as an epic poet: there he fails, as long poems in America mostly fail, because they are not content with great narratives of the existing world; they want to leave that world. Pound wants to take us out of the wasteland, the charnel house, the Heartbreak House of finance capitalism.

His way of doing this is to stun us: the language museum without walls; the past of China, Greece, Latin Europe in all the culture-splendor of their original words. The infliction of obscurity is so unyielding that sometime, if he is honest, the reader of the *Cantos* must ask (a) how much all these quotations and references are just disdain for the ordinary world in which we live, (b) how much the poem therefore corresponds to the gap between the shaman and the tribe, (c) how much, in fact, none of this is consciously demonstrative but Pound's language intoxication. In the *Cantos* this process rises to a delirium of cross-references just as in *Finnegans Wake* Joyce is so absorbed in a language entirely his own that it becomes self-reproducing.

Knowing that this intoxication is the essence does not relieve us from the contempt that shines proudly through the brilliancies of *Mauberley*. There is a frivolity in great artists—Joyce and Picasso come to mind—who take their endlessly inventive hand as the measure of reality. Yeats sadly reported his impression of the *Cantos*: "nervous obsession, nightmare, stammering confusion." Jung said of *Ulysses* that Joyce would have gone mad if he had not written it. It is true that Pound was an only child, famously spoiled, who kept his parents with him in Europe. But his belief in his own rightness was not just psychological, for like Beethoven he finally heard nothing but what he remembered. To this extent, not being deaf, he was "mad." We can see the extent and limits of this "madness" in the *Cantos* as well as in his Fascist pamphlets and radio broadcasts from Italy during the war.

Pound's problem was never conflict with himself but an excessiveness, an incessancy of verbal self-stimulation; isolated in Rapallo from much of what was happening in the great cities of Europe, and as always living on his reading, he could be more excited by anything in print than by strong drink. There has simply been no other mind like Pound's for the energy with which he assimilates, the sputtering impatience with which he turns from episode to quotation to anecdote. The shiftings of his mind are such that one feels changed by the extraordinary lyric bursts, usually in a water context which provides an extension of ordinary human sight.

> Black azure and hyaline,
> > glass wave over Tyro,
> Close cover, unstillness,
> > bright welter of wave-cords,
> . . .
>
> Glass-glint of wave in the tide-rips against sunlight,
> > pallor of Hesperus

Then one feels positively jostled by the inevitable shift.

The difficulty lies not in the huge blocks of Greek, Latin, Provençal, and Chinese flung at us—or in the elusive garbled quotations relating to the plunderings and escapades of the Renaissance swashbuckler Sigismundo da Malatesta, obviously admired for his cruel Renaissance "energy." Even if we knew everything that Pound knows, we still would not know *why* in Canto VII we go from Eleanor (presumably of Aquitaine) to

> > poor old Homer blind,
> > blind as a bat,
> Ear, ear for the sea-surge;
> > rattle of old men's voices

to Pound quoting himself on Henry James—"And the great domed head, *con gli occhi onesti e tardi.*"

All we know is that this is the order in which the voices of Pound's cherished inscriptions, memories, etc., are heard by him. They occur on the page as they occur to Ezra Pound. If the reader, informed with all of Pound's references, nevertheless asks of this automatic writing, Where am *I* going with all this?—the answer is something that has to be given him by a critic; he will not decipher it himself from the dizzily shifting references.

We can all use instruction. How many of us now look at Picasso's *Les Demoiselles d'Avignon,* hear Stravinsky's *Le Sacre du printemps,* know that $e = mc^2$, or even follow the historians' arguments about the origins of the Cold War without having been instructed by authority? Are we against interpretation, do we want to take the bread out of Hugh Kenner's mouth if we wonder just what his instruction does for us when he writes in *The Pound Era:*

> Later 1–16 and 17–27 were joined without division, and three more cantos added to make a first block of 30. The span of this no longer reaches from the Renaissance to modern times but makes a closed loop within the Renaissance, with modern extrapolations. We commence with Divus, 1538, and close with the death of Pope Alexander Borgia, 1503; close, moreover, despite this death, on a note of hope, for Hieronymous Soncinus is initiating the kind

of printing activity that will bring Divus' Homer into the public domain. Even the wreck of the Malatesta is subsumed; the quotation from Soncinus concludes. . . .

But this is supposed to be an epic, and an epic is a poem that includes history! In fact the *Cantos* are Pound's diary, the record of his amazing reading, disgorged when and how he feels like it. So the final authority of this epic belongs not to Ezra Pound but to his commentators. Whom we cannot choose but hear. The *Cantos* are not to be dismissed, bewildering as their many turns can be. To anyone sensitive to poetry and at the same time aware that "modern times" are equivalent to the sense of History as a problem inviting a solution—the Enlightenment legacy which only in our day has begun to discourage intellectuals—the *Cantos* are shattering in the *insistency* of Pound's mind, and finally they are tragic. Tragic because, like all ambitious efforts to present History within a single book, they yield us just another image of ourselves.

Eliot told us that the order of the past is transformed by every new work; everything past becomes an aspect of present taste. The greatest effect of "Eliot-Pound" was to abolish among the literary all historicism and to coerce the whole past into the fashions of the present. African masks are viewed by the museum crowd as a stimulant to Picasso's roving imagination, Confucius the perfect teacher becomes a metaphor of the "wise ruler" in Pound's myth of the perfect society, Jefferson is a counterpart to Mussolini, and his great hero John Adams becomes absolutely meaningless in the so-called Adams Cantos, 62–71. As Peter Shaw has shown in a devastating examination of what Pound did to the works of John Adams, Pound transcribed so mechanically that he reproduced even the misprints.* But one of the marks of what Harold Rosenberg called the herd of independent minds, the culture vultures who nervously pace the modern museum gathering impressions, who expertly compare one recording with another without knowing how to read music, is the lack of attentiveness that Pound's ransacking method invites.

The difference between us who nowadays accumulate too many impressions and Pound is that although he shares many of our touristy traits, he collects them at the pitch of genius, as Henry Adams did in the historical scene shifts of the *Education* and *Mont-Saint-Michel and Chartres*. Perhaps

---

The Works of John Adams, Partisan Review, 1977. Just how dotty Pound could get when the word "Adams" swam into view is suggested by the following: "[Eliot] has renounced America ever since the time of his first departure, but if he would consider the dynasty of the Adamses he would see that it was precisely because it lacked the Confucian law that this family lost the Celestial Decree." ("A Visiting Card," No. 4 of the Money Pamphlets, London, 1952.)

more than Adams, who cultivated a weary detachment, Pound is visibly tormented. History has become his agony. Joyce said: history is the nightmare from which I am trying to awaken. Joyce fled history into the interstices of language. Pound did just the opposite: he moved from the withinness of the poem out into the terror of twentieth-century history. Yet the terror is not the authoritarian state—Pound is noticeably indulgent to Lenin, as an admirer of Mussolini should be; he ignores the slaughter of so many innocents by Hitler-Stalin-Mussolini-Franco, he is obsessed by finance capitalism and the admitted lunacy and unfairness of the credit system. *Usura* (as he calls it) is his Inferno, not imperialism, racism, the ever-accelerating avalanche of war. The classical past, embodied in perfect language, has become the sacred icon. The present is by definition without value.

Pound the would-be epic writer has a driving sense of history but is really without history. Over and again he refers in the *Cantos* to Mussolini's draining the marshes and establishing corporate guilds for labor and capital; in *The Pisan Cantos*, written with gallantry in the appalling cage of an American army disciplinary unit, he refers to Mussolini as the "twice-crucified" and describes Italians as "maggots eating off a dead bullock." Did he not know how little the draining of the Pontine marshes represents in the history of Fascism? That the so-called Fascist corporations never really existed? When Hitler made his state visit to Mussolini, Italian submarines were ordered to make instant maneuvers that put whole crews in jeopardy; Pound quotes an informed source on the danger without recognizing what this implies.

The Second World War as most Europeans lived it and the war that Pound in Rapallo read about in Fascist newspapers bear no relation to each other. Pound was capable of saying in St. Elizabeth's that no man named Ezra could be an anti-Semite. But in the great work of his life, the *Cantos*, that self-announced successor to the great epic poems of Western man, we read of "fresh meat on the Russian steppes" and that the slaughter of the Jews was unfair only because so many poor Jews had to pay for the guilt *(Schuld)* of the Rothschilds, whose name means Red Shield. Schuld, Schild, what's the difference so that you get a pun in? "Poor yitts paying for / a few big jews' vendetta on goyim." This apparently is how the Second World War started, and Hugh Kenner confirms and expands on this in *The Pound Era*.

Pound's broadcasts on the Fascist radio are all available through the Library of Congress, and although the lawyers of the Pound estate have tried to keep people from quoting them, the broadcasts were published by the United States government and so are out of copyright. Hemingway said that Pound was crazy, "all poets are," and it is a fact that Pound's broadcasts were so disordered that one Italian official suspected that he was really an American agent broadcasting to the United States in code.

Pound's Fascist writings and broadcasts, his thirteen years in St. Elizabeth's in Washington, all belong to the past; no need to go over it all again, is there? Besides, everything passes so quickly nowadays, the war has been over for so long, that a student of Pound's genius may properly affirm that the Pound case, taken entire, with the flood of commentary dripping over it, represents the last act in that nineteenth-century drama of the poet as the unacknowledged legislator, the poet who presumed, once, to lead us from history as blood and tears, *mere* history, to the delectable mountains.

Eliot, saluting *Ulysses* in April 1921, said that

> in using the myth, in manipulating a continuous parallel between contemporaneity and antiquity, Mr. Joyce is pursuing a method which others must pursue after him. . . . It is simply a way of controlling, of ordering, of giving a shape and a significance to the immense panorama of futility and anarchy which is contemporary history.

Eliot was on his way to a religious solution of his personal longing for authority: the "immense panorama of futility and anarchy which is contemporary history" had to be checked *now*. None of this was useful to Joyce, who had begun by withdrawing from the two empires of Britain and the church, or to Pound, who was bored by Christianity. For a while, for quite a long while, modernism became a kind of church, and students, who knew nothing of poetry but what their teachers told them, recited in unison the wonders of myth, tension, paradox, and ambiguity, to say nothing of the horrors of "heresy." All that is over now, in a culture so speeded up in disposing of last year's cultural models that freshmen have never heard of Norman Mailer. Poor Ezra Pound, who believed in the authority of history as transmitted to us through the unique authority of literature.

Pound failed himself, not the masses who never really knew or cared about History as enchantment, idol, sorrow, trap—the History that only intellectuals can afford to worry about. In the end, in Italy, this formerly quenchless mouth snapped itself shut. *Tempus loquendi, tempus taciendi* was one of his favorite sayings. There is a time to speak and a time to shut up. And indeed he had much to be silent about. Pound spoiled his own dreams. But the anticlimax of his old age should not blind us to the radiance with which he started. Pound was the last to believe that the poet does have authority. His manic power reminds us why Plato feared the poets and wanted them out of the perfect Republic.

14

"An American Tragedy" and "The Sound and the Fury"

"Dis long time, O Jesus," she said, "Dis long time."

FAULKNER, *The Sound and the Fury*

I

An American Tragedy, published in mid-December 1925 and Dreiser's first novel since *The "Genius"* (suppressed for immorality a year after its publication in 1915), was Dreiser's one commercial success. This much Dreiser, who had been thinking of a "murder novel" since 1901, owed the newly emancipated readers who in 1925 welcomed once-forbidden literature.

An American Tragedy was brought out by the smart new firm of Boni and Liveright. Horace Liveright, who was to take over (for a time) Dreiser's scattered copyrights, was a famously vivid character and bon vivant, the model for Ben Hecht's maliciously engaging film *The Scoundrel.* Like Alfred A. Knopf, Ben Huebsch, Thomas Seltzer, Albert and Charles Boni, Pascal Covici, Bennett Cerf, Donald Klopfer, Robert K. Haas, Richard Simon and Max Schuster, and Liveright was one of the new Jewish publishers in New York who had been among the first to publish dangerous books like *Dubliners* and *Sons and Lovers.* They were as eager to establish a "tradition of the new" as the H. L. Mencken, Eugene O'Neill, Sigmund Freud, and Theodore Dreiser they now promoted. In 1900 Frank Doubleday said of the *Sister Carrie* he reluctantly published and helped to kill: "It's an immoral book; I don't like it." *Carrie* earned Dreiser $68.40.

An American Tragedy, brought out in two volumes at five dollars, had by the end of 1925 sold 13,378 copies and brought Dreiser $11,872. Not a best seller, it gave Dreiser his first substantial income from a book and a country house in Mt. Kisco. It was immediately bought by Paramount Pictures for a film to be directed by Josef von Sternberg. Dreiser rejected Samuel Hoffenstein's script, which turned Clyde Griffiths into "a sex-starved smart aleck." There was a long struggle between Dreiser and Paramount over this first film version, and the picture was not released until 1931. Patrick Kearny's Broadway stage version was produced in 1926. Many foreign editions of *An American Tragedy* soon appeared. In 1927 Dreiser, taken up by the Soviets despite his indifference to socialism, proudly reported to a friend, "in Russia the Govt publishing house has just taken over all my books (6 already published) and Stanislavsky is taking An American Tragedy and The Hand of the Potter." In May 1929 *An American Tragedy* was banned in Boston, an honor the book shared with *The American Mercury* and Voltaire's *Candide*. The *Mercury*'s editor, H. L. Mencken, was arrested for selling it on the Common; the collector of customs of the port of Boston had just confiscated thirteen copies of *Candide*.

Nineteen twenty-five was a great year. It saw the publication of Ezra Pound's first *Cantos,* Scott Fitzgerald's *The Great Gatsby,* Ernest Hemingway's *In Our Time,* Gertrude Stein's *The Making of Americans,* DuBose Heyward's *Porgy,* Sinclair Lewis's *Arrowsmith,* Willa Cather's *The Professor's House,* and Robinson Jeffers's *Roan Stallion,* and the founding of *The New Yorker.* Charlie Chaplin starred in *The Gold Rush,* Tennessee forbade the teaching of evolution, the Standard Oil Company adopted an eight-hour day, the electrocardiograph was invented, Vladimir Zworykin patented an electronic color television, and Clarence Birdseye improved the freezing of precooked foods. In Europe, Werner Heisenberg began his development of quantum mechanics. Franz Kafka's *The Trial*—he had died the year before —was brought out in the same season as Adolf Hitler's *Mein Kampf.* In Russia, Sergei Eisenstein released *Potemkin* and Lev Davidovitch Trotsky was dismissed from his chairmanship of the Russian Revolutionary Military Council.

Modern literature, advanced technology, and police states (Italy, Russia, Turkey, most of Latin America) were in the ascendancy. The heroes of the intelligentsia (a term never before used for Americans conscious of their cultural superiority) were Freud, Picasso, Stravinsky, Joyce, Eliot. In just eight years bonfires and concentration camps in Germany would begin to obliterate "modernist degeneracy." At the moment expressionism, Walter Gropius, the Bauhaus, Bertolt Brecht and Kurt Weill, Thomas Mann, Arnold Schoenberg, and the most brilliant theater in Europe thrived on Germany's seeming recovery from defeat, inflation, the fanatics of left and right. America under the somnolent eye of President Calvin Coolidge was speculation-mad, but a great many people were newly prosperous enough to be smug. Innumerable new forms of entertainment were provided by Hollywood, Broadway, radio, tabloid newspapers, and the weekly news magazine *Time,* determined to be as clever in style as any new novelist. Many of the fashionable novelists and poets, fugitives from the Middle West, scorned the moralism and provincialism into which they, like Indiana's Theodore Dreiser, had been born. He was strikingly older and supposedly an anachronism.

An American Tragedy could not have been composed and accepted before the 1920s. But Dreiser's "maddeningly" patient, lumbering style of narration, his tendency to overwhelm the reader with relentless documentation, hardly reflect the anxious preoccupation with style that founded *Time* and *The New Yorker* and saw its most effective voice in Hemingway's deceitfully simple sentences.

Edmund Wilson in his old age used to say: "I am a man of the twenties. I am still expecting something exciting: drinks, animated conversation, gaiety, brilliant writing, uninhibited exchange of ideas." In *An American Tragedy* the principal industry in "Lycurgus" is devoted to something so prewar as detachable collars. The social doings among the town's upper crust, to which Clyde Griffiths is fatally drawn, seem too innocent for the Prohibition years. No hard liquor is drunk by these leisured sons and daughters of local manufacturers. The lake parties are more athletic than sexy. There is total separation between the classes. Could a young workroom supervisor in 1925 have been prohibited from dating an employee? The nasty, snobbish Gilbert Griffiths addresses his father as "Sir," speaks of him as "the Governor." Samuel Griffiths, not knowing that the bellhop in Chicago's Union League Club is his nephew, benevolently calls him "Son." The punitive morality that brings about Clyde's undoing seems unnaturally widespread for the twenties. Dreiser drew his plot from the 1906 case of Chester Gillette, who murdered his mistress, Grace Brown, in Moose Lake. Since the book was written almost two decades later and naturally absorbed details from the present, Dreiser was careful not to specify a period.

In any event, Dreiser the pathmaker of the realistic novel, the "Hindenburg of the novel," as his supporter Mencken derisively praised him (Melville's great-grandson Paul Metcalf called Dreiser "caretaker and janitor to the new century"), seems to have conceived his novel about a murderer soon after *Sister Carrie* appeared. Raskolnikov in Dostoevsky's *Crime and Punishment* was Dreiser's favorite character in fiction. Raskolnikov (excruciatingly an intellectual, utterly different from the wistful, dreaming, easily baffled Clyde Griffiths) murders an old pawnbroker in order to demonstrate his emancipation from conventional society. Such self-sufficiency was meant to show Raskolnikov up as a "schismatic," a terrible egotist. He murders to demonstrate the triumph of his will.

The "hero" of *An American Tragedy* was to be doomed by a craving for society that kept him from having any ideas of his own. He plots murder when his pregnant working-class girl friend insists on a marriage that would bar him from the upper-class girl he has fallen in love with. Of course he will never know whether he is in love with Sondra Finchley or only spellbound by her money and "glamour." Dreiser knew from earliest childhood that poverty does not improve the character. It certainly did not improve his. Only when the seemingly passive and bewildered "Theo" became a writer did he display aggressiveness. His early circumstances had almost crushed him. A vicious elder brother, "Rome," had once "playfully" tried to drown him when they were in a rowboat. But Rome, an incorrigible savage, fascinated the timid young Dreiser, whose early wistfulness and passion for "dreaming" were incorporated in Clyde Griffiths's submissiveness to everyone above him. Rome acted out the lawlessness that appealed to the eternal hater and outsider in Dreiser.

Dreiser created many trapped, "shuffling," unrebellious men, many sweetly suffering women drawn from his mother and sisters in Terre Haute. Dreiser himself was primitive in his passions, vehement in his scorn of the conventions. Just as the dirty little secret behind Hurstwood's fall and Carrie's rise is commonplace but was forbidden to tell, so the idea behind *An American Tragedy* (still not acceptable to many people) is that you do not have to be clever in order to plan murder. By a single act that may astonish them more than it does anyone else, some people *will* think to free themselves from life as one long defeat. Dreiser lived long enough (he died in 1945) to see that murder had become as open as sex.

When the Russians took him up after the success of *An American Tragedy*, Dreiser was tickled by this evidence of world fame. But before the depression of the thirties, when he was struggling with the bad novels that were published only after his death—*The Bulwark* (1946) and *The Stoic* (1947)—and was grateful to the American Communists for making him a figurehead, it was clear that he identified with ruthless capitalists like Frank Algernon Cowperwood in *The Financier* (1912) and *The Titan* (1914). He thought "the system" as unalterable as life itself. Cowperwood's proud motto is, I satisfy myself. In *The Titan* Dreiser rhapsodized over his "villain": "How wonderful it is that men grow until, like colossi, they bestride the world, or like Banyan-trees, they drop roots from every branch and are themselves a forest —a forest of intricate commercial life, of which a thousand material aspects are the evidence."

Dreiser's unattractive diaries of the period between *Sister Carrie* and *An American Tragedy* scorn Jews, blacks, and every casualty he saw in the big city. They are a record of daily fornication interrupted by complaints about current prices. He boasted that he was outside himself and his feelings. This was not really true. Breaking down after the failure of *Sister Carrie,* he had been advised by a Philadelphia physician to keep a medical record. He kept it as if Theodore Dreiser, like the society around him, was all conditioned reflex and personal gratification.

> Greenwich Village, November, 1917: Go to corner and mail letters. Take 6th Avenue L to 53d and 8th and get off and walk to 518 West 52d (Day and Company). They sell me one gallon cider for 50¢. Take 10th Avenue car to 42d and 10th and walk over to 9th and 42d. Take 9th Avenue to 14th. Get off and carry jug to Petronelle at 303 West 4th. She is out. Stop in saloon and have one more gin rickey (25¢). Come here. Find note in mailbox from Lewisohn saying he's been here. Write him and say I couldn't be here.

None of the writers who made the American novel dominant in the 1920s was below the surface such a savage as Dreiser. All his writing life his anarchic temperament exposed him to ridicule but also aroused an amazement that anyone so crude could carry out a narrative line with such devastating power. One of his many publishers called him "an abnormal American." After 1927 it pleased this exception to the national consensus to be welcomed by Soviet writers, film and stage people officially contemptuous of the face Americans put on things. The background of all his work—from the degradation of Hurstwood to his sympathy with the "fallen" Jennie Gerhardt to his fascination with the corrupt and domineering magnate type, Cowperwood—was his sense that injustice makes society possible. It was another form of the carnage that sustains nature. To understand this is to respect fact. The thing-in-itself may save you. In the unremitting trivialities he recorded in his diaries, he demonstrated the fascination with fact that kept him from drowning in his greedy appetites and endless complaints. This was the professional habit of avid observation that fostered endless patience in carrying out a narrative. He would not stop where others did. What was not inevitable and "total" to himself alone he could not see at all.

Nothing Dreiser retained from his early life, nothing he shared with his rambunctious "outlaw" brothers and sisters, was ever to be softened or effaced. Mencken, despite his championship of Dreiser's work up to *An American Tragedy,* never understood the primitive levels (like a blind man making his way from object to object) on which a novelist must operate. Mencken, a splendid and highly comic satirist just when America needed one, was easily pleased with himself. After years of tolerating Dreiser's bêtises, he turned on *An American Tragedy*. In a characteristically jocular preface to a "memorial" edition of the novel (1946), Mencken noted that once the plot had been worked out by Dreiser, he proceeded on "reminiscence."

The wistful, doomed Clyde Griffiths was hardly the double of Theodore Dreiser. But it is typical of Dreiser's revengeful memories that he recovered from the failure of *Sister Carrie* to brood over images of ambition and murder. At first Dreiser had gone into a decline that paralleled Hurstwood's slide and came near killing him. Rescued by brother Paul the songwriter and restored at Muldoon's health farm, Dreiser suddenly became a success in the magazine business. In 1904 he joined Street & Smith, the dime-novel house; as editor of *Smith's Magazine*, he achieved a circulation of one hundred twenty-five thousand. He moved from his "moderately comfortable and autocratic position" at *Smith's* to *Broadway Magazine*, where he used his position and his new income to back a second edition of *Sister Carrie* (1907), brought out by B. W. Dodge. This sold well enough to demonstrate that there was a new public ready to welcome Dreiser's realism.

That same year Dreiser went to the Butterick Company, the firm founded on paper sewing patterns. He ran three women's magazines that specialized in "fiction, uplift, fashion." He made the impressive salary of five thousand dollars a year, and as editor of *The Delineator* announced, "We like sentiment, we like humor, we like realism, but it must be tinged with sufficient idealism to make it all of a truly uplifting character." He met Mencken when that cheerfully cynical pro was ghosting a baby-care series for Dreiser. By 1909 Dreiser was secretly editing *The Bohemian* as a diversion from his days at Butterick. Mencken, his collaborator, was warned: "no tainted fiction or cheap sex-struck articles." As always, Dreiser's real diversion, the one constant in his restless life, was women. A member of the Butterick staff, the father of a seventeen-year-old Dreiser was chasing, got him fired. Dreiser left without regret; "the big work was done here."

Sex and religion were still antagonists; Dreiser was absorbed by both. His father's harsh immigrant Catholicism had left him with a bitter hatred of the Church. When *An American Tragedy* was banned in Boston, Claude Bowers congratulated him in a *New York World* editorial. Dreiser was sure that the ban had been instigated by the Church. "I have stated over and over that the chief menace to the world today is the Catholic Church because it is a world wide organization and because chiefly it attacks intelligence—the development of the human mind in every country in the world—since for its own prosperity's sake it believes in mass stupidity." Dreiser's mother, of Pennsylvania Dutch background, had been brought up a Mennonite. She converted to her husband's Catholicism, but her pietism contributed to Dreiser's fascination with every form of radical Protestantism as he grew older.

In the 1920s nothing was more expected of literary men than a contempt for Victorian morality. Morality seemed the residue of religion, and as the only creed left to the unenlightened "booboisie," it became an easy mark for the emancipated. In presenting Clyde Griffiths as the victim of an evangelical upbringing, Dreiser in 1925 was, as usual, the Great Exception. Supercilious academics, then and later, called him a Neanderthal because he was unconscious of literary fashion.

The roots of *An American Tragedy* lie below the urban world that becomes Clyde's undoing. The book opens (no date given) on a pair of drab evangelists in Kansas City whose twelve-year-old boy is the prisoner of parents "determined upon spiritualizing the world as much as possible." The family enters the novel between the "walls" of a big city. Clyde Griffiths grows up so innocent that his first experience of the money-obsessed, pleasure-mad world in the great hotel he finds employment as a bellhop intoxicates and deranges him.

From now on nothing will exist for him except his need to replace his freakishly religious childhood with the standard American life of external success. He runs away after a car in which he is riding with drunken friends kills a little girl, and eventually he finds employment in the collar factory in upstate New York owned by his pompous uncle, Samuel Griffiths. He is first assigned to the "shrinking" room. The coldly superior Griffiths family in Lycurgus shuns him. He becomes a supervisor in the "stamping" room but is too lonely to stay away from the help, as ordered. In the evenings he meets with the poignant, all-loving and all-trusting Roberta Alden at the deserted end of her street. Roberta is the daughter of a hopelessly impoverished farmer from "Biltz" (Dreiser's names for some characters and places are wonderfully ugly). Since Clyde is related to the important Griffiths family, his pale handsomeness and appealing eyes (his most noteworthy feature) attract the interest of sprightly Sondra Finchley, whose wealthy father manufactures vacuum cleaners. Clyde's desire for Sondra, indistinguishable from his need to be accepted by her set, becomes overwhelming. When Roberta becomes pregnant and insists that he marry her, he discovers that there is no way out for him and (to his amazement) that he wishes to kill her.

Clyde accomplishes Roberta's death without actually killing her. He takes her rowing on Big Bittern Lake and is so torn by fear of the crime he wishes to commit that he allows her to drown when she falls out of the boat after he has "accidentally" struck her with his camera. He has left so many indications of his intent to commit murder that the law easily catches up with him. The local district attorney is ambitious for higher office; he is personally disfigured, grew up poor as Clyde, hates Clyde for destroying a poor girl in order to join Sondra Finchley's class. A jury of hard-faced country folk clearly takes satisfaction in sending Clyde to the chair. After almost a thousand driving pages of closeknit narrative have demonstrated to the point of pain that Clyde Griffiths never had a chance to think, dream, and be other than he is, he is executed. At the end Dreiser brings us back to the drab, beaten family of evangelists trudging away from still another forlorn prayer service. The scene is now San Francisco. A little boy—the son of Clyde's sister Esta—has replaced Clyde in the family circle. He may be another victim.

Dreiser's first and last emphasis is on enclosure. There is the dark beginning within "the tall walls of the commercial heart of an American city of perhaps 400,000 inhabitants—such walls as in time may linger as a mere fable"; the dark epilogue within "the tall walls of the commercial heart of the city of San Francisco—tall and gray in the evening shade." Enclosure is fundamental to the social logic behind *An American Tragedy*. It is a logic that Dreiser's method forces us to accept though we have abstract reasons to offer against the method and our acceptance. Even when we argue that the circle that closes around Clyde Griffiths is not necessarily an *American* tragedy, we cannot claim that the circle is not there and is not complete. Dreiser does not leave anything out of his almost one thousand pages, never leaves blank the tiniest corner of his canvas. The compulsion behind Clyde's life has transferred itself to the narrative. The inevitability that Dreiser brings to every detail is like Clyde's progress to the chair. The reader feels as trapped as Clyde.

Dreiser's reasoning is that a man has no escape from the social net if he totally accepts its values. Clyde incorporates everything meretricious and fatal to himself because, as in his evangelical youth, he has never been anything but obedient, a creature of other people's ideas. He may seem to transfer his loyalties from his parents' God to the idolatry of Sondra Finchley and everything money-wise, hedonistic, and sexy that she represents. But he still has no mind of his own. He never puts up a single value of his own against everything he dumbly embodies. He is engulfed by ambitions and fancies that personify the society he has never thought to question. Dreiser's hatred of organized religion is the key. Religion no longer has anything to do with individual promptings of faith, has become just social convention.

Clyde and Roberta are luckless lovers who know nothing of the easy freedom that a later generation would regard as an elementary right. It was typical of Dreiser's concern with everything proscribed that the pair have their first date—forbidden by company rules—meeting in embarrassment and fear at the *end* of the street where Roberta has her room. When Roberta discovers herself pregnant, a necessarily illegal abortion is such a terror that the pharmacist who sells them a fake remedy is outraged when, the pills having failed, Clyde begs for the name of a doctor willing to perform an abortion. When Clyde is in jail awaiting trial, his lawyer lights a cigarette but warns that it would look "immoral" for Clyde to smoke. In the last scenes pushing Clyde to the chair, an unaffiliated young preacher, hysterical in his piety as if to convince himself, is able to pressure Clyde to make a pitiful contrition. This preacher can do anything with Clyde; everyone has abandoned him. But he can work Clyde up to his last abjectness only because Clyde has all his life been subject to something and someone.

Did the emancipated readers of *An American Tragedy* in 1925 accept the tragedy because it mirrored a world already past? Samuel Griffiths's authority over his business is as total as his domination of his family. Once their unfortunate relative is in jail, they let him rot; once he is sentenced, they refuse to support an appeal. This cuts off his one chance. And it was still possible in this novel for the name of Clyde's young "society beauty" to be kept out of the testimony. Clyde, whom his rich relatives rejected from the first, is a victim of the class he yearned for.

The proprieties, everything pertaining to social control, finally lock Clyde in. Dreiser has not the slightest doubt of his case. The book is an extended, monumental demonstration (not a defense) of a man who had no choice because he had never made a choice. What makes the demonstration so convincing is Dreiser's peculiar inability, as with Hurstwood and Carrie, to imagine alternatives. Every detail *performs* because Dreiser cannot be distracted. He was awed by his material. Beginning the book, he said, "It seems simple. The right procession & selection of incidents should be as nothing but it just chances to be everything."

Dreiser's style is easily ridiculed, but it never gets in the way of the story. His laboriousness, his grinding repetitions, assist his aim—to lock the reader in with Clyde. He is so intent on leaving nothing blank that in describing Roberta's background, he more than fully describes Titus Alden's broken-down farm, then goes on: "the interior of the house corresponded with the exterior." Dreiser usually finds the right word, but only after scrabbling for it in full view of the reader. Yet his ability to light on some external feature as a mirror of human feeling can arrest the reader by its accidental, perhaps unconscious symbolism. The reader overlooks Dreiser's clumsiness when he provides crucial details.

In chapter 18 the isolated furtive lovers, forced to take their few pleasures away from respectable society in Lycurgus, have a few hours together near a little city strange to both of them.

> For outside of Fonda a few miles they came to a pleasure park called Starlight where, in addition to a few clap-trap pleasure concessions such as a ring of captive aeroplanes, a Ferris wheel, a merry-go-round, an old mill and a dance floor, was a small lake with boats. It was after its fashion an idyllic spot with a little bandstand out on an island near the center of the lake and on the shore a grave and captive bear in a cage.

This is the first presentiment of the role that a lake will play in the story. The "pleasure park called Starlight" is one of the "rougher" resorts, only less "strident" than others. Clyde leads Roberta "to the stand of a man who sold frankfurters." A merry-go-round is "in full blast, nothing would do but that Roberta should ride with him." He seats her on a zebra, "then stood close in order that he might keep his arm about her, and both try to catch the brass ring." The scene is "commonplace and noisy and gaudy." They are both in "a kind of ecstasy which was all out of proportion to the fragile, gimcrack scene." Every detail is as commonplace as can be. The shabby scene evokes a kind of ecstasy in the lovers because there is sudden freedom, yet it moves the reader because it is so pitiful in relation to the facts. We may smile at "It was after its fashion an idyllic spot," but we are hemmed in when "a little bandstand out on an island near the center of the lake" is immediately followed by "and on the shore a grave and captive bear in a cage."

And now the terror toward which Dreiser has been working all along is instilled in us—Clyde searches for a lake in which to drown Roberta. The whole second volume, four hundred solidly packed pages, is given over to the planning of the crime, the essential scene of Roberta's death, the unravelling of Clyde's original plan by local authorities who are quick to exploit his defenselessness, and his undoing. Melville described his last work as an "inside narrative." *An American Tragedy* is all outside narrative, and now it moves with the inevitableness of tragedy to the doom that has been waiting for Clyde all along.

Clyde, debating with himself the necessity of murdering Roberta, must still join Sondra Finchley at a lake full of "bright blue waters," a lake bounded by "small and large, white and pink and green and brown lodges on every hand, with their boathouses." But "the tall, dark, spear pines that sentineled the shores on either side . . . gave to the waters at the west a band of black shadow where the trees were mirrored so clearly." When Clyde and Sondra "motor" from one lake party of her friends to another, en route Clyde is most "strangely impressed" by the desolate and for the most part lonely character of the region. The narrow and rain-washed and even rutted nature of the dirt roads that wound between tall, silent and darksome trees—forests in the largest sense of the word—that extended for miles and miles on apparently either hand. The decadent and weird nature of some of the bogs and tarns on either side . . . dirt roads which here and there were festooned with funereal or viperous vines, . . . strewn with soggy and decayed piles of fallen and criss-crossed logs . . . in the green slime that an undrained depression in the earth had accumulated.

Dreiser has been timing the approach to Roberta's death by accumulating images of emptiness, darkness, decay. The "voice" of the evil genie that Clyde hears, counselling him to go through with his projected crime, is the voice Hurstwood hears counselling him to take the money when the safe clicks shut before he can put the money back. This voice is effective because it is so elemental; Dreiser believes that we are faithless at heart. The dreaded act is what we are dying for—and will die for. Despite his terror at even thinking Roberta dead, everything in Clyde's mind is pushing him to act. Totally at odds with himself, he steadily rows the boat into more and more remote corners of Big Bittern Lake. It is the sign of his agonized debate with himself that finally alarms Roberta and hastens her death. She moves toward him. And he, "angry and confused and glowering," moving entirely within confusion and anger with himself, wanting nothing but to be free, "flings out at her," pushes at her with the camera she tries to put down, injures her so that she screams. Whereupon he gets up, "half to apologize for the unintended blow," capsizes the boat, and, seeing her helpless in the water, lets her drown.

He has murdered her without committing murder. He has also saved himself in the way most calculated to expose his original plan. He has arranged his own fate, though it is the one thing in his life that he alone has arranged. When he is caught and is ground down by everyone eager to take advantage of his self-exposure, he is still naive enough to wonder why it is all happening to him. "He had never imagined that it was going to be like this; that he was going to suffer so." He is the unconscious prisoner—of other people—to the last. Just once in his life he deliberated long enough—to plan a crime; now he goes to the chair.

And what were the alternatives? Dreiser's logic, given the irresistible context he built up, makes the *story* irrefutable. He was in fact so consumed by the story that he never disputed the varying interpretations of *An American Tragedy*, not even the sophistries of the time that saw Clyde Griffiths, who had allowed Roberta to drown, as technically "innocent." Typically, Dreiser also refused to condemn capital punishment. He was a novelist, and this was his last good novel, his supreme novel. People preoccupied with Dreiser's famous clumsiness and crushingly old-fashioned technique missed the irony behind Dreiser's unexpected success. *An American Tragedy* was a triumph of method. The method succeeded through its total projection of a distinct point of view. Society was now everything. Hence man as man, the soul of man, man in his freedom, was still to be understood by a society just as steeped in materialism as Clyde. Man as the dupe of society is outside himself—like Clyde Griffiths, who went to his death still not knowing who he was and what he had done.

11

Dreiser was a novelist Faulkner once praised. He may have found Dreiser easier to praise than he did his contemporary and rival Hemingway, like himself a product of the modern literary revolution.* But he found Hemingway narrow. When Faulkner, to his great surprise, became a world figure in the 1950s, he told an interviewer in Japan:

> I thought that he [Hemingway] found out early what he could do and stayed inside of that. He never did try to get outside the boundary of what he really could do and risk failure. He did what he really could do marvellously well, first rate, but to me that is not success but failure . . . failure to me is the best. To try something you can't do, because it's too much [to hope for] but still to try it and fail, then try it again. That to me is success.

"Failure" was a condition that Faulkner, the descendant of "governors and generals" (the embittered Jason Compson in *The Sound and the Fury* is always throwing the past at his sorry family), was used to. He made failure a condition of the South in his fiction and of the human condition—despite all ready-made American propaganda to the contrary. "Count no 'account," folks called the young Faulkner in Oxford, Mississippi.

Failure was more habitual in the South than elsewhere for most of the eighty years (1865–1945) before "the old unreconstructed had died off." This was the period that Faulkner (born in 1897) shared with survivors and memo-

---

*Dreiser wrote as if there were no other novelists. In the bleak period following *Sister Carrie*, he told himself in his diary to read some current novels, for he might want to write another novel some day.

ries of the Confederacy. In his long chronicle, it ended only with the Second World War and the rascally poor white Snopeses taking over from the once high and mighty Compsons, Sartorises—and Faulkners. Those eighty years were also continuous in Faulkner's mind with the Highlander who with just his tartan and claymore had barely escaped to the South from the English hunting down of survivors of the last Jacobite campaign. His descendant crossed the Appalachians to the last Southern frontier—the delta country owned by Chickasaws. The Compsons acquired their land from Indians who kept Negro slaves (and buried them with their master when the master died). In his "appendix" to *The Sound and the Fury,* written seventeen years after the novel in an effort to clear away Compson history over three centuries, Faulkner introduced the Chickasaw chief Ikkemotubbe, "A dispossessed American king," who merrily changed what the French called him, "de l'homme," to "Doom,"

> who granted out of his vast lost domain a solid square mile of virgin North Mississippi dirt as truly angled as the four corners of a cardtable top (forested then because these were the old days before 1833 when the stars fell and Jefferson Mississippi was one long rambling onestorey mudchinked log building housing the Chickasaw Agent and his tradingpost store) to the grandson of a Scottish refugee who had lost his own birthright by casting his lot with a king who himself had been dispossessed.

The Chickasaws went on "to the wild western land presently to be called Oklahoma; not knowing then about the oil." In one compendious sentence Faulkner filled up two and a half centuries. Since he was a bit of Southern history himself, one who traced "my own little postage stamp of native soil" from the Chickasaws to the Snopeses, that period (vast for an American) belonged to him. The crucial eighty years marked the last time when the South could claim to be separate in culture and memory.

Given his South, his family, his class, the breaking down that coincided with Faulkner's life and became his life, it is evident that history opened up to Faulkner with his name. "Whether he wanted it or not," Faulkner liked to say. He was steeped in legends of the Highlanders, reports by old hunters of the original wilderness, the primitive isolation of Mississippi before "the Wawh," the violent separation of the races ordained by God. The "old forces" were part of him. From his earliest days Faulkner still lived the heroic and defiant past—though its decay mocked the oratory with which Southerners celebrated it. Faulkner lived with sacred history like a character in the Bible. Yet God's promise to His people had been withdrawn. Forced to live in the past, Southerners were kept from prolonging it. What remained was the "imperishable" story, one that Faulkner felt condemned and privileged to write. Only by writing could he save his awareness and extend it. Among so many failed and desperate Southerners in the "silent South," he was isolated by being a writer. He was to project his menaced sensibility onto many defeated and violent Southerners. Oxford did not like his stubborn refusal to be absorbed elsewhere.

Faulkner's sharpest characteristic as a person and as a "poet," as he first called himself, was his concealment of his idiosyncrasy, his protection of his privacy. He was one with the South in its history, but he knew it well enough to be afraid. Many a writer emerging in the twenties was glad to escape his established family. Faulkner, growing up in the poorest state in the Union, in a regressive family and an impoverished culture, started cutting ties as soon as he could. He hated school, left high school without graduating, enjoyed being a roustabout and playing the local eccentric. He enlisted in the Royal Canadian Flying Corps in 1918 but never flew. He was a special student at the University of Mississippi because of his interest in French; he worked at a bookstore in New York, where he met Elizabeth Prall, Sherwood Anderson's future wife. Anderson's slovenly independence from literary convention was a decided influence when Faulkner lived near Anderson in New Orleans's French Quarter and wrote sketches for *The Double Dealer* and other publications that were meant to deliver the South from Mencken's "cultural swamp."* Anderson said he would get Faulkner's first novel, *Soldiers' Pay* (1926), published as long as he did not have to read it himself, and he was as good as his word.

Faulkner, always hard up, was an assistant postmaster at the university, where he was fired because he neglected the customers. (He did not want to be at the mercy of every son of a bitch who needed a two-cent stamp.) After publishing a first book of poems, *The Marble Faun* (1924), *Soldiers' Pay*, and *Mosquitoes* (1927), he worked as a carpenter, a painter, a paperhanger, and was a coal heaver in Oxford's power plant. From 1932, the year he published one of his greatest novels, *Light in August*, to 1946, the year he was finally

---

*One of these sketches describes a local bootlegger's brother: "and his eyes were clear and blue as cornflowers, and utterly vacant of thought . . . and gripping tightly in one fist was a narcissus." After the broken narcissus is splinted, "His eyes were like two scraps of April sky after a rain, and his drooling face was moonlike in ecstasy." In the concluding section of *The Sound and the Fury,* Benjy has eyes this color and holds a broken flower held together with a twig and two bits of string.

"recognized," he spent half of every year writing film scripts in Hollywood in order to be able to devote himself to his own work the rest of the year.

In the twenties the New South (as it was optimistically called) saw the emergence of a typically American middle class. Local businessmen and lawyers were not displeased by the descent from glory of proud families like the Faulkners. Faulkner was disliked for rejecting all virtuous paths to prosperity, mocked for drinking himself (sometimes literally) into the gutter. The tensions that racked him were not easily relieved by whiskey, but whiskey helped to relieve them in passionately inclusive one-sentence paragraphs. In *The Sound and the Fury* (originally called *Twilight*) the Compsons have come down to a father who died of drink, a self-pitying mother who has given up on everything to become a professional invalid, a sister cast off by her husband for marrying him when she was pregnant by another man, a brother who commits suicide because he is hopelessly in love with his sister. The baby of the family is an idiot who has been castrated after frightening a little girl. Jason Lycurgus Compson IV, who has blackmailed his sister and stolen the money sent for her daughter's care, says bitterly (after he has had his idiot brother, Benjy, sent to the state asylum in Jackson), "Blood, I says, governors and generals. It's a damn good thing we never had any kings and presidents; we'd all be down there at Jackson chasing butterflies."

In one respect Faulkner in Oxford was beyond censure. A writer was generally ignored. This may have been his good fortune. Faulkner agreed with critics that his style might have been less fervid if he had had other writers around for him to talk to and compare notes with; he described his writing as "oratory out of solitude." But there was no way for Faulkner to develop except on his own lines—and Mississippi made this easy. The South even in its palmiest days before the Civil War had never seen any use for local writers. William Gilmore Simms of South Carolina, though eager to espouse the "code," was told by the plantation owners who alone could afford to buy books that they were satisfied to get their reading matter from England. Their favorite author was Sir Walter Scott. Romance consoled the defeated South until the 1920s. The premature realist George Washington Cable had had to flee to Massachusetts because of his outlandish views on the "Negro Question."

Faulkner was an exception even among Southern writers in the twenties, when the affected style and giggly double entendres of *Jurgen* passed for naughtiness from James Branch Cabell's Virginia. In some way that can be accounted for only by instinct, Faulkner (as Ezra Pound was to say of the young T. S. Eliot) had modernized himself on his own. Eliot had enjoyed "advantages" in St. Louis, had studied at Harvard, Marburg, Oxford. Faulkner did not find his stride even with his third novel, *Sartoris* (1929), though it took up the waiting theme of the failed "aristocracy." Its working title was *Flags in the Dust*, it was rejected by twelve publishers, and the published text was carved out of an enormous manuscript that everyone thought hopeless. Yet astonishingly, Faulkner's masterpiece, *The Sound and the Fury*, was published the same year. Looking back from it, one can see in all Faulkner's early work, not least in the New Orleans sketches, a jaunty need to make experiments, a wish to try himself to the limit, that prepare one for the imaginative abandon of *The Sound and the Fury*. He felt bound to certain themes but was always shifting his point of view.

Faulkner's deep sense of locale and his total involvement in its history often suggest Hawthorne. But his constant growth within himself and his particular gift for locating every narrative within the rush and beat of some embattled single voice have only one analogue in American writing. Melville was a self-educated wanderer who first wandered within each book, then from book to book. He constantly shifted and transformed himself; the motion of the sea became his image of truth. Faulkner did not continue to experiment after the extraordinary series—*Sartoris, The Sound and the Fury, As I Lay Dying, Sanctuary, Light in August, Absalom! Absalom!*—was produced in just seven years, 1929–36. In the 1950s, when he had become a world figure, Faulkner recalled of this time:

> I think there's a period in a writer's life when he, well, simply for lack of any word, is fertile and he just produces. Later on, his blood slows, his bones get a little more brittle, his muscles get a little stiff, he gets perhaps other interests, but I think there's one time in his life when he writes at the top of his talent plus his speed, too. Later the speed slows; the talent doesn't necessarily have to fade at the same time. But there's a time in his life, one matchless time, when they are matched completely. The speed, and the power and the talent, they're all there and then he is . . . "hot."

The Sound and the Fury is certainly hot. Something like Melville's incessancy of thought and commanding rhetoric, marking the proud wanderer (within his own mind) who despises the progress of society, stamps *The Sound and the Fury* with Faulkner's fundamental image—life as a perpetual breaking down. In Benjy's mind, the bottommost layer and residue of Compson family history with which the novel opens, the world is all phenomenon, things-are-just-happening. In this beginning Benjy is incapable of explaining why they are happening. He just reverberates to every call of "Caddy!" from the golf course (the land once belonged to the Compsons but was sold to send Quentin to Harvard) and every glint from the fireplace that brings back the memory of his absent sister, Candace ("Caddy"), warming him in winter.

Only as we ascend from Benjy's mind to Quentin's monologue on the day of his death, recounting *his* love for his sister; from Quentin to Jason, the maddened survivor spewing out all his bitterness; from Jason to Faulkner himself, taking over the last section, are we put into the light. We are given every why and when that have produced the downfall of the Compsons, interlocked by so much passion and rage. The novel ends in the light of Easter Sunday and the unspoken triumph (if that is the word for those who merely "endured") of Dilsey, still a slave to these degenerate whites whom she and her family will survive. But the last word and the last cry out of the book belong not only to Benjy, who bellows in protest when Dilsey's grandson drives him the "wrong" way around the Confederate monument in the center of town, but to Faulkner's wonderfully sustaining style. The whole book recounts in the most passionate detail life as phenomenon, a descent into breakdown. In the end we are saved and exhilarated by Faulkner's reconstituting all this in the speed and heat of his art.

What the novel owed to the Freudian emphasis on the interior consciousness and to the already inescapable influence of *Ulysses* (1922) is obvious. Theodore Dreiser was so awed studying the case histories in an early book explaining psychoanalysis that he exclaimed: "I feel as though I were walking in great halls and witnessing tremendous scenes." But Clyde Griffiths's tormented dialogues with himself, though they go to the bottom of his character, could have come out of a novel by Zola or Hardy. Dreiser's strength lay in the all-or-nothing determinism of the nineteenth century.

James Joyce was a great originator. *Ulysses*, like the classical epic it absorbs into a single day, is by now a fundamental reference to our civilization. But as a great epic will be, it is a labored synthesis, more demonstrative of Joyce's fabulous powers than of the Dublin that remains a project in Joyce's mind. *The Sound and the Fury* is a greater *novel*, more dramatic, more universally representative through the interior life of everyone in it. We do not know just what Faulkner owed Joyce. Joyce in the twenties affected other writers like the weather. Eliot heralded *Ulysses:* "Mr. Joyce is pursuing a method which others must pursue after him." Faulkner was not that interested in becoming a founder. It is a mistake to assume that in scrambling so many different periods of time (especially in the "Benjy" section) Faulkner wished to mystify and even to "test" his readers. Joyce joked that *Ulysses* would make him immortal because it provided endless work for professors. But Faulkner was telling the truth when he said that he had originally written a lot and even sent it off before he realized that people would actually read it. He was certainly having *his* joke when he explained that there were four different voices in his book because each of the first three had proved insufficient. What rings true to readers of *The Sound and the Fury* is Faulkner's admission that the novel began as a story in a vision. Faulkner "saw" a little girl with muddied drawers sitting in a tree, reporting to her brothers below what she could see through a window of their grandmother's funeral in the house across the way.

In another report of how the novel had begun, Faulkner said that the little girl had muddied her drawers when she had sneaked under the barbed wire dividing the Compson property. The little girl became Candace, "Caddy." The land on the other side of the fence, the future golf course, was sold to send Quentin Compson to Harvard. A fence separates the Compsons from their past.

Intimate family details lock together in the novel so that every repetition is heard in a different register, widening and deepening its effect on the reader as it does on the Compsons themselves. We share every flicker of their minds. In the concluding section, "The clock tick-tocked, solemn and profound. It might have been the dry pulse of the decaying house itself; after a while it whirred and cleared its throat six times." Everything belonging to this family makes itself heard, over and over, like the sound of that clock. Not only is there soon no "mystery" to the book, no pedantry of the kind that makes *Ulysses* so formidable; we get so caught up by the Compsons that one of the many pleasures of the book is that everything long stored up in everyone is intoned by a different character so as to advance the action. Caddy, not directly present for most of the book, is so intensely visualized by her brothers that she dominates their lives. Every sensation in Benjy's fractured mind reminds him of her. Her brother Quentin, preparing to drown himself in the Charles River, walks about Cambridge reliving every precipitous scene that he (more than she) botched at the last minute. Jason is magnetized by her, but his resentment of her freedom will not permit him to admit that he is jealous.

The charming but usually sodden father of this tumultuously incestuous family, Jason Lycurgus Compson III, a classical scholar, had long before given up and retired to his dog-eared Horace and his whiskey decanter. When his son Quentin departed for Harvard, he gave him (as cynical farewell) his ancient watch. Quentin twists its hands off in the morning of the day that will end with his suicide. But like the dead son, the idiot son, the absent daughter, the father is a constant infliction to his son and namesake, Jason. Nothing that ever happened in this family is forgotten; every offense, anything appropriated by one Compson at the expense of another, everything taken by the world to the shame of the Compsons in general, is endlessly (but variously) repeated. Finally, because their history has ended, the novel can begin—in the splintered, hopelessly yearning mind of Benjy.

Many novelists have claimed that any family can become a novel. This novel succeeds beyond all others of its time and place because the Compsons *live* time, they do not just live in it, which makes them as real as our family makes time real to us. Time is entirely fluid in the book, not an external measure against which people move. It assumes so many shapes because the force of memory plays on many people.

Any action—Quentin buying weights to keep his body down after he has jumped into the river, or Jason hysterically running after his niece Quentin after she has stolen the money that he had stolen from her care—interrupts a dream scene of reminiscence. The daughter's name "Quentin"—the departing sister's salute to the self-lacerating brother who died for love of her —itself reflects the sameness and repetition that are a constant in every family. The rapid shifts in time that Benjy lives successively, and that at first are bewildering to the reader, are soon enjoyed as the fragments that surprise our waiting consciousness. What makes Benjy so poignant is that he experiences nothing but sensations—Caddy shielding him from the cold, Caddy bringing him to the fire, Caddy crying "Stomp, Benjy! Stomp!" when they put on his galoshes. This family is in decay, but everything we see of them is bright with life, thrilling in its actuality. Dilsey near the end intones, "I seed de beginnin, en now I sees de endin." That refers to the Compsons themselves, over whom she waits in judgment without knowing that she does. But for the reader hypnotized by so much life on the page, nothing has ended. As it never ended for Faulkner, who when asked to supply an appendix clearing up the difficulties, went back to 1699 and forward to 1945 to fill in the Compson history. He spilled the book out in such ecstasy and freedom that he rewrote it as if he could not bear to leave it. He said that the book "caused me the most grief and anguish, as the mother loves the child who became the thief or murderer more than the one who became the priest. I wrote it five separate times, trying to tell the story which would continue to anguish me until I did."

Because of the war and the uncertainty of everything in sight, the twenties lived with a sharp, baleful sense of time. Secular man had supposedly triumphed, since he was ready to pay the cost of an existence totally without illusion. The hero of Dreiser's anachronistic novel had nothing to say about the circumstances that drew him down. The "sentinel" trees around the lake were still the old gods. The brave new world *entre les deux guerres* gave a demonstrative radiance to style in *Ulysses, In Our Time, Voyage au bout de la nuit, The Great Gatsby, Mrs. Dalloway.* Style was heightened consciousness, the only defense against the fatal ordering of things, our true Prometheus. Style now proclaimed the Everlasting No. In *The Sound and the Fury*, consciousness never stops addressing itself or the absent loves and foes of one's own household. Sharpened to a scream—to a murder that is never accomplished, except by brother Quentin against himself—Jason curses the world as he frantically chases after his niece, then cries, "And damn You, too. See if You can stop me." Benjy without knowing it has become nothing but "style," in the voice he cannot hear as his own. Quentin is so full of his moony, overburdened style that he cannot get relief from it or from himself (he is all too conscious of *his* style) this side of the river. Jason's hatred is so expressive that, terrible as he is, we come to love his *fluency* (certainly not him) for never letting up.

In the fourth section, where Faulkner takes over to conclude the novel, there is a good deal of charged writing, as there is in Quentin's reveries. (Quentin is grandiloquent enough to be a parody of Edgar Allan Poe on *his* last day in Baltimore.) Faulkner compares the little black preacher at the Easter morning service to "a worn small rock whelmed by the successive waves of his voice.

> With his body he seemed to feed the voice that, succubus like, had fleshed its teeth in him. And the congregation seemed to watch with its own eyes while the voice consumed him, until he was nothing and they were nothing and there was not even a voice but instead their hearts were speaking to one another in chanting measures beyond the need for words, so that when he came to rest against the reading desk, his monkey face lifted and his whole attitude that of a serene, tortured crucifix that transcended its shabbiness and insignificance and made it of no moment, a long moaning expulsion of breath rose from them, and a woman's single soprano: "Yes, Jesus!"

The blacks in *The Sound and the Fury* do not speak for themselves. The Compsons live in such echoing transmission from one mind to another that by the time we get to see them on stage in the final section, *we* are helping to complete the design. They have been in our ears all along; now we *see* them. But Dilsey must be seen first, and nothing in the prose fiction of our time could be more satisfying than her entrance, it is so much the proof of what is already in our minds.

> The day dawned bleak and chill, a moving wall of grey light out of the northeast which, instead of dissolving into moisture, seemed to disintegrate into minute and venomous particles, like dust that, when Dilsey opened the door of the cabin and emerged, needled laterally into her flesh, precipitating not so much a moisture as a substance partaking of the quality of thin, not quite congealed oil. She wore a stiff black straw hat perched upon her turban, and a maroon velvet cape with a border of mangy and anonymous fur above a dress of purple silk, and she stood in the door for awhile with her myriad and sunken face lifted to the weather, and one gaunt hand flac-soled as the belly of a fish, then she moved the cape aside and examined the bosom of her gown.

We never feel in these charged-up passages, as we do in Faulkner's later writing, that he is elaborating his text and even commenting on it. In *The Sound and the Fury* everything about this family—especially those whose servitude makes them a part of it—already fits together, so that when Faulkner comes to describe them, the inherent design is rounded out in words as charged as these lives. Faulkner also needed to take over at the end and to put his particular stamp on the book. He liked to say that his ambition was to put everything, "the world," into one sentence. Our extraordinary view of Dilsey was composed under that spell. There was a stunning contractedness that followed from Faulkner's calling himself a failed poet. "Maybe every novelist wants to write poetry first, finds he can't, and then tries the short story, which is the most demanding form of poetry. And, failing at that, only then does he take up novel writing."

It was nice of Faulkner to say that "every novelist" was like him. He could be generous to the competition, for they never got in his way. His need to pile everything on his "little postage stamp of native soil" was his tribute to style. "Art is simpler than people think because there is so little to write about." The material is all so elemental, obvious, and foreclosed that one has constantly to bring a different perspective to it, which is style. But Faulkner liked to add, "I'm still trying to put it all on one pinhead. I don't know how to do it. All I know to do is to keep trying in a new way."

The "trying" was central to Faulkner's style; he saw the novelist not as an artist capable of finishing anything but as a gambler playing for higher and higher stakes. The Compsons, he said in his appendix to *The Sound and the Fury*, were gamblers; they were wrecked as a family, out of the running in the South (except for Jason, who, as Faulkner admitted with astonished admiration, was still running). Their claim on the past was like their ancestor's claim on the future when he entered the Mississippi wilderness. Man's desire was always in inverse proportion to himself. He had to gamble everything he had—little enough—against time's closing in on him. There was "one anonymous chance to perform something passionate and brave and austere not just in but into man's enduring chronicle . . . in gratitude for the gift of time in it."

Life to Faulkner was "this pointless chronicle." "Though the one I know is probably as good as another, life is a phenomenon but not a novelty, the same frantic steeplechase toward nothing everywhere and man stinks the same stink no matter where in time." We are moved about by what Faulkner in both *The Sound and the Fury* and *Light in August* called "the Player." We seem to be without help when matched against this figure. Faulkner's "Christ figures" are an idiot castrated in *The Sound and the Fury* because he frightened some little girls (and had a sadistic brother), and the murderer Joe Christmas in *Light in August,* pursued all his life because he *may* be a "nigger." (He is finally run to earth, castrated, and bled to death by a Ku Kluxer.) In *A Fable* (1954) the illiterate French corporal who leads the mutiny against the war obviously represents Christ; he has twelve followers. After rejecting the temptation offered by the "Supreme Commander," he is shot and falls into barbed wire that crowns his head with thorns.

A Fable is more allegory than fiction. By the 1950s Faulkner was editorializing over "fables" written in his "one matchless time." Faulkner's "Christ figures" are such only in their power of suffering. One of the most wonderful touches in the conclusion of *The Sound and the Fury* shows blond Benjy with eyes the color of sunflowers sitting next to Dilsey in the Negro church. "In the midst of the voices and the hands Ben sat, rapt in his sweet blue gaze." What Faulkner evidently wanted to say in *A Fable* was that his corporal was for the salvation of the world gambling his own life against the greater power represented by Satan, the "Supreme Commander." He lost. The essence of Christ for Faulkner in the twenties, that period of great scepticism, was that we are not savable.

The potent and redemptive figure in Faulkner's mythology is the novelist. The novelist gambles his talent against the silence surrounding us. He pits himself against vacancy and unreality, replacing the silence with a world organized by himself alone. Words must somehow exceed themselves through an effort that ultimately becomes the writer's signature, his style. The failure of a class, a tradition, a way of life, was the haunting subject. Failure entered the writer's attempted grasp of a *comédie humaine* often beyond language. "I don't know how to do it. All I know to do is to keep trying in a new way."

Faulkner liked the word "immortality." He meant the novel that lasts, Ezra Pound's "literature is news that stays news." It was an ambition still fundamental to writers of the twenties, who could not conceive of immortality anywhere else. Faulkner was amazing. The novelist was his hero. He meant *the novelist,* not himself.

15

Hemingway the Painter

> Our people went to America because that was the place
> for them to go then. It had been a good country and we
> had made a bloody mess of it and I would go, now,
> somewhere else as we had always the right to go some-
> where else and as we had always gone. . . . Let the others
> come to America who did not know that they had come
> too late. Our people had seen it at its best and fought for
> it when it was well worth fighting for. Now I would go
> somewhere else.
>
> HEMINGWAY, *Green Hills of Africa*

I

One of the last photographs of Hemingway shows him wandering a road in
Idaho and kicking a can. He is surrounded by grim mountains. He looks
morose, he is evidently in his now-usual state of exasperation, and he is alone.
The emptiness of Idaho is the only other presence in the picture.

With his gift for locating the most symbolic place for himself, Hemingway was bound to end up in Idaho. And not just for the hunting and fishing.
At every stage of his life he found himself a frontier appropriate to his fresh
needs as a sportsman and his ceremonial needs as a writer. Only Henry James
among his significant predecessors made such a literary cult of travel. James
even in his sacred Europe never went very far. He certainly never sought
the last possible frontier.

Most American writer-wanderers, like Melville the sailor, Mark Twain
the mobile printer, correspondent, and lecturer, went where they were
forced to go to make a living. Hemingway for the most part chose where
he wanted to go. That was the impression he managed to leave. He did spend
his early summers "up in Michigan" because his family summered there.
Right after the First World War he was sent by the *Toronto Star* to report
still more fighting between Turks and Greeks. But his conjunction of Michi-

gan and the Balkans in *In Our Time* made these startling stories read as if *he* had chosen these experiences. There was a point to being Ernest Hemingway and to writing like Ernest Hemingway. Everything was under control like one of his sentences. He was an entirely free man. He had shaped his own career.

To summer up in Michigan was wonderful. It was also wonderful to sit in a café when Paris was "the best town for a writer to be" and, nursing a single *café crème,* to write the first Nick Adams stories in a blue-backed notebook with the stub of a pencil you shaved with a little pencil sharpener as you went along. Sharpening a pencil with a knife was too wasteful. Remembering how poor you had been, thirty years later in *A Moveable Feast,* you also made the point that "wasteful" referred to other people's prose, not E. Hemingway's. And when and where else was poverty so easy to bear that a young couple with baby could live on five dollars a day and go skiing in Austria when a story was finished? It also helped to skip lunch because on an empty stomach all sorts of hidden details in the Cézannes in the Luxembourg became sharper, easier to grasp for your writing when you were learning "to do the country like Cézanne."

Any place Hemingway sojourned in, any place he passed through, somehow took on Hemingway's attributes as an artist. He was the most extraordinary appropriator. He learned to omit many things for his famous style, but a trout stream in Michigan or a street in Paris came rhythmically to belong to Hemingway alone. Michigan became all primitive, brutish, but above all naked, like the starkness of a Hemingway story. Paris was electric, crowded, but above all derisory like *The Sun Also Rises.* No one after Maurice Utrillo established such an intimacy with Paris streets as Hemingway the foreigner did just by the loving repetition of certain names—Rue du Cardinal-Lemoine, Place de la Contrescarpe. And there were always the knowing little references—"The dancing-club was a *bal musette* in the Rue de la Montagne Sainte Geneviève"—that established Hemingway's ability to make a part of his page anything that he had first absorbed as a stranger in Paris.

He was ambitious, he was shrewd, he seemed to have worked out in advance just what he needed to get from a place, and he became contemptuous of others as soon as he had learned it. So much command of experience belonged to an imperial race. Defying his Victorian parents, and a year out of high school, he put himself on the line, went to the Italian front as a Red Cross volunteer and got himself gloriously wounded. What other solidly middle-class boy from one of "our best families in Oak Park" could at nineteen have won for himself such lasting images of war, fright, and death?

And who but Hemingway would have so indelibly recorded his wounding as his moment of truth?

> Then there was a flash, as when a blast-furnace door is swung open, and a roar that started white and went red and on and on in a rushing wind. I tried to breathe but my breath would not come and I felt myself rush bodily out of myself and out and out and out and all the time bodily in the wind. I went out swiftly, all of myself, and I knew I was dead and that it had all been a mistake to think you just died.

From now on it was his war, war was his. Reading Tolstoy's Sebastopol stories while hunting in *Green Hills of Africa* made him think of riding a bicycle down the Boulevard de Sébastopol in the rain:

> And I thought about Tolstoy and about what a great advantage an experience of war was to a writer. It was one of the major subjects and certainly one of the hardest to write truly of and those writers who had not seen it were always very jealous and tried to make it seem unimportant, or abnormal, or a disease as a subject, while, really, it was just something quite irreplaceable that they had missed.

His wounding was a shock that went straight into Hemingway's early stories and fables of the war. *In Our Time* taught him to make set passages out of the body's response to a particular blow. Mastery lay in the moment's triumph over danger; in life as in art, Hemingway needed one deliberate trial of himself after another. He made a point of seeking out violence. Clearly accident-prone, he retained his ability to turn every new accident into the confrontation of something or someone. In his bilious last years he was to say that it was good for a writer in despair to hang himself and "then be cut down without mercy and forced by his own self to write as well as he can for the rest of his life. At least he will have the story of the hanging to commence with."

This need of risk, of the ultimate challenge, became something that only an international sportsman could buy for himself. In *Green Hills of Africa* (1935) he was still boasting to a chance acquaintance:

> "And you know what you want?"
> "Absolutely, and I get it all the time."

This was the mark of a special time and a particular ego. Only the florid buccaneers of the age of enterprise had talked that way. Hemingway's crushing sense of self sought not wealth but fame—absolute distinction, to be top dog, the undoubted original and pacemaker for literary prose in his time.

Writing was everything. And the journey that Hemingway undertook, the journey into the country of the dead that Ezra Pound idly and occasionally thought he was writing in the *Cantos*, made possible that extraordinary concentration of line and progression of effect that no matter how often we reread "The Battler," "Fifty Grand," "Big Two-Hearted River," can still make us hold our breath. No other American "in our time" so captured the actual physical element. No one else so charged up the reader, for no one else was so charged up by the act of writing itself.

> Nick walked back up the ties to where his pack lay in the cinders beside the railway track. He was happy. He adjusted the pack harness around the bundle, pulling straps tight, slung the pack on his back, got his arms through the shoulder straps and took some of the pull off his shoulders by leaning his forehead against the wide band of the tump-line. Still, it was too heavy. It was much too heavy.

So Hemingway caused "real" and "concrete" to become the first essentials in the act of writing. He put life back on the page, made us see, feel, and taste the gift of life in its unalloyed and irreducible reality. It may be that all we really have and know is our consciousness, that the alternative is something we know nothing about, that the livingness of being alive is the inescapable drama of our existence. Not many writers have incarnated this in their work, have emphasized the angle of their particular consciousness so that our experience of their work becomes as elemental as their own grasp of existence. To read Hemingway was always to feel more alive. The spontaneous reaction was pleasure from the cunning way sentences fall, from the bright echoing separateness of the words, from every picture a passage put into the mind. One was brought close to some exceptional vividness.

Of all the many things Hemingway appropriated, the most celebrated was his own experience. How he hammered any triviality into place, kept it luminous with his particular gift for shining in his own light! This was what he hungered for beyond anything else, what he kept from dying. With his particular talent for saving and treasuring his experiences, for turning life into the economy of art, he brought into his sacred circle many small things insubstantial and fugitive. It was typical of him to call them "rain" and to celebrate "rain" as what did not vanish when secured in the style of Ernest Hemingway.

His minute details bring us into a world dense but never thick like that of the great nineteenth-century novels—a world stark, each detail oddly magnified, so that the bombardment gives us a sense of being violated. Like many startling achievements of modernism, this can be felt first as pain. In

A Farewell to Arms there is the confrontation on the bank of the Isonzo between the Italian battle police and the officers separated from their troops in the retreat at Caporetto. The scene excites a quiver of terror when the questioning of the hapless officers is followed by their immediate execution. It is night. The lights being flashed by the battle police into face after face bring to mind the unnaturally bright faces of the condemned being shot by the light of torches in Goya's *Disasters of War*.

They took me down behind the line of officers below the road toward a group of people in a field by the river bank. As we walked toward them shots were fired. I saw flashes of the rifles and heard the reports. We came up to the group. There were four officers standing together, with a man in front of them with a carabiniere on each side of him. A group of men were standing guarded by carabinieri. Four other carabinieri stood near the questioning officers, leaning on their carbines. They were wide-hatted carabinieri. The two who had me shoved me in with the group waiting to be questioned. I looked at the man the officers were questioning. He was the fat gray-haired little lieutenant-colonel they had taken out of the column. The questioners had all the efficiency, coldness and command of themselves of Italians who are firing and are not being fired on.

"Your brigade?"

He told them.

"Regiment?"

He told them.

"Why are you not with your regiment?"

He told them.

"Do you not know that an officer should be with his troops?"

He did.

That was all. Another officer spoke.

"It is you and such as you that have let the barbarians onto the sacred soil of the fatherland."

"I beg your pardon," said the lieutenant-colonel.

"It is because of treachery such as yours that we have lost the fruits of victory."

"Have you ever been in a retreat?" the lieutenant-colonel asked.

"Italy should never retreat."

We stood there in the rain and listened to this. We were facing the officers and the prisoner stood in front and a little to one side of us.

"If you are going to shoot me," the lieutenant-colonel said, "please shoot me at once without further questioning. The questioning is stupid." He made the sign of the cross. The officers spoke together. One wrote something on a pad of paper.

"Abandoned his troops, ordered to be shot," he said.

The "picture" is certainly very distinct—and so is the paragraphing. The "fat gray-haired little lieutenant-colonel" is on that page forever, saying with perfect contempt, "Please shoot me at once without further questioning. The questioning is stupid." Hemingway certainly learned to parody Italian, Spanish, and French with affection and respect. *Stupido* is a word of perfect contempt. Generations of students, brought up on modernism as the latest (but not the last) academic tradition, have by now learned to speak of *reduction, foreshortening, irony* in order to indicate that Hemingway makes us see, brings us close to, that scene by the river. The *seeing* is all-important; Hemingway learned many things from painters and from extraordinarily visual war scenes in Stendhal, Tolstoy, Crane, that enabled him to get Caporetto just right. But the key to the scene is Hemingway's need to show that while the questioning and the shooting are mistaken, totally unjust, as hideously wrong as anything can be, this is what stoical men "in our time," like the fat little lieutenant-colonel, accept—because they will always be superior to the stupido.

Hemingway had many gifts. His greatest gift, the foundation of all his marvellous pictorial effects, was his sense of some enduring injustice, of some fundamental wrongness at the heart of things, to which an American can still rise, and which he will endure (and describe) as a hero. "There is a great disorder under heaven," the Chinese say. Today they draw political cheer from this, since masses oppressed for centuries learn resignation. Hemingway was an American from the Middle West, "the valley of democracy." He was brought up on the old American religion of the self-sufficient individual. He knew that the public world was pushing him and everyone else toward an abyss. But he still had a private code in the twenties that, as Lady Brett said in *The Sun Also Rises* about "deciding not to be a bitch," sort of replaced one's religion. When repeated often enough in the same tone of discovery, the code became one's politics. Of course the code did not survive into the thirties, the Hitler-Stalin era, and still another world war. What in the twenties was pronounced with so much startled self-approval as a form of conduct was really a lean, wary style of writing, Hemingway's style. This style thrived on "the disasters of war" but somehow saved a few exceptional people from destruction. It was all the law and all the prophets.

Hemingway's great teacher in Paris, Gertrude Stein, was as resentful of him when he became famous as he was of her for condescending to him as she did to everybody else. Unlike Hemingway, whose sense of himself was so imperious that he became violent when he felt himself slighted in the least, Stein was never "insecure." For the most part she operated so much on a personal and domestic level that even her early writing became as indistinct as the message from the other side at a séance. Unlike Hemingway, who always conflated the personal and the political, *his* style and *the* world, Stein talked with an aphoristic brilliance that she disdained to put into her writing. Better, much better, than her taking from a French garage owner (contemptuous of his mechanics) the saying that Hemingway put at the head of *The Sun Also Rises*—"You are all a lost generation"—was her saying that in the twentieth century nothing is in agreement with anything else.

Hemingway was born near the close of the old century and was fated to become one of the great expressers of enduring disorder in this century. His sense of incongruity was everything to him and came out as an uncanny intuition of stress, of the danger point, of the intolerable pressure level in life, personal and political. Women have their bodily fears and men have theirs; both relate to the sexual organs, to sexual vulnerability and respect. Perhaps Hemingway himself did not know just where and how a famously rugged, fearless, sometimes madly aggressive sportsman developed that special fear of violation and of mutilation—it is hinted at in the encounter with a hobo in "The Battler"—that he was able to project back on the world with a burning intuition of the *world's* inherent cruelty, danger, injustice. Sexual vulnerability is a universal condition that only a Hemingway could have concealed and yet mythologized in *The Sun Also Rises* and *Death in the Afternoon.* But in the mysteriously transforming interaction between Hemingway's bruised psyche and his masculine need always to sound *positive*—something extraordinary did result. His self-disapproval at being vulnerable at all had to be hidden, but his shock at not being allowed always to have his own way made him see the world as inherently treacherous. His easy American claim to power—especially over his own life—was constantly being limited and denied. The self remained intact. But wary, very wary, it had premonitions of war after war. Hemingway was not just being cocky when he put down writers who had not seen battle. Phlegmatic types never suffered and understood as he did. (Gertrude Stein was so vain that, living under Nazi occupation in France, she felt mysteriously protected—and she was.) Responding bitterly to accusations that he was "indifferent," Hemingway memorably responded in a letter, "These little punks who have never seen men street fighting, let alone a revolution . . . Listen—they never even heard of the events that produced the heat of rage, hatred, indignation, and disillusion that formed or forged what they call indifference."

II

Society, the body politic, the "world" that makes continually for war and social disorder, works as fiercely on people's unconscious and becomes their true intuitions. This often unhinges them without their recognizing the cause as politics or common fate.

Hemingway's attraction to violence, to hunting and fishing, to war—he saw a lot of war but was never a soldier—was not just a form of hell-raising and self-testing in the usual masculine way. It was a way of coming close to certain ordeals fundamental to his generation. From the beginning, because of his upbringing as a young Christian gentleman in a suffocatingly proper suburb of Chicago—Oak Park, "where the saloons end and the churches begin"—violences fascinated him as clues to what he graphically called "in our time." Like so many great modern writers, he was of solid bourgeois background and therefore knew that, morally, the bourgeois world was helpless.

Confronting danger everywhere, he made himself one with his time by running full tilt into everything that would bring a fresh emergency into his life. And everything certainly did. Gertrude Stein laughed in *The Autobiography of Alice B. Toklas* that for a man so professionally virile and athletic, Hemingway was certainly fragile. John Dos Passos was to say in *The Best Years* that Hemingway was always having to go to bed to recuperate from his many injuries. When he did not seek damage, it sought him. From boyhood on he suffered accidents that were grotesque in their violence toward this body they did not kill. As a boy, he fell and had a stick driven into the back of his throat, gouging out part of both tonsils. In 1918, when he was a Red Cross worker in Italy distributing supplies to soldiers, a mortar shell exploded more than twenty fragments into his legs; he was then hit twice by machine-gun bullets while carrying a more seriously injured man to the rear. As a young writer in Paris during the twenties, he was clipped on the forehead by pieces of a skylight that fell just as he was standing under it. In Wyoming in 1930, his car turned over and his right arm was pinned back by the top of the windshield and badly fractured, the bone sticking through the muscle. At another time, his brother Leicester reports, Hemingway shot a shark with a rifle, but the bullets split into several small pieces of hot lead that ricocheted into the calves of both his legs. In 1949, while duck shooting in the marshes near Venice, he got a bit of shell wadding blown into his eye, and a serious infection developed; in 1953 he crash-landed in

Africa, and the rescue plane that picked him up crashed and burned; when he reached medical aid at Nairobi (just in time to read his obituaries), his internal organs had been wrenched out of place, his spine was injured, and he was bleeding from every orifice.

It is absurd to separate Hemingway from his work. He pushed his life at the reader, made his fascination with death and danger the central theme in his many pages about bullfighting, sport, and war, brought the reader closer to his own fascination with violence and terror as a central political drama. His great gift was to locate repeated episodes of violence (so linked by some profound compulsion that we anticipated the shotgun suicide) in the Turks expelling the Greeks in the lacerating inter-chapters of *In Our Time,* in the horns perforating the bullfighter (so that all the internal organs were sliced through at once) in *Death in the Afternoon,* in the very impotence of Jake Barnes in *The Sun Also Rises* and Colonel Cantwell in *Across the River and into the Trees.*

One could go on, as Hemingway certainly did, from the early story "Indian Camp," in which the Indian husband in the upper bunk cuts his throat as the doctor in the bunk below performs a cesarian on his wife with a jackknife and sews her up with nine-foot tapered gut leaders, to the ridiculously inflated episodes in the posthumous *Islands in the Stream,* where Hemingway talks of going after German submarines all by himself. The point is that Hemingway was a soul at war. He wins our assent, perhaps now more than ever, because it is the "outside" world that is increasingly violent today. Hemingway may have been as big a braggart and egotist as ever lived, but he had the stamp of the true artist. His emotions were prophetic, his antennae were out to the truth. He knew that destruction is a god over our lives, that the fear of death shapes us, that without any belief in immortality there can be no expectation of justice, so that the whole ghastly century is beginning to look like one unending chain of murder and retribution.

Hemingway's greatest gift was to identify his own capacity for pain with the destructiveness at large in our time. The artist works by locating the world in himself. Hemingway did something more: he located in himself his century's infatuation with technology, technique, instruments of every kind. Hemingway was recognized as an original, he fascinated and magnetized, because his theme was the greatest possible disturbance. His own sense of this was cold, proud know-how, professionally detached and above all concerned with applying a systematic, consistent *method* to everything he described. Obviously one attraction of sport, war, bullfighting was that each called for the maximum concentration of technique. Hemingway was clever and informed and quick to tell you what he knew. He always made a point

of giving you in the midst of a story the exact name of a wine, the exact
horsepower of a machine, even the exact moment in Paris—remember Lady
Brett's entrance in *The Sun Also Rises*—when a woman appeared in a tight
sweater and skirt so that she looked like the sides of a yacht. "She started all
that."

Hemingway liked to write, as Nick Adams liked to make camp in "Big
Two-Hearted River," from technical detail to detail. He had grown up in
a world where men still travelled by horse, took care of their horses, repaired
things themselves, walked everywhere, often grew or shot their own food.
He believed in the work of one's own hands even to the point of usually
writing by hand. It was this that led him to his great discovery of what
painting could do for writers. Newspaper work for the *Kansas City Star* and
the *Toronto Star* had taught him the first basic: to write professionally is to
write *to* somebody else's mind, and you have to lay out all the facts in an
assured, flat, knowing manner without the slightest suggestion or indecision
or demonstrative emotion about what you know. You have to "reach the
reader," said managing editors, to write for a newspaper so that said reader
will distinguish Ernest M. Hemingway from a dozen other newswriters.

The paintings young Hemingway saw in France, most intimately at
Gertrude Stein's flat, 27 Rue de Fleurus, were spellbindingly the work of an
artist's own hand, of new theories of perception, of common physical materials. Nothing could have been more instantly pleasing to his imagination and
his native sense of things. Painting was the decisive experience for an American abroad; "Europe" could seem one great painting. Painting stimulated a
young reporter, already shrewdly aware of war and sport as the stuff of
literature, to think of writing as a method. Painting was to do more for
Hemingway than it was to do even for Stein, who in the end cared for
painters more than for painting. "Genius" and "personality" were to become
her topics. Stein could not draw at all and in fact had to leave Johns Hopkins
medical school because of this and other failures in observation. Her famous
Cézannes had been discovered and bought by her erratic brother Leo, her
Matisses by Michael and Sally Stein. She kept the family collection when Leo
became infuriated by cubism and stopped buying paintings. She depended
on painting for the mental impressions that were her specialty. Unlike Hemingway, she had little feeling for the sensuous world. Her great interest was
psychology, the "bottom truth" about anybody she met. Proceeding from
psychology to composition, she became fascinated by what she felt to be the
human mind as its own self-sufficient subject. "The human mind writes what

it is. . . . The human mind consists only in writing down what is written and therefore it has no relation to human nature."

Stein was a profoundly clever theoretician, a great aphorist and wit, and a true inventor of composition based on what she called "the continuous present." Without seeing her paintings, without listening to the infatuated conversation about painting at 27 Rue de Fleurus, Hemingway might not have become Hemingway at all. As *she* was jealously to charge in *The Autobiography of Alice B. Toklas,* Hemingway was a sedulous ape, an all-too-adept pupil of other people's ideas and methods. But her comparative indifference to the subject matter of painting and the way she took off *from* painting to emphasize for psychological purposes the authority of the eye gave Hemingway the advantage over her.

Stein was fascinated by the small particular difference that distinguished identically made objects, like her Ford car, from each other. Sentences were all sentences, but each sentence was itself. She believed that the single sentence is the key to writing, and she certainly practiced what she preached: "in composition one thing is as important as another thing." As Kenneth Burke was to say, we have been sentenced to the sentence. It was *sentences* she heard from her family's black retainers. As a very bright student in William James's psychology courses, she was on the track of the individual, self-contained statement as disclosure. She was to see the sentence as orphic revelation: hers! So a sentence could become the glowing unit of a page, the building block of literature. But she was arrogant, she saw herself as a sibyl without fear or reproach, and writing through the night (in the morning Toklas would worshipfully pick up and type the scattered scrawled sheets) she heedlessly wrote straight from the ear to the paper. Her last books, like Hemingway's last books, showed the expansion and disintegration of a style founded on conversation.

Stein's genius was for conversation and especially for listening to other people's conversation. What fascinated her in the "new" painting by Cézanne and Matisse was the fact that something, anything, could be done by a temperament sufficiently self-willed—the slashing lines and thickly encrusted colors, Matisse in particular with his use of color *as* line, the thick, joyously rhythmical color building up an impression totally sufficient to the design that would satisfy the eye. Every image is made up of minute particulars. Every particular is realized through the maximum concentration and toil. The world is built up from such particulars. As the cubists soon proved, an object is a form made up of inherent forms. We go from cube to cube, atom to atom, as nature did in the long creation of every living thing that makes up the whole.

Hemingway's approach to painting was more diffident but actually closer to its sensuous content and to his own delight in method. The difference between Stein and Hemingway can be seen even in their handwriting. Her letters were tall, sprawling, arrogantly sloppy, with the large telltale spaces between words that were characteristic of her reflective mind. His letters were close, carefully and slowly shaped. They remind me of Nick Adams making camp in "Big Two-Hearted River," another demonstration of Hemingway's own planned, anxiously careful, tidy assemblage of words as objects.

> He started a fire with some chunks of pine he got with the ax from a stump. Over the fire he stuck a wire grill, pushing the four legs down into the ground with his boot. Nick put the frying pan on the grill over the flames. He was hungrier. The beans and spaghetti warmed. Nick stirred them and mixed them together. They began to bubble, making little bubbles that rose with difficulty to the surface. There was a good smell. Nick got out a bottle of tomato catchup and cut four slices of bread. The little bubbles were coming faster now. Nick sat down beside the fire and lifted the frying pan off.

Of course the great precedent to all this, Hemingway acknowledged, was *Huckleberry Finn.* The passage in which Nick Adams packs his captured trout between layers of fern reminds one of Huck planning to escape his father. He methodically lists the things he has, the things he has gained, the things he is sure of.

> The old man made me go to the skiff and fetch the things he had got. There was a fifty-pound sack of corn meal and a side of bacon, ammunition, and a four-gallon jug of whiskey and an old book and two newspapers for wadding besides some tow. I toted up a load, and went back and sat down on the bow of the skiff to rest. I thought it all over and I reckoned I would walk off with the gun and some lines and take to the woods, when I run away. I guessed I wouldn't stay in one place but just tramp right across the country, mostly nighttimes, and hunt and fish to keep alive and so get so far away that the old man nor the widow wouldn't ever find me any more.

Hemingway was naturally drawn to painting in France because it celebrated homely natural materials—like the world he knew and wanted to write about. Although he had seen the pioneer collections of the Art Institute in Chicago, it was the double experience of writing English in France and of being daily stimulated by the streets, the bridges, the museums, by meeting Gertrude Stein, Ezra Pound, James Joyce, Ford Madox Ford, that helped to form this cunningly obedient listener into the powerfully under-cutting stylist that he became. Stein said: "One of the things I have liked all these years is to be surrounded by people who know no English. It has left me more intensely alone with my eyes and my English." That is what Hemingway felt; it is his marvellous representation of this vital early expe-rience that makes his Paris in *A Moveable Feast* so beautiful, though the book is wicked in its attempt to destroy Stein, Ford, and Fitzgerald and a downright lie in its underhanded description of the collapse of his marriage to Hadley. He does not say that when he became famous he became insup-portably arrogant. He was unknown, "poor and happy," in *A Moveable Feast*, but he became ferocious in the days of fame. Fame inflamed him more than liquor and turned Stein's obedient little "ape" into an inferno of unrelenting ego. It did not make him happy. Painting at least took him out of himself.

French painting did more for Hemingway than reinforce his Ameri-can passion for technique, for method, for instruments, for utensils. It gave him, as it did a whole generation of foreign artists in Paris, a sense of what Baudelaire called *luxe, calme et volupté*. Marc Chagall, another foreigner in Paris, said: "These colors and these forms must show, in the end, our dreams of human happiness." Hemingway lived a life of danger, near-catastrophe, and was inwardly ravaged by his attraction to danger and the boozy life he led in the company of sycophants all over the world; he became a victim of his own celebrity. He was attracted to the har-mony in painting as he was influenced by the direction it gave his imagi-nation.

One of the recurrent themes in his work is the rallying from discomfort to comfort, from danger to safety, from death to life, from ordeal to escape. He was as much a romantic about himself as he was a cold-eyed observer of the world at large. In fact, he was so savagely competitive and such a brutal antagonist to other people that the pastoral, harmonious, cuddly sensations he described were as vital to his existence as the seeking of danger. Painting, even the most violent-looking painting by those whom the French once called *les fauves*, wild beasts, usually subsides into a source of peace. You can look at a Cézanne in 1906 and walk away from it disturbed, but in 1926 you will not remember what once jarred you. When Leo Stein first went to the picture dealer Ambrose Vollard to look at the Cézannes that Bernard Beren-son told him about, he had to turn them up, one after another, from a dusty pile. Leo and Gertrude Stein, usually Leo, had to talk night and day to their friends to make them *see* these paintings. When the great Stein collection was exhibited at the Museum of Modern Art in New York, the room seemed to blaze with sunlight.*

Painting far more than writing suggests the actual texture of human happiness. Hemingway understood that; what excited him, as a writer, about painting was a promise of relief from civilization, a touch of the promised land. The Hemingway hero is usually alone in nature, and the landscape he sees (and will bring back in words) is in minute particulars unseen by anyone but him. Again and again in his work this often cruel writer shows himself to be an unabashed American romantic positively melting in the presence of BEAUTY. The opening lines of *A Farewell to Arms* cast a spell. They do not altogether make sense except as pure visual impressionism, repeated and echoing Hemingway's own effort to get these "impressions" down.

> In the late summer of that year we lived in a house in a village that looked across the river and the plain to the mountains. In the bed of the river there were pebbles and boulders, dry and white in the sun, and the water was clear and swiftly moving and blue in the channels. Troops went by the house and down the road and the dust they raised powdered the leaves of the trees. The trunks of the trees too were dusty and the leaves fell early that year and we saw the troops marching along the road and the dust rising and leaves, stirred by the breeze, falling and the soldiers marching and afterward the road bare and white except for the leaves.

If Cézanne's greatness lay in the removal of his subjects from the contingent world, this opening paragraph is an imitation of that removal. It is exclusively an impression from the outside, it rests within the eye of the beholder. As an impression it is static, for it calls attention to the beholder's effort to capture one detail after another rather than to the scene of war. As so often happens in Hemingway's prose forays into war, bullfighting, marlin fishing, hunting, there is an unnatural pause in the last sentence—"leaves stirred by the breeze"—a forced transition made necessary by "painting" the scene in words. We positively see the writer at his easel.

What Stein caught from painting—it was a literary idea—was the ability of the writer to call attention to each stroke. Hemingway said that writing is architecture, not interior decoration. When he turned from the obedient pupil into the world-famous Ernest Hemingway, he made a great point, in talking about his own writing through his contempt for other people's

---

*In 1959 I saw at the Hermitage in Leningrad postimpressionist paintings bought by Russian merchants in Paris in the early 1900s. After fifty years, they were still being brought up from the cellars. Looking at them propped up against sofas, I thought of Bergotte in Proust's *La Prisonnière*, seeing his first Vermeer and saying to himself, "That is how I ought to have written."

writing, of saying that they were "unreadable." *Readable* meant the reduction of the world to a line of glitteringly clear sentences. Ironically, Stein criticized his first writings as being *inaccrochable,* not hangable on a wall, not ready to be looked at. It was she, with her thousand-page soliloquies and meanderings, who turned out to be *inaccrochable.* She longed to have a great public, like Hemingway. When she and the GIs discovered each other in 1944, she would not let a single Brewsie or Willie go.

Hemingway had the magnetic gift of fame, of arousing attention with every word, that Stein bitterly missed. He had learned his lesson from her all too well. He had in fact learned to lasso the reader, to become his eyes and ears exactly as a Cézanne or a Matisse rivets attention, obliterates everything around it. This works better in Hemingway's marvellous stories, which are consistent, all "composition," every inch of the canvas filled, than in his novels. There he often stops the action to do some scene painting and is swaggeringly self-indulgent, both in self-portraiture and as a maker of beautiful effects.

A picture is an action that must fill up its available space. Stein was fascinated by the concentration that is behind all true painting. She was always telling Hemingway: "concentrate." He certainly learned to concentrate. The inter-chapters of *In Our Time,* which tell of condemned men being carried to the gallows in a chair because they have lost control of their sphincter muscles and German soldiers climbing over a wall and being potted one two three—"We shot them just like that"—showed that Hemingway was concentrating all right, concentrating on the reader. Hemingway influenced a whole generation of journalists to become pseudoartists, especially around *Time,* where every little article was called a "story" and was rewritten and rewritten as if it were a paragraph by Flaubert instead of the usual Luceite's overemphasized account of the personal characteristics of some big shot who had made the week's cover.

Eventually, Hemingway's influence began to influence *him* too much. The famous brushwork became bloated and sometimes suggested the relaxed intention that all good American writers seek *after* writing. But Hemingway at his best understood that a short story by its very compressiveness comes nearest a lyric poem or haiku in its total intactness. A novel is by tradition too discursive, epic, and widespread. Of all Hemingway's novels, *The Sun Also Rises* has the best chance of surviving, for it is more consistent in its tone, its scene, and even Hemingway's scorn than *A Farewell to Arms,* which veers between the sheerest personal romanticism and Hemingway's desire to give an essentially lyric cast to his observations of the Italian-Austrian front in World War I.

More and more in his big books Hemingway, for all his genius at intuiting the trouble spots and danger points in human existence, used his well-developed style as a lyric diversion from his increasing sense of being closed in. The old rugged individualist had somehow known from the beginning that the coming century was going to be war on the individual. That was the dark and even ominous climate of feeling—achieved in the fewest, somehow punitive words—he got so unforgettably into his great stories, especially "Big Two-Hearted River." This story sums up the Hemingway hero's courage and despair, his furthest need and his deepest fear, in a way that also sums up the Western American's virtually sexual encounter with Nature, his adoration and awe, his sense of being too small for it, his abrupt, unfulfilled confrontation with what once seemed the greatest gift to man, but somehow always threw *him* off.

Hemingway was always a deeply personal writer. The immediacy, sometimes the deliberate brutality, but above all his vulnerability to anxiety, rage, frustration, and despair, gave him a masterful closeness to his kaleidoscope of emotions. He was by turns so proud yet so often stricken a human creature that the reader again and again surrenders to him. For Hemingway makes you feel in painfully distinct human detail how much the world merely echoes the endless turmoil in the human heart.

> Ahead the river narrowed and went into a swamp. The river became smooth and deep and the swamp looked solid with cedar trees, their trunks close together, their branches solid. It would not be possible to walk through a swamp like that. The branches grew so low. . . .
> . . . He did not feel like going on into the swamp. He looked down the river. A big cedar slanted all the way across the stream. Beyond that the river went into the swamp.
> Nick did not want to go in there now. He felt a reaction against deep wading with the water deepening up under his armpits, to hook big trout in places impossible to land them. In the swamp the banks were bare, the big cedars came together overhead, the sun did not come through, except in patches; in the fast deep water, in the half light, the fishing would be tragic. In the swamp fishing was a tragic adventure. Nick did not want it. He did not want to go down the stream any further today.

Hemingway was a painfully complex man who was indeed as gifted and, yes, as "brave" as he claimed to be. He did his work. He hauntingly intimated on paper some fundamental conflicts that like all of us he did not resolve in the flesh. Especially not in the flesh. Nor did he realize these conflicts in his novels as the great novelists have done. He was too immature and self-absorbed, in the fashion of so many gifted Americans maddened by the gap between their talent and their vulnerability. What made Hemingway important, what will keep his best work forever fresh, was his ability to express a certain feeling of hazard that men in particular do not suffer any less because they go out of their way to meet it. Who is to say how much this sense of hazard, peril, danger, with its constant rehearsal of the final and perhaps only real battle—with death as the embodiment of a universe that is not ours alone, that may not be ours at all—who is to say how much Hemingway sought it out for his natural subject matter as much as it constantly whipped *him* to prove himself again and again? In Gregory Hemingway's memoir, he says that he felt

> relief when they lowered my father's body into the ground and I realized that he was really dead, that I couldn't disappoint him, couldn't hurt him anymore. . . .
>
> I hope it's peaceful, finally. But oh God, I knew there was no peace after death. If only it were different, because nobody every dreamed of, or longed for, or experienced less peace than he.

This is the truth about Hemingway that all the carousing and boasting could not conceal. Yet it is a truth that every reader recognizes with gratitude as being at the heart of the darkness that Hemingway unforgettably described: the sense of something irremediably *wrong.* Against this, Hemingway furiously put forth his dream of serenity, of Nature as the promised land, for which composition—the painter's word that he picked up as his ideal—suggested the right order of words in their right places. As Ford Madox Ford put it so beautifully in his introduction to *A Farewell to Arms,* "Hemingway's words strike you, each one, as if they were pebbles fetched fresh from a brook. They live and shine, each in its place. So one of his pages has the effect of a brook-bottom into which you look down through the floating water."

Nature as a nonhuman ideal has always been an American's romantic dream. All the great American landscape painters have always portrayed Mother Nature as too big for the solitary man on the cliff looking down. By contrast, as Malraux wrote in *Man's Fate,* painting to Orientals has been the practice of "charity." Charity is hardly what Hemingway found in the world or what he sought from painting. There is no charity in his writing at all, serenity on occasion, a rally, a promise of peace. He was a tough, sharp realist about other people, for in portraying himself so exhaustively, he portrayed us and the pitiless century into which we were born.

Retrospect, 1932:
The Twenties and the
Great American Thing

Art invariably grows out of a period when, in general, the
artist admires his own nation and wants to win its approval. This fact is not altered by the circumstance that
his work may take the form of satire, for satire is the subtle
flattery of a certain minority in a nation.

Show me a hero and I'll write you a tragedy.

FITZGERALD, *Notebooks*

I

In June 1932, a discouraged month and year in the history of the United
States, John Roderigo Dos Passos sat down in his Provincetown house at the
end of Commercial Street to write a preface to his antiwar novel of 1921, *Three
Soldiers,* published when he was twenty-five.

Three Soldiers was being reissued by the Modern Library, a reprint series so inclusively "modern" in its taste that Petronius's *Satyricon* was in it
along with Renan's *Life of Jesus* and John Reed's *Ten Days That Shook the
World.* The reissue of *Three Soldiers* was a tribute to Dos Passos's emerging
reputation in the 1930s as a solidly "social" novelist with distinctly radical
views. His trilogy *U.S.A.,* to be completed in 1936 with *The Big Money,* had
already taken shape with *The 42nd Parallel* (1930) and *1919* (1932). *There
would be no more lost generations!* In his preface, "Dos" responded to the
honor with heartfelt memories of the hopes with which he had written
Three Soldiers:

The memory of the spring of 1919 has not faded enough. Any spring is a time of overturn, but then Lenin was alive, the Seattle general strike had seemed the beginning of the flood instead of the beginning of the ebb, Americans in Paris were groggy with theatre and painting and music; Picasso was to rebuild the eye, Stravinski was cramming the Russian steppes into our ears, currents of energy seemed to be breaking out everywhere as young guys climbed out of their uniforms, imperial America was all shiny with the idea of Ritz, in every direction the countries of the world stretched out starving and angry, ready for anything turbulent and new, whenever you went to the movies you saw Charlie Chaplin. The memory of the spring of 1919 has not faded enough to make the spring of 1932 any easier.

But it *was* 1932, and American radicals were countering the national breakdown with militant new hopes of their own. Dos Passos, in the spirit of the thirties, dutifully went on:

Today, though the future may not seem so gaily colored or full of clanging hopes as it was thirteen years ago . . . we can at least meet events with our minds cleared of some of the romantic garbage that kept us from doing clear work then. Those of us who have lived through have seen these years strip the bunting off the great illusions of our time, we must deal with the raw structure of history now, we must deal with it quick, before it stamps us out.

The left-wing novelists of the thirties never matched Dos Passos's springy style and inner gaiety. But his contempt for the "romantic garbage that kept us from doing clear work then" was right in style and dominated left-wing literary thinking about the decade just past. By 1933 the great United States, with a quarter of its work force unemployed, thousands of people wandering the roads looking for a job, food, shelter, and a desperately pragmatic F.D.R. trying any stratagem with which to keep America together, was a country of punctured illusions and was virtually bankrupt. Roosevelt, who had not been superior to the speculative madness of the twenties, now decried the period as an "age of mammon, full of self-seekers."

If you travelled about the country as madly as John Dos Passos always travelled, and were sensitive to common, unliterary persons (unlike his friends E. Hemingway and e. e. cummings), you put them into your books. Dos Passos was not contrite about the "jazz age" like his friend Scott Fitzgerald, who by 1936 was regaling the readers of *Esquire* with the news of his "crackup." Nor was he so heavy-footed in the direction of Communism as Theodore Dreiser, whose *Tragic America* (1931), the usual writer's journey through depression America, would not replace *An American Tragedy* in the affections of those who obstinately respected Dreiser as a storyteller despite the great man's untrustworthy mind and derivative opinions. On the other hand, Dos Passos was not so smug as that great satirist of the American scene, H. L. Mencken, who never seemed to know that there *was* a depression, and who made light of Hitler as if he were just another redneck demagogue from the Deep South.

Dos Passos, though a distinctly upper-class product of Choate, Harvard, and the Norton-Harjes Volunteer Ambulance Service, and a diffident, elusive, elaborately hesitant character in public, was the grandson of a Portuguese shoemaker from the island of Madeira. The shoemaker's son, John Randolph Dos Passos, was born early enough in the nineteenth century to be a drummer boy in the Civil War, a dominating corporation lawyer in the palmiest days of the age of enterprise, and counsel to the American Sugar Refining Company when the Havemeyers controlled virtually all the sugar refined in the United States. He was a Republican stalwart, an authority on the law of the stock exchange, and the author of *Commercial Trusts: The Growth and Rights of Aggregated Capital.* "It is a primary object of every well-founded government to encourage the acquisition of individual fortunes."

The "early" Dos Passos, with his sardonic view of American capitalism and American character, had good reason to scorn official pieties. Born in a Chicago hotel room in 1896, Dos Passos was the illegitimate son of a forty-two-year-old Southern gentlewoman, Lucy Sprigg Madison, and the fifty-one-year-old John Randolph Dos Passos, who was a married man unable to divorce his Catholic wife. Lucy was the widow of a man named Madison, and until her son was sixteen—his birth was never registered—he was known as John Roderigo Madison. The father, a great figure in respectable business and political circles of the time, tried to hide his son's existence. Mother and son were forced to live abroad, and the son remained John Roderigo Madison for two years after his parents were finally married.

John Randolph Dos Passos, the self-made son of the Portuguese shoemaker, was an extraordinary character; whatever pains he inflicted on his isolated sensitive son, he was a godsend to a future novelist. It is easy to see why the novelist derided authority figures who resembled his innocently pompous father, why he was obsessed about American history, which immigrants' children used to consider the great romance. Lucy and little John Madison had to be kept out of the way. Dos Passos had even more of a "hotel childhood" than Henry and William James: mostly in Brussels and London, with furtive visits to the father in Washington and Virginia. It was from growing up among foreign languages that Dos Passos became convinced that ordinary speech is the index to a society; he was to say in his most famous book, "But mostly U.S.A. is the speech of the people." With his earliest feeling that "the voyages never stopped," he was to register in his prose not just the speedup of history but his Victorian mother's attempts to escape the "shame" of her son's illegitimacy. For the rest of his life Dos Passos was to think that the way out of any problem was to keep moving. The constant movement of his characters was to be more memorable than their personalities. The rapidly flashing, image-crackling style of physical sensation he developed not only came out of the painful but exciting unsettlement of his early years; it became his way, in the early Camera Eye sections of *U.S.A.* that relate the author's personal experiences, of blurring everything he still needed to conceal. Dos Passos clearly felt himself to be a special case, thrown into a succession of contradictory situations and scenes, to which a highly stylized literary response was sufficient. Even the "Jeffersonian" tracts he wrote after his disillusionment with the left, books that were politically simpleminded, were invigorated by the physical images that dizzyingly moved his style.

Dos Passos was a naturally impressionistic talent deeply influenced by painting and poetry; *U.S.A.* was to interpolate biographical and historical pictures of American life in free verse. Dos Passos would always depend on some fast-running mixture of prose and verse to project the many "pictures" of travel he carried in his head. At Harvard, he offered his famous teacher of composition, Charles T. Copeland, an exercise called "Trains: Fragments of Mémoires" (collage and the use of French words were a lifelong habit), in which he described endless travel as "the trembling joy that is akin to terror."

Dos Passos was later to write that his "continuously scuttling about the world was ridiculous—like a cockroach running away from the light." He had difficulty in talking to strangers but a gift for friendship with Europeans (and his literary peers in America) that somehow put him in the most eventful places at the most interesting times. The "cult of experience" so important to writers in America had no more anxious devotee than Dos Passos. Just out of Harvard in 1916, he roamed Spain, studying architecture. As a volunteer ambulance driver he saw French soldiers drugged with agnol, a combination of rum and ether, go into the most terrible battles. As a Red Cross driver in Italy, he met another Red Cross driver, Ernest Hemingway, who during the Spanish Civil War was to irritate Dos Passos into conservatism. Dos Passos was even in Russia just when certain days shook the world. He got into the army medical corps by persuading an examiner to let him memorize the eye chart, travelled back and forth between America and Europe during the most restrictive war conditions, got to the Near East with handy advice on where to go and whom to see from the famous explorer Gertrude Bell.

Dos Passos's career would have been nothing without what one of his last books called "Mr. Wilson's War." When Woodrow Wilson saved an exhausted England and France by taking America into the war, he certainly saved Dos Passos and his friends Cummings and Edmund Wilson from being safe and bored at home. Dos Passos, even in his last years among the Virginia gentry in Woodrow Wilson's native state, kept a grudge against the great war leader who separated America forever from its supposed age of innocence. There is a legend that Hemingway as a Red Cross worker on the Italian front once impersonated an American soldier in order to lull the war-weary Italians into the belief that the Yanks were already at the front. It was natural for Hemingway, Dos Passos, Cummings, Edmund Wilson to deride the rhetoric (penned by his very own hands) with which the president of the United States had told Congress that

> it is a fearful thing to lead this great peaceful people into war, into the most terrible and disastrous of wars, civilization itself seeming to be in the balance. But the right is more precious than peace, and we shall fight for the things which we have always carried nearest to our hearts . . . to make the world itself at last free.

But if "Professor Woodrow Wilson" (as Ivy League rebels regularly called him) had not thought and written in that imposing style, Hemingway and friends would not have formed *their* style in opposition to such public rhetoric. In *A Farewell to Arms,* published eleven years after the war ended, an Italian soldier-patriot protests to the cynical American hero: "What has been done this summer cannot have been done in vain." Our hero (it is never *his* war; he is just there for the experience):

> I did not say anything. I was always embarrassed by the words sacred, glorious, and sacrifice and the expression in vain. We had heard them, sometimes standing in the rain almost out of earshot, so that only the shouted words came through, and had read them, on proclamations that were slapped up by billposters over other proclamations, now for a long time, and I had seen nothing sacred, and the things that were glorious had no glory and the sacrifices were like the stockyards at Chicago if nothing was done with the meat except to bury it. There were many words that you could not stand to hear and finally only the names of places had dignity.

"You and me, Rinaldi," Frederic Henry says confidently to his surgeon friend, "we've made a separate peace." In the brilliantly satiric "The Body of an American" section of *1919* that sums up his outrage at "Mr. Wilson's War" by constructing the life and death of the Unknown Soldier who was buried at Arlington, Dos Passos concludes his description of the funeral rites by dryly adding, "Woodrow Wilson brought a bouquet of poppies."

Dos Passos had also made a separate peace, had fought a separate war. Only an American could have lived the Great War as if it were just material for a book. The ghastliness of the mass slaughter in Europe never meant so much to another ambulance volunteer, e. e. cummings. Cummings was imprisoned in "the enormous room" for saucily rejecting official demands that he dissociate himself from his friend Slater Brown, who had mocked the French in his letters home. Cummings made literary capital of his temporary imprisonment—from which he was rescued thanks to the intervention with Woodrow Wilson of Cummings's father, a minister and Harvard professor. Sergeant Edmund Wilson of the AEF medical corps was perhaps more troubled by the war itself; he certainly saw more corpses. Characteristically, Edmund Wilson in old age proudly noted in his journal that, always impelled to write protests against various officials of the United States government, he had written his first protest while still in the army. In *1919* an ambulance driver keeps crying out in astonishment and delight—"Fellers, this ain't a war. It's a god-damned whorehouse!" Dos Passos as an ambulance driver sailed for Europe in June 1917 "amid a lot of patriotic fanfare; a band playing a hula-hula on the docks and people dancing among the luggage at boatside and singing anti-German songs."

"Dos" was looking forward to a revolution in Europe. Although "the" revolution never came to Western Europe, the sense of new things opening up everywhere as "guys climbed out of their uniforms" helped to promote the irretrievable memory of the 1920s as a golden age for modern art, free expression, and American individualism. The century was new, Americans were still such a new factor in the world that they seemed new even to themselves. One thing they took for granted: America was unique. For those born in the last decades of the nineteenth century and now prepared to take over the twentieth, the buoyancy and confidence displayed by so many Americans at large were irresistible even to Europeans. Picasso said of his friends the Gerald Murphys (Dick Diver in *Tender Is the Night* had the anxious soul of the author but the physical appearance of Gerald Murphy) that with them it was *toujours festin*. The buoyancy and openness of Americans (especially in Europe) had led the painter Georgia O'Keeffe to situate the new century perfectly as the time of "the great American thing." The photographer and surrealist painter Man Ray, born of immigrant parents in Philadelphia under a very different name, was one of many Americans who felt that they had discovered themselves as artists in the Paris of the twenties.

In his old age, still sticking to Paris as the sacred ground where he had recreated himself, Man Ray gratefully remembered the postwar period:

> Everything about the place struck me as being just about right. I had the feeling that this was the best possible place in the world for the artist to live and work; and at the time it was. There was so much of the past and the immediate present brought together on one plane that nothing seemed left to be desired.
>
> And there was no feeling of being isolated from America.

No other group of working artists in Europe so cheerfully celebrated themselves as Americans did. Virgil Thomson from Kansas City commemorated the special moment of this, the joyous season, when he said of his infinitely joyful *Four Saints in Three Acts,* written to lines by Gertrude Stein, that the theme was "the working artist's working life, which is to say, the life we both were living. The work was to center about figures similar to Joyce and Stein, surrounded by disciples in their respective Parisian courts in the rue de l'Odéon and the rue de Fleurus." Thomson said in his program notes to the recording of *Four Saints* made in the 1970s, "I am sorry now that I did not write an opera with her every year. It had not occurred to me that both of us would not always be living." He called his composition "the acoustical support of a trajectory, of a verbal volubility that would brook no breaking." He wanted particularly to evoke "the inner gayety and mystical strength of lives consecrated to a non-material end."

Margaret Anderson from Indianapolis founded *The Little Review* in Chicago in 1914. It was the best of the transatlantic reviews in Paris until it expired there in 1929. Between these significant dates she published for the first time many now-classic pieces by Joyce, Eliot, Yeats, Pound, Hemingway, Stevens, Williams, Sherwood Anderson, Stein, Ford, Hart Crane—works that she was gladly given for nothing at a time when many of them were being rejected everywhere. This was a tribute to a spirited American who had founded *The Little Review* on nothing but her desire for "conversation with the best creative opinion" of her time. The conversation had to be with people as spirited as herself.

Margaret Anderson never lost the faith in "life as a work of art" that was fervently believed in, at least in Paris in the twenties, by Americans undistracted by children, anxieties about money, political despotism, racial persecution. "Life as a work of art" was a genuine conviction to certain extremely sensitive and unusual people for whom personal love and "perfect taste" added up to the ideal harmony usually achieved only in works of art. But as a daughter of the Midwestern business class in the 1890s, Margaret Anderson was important to defiant new Americans in the arts. They displayed the bristling independence, the striking self-confidence, the shrewd resourcefulness that founded so many innovations in art as well as in science, business, technology. The gumption, decisiveness, and intuition that maintained *The Little Review* made Margaret Anderson another of those American pioneers, in all fields, whose biographies Dos Passos wrote into *U.S.A.*

There was a gaiety on the part of writers and intellectuals that every woebegone later generation reads about with envy. The young Edmund Wilson, meeting Dos Passos at the offices of *Vanity Fair*, turned a somersault as they were waiting for the elevator. Dos Passos plunged into Greenwich Village with a special excitement about New York's brilliance and turmoil that led to his first notable novel, *Manhattan Transfer*. He joined the radical playwright John Howard Lawson in the New Playwrights Group and somehow wrote *The 42nd Parallel* between travels to Latin America and repeated forays into France and Spain.

The execution of Sacco and Vanzetti in 1927, the Great Crash, the powerful example of Edmund Wilson, were radicalizing influences on Dos Passos. (Wilson was undergoing the trial by Marxism that resulted in *To the Finland Station* but that would not last out Stalin's bloody career.) Dos Passos was never a Marxist, was never so interested in Marxism as Wilson became in the 1930s; he was always more "agin the system" than *for* anything in particular except personal freedom and the "working-class stiffs" whom he tended to romanticize. He clearly put himself into the homeless boy Vag—like himself, forever on the road—who opens and closes the *U.S.A.* trilogy. Dos Passos's scorn for the ruthless methods of American business, his growing regard for Jefferson and agrarian democracy, had less to do with political thinking than with his personal myths; he was always an upper-class man who had been deeply humiliated in childhood. Among the "typical" Americans with whom he peopled *U.S.A.*, he remained a loner ruthlessly dramatizing a mass society that was without the slightest tinge of love.

Dos Passos's digs at the Communist faithful at the end of *The Big Money* show that he was fast losing whatever sympathies he may have felt for Communist friends like John Howard Lawson. In the Spain of 1937 such sympathies were dashed forever by the secret murder of his friend José Robles, a Spaniard teaching at Johns Hopkins who had gone home to serve in the Loyalist Ministry of War during the Civil War. Like Dos Passos, Robles was averse to authoritarian methods; he was shot, apparently by Communist militia. Dos Passos suspected that Robles had protested political intervention by the Russians. In the feverish, overwrought Madrid of 1937, Dos Passos was horrified by the conspiracy of silence about Robles's fate; he came to hate Communists everywhere and the nefarious statist philosophy he saw behind the New Deal.

Dos Passos soon turned sharp right and wrote tracts, novels, biographies in an increasingly somber attempt to offer for the political salvation of a mass society the example of Thomas Jefferson and the aristocratic republicanism of the eighteenth-century Virginia planters. His one lasting book, *U.S.A.*, continued to dazzle readers as *the* American experimental novel of the 1920s. Dos Passos's fluid originality as a stylist, his ability to bring the whole new century into his trilogy, made it not at all ludicrous for Jean-Paul Sartre, a harshly demanding critic, to say in 1938: "Dos Passos has invented only one thing, an art of story-telling, and that is enough. I regard Dos Passos as the greatest writer of our time."

Whatever that meant in 1938—Hemingway in Toots Shors's talked about knocking Tolstoy out of the ring, but no one cared any longer about being or even naming "the greatest writer"—*U.S.A.* brilliantly succeeded as novel because it reflected the inventiveness of the twenties and the "religion of the word." Dos Passos had written a "collective" novel about "the march of history" with mass society as his protagonist. But with his gift for putting on display all the social events and stylistic novelties of his time, he made his trilogy seem the work of many American minds. In the gray and anxious 1930s, *U.S.A.* reflected the buoyant twenties as freshness and irreverence. It offered no bright hopes for the future, and the Communists were right to complain that it lacked a political direction—theirs. But like certain Elizabethan playwrights and Italian painters of the Renaissance, Dos Passos was less a great artist than one of several hinges operating the same great door. That door did open to "the great American thing." There would yet be an American literature and art equal to the promise of American life. Without Dos Passos's invention of his cinematic machine to record the momentum carrying an industrial mass society headlong into moral chaos, a good deal of our present sophistication in fiction, in the classy new journalism, even in the formal writing of American history, would not exist. Dos Passos was a writer whom other writers will always imitate without knowing it. He created a tight-lipped national style that was above all a way of capturing the million alternatives of experience in America.

The "big money" all around them certainly stimulated writers in the twenties. John O'Hara, who came in just at the end of his favorite decade and was never really a part of it—except in his envy—said that the development of the United States in the first half of the twentieth century was the greatest possible subject for a novelist. Scott Fitzgerald, O'Hara's icon, was fascinated by the rich but thought them as tragic as everyone else in this society of excess. Dos Passos, though he was swept along by American history, thought that the function of art was to resist.

John O'Hara just admired the rich; he did not have the intellectual breeding of the writers he admired. Nevertheless, it is a fact that the secret strength of the 1920s was the reliance on American power as the greatest of social facts. There was a respect for status, an innate sense of social class, that would distinguish Dos Passos and friends from those writers after another war—Saul Bellow, Ralph Ellison, Carson McCullers, Norman Mailer, Flannery O'Connor—who grew up in depression and war, who would never think the United States to be so unique in history as Hemingway and friends used to think it was. Writers emerging in the 1940s, too late to take in the legends of America's special destiny, were quickly persuaded that history sooner or later becomes the same. And all history is essentially obscure and problematical, in some ways too "cunning" ever to be fully understood by the individual novelist, who can no longer feel that history is on his side— that *he* can depend on history to hold him up, to supply him effortlessly with material, to infuse him with the vitality that only confidence in one's subject can.

Dos Passos was still in the groove of Henry James's firm belief that "the novelist succeeds to the sacred office of the historian." The old faith that History exists objectively, that it has an ascertainable order (if no longer a purpose), that it is what the novelist most depends on and appeals to, that History even supplies the *structure* of the novel—this is what distinguishes the extraordinary invention that is *U.S.A.* from most novels published after 1940. And it is surely because History as order—to say nothing of History as something to "believe" in—comes so hard to later writers that Dos Passos sometimes resembles one of those early movie directors resurrected for his "technique" at the Museum of Modern Art.

Most oddly for someone with his "esthetic" concerns, Dos Passos in *U.S.A.* was sympathetic to the long tradition of radical dissent in America. *The 42nd Parallel* opens on the story of Mac, a typically rootless Wobbly and "working-class stiff" of the golden age of American socialism before 1917. *The Big Money* ends on the struggles of Mary French (and John Dos Passos) to save Sacco and Vanzetti in 1927. To round out his trilogy when it was finally published in a single volume, Dos Passos added, as preface and epilogue, his sketches of the young man, hungry and alone, walking the highways. Vag, the American vagrant, expresses Dos Passos's fascination with the alienated, the outsider, the beaten, the dissenter: the forgotten in American history (with whom he would finally include Thomas Jefferson). Mac, the American Wobbly and drifter at the beginning of *U.S.A.*, is as much an expression of what has been sacrificed to American progress as Mary French, the middle-class Communist, is at the end of the last book. These solitaries, along with the young man endlessly walking America, frame this enormous chronicle of disillusionment with the American promise. The loner in America, the homeless like himself when young, interested Dos Passos as examples (not as fully exposed, interesting individual souls) long before he became interested in the American as protester. And despite his revulsion from the radical-as-ideologist, the Communist-as-policeman (at the end of *The Big Money*, the lonely Mary French identifies with a Stalinist orthodoxy to which she will fall victim), Dos Passos remained fascinated with the true dissenter, whether on the highway or, like Thomas Jefferson, alone in the White House.

Although Dos Passos's sympathies, at least in *The 42nd Parallel*, were clearly with radicals who were off the main track, he did not particularly like them. It was inventors like the Wright brothers, scientists like Steinmetz, intellectuals of the highest creative ability like Veblen, politicians with rare moral courage like La Follette, who became the heroes of his "biographies" in *U.S.A.* And rousing as Dos Passos's prose stanzas were in style, even these heroes remained *careers*. There are no such heroes and heroines among the fictional characters of his novel; they are mediocre, futile, forgettable. The tonic edge of *U.S.A.*, its stylistic dash and irony, its gay inventiveness, finally reflect Dos Passos's own practicality in getting down the sweep of the national existence in our century. The people are just case histories—as more and more Americans are to themselves. But Dos Passos's own sense of his art as something new is one of the great themes of the books—a tribute to the original structure of the novel.

What Dos Passos created with *U.S.A.* was in fact another invention—another American *thing* peculiar to the openness and stress of American life, like the Wright brothers' airplane, Edison's phonograph, Luther Burbank's hybrids, Thorstein Veblen's investigation of the leisure class, Frank Lloyd Wright's first office buildings. All these fellow inventors are celebrated in *U.S.A.* We soon recognize that Dos Passos's contraption, his new kind of novel, is in fact (reminding us of Frank Lloyd Wright's self-dramatizing Guggenheim Museum) the greatest character in the book itself. We find that our primary pleasure in the book is in its scheme.

A real ingenuity went into *U.S.A.* Dos Passos invented a remarkable tool for evoking the simultaneous frames of existence. History in the most tangible sense—what happened—is obviously more important in Dos Passos than the people to whom things happened. The matter of the book is always the representative happening and person, the historical moment illustrated in its catchwords, its songs, its influences, above all in its speech. What Dos Passos wanted to capture above anything else was the echo of what people were saying, exactly in the style in which *anyone* might have said it. The artistic aim of his novel was to catch the litany, the tone, the issue of the time in the voice of the time, the banality, the cliché that finally becomes the voice of mass opinion. The voice that might be *anyone's* voice reduces human uniqueness to the vibrating resemblances of history "in our time." All becomes newsreel. In the flush of Wilson's New Freedom in 1913, Jerry Burnham the professional cynic says to Janey Williams, "I think there's a chance we may get back to being a democracy." Mac and his comrades talk about "forming the structure of a new society within the shell of the old." Janey Williams's "Popper" grumbles, "I don't trust girls nowadays with these here ankle-length skirts and all that." Eveline Hutchins, who will find life just too dreary, thinks early in the book, "Maybe she'd been wrong from the start to want everything so justright and beautiful." Charley Anderson, leaving the sticks, thinks, "To hell with all that, I want to see some country."

1919, the second volume of the trilogy, is sharper than *The 42nd Parallel*. The obscenity of "Mr. Wilson's War" is its theme, and since the war is the most important political event of the century, Dos Passos rises to it with a brilliance that does not conceal his fury behind it. His contraption is running better with practice. Apart from the book's unforgettable ironic vibrations as a picture of waste, hypocrisy, debauchery, *1919* (Dos Passos growing into his style) shows History as a bloody farce, now unspeakably *wrong*, a mockery of the hopes associated with the beginning of the century. The fictional and historic characters come together on the same plane. One character is both "fictional" and "historic": the Unknown Soldier. He is fictional because no one knows who he is; yet he was an actual soldier, picked at random from so many other dead soldiers. The symbolic corpse has become for Dos Passos the representative American. His interment in Arlington Cemetery Dos Passos blazingly records in "The Body of an American," the prose poem that ends *1919* and is the most brilliant single piece of writing in the trilogy:

> they took it to Châlons-sur-Marne
> and laid it out neat in a pine coffin
> and took it home to God's Country in a battleship
> and buried it in a sarcophagus in the Memorial Amphitheater in the
>   Arlington National Cemetery

and draped the Old Glory over it
and the bugler played taps

What above all else invests *1919* is the contrast of the official and popular idealism with the hysterical hedonism of young gentlemen in the ambulance service. The echoes of popular speech are now our last ties with the doomed. This monument to a generation sacrificed is built up out of those mythic quotations and slogans that make up the book in its shattering mimicry. "In Paris they were still haggling over the price of blood, squabbling over toy flags, the river-frontiers on relief maps"; "tarpaper barracks that stank of carbolic"; "the juggling mudspattered faces of the young French soldiers going up for the attack, drunk and desperate, and yelling *à bas la guerre, mort aux vaches, à bas la guerre*"; "an establishment where they could faire rigazig, *une maison propre, convenable, et de haute moralité*"; "did Meester Veelson know that in the peasants' wargrimed houses along the Brenta and the Piave they were burning candles in front of his picture cut out of the illustrated papers?"

The Versailles Peace Conference is reduced to the style of Dos Passos's generation—"Three old men shuffling the pack, dealing out the cards."

Woodrow Wilson is caught forever when he says in Rome, "It is the greatest pride of Americans to have demonstrated the immense love of humanity which they hear in their hearts." Dos Passos's mimicry is brought to a final pitch of indignation in the person of the Unknown Soldier: *"Say feller tell me how I can get back to my outfit."*

He *is* anybody—and (as Dos Passos thought in 1932) everybody. In "The Body of an American" we can see that this is not so much a novel of a few lives as it is an epic of the mass society that has replaced "our storybook democracy." In other famous American books about democracy—*Representative Men, Leaves of Grass, Moby-Dick*—the subject is that dearest of all American myths, the self-made man as hero. Unlike these great romantic texts of what Whitehead called the "century of hope," *U.S.A.* does not raise any of its characters to hero. Dos Passos's subject is the degradation of democracy into mass society, of politics into sociology. His conviction is that the force of circumstances—call it the State, and "war is the health of the state"—is too strong for the average man, who may never rise above mass culture, mass superstition, mass slogans.

Completing his trilogy in 1936 with *The Big Money,* an account of the boom, Dos Passos portrayed a society gone mad with greed. The only fictional character in *The Big Money* who gets our respect is Mary French, the doctor's daughter and earnest social reformer who becomes a fanatical

Communist in her rage over Sacco and Vanzetti. The emotions of the Sacco-Vanzetti case provide Dos Passos with his clearest and most powerful memories—"*all right we are two nations.*" But Mary French is giving her life to the Communist Party. The chips are down; the only defense against the ravages of our century is personal integrity.

U.S.A. was distinguished by its clarity, its strong-mindedness, the bold and sharp relief into which it put all moral issues, all characterizations—all human destiny in America. There were no shadows in the book, no approximations (except of individual character), no fuzzy outlines. Everything was focussed, set off from what was not itself, with that special clarity of presentation which Americans valued above all else in the arts of communication. Yet by the end of his book Dos Passos had made it clear that although the subject of his book was democracy itself, democracy had meaning for him only through the superior man, the intellectual-elect, the poet who can never value what the crowd does. The philosophy behind *U.S.A.* was finally at variance with its natural interest, its subject matter, its greatest strength—the people and the people's speech. *U.S.A.* turned out to be a book at war with itself. It was bright with the artistic confidence of the twenties and always so distinct in its effects as to seem simple in its values. Its America was finally all external. Not a single character Dos Passos imagined mattered to him in the slightest. When he was through with the radical mood, he was ready for no other American mind and hero but Thomas Jefferson. Mass society now equalled America—and modern America was Dos Passos's adversary. What was begun with the high spirits of "Mr. Wilson's War" was concluded with the energy of disenchantment. Dos Passos wrote like a stranger in his own country.

11

Second Lieutenant Francis Scott Key Fitzgerald (Princeton '17) never made it overseas during "the late unpleasantness." That was only one of his many losses, chagrins, and heartbreaks in a career that resembled a cometlike sweep (with final descent) through the American heavens. His career was peculiarly public, for almost everybody who admired his writing came to read both life and work in the same light—the light that Fitzgerald trained on himself. With his special feeling that he was handsomer, more gifted, more open to life than any other man in sight (but the gods smiling on him were really competitive Americans), Second Lieutenant Fitzgerald never forgot that he had actually been marched up the gangplank to a transport—and had been marched down again. At Princeton he could not hope to compete with football heroes like the immortal Hobie Baker or the star of his own day who *wearing a bloody bandage around his head kicked a goal from behind his own goal post.* Blond and handsome as Fitzgerald was, with the famous blue-green eyes and drooping eyelashes (to say nothing of his being eager, voluble, gifted), he was only five foot eight and slight, and he "took things hard." The slightest mishap was a loss that made him undergo everything "Wellington felt at Waterloo." He was always more charged up than the occasion seemed to warrant. He could put a "presentiment of disaster" into the slightest short story. The real disasters were to fall on him in carloads. But even when he was reciting his "crack-up" in *Esquire* to the jeers of the many who hated him for his talent, he saw himself in the best light, the right light. By "taking things hard," he wrote, he created "the stamp that goes into my books so that people can read it blind like Braille."

He did not get to Europe until *This Side of Paradise, Flappers and Philosophers, Tales of the Jazz Age, The Beautiful and Damned*—all published in 1920–22—had made him newsworthy, luridly successful, and the voice of the "jazz generation." He had had to be successful, he wrote in the bitter thirties, in order to win the girl. He won the girl—a wife amazingly his spiritual twin, so talented, spoiled, endlessly driven, and demanding, like Fitzgerald himself, that they seemed born to excite and destroy each other. Sensation was necessary to him; Zelda, like the bottle, provided continual sensation. But it was also typical of his respect for his craft that he was able to begin the novel that first made him famous, *This Side of Paradise*, while sitting on cracker barrels at an officers' training camp in Kansas. Near the end of his life he was to produce his most deeply felt novel, *Tender Is the Night* (1934), while struggling against a mountain of debt, his notoriety as a drunk and a has-been, and his despair over his schizophrenic wife, who was institutionalized until her death in a fire. Just before he died in Hollywood, he was doggedly writing at the uncompleted *The Last Tycoon*. Edited by his classmate Edmund Wilson (who had never fully appreciated him before) and published in 1941 in half-skeletal form, it proved to be subtler about the social facts in Hollywood and more luminous and sharp-edged in its creation of individual character than anything else in sight.

Fitzgerald was certainly dogged—in the use of his talent, as much as in throwing his life away. His doggedness as a writer was like his wildness in the pursuit of pleasure, like his flickering sense of doom, like the "presentiment of disaster" he was so proud of getting into a story. In the twenties he felt unlimited, sacred to himself. Everything that happened to him seemed a release into the great world as well as a kind of early warning system. He saw himself as the glowing center of a period distinctly made for him—and one that by the same token was treacherous, like the sudden evil in a fairy tale. Fitzgerald's burning sense of self, with all the drama this brought to his legendary rise and fall, was not unusual among American writers. It was paralleled by many a modern prima donna of the American novel, from Mark Twain to Hemingway and Thomas Wolfe. They reacted on each other with mutual fascination and revulsion; being a *novelist* in the twentieth century could make everything about another writer not only unwelcome but positively repellent.

What made Fitzgerald stand out, even in the personalized twenties, was such a vehemence of self-absorption and self-assertion as to make him feel that he had created himself. He was to say of his most famous character, Gatsby, that he was his own Platonic conception of himself. The ultimate loneliness of Gatsby pursuing his impossible dream was Fitzgerald's unmistakable omen of what so much illusion, so much "unlimitedness"—in the mind alone—did to that precious sense of self that was one's whole life and every resource.

But as Fitzgerald also made clear in his books, he had been born into an age that assisted every illusion. Just as he was the central subject and best historian of his personal drama, so he instantly found an audience that, like his wife, seemed a correlative of himself. When he died a "failure" in 1940, many of his books were out of print. But with his genius for symbolization, he nailed history to himself even in death. Not only did he become a legend as writer, man, and frantic lover of his own wife; *Gatsby* and *Tender,* both infinitely readable, sank so deeply into the national consciousness that they came to seem not just "personal" but an allegory as well as a scenario of American fortune.

How did Fitzgerald the "spoiled child," the famously immature young wastrel of the twenties, manage to get such a hold of his readers, then and long after his death, that certain lines, passages, scenes in his novels became not just favorite quotations but unforgettable attachments to one's own life?

A breeze blew through the room, blew curtains in at one end and out the other like pale flags, twisting them up toward the frosted wedding-cake of the ceiling, and then rippled over the wine-colored rug, making a shadow on it as wind does on the sea.

The only completely stationary object in the room was an enormous couch on which two young women were buoyed up as though upon an anchored balloon. They were both in white, and their dresses were rippling and fluttering as if they had just been blown back in after a short flight around the house.

. . .

> There was music from my neighbor's house through the summer nights.
> In his blue gardens men and girls came and went like moths among the
> whisperings and the champagne and the stars.

It was because he "cared" so much but never slopped over. He had a
talent for plot that fell into melodrama; he knew how to objectify, frame, and
even satirize the very figure, his great Gatsby himself, who carried the weight
of so much yearning for the green light at the end of Daisy's dock. The
period, with all its dreamlike extensions of the self, was certainly his objective
correlative. Fitzgerald became the twenties and the twenties became a version of F. Scott Fitzgerald. He put himself radiantly on the map of his time,
stretched all his caprices across the American landscape. Now, when no one
(especially no one and his wife) would think of riding on top of a taxi or
throwing himself into the fountain at Union Square as well as the one in
front of the Plaza, a later generation reads with envy, stupor, disbelief, about
the kind of assertiveness and self-aggrandizement, the sheer display of "temperament," that went with the period.

But then Scott Fitzgerald from St. Paul remains the only Proust of
luxurious upper-class landmarks in New York like the Plaza Hotel. New
York was dreamland to Fitzgerald. It represented his imagination of what is
forever charming, touched by the glamour of money, romantically tender,
and gay. No writer born to New York's constant pressure has ever associated
so much beauty with it—can ever think of New York as the Plaza Hotel.
Fitzgerald felt about New York what a man might feel about a woman too
exciting to be trusted. New York was the pleasure capital, the fulfillment of
all possible dreams in St. Paul—New York was much more beautiful to
Fitzgerald than was Paris. But by the same token it was as unreal as Gatsby's
too-glamorous life on Long Island, as subtly corrupt and even as canniballike
as Meyer Wolfsheim's cuff links of human molars, Meyer Wolfsheim describing (over "a succulent hash") the murder of the gambler Rosenthal.
"Then he went out on the sidewalk, and they shot him three times in his full
belly and drove away."

Fitzgerald never wrote very much about St. Paul, and he certainly never
wrote about it as brilliantly as he did about New York and Long Island in
The Great Gatsby. He had the feeling for the textures and lights of the great
metropolitan glitter that the enraptured provincial once got from the great
New York feast. No wonder that Fitzgerald wrote of "the enchanted metropolitan twilight," of forms leaning together in taxis, of New York on summer

afternoons as "overripe, as if all sorts of funny fruits were going to fall into your hands," of blacks in cream-colored limousines being driven by white chauffeurs across the Queensboro Bridge. For Fitzgerald all paradoxes were just spectacles. The name of the American dream was New York.

What is most striking about Fitzgerald in the twenties is his alliance with its élan vital. It was one of his boasts and premises—his and Zelda's—"never to be too tired for anything." He had an old-fashioned gift for hero worship, a sense of the ideal, that led him to say to an incredulous Edmund Wilson when they were still at Princeton, "I want to be one of the greatest writers who ever lived, don't you?" When Joseph Conrad visited the United States and was secluded on the Doubleday estate, Fitzgerald was unable to see him but, humble as Gatsby, waited on the lawn for the merest sight of the great man.

European writers and artists in the twenties, many of them far deeper and more comprehensive in their talent, not so everlastingly "personal" as Fitzgerald, never achieved (or wanted) so much identification with a *period*. But the twenties were America's reprieve from puritanism and provincialism, or so Mencken led his superior readers to believe. Mencken had a spectacular ability to turn into personal "prejudices" his own prose comedy of the American Scene: " 'If you find so much that is unworthy of reverence in the United States, then why do you live here?' 'Why do men go to zoos?' " The offhandedness, a delight in destructiveness and even in sadism, were to mark the buffoonery of Dada, the music-hall humor of the Brecht-Weill period in Berlin, the sudden (and soon eclipsed) tomfoolery even of Russian artists in their one brief period of "experiment" just after the revolution. What was being attacked was the bourgeois nineteenth century and the "fixed thing" that D. H. Lawrence called Victorianism. Fitzgerald "adored" the rich because he needed them for the comedy of manners that would show them up at the end. The Europeans knew that after such a war, as only they had lived through, a new order was inevitable. Barbusse and Brecht became Communists, Céline (like Mussolini and Hitler, of the same "front generation") a Fascist. The "men of 1914" found their inspiration, their language, much of their audience, in the recall of the trenches that never left a generation. Those who fought and bled on the soil of their own country, like the French, would never forget such scenes as La Ravine de la Mort at Verdun. Though most of it was in French hands, it was enfiladed by a German machine gun at each end, which exacted a steady toll—on corpses. Day after day the German "heavies pounded the corpses in this gully, until they were quartered, and re-quartered; to one eye witness it seemed as if it were filled with dismembered limbs that no one could or would bury. . . . The compressed area of

the battlefield became an open cemetery in which every square foot contained some decomposed piece of flesh."*

The violence of 1914–18 seeped, just a little, into every American writer
who (unlike Dreiser or Sinclair Lewis) experienced the war as the great
adventure of his generation. Europe in its national savagery was just one part
of that adventure and of a writer's initiation. In *Tender Is the Night* Dr. Dick
Diver, who found in the war his chance to train as a psychiatrist in Switzerland and no more knew the war than the Scott Fitzgerald who wistfully
craved "material," takes his new love, Rosemary Hoyt, on a tour of the
battlefields. He grandly—too grandly!—tells the "child" what it was all
about:

> "All my beautiful lovely safe world blew itself up here with a great gust of
> high explosive love," Dick mourned persistently. "Isn't that true, Rose-
> mary?"

And earlier:

> "See that little stream—we could walk to it in two minutes. It took the British
> a month to walk to it—a whole empire walking very slowly, dying in front
> and pushing forward behind. And another empire walked very slowly back-
> ward a few inches a day, leaving the dead like a million bloody rugs. No
> Europeans will ever do that again in this generation."

Mourning persistently as he croons his litany over fighting he never saw,
Dick Diver historically proclaims his failure as a man and his submission to
the rich, crazy wife whose real attractiveness for him has been in his ability,
as a physician, to take her over. Of course she takes him over. Dr. Diver on
the subject of war is as fancy as the casualness which Nick Carraway and
Gatsby exchange in chapter 3 of *The Great Gatsby*.

> "Your face is familiar," he said, politely. "Weren't you in the First
> Division during the war?"
> "Why, yes. I was in the Twenty-Eighth Infantry."
> "I was in the Sixteenth until June nineteen-eighteen. I knew I'd seen you
> somewhere before."

The tone of this is pure swank—as many far-distant peaks of American
status were for Fitzgerald, though he invariably found the right social tone
for his own wistfulness. Compare this with the scene in Robert Graves's
Goodbye to All That in which the orderly bearing the necessary ration of rum
to the troops is trodden into the ground because he falls with the drink; the

---

*Alistair Horne, *The Price of Glory: Verdun 1916*, 1979.

scene in Céline's *Journey to the End of Night* in which Bardamu describes the decapitation of the sergeant in the road just as war begins. Fitzgerald's war is a bit of a joke, a "phantom" like Jay Gatsby, who was real only as the Platonic conception of himself.

Still, no one caught the uproar of the great American party in the twenties as Fitzgerald did. How could a period be epitomized as an unending party? What was it about "Mr. Wilson's War," as some wild joy from it seeped into the twenties, that made mischievousness, provocation, "smartness" so important to this generation? Only the dissociation produced by alcohol could carry people beyond their old limits. (When he tapered off in later periods, Scott Fitzgerald's idea of sobriety was to consume thirty bottles of beer a day while working.)

What was it about the twenties that made Fitzgerald picture an even heavier drinker, Ring Lardner, drinking all night in a slow, methodical effort to destroy himself? Obviously the twenties did seem to many gifted people a "release" from private bonds. It was a period in which widespread poverty (in the wrong class) found no interest, in which the poor had no one to identify with, in which the editor of *The Dial* apologized to James Joyce for America's "Presbyterian Post Office." Much of the "release" was an expression, at last out in the open, and in concert, of that scepticism which had been filling up the consciousness of the "elect" ever since the dying of the old gods. And in the twenties the elect were at last acceptable to a middle-class audience that had not been "sophisticated" before. That audience was not created by writers, but the new writers bolstered its scepticism and gave status to its self-regard. Walter Lippmann complained of the "modern" period that "it is useless to command where there is no one to obey," but Lippmann the Freudian and ex-liberal had the influence of an Emerson in this period. The "booboisie" consisted of everybody who did not enjoy the raillery of Lippmann, Mencken, Sinclair Lewis, Theodore Dreiser—and Scott Fitzgerald.

Fitzgerald, more than Mencken or Hemingway or Dos Passos, loved America and attached himself to its myths. (No one else in his generation so seriously took American history as *his* history.) At the same time, he had this extraordinary and perhaps self-destructive gift of feeling himself to be the center of the universe and so a marked man. He was the reason for everything in sight yet was the wallflower-observer; he was Frank Merriwell on the mound yet was a half-Irish, ultimately dubious "outsider." He was the center of things and its everlasting margin.

So much doubleness was irresistible to Americans and was irresistibly American in an age whose scepticism had by no means replaced the native romanticism. The epigoni of the modern movement featured the ironic personality—the man eager to display his critical sense, his intellectual edge and inviolable aloofness. Some withholding of oneself became the essential mark of the "new intellectual." Only a superb if raddled artist like Scott Fitzgerald could "in an age of mammon" have been so generous with himself as to equate desperately needed energy with "emotional capital." Only an American would have equated best-sellerdom with "success" as a writer. But only a Scott Fitzgerald living so much on his psychic resources would in his "decline" during the 1930s have talked so much about "emotional bank-ruptcy," of having "invested" in another human being. The importance of "vitality" was that the world rewarded it. Zelda said right after their marriage that it seemed to put them into "the great, shining stream of life."

Despite all the rueful sounds Fitzgerald was to make in *The Crack-up* about wasting and spending in the twenties, his heyday was distinctly a period of joy if not of hope. There was joy because people who had often felt out of things, like Scott Fitzgerald, were now in the "big money" and were spending it, "as if," the envious and resentful grumbled, "there were no tomorrow." There was joy because the war-liberated ex-puritan Ameri-can self from bitterest poverty in Minnesota could now, like Gatsby, buy as many shirts, and in as many colors, as his heart desired. (When Daisy Buchanan in Gatsby's bedroom laughed and cried over Gatsby's many shirts falling in the air, she came nearer to loving Gatsby than she ever would again.) And there was joy in this heady new American weather because the self seemed unlimited in its possibilities, its pleasures, its sense of itself.

Not for the twenties was it "the century of the common man"—common because always being manipulated. Before the Great Depression, Hitler, Stalin, the new Technological Revolution, the Holocaust, the heartlessness of mankind was taken for granted, not "the banality of evil." The protracted existence of mankind was not in question, nor was the value of existence itself. In the early 1960s Evelyn Waugh confided to his diary the need to "abjure the realm; to make an interior act of renunciation and to become a stranger in the world; to watch one's fellow countrymen, as one used to watch foreigners, curious of their habits, patient of their absurdities, indiffer-ent to their animosities—that is the secret of happiness in this century of the common man."

The greatest writers of the century had begun with the crisis of the thirties to abjure the realm indeed—in contempt for humanity. Eliot as editor of *The Criterion* thought he had to choose between Communism and Fas-cism, and he favored Fascism. Yeats said proudly, what we are preparing here, behind our screen of bombs and smoke . . . [is] a substitution of the historical sense for logic. The return will be painful and perhaps violent but many educated men talk of it and must soon work for it and perhaps riot for it. . . .

Politics are growing heroic. . . . A Fascist opposition is forming behind the scenes to be ready should some tragic situation develop. I find myself constantly urging the despotic rule of the educated classes. . . . It is amusing to live in a country where men will always act. Where nobody is satisfied with thought.

The Fascist countries know that civilization has reached a crisis, and found their eloquence upon that knowledge. . . . The danger is that there will be no war, that the skilled will attempt nothing, that the European civilization, like those older civilizations that saw the triumph of their gangrel stocks, will accept decay.

The commonest saying among "post-modernist" writers occurs in Carson McCullers's *Reflections in a Golden Eye:* "Everyone she had known in the past five years was somehow wrong." Modernism would become its own tradition after the 1920s, the only chic tradition left in the academy. But modernism as the expression of an elite that believed in nothing so much as freedom and venerated nothing but the individual personality would soon dissipate into the modern American passion for equality—perfect, total, and continuous between the sexes, classes, races, creeds. The "golden" twenties were such only for a small group, typified by the very title—*Tender Is the Night*—that its most elegiac historian used for a novel published when the goldenness had turned derisive of its cruel holiday in *The Sun Also Rises*. But it left the memory of something soon inconceivable—some ancient belief in freedom at all costs, freedom for the sake of nothing but the enjoyment of one's freedom. This marks in the generally upper-class writers of the twenties an attitude inseparable from the vitality, ingenuity, and openness to new experience that had been the mark of an American elect since the days of the Puritan migration and that helped, in the hands of a minority, to bring about the American Revolution and, with that remarkably self-sufficient man Emerson, our literary independence.

Emerson's great theme was that the freedom of the individual soul is the only guarantee of truth. As D. H. Lawrence rapturously wrote of American literature before he saw America—"The leaving of the soul free unto himself, the leaving of his fate to her and to the loom of the open road." But "soul" was no longer a term Americans could use. The dying writer in Hemingway's "The Snows of Kilimanjaro" bitterly remembered—"It was not so much that he lied as that there was no truth to tell."

Hemingway in that story made fun of Fitzgerald for calling the rich "different." But Fitzgerald never doubted that there *was* truth to tell, and that the individual could ultimately trace truth to its hiding place in personal experience. Fitzgerald for all his ambitious worldliness remained spiritually innocent; that was one benefit of "always taking things hard." He was also perpetually in love and was a man who above all else believed that love was destiny and had its rewards. Of course his "dream" was one of possession. As the fable of Gatsby unrolled, the attempted possession turned into a joke against himself and the making of his disaster. And it is true that just as Gatsby was some ultimate expression of the American dream, so that dream often has no content but "I want! I want!" Gatsby was not a character but an idea of the everlasting self-creation that Americans have mastered. It was not enough for him to turn Jimmy Gatz into Jay Gatsby; he had to become a symbol of the great dream *and* its foolishness. It was typical of Fitzgerald's regard for the "idea" that Gatsby died without learning just how foolish he was. When Nick Carraway tries to settle him with "you can't repeat the past," Gatsby triumphantly cries, "Of course you can!"

Every wish and feeling Scott Fitzgerald had was so important to him that it stretched over the visible world. He could never convey the importance to himself of being F. Scott Fitzgerald except as an author framing and interpreting the many different sides of himself. But if Gatsby was ultimately nothing but an "idea," only life *as* idea, a specter of the self, could have conceived of Daisy Buchanan's leaving her faithless, tyrannical, but indispensable husband. Only Fitzgerald with his "willingness of the heart" would have been able to write in the lowest pit of his despair—"France was a land, England a people, but America, having about it still that quality of the idea, was harder to utter—it was the graves at Shiloh and the tired, drawn, nervous faces of its great men, and the country boys dying in the Argonne for a phrase that was empty before their bodies withered. It was a willingness of the heart."

Fitzgerald had this willingness of the heart as no one else did in his day. And because he knew all too well how to love—to the point of despair, out of his sheer inability to do anything *but* love—he alone among the fancy minds and sceptics of his generation became a writer to love. The feeling that he got into that sad, sad novel *Tender Is the Night* was such that even the acrid Hemingway was astonished to find, as so many readers have, that *Tender* gets better with each reading. It also becomes more personal and transparent— *too* personal.

One of the greatest and most terrifying of Fitzgerald's contemporaries, Louis-Ferdinand Céline, denied that his own brutally powerful work could last. "No, no! Great art is not personal like that!" Fitzgerald was unweariedly, insatiably, worrisomely personal. Dick Diver's need to marry Nicole is not convincing, but since it is explained by Fitzgerald's need to marry Zelda, we accept the one as we accept the other. So much has the life of F. Scott Fitzgerald—not without the help of his work!—become the legend that embraces his work.

Fitzgerald the perfect "representative man" of the twenties accomplished something that no one else did at the time: he included America in his romanticism. It was not just literary fame, love for woman, and other accomplishable goals that became his greatest dream and myth. It was his crowded, sprawling, disordered, increasingly pointless-seeming country. At the end of *Gatsby* Nick Carraway still loves America—if only in a vision of the West's last magic island before the people came—as he loves no human being after the disclosure of so much evil. In the end Scott Fitzgerald possessed no other human being, but he did declare his greatest wish. Because American writing is personal—like this:

> For a transitory enchanted moment man must have held his breath in the presence of this continent, compelled into an esthetic contemplation he neither understood nor desired, face to face for the last time in history with something commensurate to his capacity for wonder.

Index

About the Author

Alfred Kazin's book *On Native Grounds* changed
the entire direction of current and retrospective literary
criticism in this country. He has written numerous other
books of criticism, and has been editor of many collections
and critical studies. He has taught at Harvard, the
University of California, Smith, Black Mountain College,
the University of Minnesota, the City University of New
York, and other universities here and abroad. His other
works include *New York Jew, Starting Out in the Thirties, A
Walker in the City, The Inmost Leaf, Contemporaries* and *Bright
Book of Life*.